WORLD OF
Myths

THE · LEGENDARY · PAST

WORLD OF
Myths

VOLUME TWO

Introduced by
FELIPE FERNÁNDEZ-ARMESTO

THE BRITISH MUSEUM PRESS

The five titles included in this Volume Two compilation
are also available in individual paperback editions:
Mesopotamian Myths Henrietta McCall
Persian Myths Vesta Sarkhosh Curtis
Chinese Myths Anne Birrell
Aztec and Maya Myths Karl Taube
Inca Myths Gary Urton

The five titles included in the Volume One compilation
are also available in individual paperback editions:
Greek Myths Lucilla Burn
Roman Myths Jane F. Gardner
Norse Myths R. I. Page
Egyptian Myths George Hart
Celtic Myths Miranda Green

Other titles in The Legendary Past series:
Etruscan Myths Larissa Bonfante & Judith Swaddling
Hindu Myths A. L. Dallapiccola
Russian Myths Elizabeth Warner

© 2004 The Trustees of The British Museum
Introduction © 2004 Felipe Fernández-Armesto

First published in 2004 by The British Museum Press
A division of The British Museum Company Ltd
46 Bloomsbury Street, London WC1B 3QQ

A catalogue record for this book is available from
the British Library

ISBN 0 7141 5018 5

Designed by Gill Mouqué, Diane Butler and
Martin Richards
Jacket design by Jim Stanton

Typeset in Sabon by The Bath Press, Avon
Printed in Great Britain by Goodman Baylis Ltd

Contents

Introduction

Felipe Fernández-Armesto

If you want to know people, learn their myths. No one can ever make sense of a people's history without seeing it through their eyes – and therefore through the occlusions of myth. It is impossible to begin to understand, and impossible, therefore, fully to appreciate, the art of a culture without being able to decode its symbols and unravel its allusions. The way peoples behave is affected far less by the facts of their formation than by the falsehoods they believe. Myth becomes reality because, if people believe it with sufficient passion, they act under its influence and shape the world in deference to it.

As an object of study, myth has lost ground since the heroic scholarship of Victorian times. But its importance is inescapable. We all have myths: stories to situate us in history, morality and nature – the trammels of time, the axis of good and evil, the meshwork of the ecosystems of which we form part. Without myths, we should not know who we are, how to behave, or how to differentiate ourselves from other communities. We should probably be at a loss – even more bewildered than we already are – about how to exploit the earth and which other species to eat, for myths played a part in validating our ancestors' decisions on all these matters – decisions by which we remain conditioned, if not bound.

In this new volume of *The Legendary Past* the myths reviewed may seem random. Mesoamerica may appear, at first glance, to have little in common with Mesopotamia. The environments of the river valleys of China, the low plateau of Iran, and the abrupt topography of the Andes might have been selected specifically for contrast. Nor is there much consistency in the contributors' treatment of this startlingly assorted material. The specialist authors take fascinatingly different approaches to the study of their subjects. Gary Urton treats Inca myths as historical documents, anatomising the sources which confide to us, in all cases, late and opaque versions. Henrietta McCall, too, is interested in the history of scholarship in the field she covers – Mesopotamian myths – but is able to show more confidence in retelling the most evocative stories, selected with an eye particularly alive to potential comparisons with the myths of other cultures. Karl Taube has the task of covering contrasting areas: the Aztec world, whose myths we know, like those of the Inca, only through colonial-era reports, and that of the Maya, who have left an enormous amount of epigraphic and manuscript material of their own. In tackling Persian and Chinese myths respectively, Vesta Sarkhosh

Curtis and Anne Birrell face problems of *embarras de richesses*. The former deals with them by deft summaries of the texts, the latter by taking an ethnographer's approach and selecting myths that illustrate themes in ancient Chinese intellectual and social history.

The contents of this book, then, are various, and the contributors individual in their approaches – but that is no reason to repine. There is no 'key to all mythologies'. The search for one – satirised in George Eliot's *Middlemarch* – was a Victorian snark-hunt: a scientistic illusion, based on the expectation that myths would yield, like the lineages of species, to a single, cosmic theory. Myths are different – as dappled as the cultures from which they arise. Comparisons can be made at random. The selection of material may as well be arbitrary, since it can never be comprehensive or fully systematic. The myths reviewed in this volume are all the more interesting because they are unconnected: those of the Andes developed, as far as we know, in isolation from those of Mesoamerica, and those of the New World, until the sixteenth century, arose independently of those of Eurasia. Communications between China and Persia were tenuous during the formative periods of those cultures' respective myths. Only Persia and Mesopotamia were normally in close touch. So there are no limits to the ways in which we can classify the contents of this book. I suggest we look in turn at each of the three contexts which myths serve to make sense of: history, morality and nature.

Myth and history

In relation to history, myths are versions of the past which explain the present: they forge our sense of who we are, how we got here, and how we fit into a world full of communities different from our own. Myths are usually, though not necessarily, false; they are always more than merely true. They depend for their power not on their truth but on how much we need them. Many histories, therefore, are mythical, and all myths are historical. They are evidence for what matters to the communities which create and recall them. Old-fashioned history books used to begin with myths, recounting the stories that communities told about their own origins. Persia's Shahnameh is such a book, seamlessly linking history to an imagined past, beyond memory. So is the *Popol Vuh*, the precious collection of stories of the *Quiché Maya*, in which the tales of creation, procreation of the race and the deeds of culture-heroes blend with historical data about the highland dynasties.

The collection of Andean myths known as the Huarochirí Manuscript, compiled in the late sixteenth and early seventeenth centuries, is one of our most precious sources for understanding the history of Inca Peru, because it apostrophises the rivalries and discloses the priorities of peoples between Cusco and the coast. In China, between the myth of the Xia dynasty and the well-documented history of the Zhou, lies a tissue of legend, archaeologically verifiable in patches, and occasionally illuminated by the slanting light of surviving oracular texts: the Shang period occupies a formative millennium of the Chinese past, from which it is hard to unpick memory from imagination. The Mesopotamian Epic of Gilgamesh is a work seemingly of pure imagination, but its hero shares the name of an historically verifiable king, recorded as the fifth king of the city of Uruk in the twenty-seventh century BC. The poem quotes a proverbial saying about him: 'Who has ever ruled with power like his?' Some of the genuine wonders of the city – its walls, its gardens, the pillared hall of the sacred precinct which, as in all cities of lower Mesopotamia, was built at its heart – appear in the verses. Myths track time. In the Books of Chilam Balam of the Yucatec Maya, history and prophecy merge in an endlessly repeated cycle. In the multiple creation myths of the Aztecs, the world is constantly extinguished and renewed.

Themes recur in the myths of widely separated peoples – and, therefore, repeatedly in the course of this book – because some human experiences and some historical problems transcend culture. Paradoxically, the problem of cultural multiplicity is one of these, for every culture is aware of others, puzzlingly different in norms and values, speech and beliefs, taste and technology. One of the great unsolved problems of the human past, indeed, is why it is so variegated: other social animals, such as apes, ants and elephants, have so much culture in common, whereas humans – all of whom had a common ancestor and therefore a common culture only 150,000 years ago – have grown profoundly unalike in how they think and behave. One of the great tasks of the mythmakers, therefore, has always been to explain the differences. Another has been to justify them from the point of view of their respective communities. This usually means asserting the superiority of one culture over others.

So myths of identity dominate the legendary past. Divine or heroic progenitors found uniquely virtuous lineages, sanctified by divine selection: the Jews are God's chosen people; the Japanese are descended from the sun goddess; Ahura Mazda forms the Iranians from Gayomartan, the first mortal. Origin myths often combine assertions of the uniqueness of a particular community with claims to legitimacy of possession of its lands. A divinely ordained sign – an eagle feasting in its bone-strewn eyrie – guided the Aztecs to their homeland. In the *Popol Vuh*, the sacred book of the highland Maya, the sun in person brings the migrations of the Quiché to an end. The Inca – in common with many native American peoples – emerged, according to their own myth, from a cave, as if from the womb of the earth, to occupy the rich valley of Cusco.

Imperilled peoples still reach for myths like these in self-reassertion and sometimes reject the objectivity of archaeology as a hostile intrusion. When Hugh Brody sat on Canada's Royal Commission on Aboriginal Peoples, his workshop got 'stuck in an intellectual quagmire', because a Cree PhD student argued that archaeologists were ignorant and that native origin myths were unarguably consistent. Almost everywhere, she pointed out, the ancestors emerged from pre-human origins in the places their descendants occupied. They did not have to cross Ice Age Beringia to reach America. They just belonged. The fact that a myth occurs often is evidence of its utility, not its truth.

Myths identify communities by identifying enemies. Identity depends on self-differentiation from the other, and myths are always full of malign alterity. When the Turks appeared as would-be conquerors on the frontiers of Iran, people identified them with the Turya, contenders for divine favour in Iranian myth. Zoroastrians are enemies in Persian myths of Islamic origin. In Gilgamesh, the transformations of the hero's relationship with Enkidu – the hairy wild man – recall the transition from enmity to alliance between the agriculturists of lowland Mesopotamia and some of the pastoralist hill peoples who surrounded them. After suitable acculturation – rogering, razoring and robing – Enkidu becomes Gilgamesh's sidekick. In the Huarochirí Manuscript, the warfare between the divine occupants of the shrines of Pariacaca and Huallallo matches the mutual hatreds of highlanders and lowlanders. Much of the work is a symbolic narrative of past wars, in which the Checa, the people to whom the Huarochirí stories belonged, recalled the alliances and grievances which first bound them to the Inca, then separated them in hostility. The ballgame which the Popol Vuh describes vividly, with all the pace and passion of a ringside commentary, is an analogue of warfare. The Books of Chilam Balam, collected among the Maya of Yucatan, represent as prophecy what are really historic resentments between rival Maya lineages.

The morals of myth

The passion invested in myths make them seem worth fighting for. Indeed, the truth about any community is usually disappointing: unheroic, flawed, disfigured by violence, exploitation, tyranny and greed. But, as well as situating people in history, myths locate them in a moral universe. Our myths make us feel like the heirs of heroes. They inspire self-betterment by trailing exemplars before our eyes. Over and over again, heroes contend with a demon-haunted universe, in which evil is as dispersed among many agents as the air is filled with flies.

Morality is cultural, but the idea of goodness is universal. Belief in a universal ethos or standard of judgement, by which, as a matter of principle, good can be distinguished from evil, is so common among humankind that it is likely to be of very great antiquity. In most societies' origin myths, it is represented as one of humankind's earliest discoveries or revelations. In the Genesis story, it is man's third step – after acquiring language and society – to distinguish good and evil. And the episode dominates the story disproportionately.

The attempt to wrestle with the reality and mutual exclusivity of good and evil informs common conceptions of a twofold cosmos, satisfyingly symmetrical and therefore orderly, regulated by the balance or flow between two conflicting or complementary principles. Some of the earliest creation myths we know of, including those of the ancient Sumerians, represent the world as the result of an act of procreation between earth and sky. The idea probably started a long time before it was first documented. Indeed, although anthropologists have found many conflicting descriptions of the cosmos, it does seem that many, perhaps most, peoples inhabit a world, envisaged by the remotest ancestors they know of, which they see as in uneasy equipoise or complementarity between dual forces, such as 'male' and 'female' or 'light' and 'darkness' or 'evil' and 'good'. A past generation of scholars interpreted the cave paintings of Ice Age Europe as evidence of a dualist mental world, in which everything the hunters saw was classified in terms of gender: but the phalli and vulvae they detected in the designs seem equally likely to be weapons and hoofprints, or even part of some unknown code of symbols.

The image of a twofold universe obviously shapes the myths and morals of people who believe in it. Over the last three thousand years, it has been rejected in most new systems of thought which have claimed to describe the universe: but the exceptions include Daoism, which has had a formative influence on China and made major contributions to the history of thought in many parts of the world, and Persian Zoroastrianism. Two of the Chinese creation myths Anne Birrell highlights below describe the emergence of Yin and Yang from cosmic chaos. The attempt to confront the problems of ethics shines through Persian ways of imagining the world. Christianity has absorbed a lot of influence from the same tradition, including the notion or, at least, the imagery of a perpetual struggle of angelic powers 'of light' against satanic forces 'of darkness'.

The *Popol Vuh*, too, seems animated by a dualist notion of good and evil. The realm of Xibalba, where the hero twins travel to play the ballgame, is an apparently underground realm of sinister lords, served by creatures of the night. The twins engineer their own transformation by plunging into a pool – to the deluded glee of the evil lords – from where they emerge in the guise of poor conjurers. They entertain the lords of Xibalba to a mock dismemberment act, not unlike the modern conjurer's standby, sawing-the-lady-in-half. In the mounting excitement, brilliantly evoked in the surviving version, the lords volunteer to take part in the act themselves, with predictable results. Bereft of their leaders, the people of Xibalba submit to the twins. Is this a description of a primeval cosmic struggle or merely an episode in a chaotically plural universe? Or a millenarian prophecy? Or an essay in propaganda directed against a real-life enemy?

Ecologies of myth

Myths enflesh the environment. In the *Popol Vuh* the hero twins use their magical sympathy with other creatures to hold the lords of Xibalba at bay. In the torture chambers of the underworld, glow-worms, wasps and jaguars help the twins survive. A rabbit intervenes to help when the evil lords cheat at the ballgame. The wind, which inflicts extremes of climate, was the great

enemy of the peoples of the Iranian plateau. So the culture-hero Yima establishes a realm invulnerable to wind 'either cold or hot'. The founder-king
Haoshanha procures the help of the water goddess in defeating demons. The
myths of the Andean world are only fully intelligible in the context of the
dazzling environmental diversity created by abrupt topography, in which
temperature, sunshine and rain all vary tremendously across contiguous
altitudes, and slopes and valleys carve eco-niches for peculiar life forms: the
consequences include teemingly rival communities.

Nowhere, among the worlds of myths traversed in this book, is the
physical context more palpable than in China and Mesopotamia. The Chinese
and Mesopotamian myths described below by Anne Birrell and Henrietta
McCall took shape in similar environments, in soils dried by climate change,
yet vulnerable to the unpredictable flooding of great rivers: the Tigris and
Euphrates in Mesopotamia, the Yellow River in China. At times floods
washed away dikes and overflowed ditches. At others, desert sandstorms
choked the farmers and buried their crops.

The writers of Mesopotamian literature – the earliest imaginative literature in the world to survive in written form – described an environment
dominated or, at least, shadowed by gods of storm and flood. Nature was
purposefully malevolent. The sun blinded people and set lands ablaze. In the
wind, earth shattered 'like a pot'. 'Will ripe grain grow?' asked a proverb.
'We do not know. Will dried grain grow? We do not know.'

In lower Mesopotamia, the rivers fell through a parched landscape from
a distant land of rain, like trickles across a windowpane. Even with irrigation,
the summers were too harsh and dry to produce food for the early cities,
and they had to rely on winter crops of wheat and barley, onions, linseed,
chick-peas, sesame and vetch. Rain fell more often than today, but was largely
confined to winter, unleashed by ferocious storms that made the sky flare
with sheet lightning. 'Ordered by the storm god in hate', according to a poet,
'it wears away the country'. The supreme god, Ellil, 'called the storm that will
annihilate the land, … the hurricane howling across the skies, … the tempest
which, relentless as a floodwave, devours the city's ships. All these he gathered at the base of heaven and he lit on either flank the searing heat of desert.
Like flaming heat of noon, this fire scorched.' The floods which created the
life-giving alluvial soils were also life-threateningly capricious. Storm and
flood were humans' commonest enemies in Mesopotamian myth.

Meanwhile, earth and water – the benign forces which combined to
create the alluvial soil – were celebrated in verse: Earth, a zealous, jealous
mother, yielded nourishment, suckled infants, guarded embryos. Water, to
awaken the land's fertility, was a male god, Ea or Enki, empowered 'to clear
the pure mouths of the Tigris and Euphrates, to make greenery plentiful, to
make dense the clouds, to grant water in abundance to all ploughlands, to
make corn lift its head in furrows and to make pasture abound in the desert'.
But these were subordinate deities, at the beck and call of storm and flood.

Chinese myths are full of parallels. The Yellow River collects rain in the mountains of Shaanxi. Where it disgorges, the stream broadens suddenly and periodically overflows. Here the climate has been getting steadily more arid for millennia. The region today is torrid in summer, icy in winter, stung by chill, gritty winds and rasped by rivers full of ice. The winds blow dust from the Mongolian desert over the land, creating a friable, yellow earth which is almost sterile if unwatered. Rapid thaws bring implacable torrents. Against this background, the natural forces personified in Chinese myths are unsurprising. The warfare of the gods resounds with thunder and kicks up dust. Gong Gong (Common Work) makes the waters crash against the sky. Nu Gua (Woman Gua) dams the floods with ashes. Gun (Hugefish) steals protoplasm from the gods to repair the flooded world. His son – Yu the Great (Reptilian-Pawprint), who crafted China from the floodplain of the Yellow River – mastered the god of the Huai River, stronger than nine elephants, by chaining him and leading him to the distant mountains. In a more prosaic version, he 'mastered the waters and caused them to flow in great channels'. This legendary engineer made China possible by digging the channels where flood control and irrigation coagulate. Yi, the magnificent Archer, downed the suns that parched the earth. Tang the Conqueror gave his own life as a burnt offering for rain. Personifications of rain and drought contend for mastery of the world in the myth cycle of Nu Ba (Woman Droughtghoul), and Zhu, the crimson owl of the south who brings hot weather, spells ill omen for officials in whose district he appears.

The conditions the myths evoke were the real conditions of the first era of Chinese agriculture. When farmers first began to till these lands they were still a sort of savanna, where grasslands were interspersed with woodland. Three or four thousand years ago, water buffalo were still plentiful: their remains have turned up in strata of the era, together with other creatures of marsh and forest, such as the elaphure and water deer, wild boar, silver pheasants, bamboo rats and the occasional rhinoceros. Ancient songs collected in the *Classic of History (Shu jing)* rhapsodise on the toil of clearing weeds, brush and roots. 'Why in days of old did they do this task? So that we might plant our grain, our millet, so that our millet might be abundant'. The legendary ancestor of the most successful lineage of the time was called Hou Ji (Sovereign Millet). In folk memory, when he planted it,

> It was heavy, it was tall,
> it sprouted, it eared ...
> it nodded, it hung ...
> Indeed the lucky grains were sent down to us,
>   The black millet, the double-kernelled,
>   millet pink-sprouted and white.

In Shang times, in the second and third millennia before the Christian era, this agriculture sustained what were perhaps already the densest populations in the world and kept armies of tens of thousands in the field. The earliest known cultivators cleared the ground with fire before dibbling and sowing, harvesting each panicle by hand and threshing seeds by rubbing between hands and feet.

The present and future of myth

Memory and imagination are kindred processes. In bardic transmission, they fuse. The older our memories, the more imagination warps them. When catastrophes or traumas interrupt the transmission, myths are fragmented and pieced together in new ways. It happened, for example, in the Spanish conquest of the New World. Afterwards, people in colonial society who were struggling to understand what had happened distorted the old myths: instead of myths of validation, which boosted the confidence of the Aztecs and Inca and fortified their aggression, they invented myths of self-subversion: supposed legends of 'returning gods' – for which there is no pre-conquest evidence – and auguries of doom, which were in fact copied from European books. Among the Maya, Christian missionaries' successful challenge to indigenous religion left its mark on the language and construction of the creation stories in the *Popol Vuh*. 'Dios' joined the gods of the 'jaguar prophets' who wrote the Books of Chilam Balam. Don Cristobal Choque Casa – probably one of the indigenous compilers of the Huarochirí manuscript – prided himself on his Christianity, but in a nightmare he dreamed of sacrificing to the old gods in a neglected shrine, which had become the abode of bats and a place for illicit assignations.

Today, I think, we are witnessing a similar but global episode of discontinuity in the transmission of mythic traditions. The syncopations of modernity – the accelerated pace of change, the deracination of traditional societies, the evanescence of ancient states, the fast turnover in new technologies, the upheavals and destructiveness of modern revolutions and wars – have expunged some cherished myths and plunged others into the crucible. Re-crafted and re-combined, they re-emerge, transmuted by the alchemy of imagination into a genre called 'fantasy', which now dominates video monitors and cinema screens.

Their power does not end. In post-industrial society we have reverted to mythopoeia of our own making. Myths forgotten by most people are revived by the bards of our age. Tolkien ransacked Celtic and Germanic myth for *The Lord of the Rings*, and the works which most seem to entertain today's Western children and adolescents are the myth-steeped works of Terry Pratchett, Philip Pullman and J. K. Rowling. Capricious reconstructions of ancient monsters, immemorial adventures and cosmic wars now flit and flicker through computer games. Paradoxically, perhaps, the power of technology – which, for most consumers, is as unintelligible as magic – has reinforced the power of myth.

Suggestions for further reading

J. G. Frazer, *The Golden Bough*, is the greatest monument of Victorian mythology. L. H. Grey and J. A. MacCulloch (eds), *The Mythology of All Races*, which began to appear during the First World War, is still an insuperable quarry. M. Eliade, *The Sacred and Profane* and J. Campbell, *The Hero with a Thousand Faces* are curious examples of the abiding effort to systematise myth. C. Lévi-Strauss, *The Savage Mind*, W. D. O'Flaherty, *Other People's Myths*, and I. Okwepo, *Myth in Africa* open modern anthropological insights. The psychology of myth has inspired classics including C. G. Jung, *Essays on a Science of Mythology*, and *Man and His Symbols*, and C. Lévi-Strauss, *Myth and Meaning*. So has the sociology of myth: E. Durkheim, *The Elementary Forms of the Religious Life*.

MESOPOTAMIAN

Myths

HENRIETTA McCALL

Acknowledgements

I am most grateful to Dr S.M. Dalley of Oxford University for her kind and helpful criticisms of the text, and to Dr Roger Moorey of the Ashmolean Museum and Christopher Walker, Dr Dominique Collon and Judy Rudoe of the British Museum for their help with the illustrations. I also thank my husband Christopher for his continuing help and support.

Author's note

Where possible, the Akkadian text has been reinforced using fragments and duplicates, but many gaps still remain. Parallel passages sometimes allow them to be filled, and square brackets [ ] indicate where such words have been inserted. Where this has not been possible, missing words and phrases are noted by . . . and untranslatable terms are rendered as transliterations in italics.

Picture credits

p. 8: (left) W. Blunt, *Pietro's Pilgrimage*, London 1953; *(right)* British Museum; *p. 9: (left)* E. Flandin and P. Coste, *Voyage en Perse*, Paris 1851; *(right)* BM ANE 118885; *p. 10: (top)* BM P&E 1976,9-3,1; *(bottom)* BM P&E 1987,3-2,1; *p. 11: (left)* BM; *(right)* BM P&E 1987,1-9,1; *p. 13: (left)* BM; *(right)* E.A. Wallis Budge, *Rise and Progress of Assyriology*, London 1925; *p. 18:* BM ANE K3375; *p. 19: (left)* BM ANE 124867; *(right)* M.E.L. Mallowan, *Nimrud and its Remains*, London 1966; *p. 21:* BM ANE 118822; *p. 24:* E. Unger, *Babylon: die heilige Stadt nach der Beschreibung der Babylonier*, Berlin 1931; *p. 25: (top)* BM ANE 89115; *(centre)* BM ANE 89110; *(bottom)* BM ANE 132257; *p. 26: (top)* Iraq Museum, Baghdad, IM 15218; *(bottom)* BM ANE 89311; *p. 28: (top)* G. Loud, *The Megiddo Ivories*, Chicago 1939, pl. 4; *(bottom)* The Pierpont Morgan Library, New York, 653; *p. 29: (top)* BM ANE 124543; *(bottom)* BM ANE 102416; *p. 30:* BM ANE 124655; *p. 31:* P. Thureau-Dangin and M. Dunand, *Til-Barsip*, Paris 1936; *p. 32:* BM ANE 78260; *p. 37:* E. Ebeling and B. Meissner, *Reallexicon der Assyriologie*, Berlin 1928; *p. 39:* BM ANE 116624; *p. 40:* BM ANE 103226; *p. 42:* BM ANE 89435; *p. 44:* M. von Oppenheim, *Tell Halaf: A New Culture in Oldest Mesopotamia*, London and New York 1933; *p. 48:* G. Contenau, *Manuel d'Archeologie Orientale*, vol. II, Paris 1931; *p. 51: (top)* BM ANE 118932; *(bottom)* BM ANE 122125; *p. 52: (top)* BM ANE 22961; *(bottom)* Oriental Institute of the University of Chicago, A18161; *p. 55:* Babylon/D. Collon; *p. 56:* Unger *(ibid.)*; *p. 59:* Ur 18122; *p. 61:* BM ANE 129480; *p. 64:* D. Bell-Scott, from H. Frankfort, *The Art and Architecture of the Ancient Orient*, London 1954; *p. 67: (left)* The Pierpont Morgan Library, 689; *(right)* BM ANE 103226; *p. 69:* BM ANE 123279; *p. 73: (top)* P. E. Botta and E. Flandin, *Monuments de Nineve*, Paris 1849–50; *(bottom)* BM GR 1897.4-1.872; *p. 74:* Ebeling and Meissner *(ibid.)*; *p. 75:* Botta and Flandin *(ibid.)*; *p. 76:* C. De Bruin, *Travels into Muscovy, Persia and part of the East Indies*, London 1737.

Contents

The Mesopotamian World

Babylonia

Baghdad
Ishchali
Sippar
AKKAD
Babylon
Borsippa
Kish
Nippur
Shuruppak
SUMER
Uruk
Larsa
Ur
Eridu

PERSIA
Persepolis

URARTU

ELAM

Susa

PERSIAN GULF

Behistun

LAKE VAN

Tigris
Khorsabad
Nineveh
Nimrud
Arba'il
Ashur
ASSYRIA
MESOPOTAMIA
Euphrates

BABYLONIA

Til Barsip
Harran
MITANNI
Mari

Ebla
Emar
SYRIA

Boğazköy

TURKEY

Ugarit

CYPRUS

Megiddo

MEDITERRANEAN SEA

EGYPT

Tell el-Amarna

Introduction

Mesopotamia, that ancient land comprising Assyria in the north and Babylonia in the south, is to many unfamiliar territory. Some aspects are of course well known from its biblical connections: the glories of Nineveh and Babylon, the bloodthirsty nature of the Assyrian warriors, the magical power of the Babylonian diviners, the rich and powerful merchants, the luxurious and sensual lifestyle. The names of Hammurabi, Nebuchadrezzar, Tiglath-Pileser, Ashurbanipal and Sennacherib are potent ones. The mighty reliefs in the British Museum and the Louvre tell of victory, order, authority; they show battle preparations, fighting, sieges, chariots and splendid lion hunts. As befits the sheer size of these reliefs, their guardians are truly monumental: colossal winged bulls and lions, five-legged and immaculately curled and harnessed. Much of what we know of those ancient civilisations is what those who lived there so long ago wanted us to know. It is propaganda on a grand scale.

But it is quite another matter when it comes to records that were not deliberately meant to speak to posterity. Mesopotamia has yielded vast collections of clay tablets which record everything from the simplest sheep count to the most arcane divination procedure. These make up a corpus representing matters of current interest amongst the people of their day. Such things are not easy to digest or to interpret in a world far removed from their origins. For that reason perhaps they are of all the greater interest.

Though much of the information in these tablets may be thought of as mundane, they include amongst them a small proportion of tablets which can properly be described as literary. In them are told stories which are for the most part still unfamiliar, though in antiquity some at least were well known. These stories survived unread from about the time of the birth of Christ until halfway through the last century when Akkadian, the language in which they were written, was first deciphered. The story of their decipherment and impact is told in the first chapter of this book.

In the longest myth, the **Epic of Gilgamesh**, the hero Gilgamesh is a semi-divine king of Uruk, who, after the death of his friend Enkidu, goes in search of eternal life, a quest which takes him to Ut-napishtim, the survivor of a great flood. A flood sent to punish mankind is also a theme in the myth of **Atrahasis**. The **Epic of Creation** tells of the world's beginnings and of the building of the great city of Babylon under the protection of its god Marduk. Shorter myths are the **Descent of Ishtar to the Underworld**, in which the goddess Ishtar goes down to visit her sister Ereshkigal, the queen of the underworld, and almost fails to return. A similar myth in many respects is that of **Nergal and Ereshkigal**, in which Nergal descends to the land of no return and seduces its queen. The **Epic of Erra** tells of Babylon in decline, its patron god temporarily absent; **Etana**, of a childless king in search of a magical plant that will ensure him an heir; **Adapa**, of a priest of Ea who deliberately breaks the wing of South Wind and is taken to heaven to answer for his behaviour; and the **Epic of Anzu** relates the story of a wicked bird who snatches from the god Ellil the Tablet of Destinies (which bestowed supreme power on the one who held it), and is slain in glorious combat by the god Ninurta.

All the myths concern the gods and people of Mesopotamia, most of whom behaved – well or badly – in a way that was reassuringly familiar to their audience. The more exciting and unpredictable parts of these myths tend to occur in locations which would have been extraordinary, but real enough to command attention: in forests, by the sea, in the mountains. The pace of the action is always slow moving, and quite often presaged by dreams and warnings or even described in advance by another character, so there are few surprises and little suspense. Fixed epithets abound, which increase the stately character of the texts.

The translations given in this book preserve the lengths and order of the lines on the tablets. Rhyming verse as we would define it is not apparent, but literary devices such as puns, alliteration and onomatopoeia all help to create internal rhythms.

The way in which sequential ordering is used, and the device whereby an action is repeated once, twice, a third time, and so on, in order to heighten dramatic tension, has been maintained in the excerpts given here. In the same spirit, the temptation for the translator to use several different adjectives when the Akkadian limits itself to one, or to embroider the text for a more sophisticated modern audience, has been avoided. The translations reflect, as far as is possible, the rock-hard impact and subtle qualities inherent in the originals.

I am deeply indebted to Dr S. M. Dalley of Oxford University for the translations, which have been taken from her book *Myths from Mesopotamia* (Oxford, 1989).

Discovery and decipherment

In the first half of the seventeenth century, an urbane and well-educated Italian nobleman called Pietro della Valle made a spectacular journey to the east, a journey which began in Venice and took him to Constantinople, Alexandria, over the Sinai desert, back to the pyramids, across Palestine by caravan, to Damascus, Aleppo and Baghdad. There he married a beautiful Nestorian Christian and a year later set off once more with his bride. They went to Isfahan and Persepolis, the capital city of the Achaemenid Dynasty of Persia (559–331 BC), the glories of which della Valle was one of the earliest travellers to describe. He also copied a number of inscriptions carved on the palace doors in three different versions of a strange wedge-shaped script.

Twelve years later he returned to his native Rome, having visited India en route. His wife had died some ten years earlier and her embalmed body had accompanied him ever since. Also with him were his copies of the inscriptions from Persepolis. It was the first sight in the West of that exotic cryptic script.

In 1700 the Regius Professor of Hebrew at Oxford, Thomas Hyde, wrote about della Valle's acquisitions in a paper entitled 'Dactuli pyramidales seu cuneiformes' (signs of pyramidal or wedge-shape), and it was as cuneiform that this wedge-shaped script came to be known. Decipherment, however, lay some time in the future.

The German Georg Friedrich Grotefend realised that the three versions of della Valle's Persepolitan inscription represented three separate languages: Old Persian, Elamite and Babylonian, none of which was understood. Grotefend decided to begin with the Old Persian version and by 1802 was able to present a convincing transliteration. Meanwhile, scholars in France, Germany and Denmark were also working on the same inscription, a further copy of which had been made by a Dane, Carsten Niebuhr, and published in 1772.

It was, however, an Englishman, Henry Creswicke Rawlinson, who was the first to present a convincing translation of an Old Persian inscription in a paper he read to the Royal Asiatic Society in London in 1838. Only three years earlier he had, according to an autobiographical note, begun 'the study of the cuneiform inscriptions of Persia, being then stationed at Kerman-shah ...'. During 1835 and 1836 Rawlinson had copied the Old Persian part of a trilingual inscription carved high on the side of a mountain at Behistun (Bisitun) in western Iran. In 1844 he scaled the same mountainside again to tackle the Babylonian part of it. It took him three years: with the help of an agile local boy he was winched up the perpendicular rock-face by means of ropes and ladders and then hung precariously 300 ft (100 m) above ground, first cleaning the inscriptions and then copying them. Within two years he had correctly deciphered 246 individual signs of an approximate total of 600. His pioneering work was published by the Royal Asiatic Society in 1852.

Meanwhile, interest in Assyrian matters was growing in Europe. In March 1843 Paul Emile Botta had begun to excavate at Khorsabad, built by Sargon II at the end of the eighth century BC to be his new capital. Almost immediately Botta began to uncover limestone slabs sculptured in relief. In 1845 Austen Henry Layard began digging at Nimrud, biblical Calah, built as his new capital by Ashurnasirpal II in 879 BC. Almost straightaway, Layard too struck treasure: immense stone panels inscribed with horses and riders, abject captives, sieges, attacks on fortified cities, warriors fording rivers, archers on chariots. There were also scenes of lion hunts, and a strange anthropomorphic image of an hawk-headed deity, 7 ft (over 2 m) high. Some of the panels were additionally inscribed with cuneiform. In 1846 Layard was joined by an assistant, Hormuzd Rassam, brother of the British vice-consul at Mosul. Together they uncovered large fragments of colossal winged bull-men, and yet more inscribed stone panels. A large collection of these objects, including the Black Obelisk of Shalmaneser III, were sent – not without difficulty because of their bulk and weight – to the British Museum. Meanwhile, Botta's finds had found their cumbersome way to Paris.

In June 1847, when the colossi and great reliefs arrived in London, it was by no means certain how the public would react. What interest there was in the Assyrians was based on their bad reputation, fostered by the Bible

Pietro della Valle

Henry Creswicke Rawlinson

Drawing (above left) showing the tripartite cuneiform inscription high on the cliff side at Behistun; (right) the Black Obelisk of Shalmaneser III.

and by classical authors and scholars. The Assyrians were seen not only as vain and violent marauders intent on rape and pillage, but also as loose, debauched and immoral in their home life. This was hardly likely to appeal to the Victorian public. But in fact they found the exhibition very much to their taste, the sheer size and confident execution of the objects suggesting another much earlier empire based on the same unshakeable faith in its own enduring permanence. The public flocked to the British Museum, encouraged by *The Illustrated London News* with a full-page spread and several fine line illustrations: 'The recent excavations and discoveries' would excite the curiosity 'not only of the antiquarian but of all scriptural students, from the illustration which they afford of passages in Holy Writ ...'; the magazine went on to give a minute description of the eleven panels. In late August there was a second arrival of some fifteen further items. *The Illustrated London News* made the comment, despite five further line drawings which rather belied it, that 'this second collection of sculptures is deficient in that poetical and historical interest which so eminently distinguished the previous arrival

...'. In 1849 Layard published *Nineveh & Its Remains*, his own account of the excavations, and in its first year the book sold eight thousand copies, which would, according to Layard, 'place it side by side with Mrs Rundell's Cookery'.

In 1851, at the time of the Great Exhibition, Assyrian revival was in full flood. Jewellery was made displaying motifs from the huge stone tablets, and the London firm of Henry Wilkinson & Co. produced electroplated wine coolers engraved with human-headed bulls and an Assyrian king. The winged bull or lion on a bracket became a fairly common architectural feature both in England and France. A 'winged bull from Nineveh' made an appearance

Silver gilt casket (above) presented to Austen Henry Layard in 1853. The front shows a scene of King Ashurbanipal lion-hunting, with a winged bull to the left and a winged lion to the right.

Gold and enamel bracelet (below) in the Assyrian revival style. Made in London about 1872.

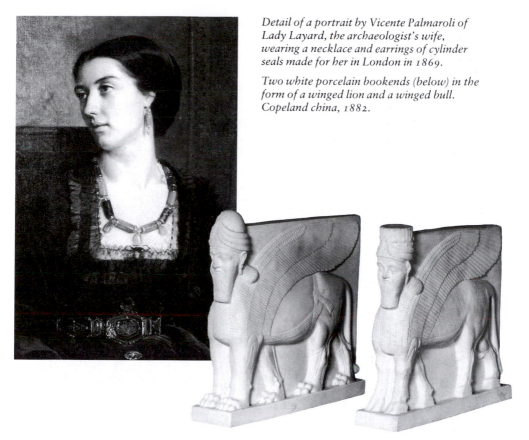

Detail of a portrait by Vicente Palmaroli of Lady Layard, the archaeologist's wife, wearing a necklace and earrings of cylinder seals made for her in London in 1869.

Two white porcelain bookends (below) in the form of a winged lion and a winged bull. Copeland china, 1882.

in a popular song and, in 1880, Maj.-Gen. Rawlinson himself was gently lampooned by Gilbert and Sullivan: in *The Pirates of Penzance* the modern major-general sang, 'I can write a washing-bill in Babylonic cuneiform'.

Thus, by the time Rawlinson published his Behistun inscription in 1852, some familiarity already existed together with a growing interest in the ancient Assyrian civilisation. In 1853 the Assyrian Excavation Fund was founded and sponsored W. K. Loftus to excavate at Warka, ancient Uruk. But it was not until twenty years later that the new skill of reading cuneiform tablets at last made it possible for scholars to try interpreting this ancient civilisation.

George Smith was only seven years old when the first objects from ancient Mesopotamia arrived at the British Museum. He was born in 1840 and received little formal education before being apprenticed into the trade of bank-note engraving. Early on, however, he became fascinated by Assyriology and before he was twenty had become such a familiar figure at the British Museum that no less a personage than Henry Rawlinson himself took an interest in him, allowing the young man to use his own room, where he could work on clay tablets. Such was the calibre of his work that, in 1867, Smith was appointed an assistant in the Assyriology section of the Museum, and in 1871 he published *Annals of Assurbanipal*.

Smith had also been busy cataloguing the collection of tablets in the Assyriology section according to subject matter. Into the compartment labelled 'Mythological and Mythical' he put together some eighty tablets from the library of Ashurbanipal at Nineveh, and when he had collated one of them and begun to translate, he suddenly realised he was reading the familiar story of the Flood. He was so overcome with excitement that he rushed around the room and began tearing off his clothes.

Some months later on 3 December 1872 he read a paper to the Society of Biblical Archaeology. His announcement caused a flurry of excitement: a heathen text, apparently anticipating Noah's Ark. His audience was all agog.

The owner of the *Daily Telegraph*, Sir Edwin Arnold, offered the British Museum a thousand guineas to allow Smith himself to go to Nineveh in search of the rest of the tablet. Smith set out in January 1873, but it was not until the beginning of May that the necessary formalities were agreed with the Ottoman governor in Mosul. Once Smith began work, turning over the debris of previous excavations and searching out fragments of inscribed material, he was almost immediately rewarded. It was his custom to spend his evenings going over the day's finds and, on the fifth evening, he found to his 'surprise and gratification' that one of the fragments he had just wiped clean contained the best part of seventeen missing lines apparently belonging to the first column of the Flood tablet and 'fitting into the only place where there was a blank in the story' of Gilgamesh.

Later that year Smith returned once more to Nineveh. As he later recounted in a letter to the *Daily Telegraph* (4 March 1875), he had taken home with him from his first expedition another interesting fragment, apparently unrelated to the Epic of Gilgamesh. When he found time to look closely at it, he realised with mounting excitement that this one was 'part of the Chaldean story of the Creation', and he determined to find as much of the rest as he could. On his second expedition, by a similar stroke of luck, he discovered in the debris where he had found the missing fragment of Tablet XI of Gilgamesh 'another portion belonging to this story, far more precious ... This turns out to contain the story of man's original innocence, of the temptation, and of the fall'.

Smith had stumbled upon fragments of another myth which we now call the Epic of Creation. Piecing these together in the British Museum, he was able to draw parallels with the biblical account of man's creation in Genesis. He promised the readers of the *Daily Telegraph* that 'when my investigations are completed I will publish a full account and translation of these Genesis legends, all of which I have now been fortunate to find ...'

Unfortunately, Smith was unable to fulfil his promise. On his third expedition to Nineveh he contracted a virulent strain of fever and died in Aleppo on 19 August 1876, aged thirty-six.

The interest aroused by his work did not die with him. In 1885 O. C. Whitehouse published an English translation of Eberhard Schrader's popular

George Smith   *Professor Doctor Friedrich Delitzsch*

work *Die Keilinschriften und das alte Testament* (*The Cuneiform Inscriptions and the Old Testament*), which went into a second edition in 1888. Schrader's original work went into three editions, and in 1903 was entirely rewritten by H. Zimmern and H. Winckler. The latter then published his own book on those cuneiform inscriptions which illustrated biblical material.

In Germany a storm of controversy arose when the leading figure in Assyriology of the time, Friedrich Delitzsch, delivered a lecture entitled 'Babel und Bibel' on 13 January 1902 to the German Oriental Society, whose audience included Kaiser Wilhelm II. This lecture became an historic event. Delitzsch's new and exact translations showed that the Bible was not, as previously thought, the world's oldest book but was in fact preceded by literature from a much earlier epoch. There were great similarities between the two ancient worlds, but the Old Testament could in his view no longer be regarded as unique and therefore as pure revelation. In fact, Delitzsch's work questioned the fundamental authority of the Old Testament. Such was the outrage at the first lecture that a year later Delitzsch gave a second, urging theologians to take a balanced view in dealing with what they saw as attacks on cherished portions of the Bible, and to make provision for the teaching of Assyriology: 'There is no need to swallow everything whole, nor to toss the Bible on the shelf as antiquated rubbish'.

This was not enough for the Kaiser who, perhaps wishing to disassociate himself from his earlier enthusiasm, wrote to the weekly review *Grenzboten* on 19 February 1903 describing it as 'a great mistake' that Professor Delitzsch should have approached the question of revelation in such a 'very polemical spirit'. 'Religion', he wrote, 'has never been the result of science, but the outpouring of the heart and being of man from his intercourse with God.'

A week later *The Times* in London printed a long defence of Delitzsch by his 'friend and fellow worker in the field of Assyrian research for more than twenty-five years', W. St Chad Boscawen, who said Delitzsch was the victim of an imperial attack strong enough to unseat him from his chair at Berlin University because, as a 'mere historian and Assyriologist', he had 'dared to enter the world of theological and religious conclusions and hypotheses'.

Less controversial was a work of translation published in 1909, which became the standard reference for biblical scholars. This was Hugo Gressmann's *Altorientalische Texte und Bilde zum alten Testament* ('Old Oriental texts and images of the Old Testament'). Less than twenty years later, in 1926, an entirely new edition was necessary because of discoveries of new texts and improved understanding of old ones. The quantity of translations presented to readers had almost doubled.

The first English collection of cuneiform texts, *Cuneiform Parallels in the Old Testament*, was published by R. W. Rogers in 1912. The available material was given both in transliteration and in translation. This was followed in 1916 by G. A. Barton's *Archaeology and the Bible*, which contained translations interspersed with notes drawing attention to biblical parallels. This book was periodically revised; a seventh edition appeared in 1937. A further major landmark was the publication in 1950 of *Ancient Near Eastern Texts* by the Princeton University Press, almost exactly a century after Rawlinson published his Behistun inscription. This large collection of texts was chosen on the basis that they were parallels to, or illustrative of, certain passages in the Old Testament. Criteria for inclusion were the appearance of a biblical name, the treatment of a biblical theme, or that the text represented a type of literary form (such as a prayer, lamentation or ritual) prominently featured in the Old Testament.

From this it can be seen that for a long time the overriding interest in texts from Mesopotamia was in their biblical connection. Throughout the nineteenth century, authentication of the Bible had been a major preoccupation among the reading classes. This preoccupation became paramount halfway through the century, when scientific progress began to compete with religious belief. Darwin's *Origin of Species*, supported by pioneer work in dating fossils, proved that the earth was millions rather than thousands of years old, and that life had evolved over that long period and had not been created in a single week. This made people question for the first time the literal truth of the Bible. And they found such questioning very disturbing. At the same time, they wanted 'proof' or otherwise of such events as Noah's Flood. It was not surprising, therefore, that the newly legible myths from Mesopotamia which seemed to offer that proof made such an impact when they first came to public attention. Nowadays they are considered in their own right as a literary corpus with its own independent merits. There will always be an argument, however, for comparison with Old Testament texts, not only for the light this can shed on the Bible, but also because such a comparison provides a unique opportunity for observing Mesopotamia from the outside.

Definitions and literary tradition

Collecting together the myths available to us today was the work of many decades. Luck, fate and chance, as well as the more scientific approach to excavation adopted in recent years, have all played their part. The table overleaf summarises such information as we have for each of the myths which make up the main corpus of Babylonian literature. Because the available material is patchy and we need to rely to a great extent on our own applied criteria, particularly in trying to assess the time of a composition, the information provided must inevitably be somewhat uneven, and we must be prepared to leave some blanks. Otherwise we run the risk of assuming too much and drawing false conclusions. Perhaps further research and discovery will enable some of the blanks to be filled in.

A glance at the table will reveal how often the place of discovery is Nineveh. The royal libraries uncovered there have indeed provided much of the material available to us, some of it in the best preserved condition, but Nineveh was only one of the many sites all over Mesopotamia where libraries and archives existed. Excavation almost anywhere will turn up at least a few tablets, even if they only record numbers of cattle and household lists. Collections of tablets were made at all periods and their remains have been found in Ashur and Harran in the north and Babylon, Ur, Nippur, Uruk and Borsippa in the south.

The existence of these collections is to some extent the result of the way scribes were trained; this remained virtually unchanged for two millennia. It included the faithful copying of texts over and over again. Scribes throughout the country probably became the owners of the texts they had copied during their apprenticeship and thus practically identical copies of texts were taken to different locations. We should distinguish, however, between collections of school exercises such as those found at Sultantepe (complete with some schoolboy howlers); administrative archives, such as those found *in situ* at Ebla and scattered at Mari; and a 'true' library, that is a deliberate collection of fine literature brought together for the motive of collection itself, probably in a palace or temple.

We should also be aware that, although the durability of clay tablets and their widespread distribution patterns may be good news for modern scholars, haphazard discovery, inept excavation methods and the occasional use of more ephemeral wax-covered wooden boards are less so. Some very popular texts may never have been found at all, and we may be misled into

Evidence of the Myths

MYTH	NUMBER OF TABLETS / APPROXIMATE LINE LENGTH		CHIEF LOCATIONS OF DISCOVERY IN MESOPOTAMIA
Epic of Gilgamesh	12 tablets		Ur, Sippar, Ishchali
	3000 lines		Nineveh (Libraries of Sennacherib and Ashurbanipal)
Epic of Creation	7 tablets		Nineveh
	1000 lines		Ashur, Kish Sultantepe
Epic of Erra	originally 5 tablets (two-thirds preserved)		Assyria: Nineveh, Ashur, Sultantepe Babylonia: Babylon, Ur, Tell Haddad
	c. 750 lines		
Etana	substantial fragments only		Ashur
	originally c. 450 lines		Nineveh
Adapa			Nineveh
	c. 120 lines		
Anzu	3 tablets		Tarbiṣu, Sultantepe Nineveh
	720 lines		
Descent of Ishtar			Ashur
	150 lines		Nineveh
Nergal and Ereshkigal			Sultantepe
	750 lines		
Atrahasis	3 tablets		Sippar
	originally 1245 lines		Nineveh

NOTE: Times of composition are not necessarily analogous to chief locations of discovery; some tablets uncovered at the main sites (particularly royal libraries) were copies of much earlier texts. Arrows pointing from times of composition relate to specific location(s).

TIMES OF COMPOSITION	OTHER LOCATIONS OF DISCOVERY	OTHER VERSIONS
— Old Babylonian period (5 tablets), early 2nd millennium BC	Boğazköy, Megiddo, Ugarit, Emar, Elam	Early Sumerian c.2150 BC Also translations into Hittite, Hurrian, Elamite
— Old Babylonian period? — 7th century BC		
c.9th–7th century BC		
Old Babylonian period ——→ Susa — Middle Assyrian, 13th century BC — Neo-Assyrian, mid 1st millennium BC	→ Susa	
15th, 14th century BC ——→ Tell-el-Amarna — late 2nd millennium BC	→ Tell-el-Amarna	
Old Babylonian period; Standard Babylonian, 7th century BC	Susa	Sumerian; story probably familiar to Hurrians
— end 2nd millennium BC — 7th century BC		Earlier and longer (410 lines) Sumerian version: Descent of Inanna
15th century BC ——→ Tell el-Amarna (shorter version: 90 lines) — 7th century BC	→ Tell el-Amarna (shorter version: 90 lines)	
— Old Babylonian period, probably before 1645 BC – 8th–7th century BC		

The Epic of Gilgamesh: Tablet XI, the 'Flood Tablet'.

believing that some texts were more popular in antiquity than they actually were, just because so many fragments of these have come to light.

How representative of the literary tradition as a whole is the literature which has survived? Royal libraries, in particular that of Ashurbanipal in Nineveh, provide one of the best clues. Recent research into some Neo-Assyrian (1000–500 BC) administrative records has revealed a high level of organisation within royal libraries, with acquisitions and accessions enthusiastically sought and carefully recorded. Literary works were arranged in terms of title and genre, the quantity in which the text was available and by description of its material. This could be in one of four categories: a full-sized clay tablet, divided into two or more columns; a smaller tablet, of just one column; a wax-covered writing board, consisting of two or more leaves; or a single-leaf writing board.

These records also make it clear that private collections in Babylonia were extensively used to build up the Ninevite private libraries, particularly after the fall of Babylon in 648 BC. Ashurbanipal himself supervised some of the acquisition, and a royal letter to the governor of Borsippa, explicitly commandeering all kinds of literary works from the temple and private libraries there, is almost certainly from him.

A wax-covered writing board in three parts, here shown opened out, found in a well at Nimrud. Each section was hinged so that it could be folded up.

The head of King Ashurbanipal, a detail of a limestone panel depicting a scene of warfare. It was in his library at Nineveh that most of the texts we have were discovered.

Because they were carefully excavated, the administrative archives of Ebla give a good insight into the nature and organisation of such archives. At Ebla tablets were stored on wooden shelves and were indexed. The contents or titles of individual tablets were recorded on the tablet edge to make them easier to find when stored on a shelf. If no shelves existed, tablets were placed in jars or baskets with an explanatory tag attached.

Literary tablets tended to have space reserved in the last column for a colophon. This contained the sort of information which a modern book provides on its title and imprint pages. The colophon might contain some of the following information: the title of the work; the name of the owner; the name of the scribe; the date of the work; comments on the original from which the scribe had copied; a declaration of secrecy; and an invocation of curses against any unauthorised person removing the tablet.

Sometimes the colophon was merely a shortened first line of the work in question plus the number of tablets in a series. For example, for the Epic of Gilgamesh it reads: 'Of him who found out all things [its first line] Tablet I, II, III [and so on].'

Texts were written in wedge-shaped cuneiform script on clay tablets, usually square or rectangular in shape, or sometimes on wooden boards. Clay was always readily available in Mesopotamia and easy to model into the required shape. The scribe used a stylus cut from a reed or perhaps one made of ivory or metal. It was trimmed at an angle or into a round end, either of which affected the style of the script. The scribe used the flat front side of the tablet first and, if necessary, continued on the back, which was slightly convex. After the tablet had been inscribed it was quite often just left to dry out, especially when the inscription was not intended for permanent record. Sometimes, however, it was baked so that it became virtually indestructible. Many of the tablets left unbaked in antiquity survive today, some of them only by lucky accident: the rooms where they were stored were deliberately burned by foreign conquerors and the heat thus baked the tablets, which might otherwise have gradually disintegrated in the damp conditions often prevalent in Iraq.

Only a very small percentage of the written material uncovered need concern us here, since most of it does not fall into the category of myth. Indeed, only a very small part of the whole corpus is 'literature' as we would understand it. Within this definition, however, we should include the few royal inscriptions, called 'Letters to the God' because of their introductory dedication and greeting to the god. Hard fact and pure historical information are perhaps their least merit, their content being selective, but they are distinguished by their highly poetic language. Particularly in descriptions of the prevailing countryside and the battles themselves, hyperbole paints a vivid picture. In his Letter to Ashur and the other gods who inhabit the city of Ashur, Sargon II describes his eighth campaign in 714 BC against Urartu, telling how his troops (with the help of the gods Shamash and Marduk) jumped the Lower Zab 'as if it were a ditch'. Simirra, 'a great finger of a mountain', is 'struck upright like the blade of a lance'. Battle troops are 'valiant eagles'. It is impossible to draw precise parallels, but this and other Letters to the God undoubtedly reflect established literary tradition. The Letters were probably intended to be read aloud to an audience; thus they are intense and alive, the action runs along apace, and their description of people, places and events is very realistic.

We should also consider a particular literary tradition which survived from Sumerian times: the Dialogue Text. This was a form of popular entertainment, which may even have been enacted or recited at court, whereby two opposing points of view were put forward by two personified contestants who argued their respective merits, e.g. The Tamarisk and the Palm, The Grain and the Wheat, The Ox and the Horse, Summer and Winter. These texts followed a stereotyped form; after an introduction saying who the disputants were and how they fitted into the great cosmological order, the grounds of their particular argument were established. Then came the contest proper, during which each side extolled its own merits while pointing out the failings of its adversary. The argument was referred to a god who pronounced judgement, which the two contestants readily accepted, departing from the scene the best of friends.

Relief showing King Sargon II in conference with a palace official.

This sort of competitive sparring was sometimes reflected in myth, as for example in Tablet VII of the Epic of Gilgamesh, when Enkidu first curses Shamhat the harlot with great curses ('The drunkard shall soak your party dress with vomit') and afterwards, following an intervention from the god Shamash, takes the polar opposite position:

> 'My utterance, which cursed you, shall bless you instead.
> Governors and princes shall love you ...'

Another form of dialogue potentially more intellectually satisfying, was a text we call the Babylonian Theodicy, although copies are extant from both Babylonia and Assyria. This is a dialogue in twenty-seven stanzas between a sceptic and a pious man, who alternately present their views on life in a polite and ceremonious way. Unfortunately, the dialogue is extremely repetitious and does not make much sense, ending somewhat lamely when the sceptic asks:

21

'May the god who has abandoned me give help
May the goddess who has forsaken me show mercy.'

The Dialogue of Pessimism presents perhaps the first instance of that situation comedy stand-by, the servant who is more nimble-witted than his master. To each of the twelve commands which the master issues, the servant replies with a witty riposte. When the command is countermanded, the servant neatly changes his riposte, showing there are two ways of looking at every situation. Some of the stanzas are somewhat abstruse, but it is clear that the intention was to amuse.

'Servant, obey me!'
'Yes, my lord, yes.'
'A woman will I love.'
'Yes, love, my lord, love. The man who loves a woman forgets pain and trouble.'
'No, servant, a woman I shall not love.'
'Do not love, my lord, do not love. Woman is a pitfall, woman is an iron dagger
 – a sharp one! – which cuts a man's neck.'

Such verbal wrestling occurs in conversations in myth, for example in Tablet VI of the Epic of Gilgamesh when the goddess Ishtar, overcome by Gilgamesh's beauty, offers herself to him along with a variety of rich rewards, only to be rejected in very colourful and exaggerated terms.

The Poor Man of Nippur is perhaps the most appealing tale outside the category of myth, with farcical overtones. The text was found at Sultantepe and a further fragment was uncovered from Ashurbanipal's library. It concerns a poor man taking revenge on the mayor of Nippur, who has taken his last goat. Three tricks are played, all of which result in the mayor receiving a sound beating, no doubt to the gratification of the audience. There is little repetition here and the fast-moving story points to the moral that those in high places have a duty to behave honestly.

The most important legacy of the literary tradition of ancient Mesopotamia, however, is its myths and legends, for which it was famed even in antiquity. We should perhaps define our terms here. If myths concern divine or semi-divine beings, legends concern historical or semi-historical beings. There are sufficient fragments extant to tell us there was a later epic tradition which related to the royal exploits of known historical kings, which we should describe as legends. But what concerns us here is myth: although Gilgamesh and Etana were known kings whose names appear on the Sumerian king list, they are, like Atrahasis and Adapa, semi-divine. Others of the myths recounted here solely concern the gods, in heaven and in the underworld, and great cosmological upheavals. The events described go back to the dawn of civilisation before – at least according to the Epic of Creation – there were any gods at all, nor any destinies decreed.

Gods and mortals, authors and audience

From around 3000 BC there is archaeological evidence for the beginning of walled cities in Mesopotamia, and for the building of temple complexes within them. These temples were built for the cult of a particular god; for example, the Sumerian city of Eridu for the god Enki. Because life was precarious, it was prudent for cities to be guarded by a special god who was responsible for both the city and its people. The temple was his house, and rituals of feeding, clothing and washing the god were carried out within the sanctuary. With the god lived his spouse and sometimes his children.

As more cities were built, the number of cult centres increased. Later cities adopted gods, made claims on their behalf and bestowed epithets on them with little regard for what had gone before. Some names and epithets were accretions of several early gods and goddesses. This meant the pantheon of gods, the basic structure of which went back to the third millennium, was full of paradox and repetition.

Gods

The more important and famous gods make frequent appearances in the myths. They include the following:

Anu, the sky-god, was originally chief god in Sumerian times. He was sometimes described as Ishtar's father. His spouse was **Antum** and his cult city was Uruk. **Ishtar** (Sumerian **Inanna**), the goddess of love, sex appeal and war, is described in one Sumerian text as the one whom not even 120 lovers could exhaust. Under various names she became the most important goddess throughout western Asia. Her sacred beast was the lion and her cult centres were at Uruk, Kish, Agade, and Arba'il.

Ellil, Anu's son, later replaced his father and became king of the gods. To him belonged the Tablet of Destinies by which the fates of men and gods were decreed. His spouse was **Mulliltu** or **Mylitta** (Ninlil) and his cult city was Nippur.

Ea (Sumerian **Enki**) was lord of the Apsu, the domain of sweet water beneath the earth. He was the source of all secret magical knowledge and instructed mankind in the arts and crafts. His spouse was **Damkina** and his cult centre was Eridu.

Imaginative reconstruction of Babylon in the time of Nebuchadrezzar II (605–562 BC), showing a bridge supported by five stone piers over the Euphrates, the great ziggurat on the left and to the right the temple of Marduk, Esagila.

Marduk was Ea's son. During the Kassite period he was elevated to the top of the Babylonian pantheon. His cult centre was naturally Babylon. **Nabu** was Marduk's son, the patron of scribes and a god of wisdom. His popularity reached a high point during the first millennium. His cult city was Borsippa.

Sin, the moon-god, was also described as Ishtar's father. He governed the passing of the months. His symbol was the crescent moon and he was worshipped at Ur and Harran. **Shamash** (Sumerian **Utu**), the sun-god, was judge of both heaven and earth. His symbol was the sun disk and his cult centres were Sippar and Larsa.

Adad, the weather-god, not only controlled storms but also the life-giving rain. His symbol was forked lightning and his animal the bull, which bellowed like thunder. **Dumuzi** (later known as **Tammuz**) was Ishtar's lover, a pastoral god. He protected seasonal fertility.

Impression (left) from a greenstone seal, showing the god Ea with water and fish streaming from his shoulders, his two-faced vizier to his left, to his right a bird (perhaps Anzu) and a winged Ishtar above the sun-god Shamash.

Cylinder seal impression (above) showing the sun-god Shamash with rays rising from his shoulders, and brandishing a saw, symbolic of his role as judge.

Impression from a chalcedony seal, showing a worshipper before the god Adad standing on his sacred bull. Winged human-headed bulls flank the shrine.

25

Black stone cylinder seal impression (right) showing the god Nergal, and dedicated to him. He brandishes his characteristic double lion-headed mace.

Impression (below) from a blue chalcedony seal showing a shaven-headed priest before the symbols of various deities.

Ereshkigal was the queen of the underworld. **Namtar** was her vizier, a much-feared god of plague who could let loose any one of sixty diseases. **Erra** or **Nergal** was the god of plague and war. **Ninurta** was a war-god and a patron of the hunt. He is the hero of the Epic of Anzu. **Nin-hursag** (also known as **Aruru** and **Mammi**) was the great mother goddess, sometimes described as the spouse of Nergal.

The **Annunaki** (**Anukki**) were the old Sumerian gods of fertility and the underworld, where they later became judges. The **Igigi**, often paired with the Annunaki, were the Sumerian group of sky-gods, headed by Ellil.

The temples in which the gods were worshipped were run by a priestly hierarchy, although we know very little about its precise arrangement. A priest called a *šatammu* probably headed the administrative side and another, an *en*-priest, the spiritual side. We know that sons often followed their fathers into priestly service one generation after another.

Throughout Mesopotamian history exorcists and diviners have played a significant part, and all over the ancient world the skills of the Babylonian diviners were very highly regarded. Techniques varied, but the more common ones were the observation of animals' entrails; the effect of oil on water; the pattern of smoke from incense; the behaviour of birds and other animals, especially about the city gates or within the temple precinct; and celestial and meteorological phenomena.

Religion played a great part in the everyday lives of ordinary people. On a personal level, they attached themselves to a particular god or goddess and offered prayers and sacrifices in return for intercession with the other gods and protection from evil spirits. There is a vast fund of spells and incantations, which sometimes used passages from myths. Even though ordinary people were denied access to the innermost sanctuaries of the temples, they were observers of the great religious processions. The enormous enclosure around the ziggurat at Babylon was probably designed to enable a large crowd to watch the ceremonies from a suitable distance.

Mesopotamian attitudes towards death are largely known from myths and epics. There was no promise of an afterlife, as in ancient Egypt, and it seems that death was accepted in a resigned and matter-of-fact way – the obvious exception being, as we shall see, Gilgamesh, who railed furiously against his friend's death which had been presaged by alarming dreams. The living made commemorative figurines of the dead, as Gilgamesh did for Enkidu. Burials, apart from early royal burials, took place in the house of the dead person, who was put under the floor with his favourite possessions. Corpses left unburied and denied the normal offerings of water by surviving relatives were thought to become restless ghosts who could harm the living. There were no public cemeteries.

Mortals

The people of Mesopotamia, even from earliest times, tended to live in cities. Apart from the basic advantage of security provided by numbers, this allowed the centralised organisation and maintenance of a canal network with artificial irrigation and drainage in a land where rainfall was extremely sparse. Despite the dry climate, the land was potentially very fertile and, regularly watered, could support several harvests a year. The principal crops were cereals and dates. The livestock included sheep, goats and cattle, and the soil was rich in clay which, when dried, was used not only for clay tablets but also for all building construction.

Early cities showed a pattern which repeated itself throughout Mesopotamian history. They consisted of three main parts: a walled inner area containing the temple, the palace, the houses of royal officials and those of citizens; the suburbs encompassing farms, fields, orchards and date groves; and the harbour area, which was the centre of commercial activity. Every city also

*Ivory inlay from Megiddo
showing a victorious homecoming
and feasting.*

had gates through the outer wall, and the area in front of these was used as a gathering place as well as for the transaction of business, law-giving and money-changing. This was also where scribes sold their skills.

The fortunes of cities periodically rose and fell, sometimes as a result of changes in water-courses. Even the splendour of a city such as Ur was intermittent: by the Middle Babylonian period, it was more or less a ruin. Larsa and Ashur disintegrated, though the latter revived in Parthian times, and the great city of Akkad literally disappeared without trace. Most cities only became truly rich and famous in periods of victory, when lavish spending was made possible by the spoils of war and luxury items such as spices, scent, wine, fine cloth and exotic animals reached them.

The inhabitants of cities could be divided into two main groups: those few who benefited from court and temple connections which gave them the use of their own means of production, and those who were wholly dependent on the temple and palace organisations. Most of the means of production were under the control of the vast temple complexes and the royal palaces, although private individuals owned land as well. Both temple and palace derived their income mainly from agriculture, either directly or through the payment of rates and taxes. Central administration received most income and redistributed it. Both organisations supported a large number of personnel who were 'paid' with food, clothing and so on.

Those who were dependent, to a greater or lesser extent, upon the temple and palace organisations can perhaps be categorised as peasants, craftsmen, slaves and merchants, whose exact status varied at different periods. A further

*Cylinder seal impression
showing a ploughing
scene. Barley was the
principal crop.*

Detail (above) from the palace reliefs of Ashurnasirpal at Nimrud, showing soldiers crossing a river by means of inflated animal skins.

Cylinder seal impression (left) showing a palace or temple facade with animals to the right.

very important class within this society was the scribes, whose calling always carried prestige. There is no definite evidence to tell us how candidates for this group were selected, but they were frequently the sons and relatives of city princes and governors. There is only one known instance of female scribes, at Mari, where evidence from lists of rations allotted to palace workers reveals some nine female names. Unfortunately there are no details of their social standing, training, or the type of work they did.

Peasants were engaged in a number of occupations, mainly agricultural. They sowed, reaped and threshed barley, sometimes several times a year where the land could support it. They also tended herds, mainly sheep and goats of several varieties. They milked cows, ewes and goats, and made butter and cheese. Farmyards usually contained ducks and geese; hens were common only in later periods. There was in addition a great deal of seasonal nomadism.

Craftsmen followed more varied occupations, many of which were hereditary, the skills being passed by father to son. Some were engaged in the cloth trade: bleaching, spinning and dyeing. There is archaeological evidence for spindle-whorls at all early settlements. Other craftsmen were tanners. Leather and skins were used in making shields and harnesses, small boats, drinking bags, pouches for milk and butter, and sandals. Skins were also inflated for crossing rivers.

Craftsmen could also be potters, although this occupation had a rather

Detail from bands of embossed bronze from the Balawat Gates in the reign of Shalmaneser III. Bound captives are brought to the capital.

low profile. As early as the sixth millennium, a large variety of rather dull pottery was being made throughout Mesopotamia. Potters' wheels were in widespread use soon after 4000 BC. More important were metal-workers. Before 7000 BC there is evidence that native copper was being made into simple tools, and by 6000 BC lead and copper were being smelted. There is evidence for metal casting during the latter part of the fifth millennium.

Carpenters made chariots, sledges and ploughs, and there were also stone-carvers, brewers, jewellers, scent-makers, confectioners, bakers and basket-makers.

As for slaves, these could be roughly divided into two categories: slaves belonging to private individuals and those owned by the temples or palaces. Those in the first group were often born or perhaps adopted into the house where they were enslaved. The famous Law Code of Hammurabi (king of Babylon from 1792 to 1750 BC) makes it apparent that, certainly in the Old Babylonian period, slaves enjoyed a special status. The Code also tells us that sometimes people sold themselves, their wives and children into slavery if they were unable to pay a debt. Once the debt was repaid, they regained their former status. While in slavery, their position was protected to some extent by the Code and their relationship with their masters was based on mutual obligation.

Many slaves came into the country as prisoners of war. Assyrian reliefs depict such people being led to the capital, often with their wives and children. Foreign slaves were particularly prized for their artistic skills, and often for the beauty of their women, but mainly their work was domestic, and they helped in the fields at harvest time.

The Old Testament speaks with loathing of the merchants of Babylon and Nineveh. These merchants occupied an important place in society, since Mesopotamia was poorly provided with mineral resources. As it lacked any stone suitable for building or for sculpture and had no gold, silver, copper or timber, or other precious items such as lapis lazuli, cornelian, rock crystal and turquoise, all these had to be acquired through trade. Trade was therefore crucial and the great rivers between which Mesopotamia lay, the Tigris and the Euphrates, served as major trading routes. Merchants engaged in two different types of trade: city and inter-city, and foreign trade, whereby textiles and food staples such as dates were traded for those commodities lacking in Mesopotamia, particularly metals.

Texts from Mari reveal routes which link the Mediterranean and Anatolia to the Persian Gulf. At that period trading caravans had royal protection and foreign merchants travelling from court to court were treated with honour. This, however, did not become the general situation in Mesopotamia until the time of Sargon II (721–705 BC). Not only did trade enhance living standards, it also served to spread the influence of Mesopotamian civilisation. With the exchange of goods doubtless went an exchange of ideas and stories.

Scribes were trained in schools which were nearly always attached to temples. There is a record of only one independent establishment, at Ur. Scribal training was long and repetitive and because of the very complexity

Mural painting of scribes, from Til Barsip on the Middle Euphrates in the reign of Tiglath-Pileser III (744–727 BC).

A typical school tablet, showing three registers of signs.

of cuneiform – over five hundred variable signs – it required not only application and patience, but intelligence. Teaching relied on the memorisation of lists of words and signs copied over and over again, and such training began early in boyhood. Even outside the borders of Mesopotamia scribes were carefully trained, and bi-lingual syllabaries and lexical lists have been found in the Hittite capital of Boğazköy.

The school curriculum was apparently standard and changed little over the millennia. A Sumerian literary document describes the reaction of a school-boy and also the behaviour and attitude of his teachers and parents. Written perhaps as early as 2000 BC, it was a highly popular composition and repeatedly copied. The schoolboy in question read his tablet, ate his lunch, prepared and wrote another tablet, and was assigned oral and written work, but, unfortunately for him, his work was not up to standard and he was caned by various teachers. The boy's parents then invited his teacher home, where he was feasted and presented with gifts. After this his attitude changed; he waxed lyrical about his pupil's abilities and Nissaba, the goddess of schools and scribes, was exhorted to show favour to the boy's reed.

Authors

The scribes copied the texts, but who were the original authors of the creative literature? Unfortunately, any answers to this question are bound to be conjecture, since our evidence is meagre and has to be carefully interpreted.

The very fact that creative writing exists at all presupposes that there were individual authors at work, but cuneiform literature hardly ever names them. Traditionally, authorship of the oldest works was attributed to sages sent out before the Flood by the god Ea to bring civilisation to mankind. After the Flood, authors were honoured with sage-like status, which gave their work the strong foundations of great antiquity and divine inspiration. But these authors did not mention their own names and throughout the whole of Mesopotamian literature there are only two possible exceptions to this rule. The first is Kabti-ilani-Marduk, who professes to have drawn up the tablets of the Epic of Erra – although he says he received the entire work in a vision, which rather weakens his claim to original authorship. The author of the Epic of Gilgamesh is recorded in a first-millennium catalogue of cuneiform literature as Sin-leqi-unnini ('Oh-Sin-accept-my-prayer'), an exorcist-priest who probably lived in Uruk. His name has been traced back to the Middle Babylonian period (1600–1000 BC) when Babylon was ruled by the Kassites and, since this was a time when the epic was standardised, it is probable that Sin-leqi-unnini was the recorder of a definitive version rather than its original author. His version was influential enough, however, to ensure that his name is permanently associated with the epic.

It is perhaps not surprising that a civilisation which produced from earliest times syllabaries and lists of cuneiform signs, and bi-lingual tablets of Sumerian words with their Akkadian equivalents, should also have produced a catalogue of authors. Such a catalogue, albeit fragmentary and somewhat obscure, was found in Ashurbanipal's library. It lists works and ascribes them to named scholars, and also identifies four classes of authors: gods; legendary humans and humans of great antiquity; humans with no indication of family origin; and humans with indication of family origin, described as 'son' of an ancestral figure.

The first two categories underline that, in Mesopotamian eyes, true authenticity must derive from divine inspiration and/or great antiquity. These apart, there remain various names, all of whom are said to be scholars of particular cities and to possess priestly titles. It would be fascinating to trace both the ancestors and descendants of those names, with indications of family origin, but this would require a great deal more information than we have. The catalogue does, however, show that the Mesopotamians themselves were interested in the identity of the chief scribes of the temple schools and considered them to be the authors of the compositions.

In fact, even if the works in question were signed, it is probable that we would consider most of the versions we have as compilations rather than originals. It is clear that generations of story-tellers and scribes have added and omitted passages as seemed appropriate or topical at the time. Few works bear the imprint of a single personality. The Epic of Gilgamesh itself has been described as a 'stitch-up job', and it certainly reveals some techniques used to give cohesion and continuity to the whole. Sometimes the joins are less than smooth.

Audience

If the authors themselves are hard to trace, the identity of the audience or readers must be pure conjecture. We know that only a tiny percentage of the population were literate, and thus access to literature by the rest must have depended upon someone who could read, i.e. a scribe. So how did the general public indulge its taste for literature?

In the case of the Letters to the God described in the previous chapter, their style and content suggest that some at least were meant to be read out aloud to an assembly of citizens, rather than silently deposited in the sanctuary before an elite congregation. Some of the Letters show a careful build-up of tension: after the assessment of a deadly foe, a crisis when all looks hopeless, a sudden divine intervention brings sure triumph. Then there is the language which, as we have seen, is extremely stirring and full of vivid similes. There are also fanciful descriptions of the marvels of 'abroad'. This all points to an audience sophisticated enough to be aware not only of its own traditions but of the existence of others, and thus to be able to make comparisons and contrasts. Because of their trading links, Mesopotamians knew about foreign lands and were able to take a wide view of what was happening outside their own borders. As for the lively descriptions of the beauties of nature, this only makes sense if an audience is actively participating, and it is not hard to imagine gasps of wonder and amazement at some of the wilder flights of fanciful report. Sometimes there are quite technical details, of weaponry manufacture for example, and once more this points to an audience whose members included master craftsmen familiar, for example, with how much metal went into making a decent axe.

To refer to the audience as an 'assembly of citizens' is necessarily some- what vague, since we cannot know exactly who was privileged enough to hear these readings. It probably depended to some extent on where they took place: at court, in temples at festivals, or even around caravan campfires. Clearly, different locations would have commanded different types of audiences.

But what of the audience for imaginative literature – the written versions of the myths and legends? Was it the same 'assembly of citizens' who heard the stories that we have uncovered from the ancient libraries, and which therefore bear the stamp of official acceptance? Or was this a more elite section of society – temple and palace personnel, for example?

These texts provided for us by the accident of discovery are subtle and esoteric, much more so than the Letters to the God. Although the locations in the stories can be specific (for example, Uruk and the Lebanon in the Epic of Gilgamesh, Babylon in the Epic of Creation and Nippur in the Epic of Anzu), and the plot can describe a definite historical event (for example, the building of Uruk's city walls and the foundation of Babylon), and the heroes can be famous and real people (for example, Gilgamesh and Etana), all are presented in an idealised fashion. There is little prosaic detail. Plots are unimportant; in some cases they are practically non-existent. The action moves slowly and is quite often halted altogether for consideration of the beauties of nature and the wonders of the cosmos, as well as the interpretation of highly cryptic dreams. All this results in a sophisticated form of literature not necessarily easy of access, especially when the added subtleties of language and style, the artful puns and elaborate repetition are taken into account.

This raises the question of a vernacular literature existing alongside the literary texts. Unfortunately, there is very little hard evidence for an oral tradition, but it must have existed. Isolated tablets surviving in single copies suggest an abundance of love songs, courtly tales and legends, topical, popular and bawdy stories, riddles, animal lore and parables. Probably versions of these were sung, told and performed not only at court but in more humble surroundings. The second-millennium royal courts at Ur, Isin, Larsa and Babylon harboured scholars and poets, and these places were probably centres of creativity in this genre at other times as well. And because of their ephemeral and topical nature, these stories may have been recorded (if at all) on something less durable than baked clay tablets. Papyrus and leather, for example, do not long survive damp conditions, and waxed boards are prone to damage.

It is possible that the preserved literary tradition may sometimes have been sung, to the accompaniment of a harp or lyre, by trained professionals who had learned the words by heart. As for public oratory, it is only the Epic of Creation which specifically states that it is to be recited – as part of the ritual on the fourth day of the New Year's Festival in Babylon.

That there is a connection between myth and ritual is certain, but fashions change in the interpretation of how close a link there is. Biblical scholars at the beginning of this century, influenced by the theories of J. G. Frazer, author of *The Golden Bough*, believed that all myths originated from rituals, but that view is now treated with more caution. We cannot know in many instances which came first, the myth or the ritual, and there are certainly myths in other cultures which have no apparent ritual association at all. The relationship between the two is complex and variable. In the Near Eastern context, it is important to bear in mind the possible ritual associations, but also to remember that except in specific cases – for example, in the last part of the Descent of Ishtar to the Underworld, where a fertility ritual involving the god Dumuzi is intended, and in the Epic of Creation – such connections may be slight, casual or even non-existent.

Gilgamesh and the Flood

Most of the twelve chapters of the Epic of Gilgamesh were found during the last century at Nineveh in the ruins of the temple of Nabu and at the palace library of Ashurbanipal. At the beginning of this century, Bruno Meissner purchased a large fragment of the epic from a dealer in Baghdad. It had been found in the ruins of ancient Sippar (modern Abu Habba) and contained part of the Old Babylonian version of Tablet x. Then, in 1914, the University of Pennsylvania bought from an antiquities dealer a fairly complete six-column tablet containing the Old Babylonian version of Tablet II. At about the same time, Yale University acquired from the same dealer a continuation of the Pennsylvania Tablet inscribed with Tablet III. Shortly before the First World War, a team of Germans excavating at Ashur found a considerable fragment of the Assyrian version of Tablet VI and, in the 1928–9 season, they discovered at Uruk two rather smaller pieces belonging to Tablet IV. Despite this serendipity, it is not possible to restore the entire epic without gaps, but we do have some three thousand lines of the main epic as well as four separate Sumerian stories, some parts of which are incorporated in Akkadian into the main epic.

We know almost certainly that Gilgamesh was a youthful ruler of Uruk during its First Dynasty (around 2600 BC). The Sumerian king-list assigns to him a reign of 126 years. He was said to be the son of the goddess Ninsun, whose husband was the king Lugalbanda. But although the epic says that Lugalbanda was Gilgamesh's father, the Sumerian king-list tells us his father was 'a high priest of Kullab' (a district within Uruk). This made Gilgamesh at least semi-divine. His most famous accomplishment was the building of the city walls around Uruk, mentioned in the epic and confirmed by a later ruler of the city, Anam, who recorded his own rebuilding of the walls which he described as 'an ancient work of Gilgamesh'.

The epic opens with a brief declaration of the deeds and fortunes of its hero, a scene-setting device which establishes Gilgamesh as great in knowledge and wisdom, as one who brought information from before the days of the Flood, and as one who went on a long journey in search of immortality, became weary and resigned, returned home and engraved on a tablet of stone all that he had done and suffered, and then completed the building of the walls of Uruk and its holy temple Eanna, the home of the goddess Ishtar.

This framework is then filled out with the story proper, which begins with a rampant Gilgamesh exercising *droit de seigneur* over all the nubile maidens in Uruk while forcing all its able-bodied young men to work on the city walls and the temple. Eventually the inhabitants of Uruk invoke the mother of the gods, Aruru, urging her to create a rival to Gilgamesh.

> Aruru washed her hands, pinched off a piece of clay, cast it out into open country.
> She created a primitive man, Enkidu the warrior: offspring of silence, sky-bolt
>   of Ninurta.
> His whole body was shaggy with hair, he was furnished with tresses like a woman,
> His locks of hair grew luxuriant like grain.
> He knew neither people nor country; he was dressed as cattle are.
> With gazelles he eats vegetation,
> With cattle he quenches his thirst at the watering place.
> With wild beasts he satisfies his need for water.

The primitive man Enkidu is one of the most important characters in the epic. But first he must be tamed. This is done by the harlot Shamhat; she reveals to him her many attractions and, after six days and seven nights of love-making, Enkidu is changed:

> Enkidu had been diminished, he could not run as before.
> Yet he had acquired judgement, had become wiser,
> He turned back, he sat at the harlot's feet.

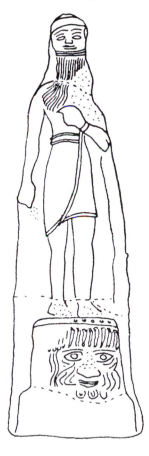

Possibly a representation of the hero Gilgamesh, standing on the head of the vanquished Humbaba. Despite the fact that this is the longest and best known myth, pictorial representations are scarce and difficult to verify.

The harlot was looking at his expression,
And he listened attentively to what the harlot said.
The harlot spoke to him, to Enkidu,
'You have become profound, Enkidu, you have become like a god.
Why should you roam open country with wild beasts?
Come, let me take you into Uruk the Sheepfold,
To the pure house, the dwelling of Anu and Ishtar,
Where Gilgamesh is perfect in strength,
And is like a wild bull, more powerful than any of the people.'

Enkidu agrees to go to Uruk so that he can challenge Gilgamesh and show him that even one born in the open country can be superior in strength. But Shamhat tries to persuade Enkidu that Gilgamesh wants to be his friend:

'Let me show you Gilgamesh, a man of joy and woe!
Look at him, observe his face,
He is beautiful in manhood, dignified,
His whole body is charged with seductive charm.
He is more powerful in strength of arms than you! He does not sleep by day
    or night.
O Enkidu, change your plan for punishing him!
Shamash loves Gilgamesh,
And Anu, Ellil, and Ea made him wise!
Before you came from the mountains,
Gilgamesh was dreaming about you in Uruk.'

Tablet I ends with two dreams of Gilgamesh, about a sky-bolt and a star. Both are interpreted to mean that a strong partner will come to him and that they will love one another. But despite these good auspices, Tablet II begins with Enkidu in fighting form, waylaying Gilgamesh on his way to yet another amorous assignment.

Enkidu blocked his access at the door of the father-in-law's house,
He would not allow Gilgamesh to enter.
They grappled at the door of the father-in-law's house,
Wrestled in the street, in the public square.
Door-frames shook, walls quaked.

The outcome of the wrestling match is that the two protagonists recognise that they are not meant to fight but to be friends; almost immediately they decide on a joint venture, to kill the giant of the Pine Forest, Humbaba (or Huwawa in the earlier version), 'whose shout is the flood-weapon, whose utterance is Fire, and whose breath is death'. The great counsellors of Uruk advise against such a foolhardy plan of action, but at the beginning of Tablet III they have become reconciled to the venture and their advice is practical.

'Do not trust entirely, Gilgamesh, in your own strength.
When you have looked long enough, trust to your first blow.
He who leads the way will save his comrade.
He who knows the paths, he will guard his friend.
Let Enkidu go in front of you,
He knows the way of the Pine Forest.
He can look at the fight and instruct in the battle.

The face of Humbaba, the giant of the Pine Forest.

Let Enkidu guard the friend, keep the comrade safe,
Bring him back safe in person for brides,
So that we in our assembly may rely on you as king,
And that you in turn as king may rely on us again.'

The exact location of the Pine Forest is not certain. An earlier Sumerian version of this part of the epic suggests that it was to the east of Mesopotamia, possibly near the Zagros mountains on the borders of Elam, but the later version states that it was to the west of Mesopotamia in the Lebanon. We do have some idea what Humbaba looked like: a clay head, probably from Sippar and now in the British Museum, bears an inscription saying it is he, and very unpleasant he is with his fat-encircled face.

Taking heed of the counsellors' words, Gilgamesh and Enkidu consult Ninsun, the great queen. She makes a smoke-offering to the sun-god Shamash for Enkidu to protect his friend so that Gilgamesh may return safely.

Tablet IV, unfortunately in bad condition, describes how the two friends set off, eat their rations, and set up camp. True to both epic tradition and his own character, Gilgamesh has two 'extremely upsetting' dreams, which Enkidu interprets to mean that their expedition against Humbaba will be successful.

Tablet V sees the arrival of the friends at Humbaba's lair. It is splendidly described for a Mesopotamian audience, to whom forests would not have been familiar:

They stood and admired the forest,
Gazed and gazed at the height of the pines,
Gazed and gazed at the entrance to the pines,
Where Humbaba made tracks as he went to and fro.
The paths were well trodden and the road was excellent.
They beheld the Pine Mountain, dwelling-place of gods, shrine of Irnini.
The pines held up their luxuriance even on the face of the mountain.
Their shade was good, filling one with happiness.
Undergrowth burgeoned, entangling the forest.

Humbaba approaches and is scornful of his visitors: 'You are so very small that I regard you as I do a turtle or a tortoise . . .'

All seems hopeless; Gilgamesh despairs. As we shall see, it is common in Mesopotamian myths that, just when disaster threatens, the gods intervene with divine weapons and turn the tables against the enemy.

Shamash summoned up great tempests against Humbaba,
South Wind, North Wind, East Wind, West Wind, Moaning Wind,
Gale, *saparziggu*-Wind, *imhulla*-Wind, . . .-Wind,
Asakku, Wintry Wind, Tempest, Whirlwind,
Thirteen Winds rose up at him and Humbaba's face grew dark.
He could not charge forwards, he could not run backwards.
Thus the weapons of Gilgamesh succeeded against Humbaba.

Humbaba pleads for his life, but Enkidu persuades Gilgamesh to finish him off. They decapitate the ogre and place his head on a raft which the Euphrates will carry down to Nippur.

Back in Uruk, Gilgamesh washes and changes into a clean robe and a sash. His glamour is too much for the goddess Ishtar:

And Ishtar the princess raised her eyes to the beauty of Gilgamesh.
'Come to me, Gilgamesh, and be my lover!
Bestow on me the gift of your fruit!
You can be my husband, and I can be your wife.
I shall have a chariot of lapis lazuli and gold harnessed for you,
With wheels of gold, and horns of *elmēšu*-stone

Cylinder seal (left) with its impression, showing a nude goddess, possibly a Syrian version of Ishtar, wearing elaborate jewellery.

You shall harness *ūmu*-demons as great mules!
Enter into our house through the fragrance of pine!
When you enter our house
The wonderfully-wrought threshold shall kiss your feet!'

But Gilgamesh is not tempted by the goddess and, with devastating frankness, lists the fates that have befallen her previous lovers: Dumuzi, still weeping; the colourful *allulu*-bird, whose wing she broke; the lion, for whom she dug seven-and-seven pits; the horse she whipped, goaded and lashed, and decreed that he should gallop seven leagues non-stop; the shepherd; the herdsman; the chief shepherd who was turned into a wolf; and lastly, her father's gardener, Ishullanu, who brought her baskets of dates, and whom she turned into a frog. 'And how about me? You will love me and then treat me just like them!'

Ishtar is not used to such plain speaking; she storms up to heaven and demands of her father, Anu, the Bull of Heaven to help her strike down Gilgamesh. Her terrible threats – 'I shall set my face towards the infernal regions, I shall raise up the dead, and they will eat the living, I shall make the dead outnumber the living!' – prevail, and she enters Uruk with the reins of the Bull of Heaven in her hand.

Down beside the river the Bull snorts, and a chasm opens up into which a hundred young men of Uruk fall, then two hundred, then three hundred. It snorts again and another chasm opens up, into which another hundred young men of Uruk fall, then two hundred, then three hundred.

> At its third snorting a chasm opened up,
> And Enkidu fell into it.
> But Enkidu leapt out. He seized the Bull of Heaven by the horns.
> The Bull of Heaven blew spittle into his face,
> With its thick tail it whipped up its dung.

Half-blinded, Enkidu calls on Gilgamesh, who plunges his sword into the Bull's neck. They pull out its innards.

> Ishtar went up on the wall of Uruk the Sheepfold.
> She was contorted with rage, she hurled down curses.
> 'That man Gilgamesh who reviled me has killed the Bull of Heaven!'
> Enkidu listened to Ishtar saying this,
> And he pulled out the Bull of Heaven's shoulder and slapped it into her face:
> 'If I could only get at you as that does,
> I would do the same to you myself,
> I would hang its intestines on your arms!'
> Ishtar gathered the crimped courtesans,
> Prostitutes and harlots.
> She arranged for weeping over the Bull of Heaven's shoulder.

Gilgamesh summons the craftsmen of Uruk to admire the horns and then to decorate them. He dedicates them to his father Lugalbanda. The two heroes wash in the Euphrates and ride in triumph through the streets of Uruk. This is the high point of the epic.

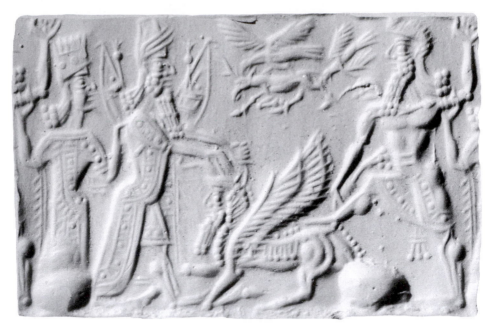

Impression from a blue chalcedony seal, possibly showing Gilgamesh and Enkidu slaying the Bull of Heaven, with the goddess Ishtar trying to prevent them.

Tablet VII is not well preserved and about twenty lines at the beginning are missing. Fortunately they can be partly filled in from a Hittite version, and they reveal Enkidu recounting his dream the morning after the great fight with the Bull of Heaven. The dream's portent is clear.

'O my brother, what a dream I saw last night!
Anu, Ellil, Ea, and heavenly Shamash were in the assembly.
And Ea said to Ellil, "As they have slain the Bull of Heaven,
So too they have slain Huwawa, who guarded the mountains planted with pines."
And Anu said, "One of them must die."
Ellil replied: "Let Enkidu die, but let Gilgamesh not die."'

Gilgamesh listens to his friend's words, 'and his tears flowed'. He goes to offer prayers to the great gods. Enkidu curses his fate, and particularly he curses Shamhat for corrupting him in the first place. Shamash replies on her behalf:

'Enkidu, why are you cursing my harlot Shamhat,
Who fed you on food fit for gods,
Gave you ale to drink, fit for kings,
Clothed you with a great robe,
Then provided you with Gilgamesh for a fine partner?
And now Gilgamesh, the friend who is a brother to you
Will lay you to rest on a great bed
And lay you to rest on a bed of loving care,
And let you stay in a restful dwelling, the dwelling on the left.
Princes of the earth will kiss your feet.
He will make the people of Uruk weep for you, mourn for you,

And he himself will neglect his appearance after your death.
Clothed only in a lionskin, he will roam the open country.'

Enkidu's anger abates; he forgives Shamhat. He falls ill and dreams again of his own death and descent to the underworld. For twelve days he lies in bed and grows weaker. In a moving speech at the beginning of Tablet VIII, Gilgamesh bids farewell to his friend. He lists all who will weep for him: the elders of Uruk, the open country, the field, the myrtle, pine and cypress trees:

'They shall weep for you, the bear, hyena, leopard, tiger, stag, cheetah,
Lion, wild bulls, deer, mountain goat, cattle, and other wild beasts of the open
    country,
It shall weep for you, the pure Euphrates,
With whose water in waterskins we used to refresh ourselves.
They shall weep for you, the young men of the broad city, of Uruk the Sheepfold,
Who watched the fighting when we struck down the Bull of Heaven...'

But Enkidu can no longer hear:

'Now, what is the sleep that has taken hold of you?
Turn to me, you! You aren't listening to me!
But he cannot lift his head.
I touch his heart, but it does not beat at all.'

Enkidu has died and Gilgamesh sends a shout throughout the land, a shout for a precious likeness to be fashioned of his friend, of copper, silver, jewels, lapis lazuli and gold. The rest of the tablet is very broken but what remains suggests that it is concerned with the funeral rites of Enkidu.

Tablet IX reveals a distraught Gilgamesh roaming the open country, terrified of death. He decides to go to see Ut-napishtim, who with his wife is supposed to have survived the Flood and to know the secret of eternal life. The journey is hazardous: lions lurk in the passes, and the gate to the towering mountain of Mashu, through which he must pass, is guarded by Scorpion-men 'whose aura is frightful, and whose glance is death. Their terrifying mantles of radiance drape the mountains.'

At first Gilgamesh's reception is hostile, but in a very broken passage he obviously manages to convince the Scorpion-man and his woman that he must pass through their gate, even though:

'It is impossible, Gilgamesh ...
Nobody has passed through the mountain's inaccessible tract.
For even after twelve leagues ...
The darkness is too dense, there is no light.'

In a highly stylised passage in which three nearly identical lines are repeated, building tension in a most effective way, Gilgamesh progresses through this ancient slough of despond:

When he had achieved one [two/three/four etc.] leagues[s]
The darkness was dense, there was no light,
It was impossible for him to see ahead or behind.

Sculpture of a scorpion-man, with coiled tail and splayed pincers, from Tell Halaf in Syria.

The unknown audience can almost be sensed counting its way through the dark miles. Suddenly Gilgamesh comes out into bright sunshine and a jewelled garden, the description of which is unfortunately missing about twenty-four lines. It begins:

> All kinds of thorny, prickly, spiky bushes were visible, blossoming with gemstones.
> Carnelian bore fruit
> Hanging in clusters, lovely to look at,
> Lapis lazuli bore foliage,
> Bore fruit, and was delightful to view.

Many different kinds of trees and semi-precious stones are mentioned and in the distance can be glimpsed the sea, probably the Mediterranean off the Phoenician coast. There lives Siduri, the divine ale-wife.

Tablet x begins with an introduction to Siduri. Her profession of beer-seller is well attested in the second millennium. There is nothing of the jolly barmaid about her, however; she is almost a prophetess here. At first, when she sees Gilgamesh, she locks herself behind her door because she thinks he may be an assassin. Certainly he looks very different from the splendid young man in clean robes and a sash who proved so irresistible to Ishtar.

> Clad only in a lionskin . . .
> He had the flesh of gods upon his body,
> But grief was in his innermost being.
> His face was like that of a long-distance traveller.

Gilgamesh accosts Siduri and tells her that he (and presumably Enkidu – the tablet is very fragmentary here) are the ones who destroyed Humbaba in the Pine Forest. The ale-wife seems to know all about them, including the killing of the Bull of Heaven, but she does not believe this can be Gilgamesh. He replies:

'How could my cheeks not be wasted, nor my face dejected,
Nor my heart wretched, nor my appearance worn out,
Nor grief in my innermost being,
Nor my face like that of a long-distance traveller
Nor my face weathered by cold and heat . . . ,
Nor roaming open country, clad only in a lionskin?
My friend whom I love so much, who experienced every hardship with me –
Enkidu, whom I love so much, who experienced every hardship with me –
The fate of mortals conquered him! Six days [and] seven nights I wept over him. . . .'

Gilgamesh then asks the ale-wife the way to Ut-napishtim, saying:

'If it possible, I shall cross the sea;
If it is impossible I shall roam open country again.'

The ale-wife tells Gilgamesh that there has never been a ferry of any kind, from time immemorial, and that only Shamash has ever crossed the sea:

'The crossing is difficult, the way of it very difficult.
And in between are lethal waters which bar the way ahead.'

She suggests that he look for the boatman, Ur-shanabi, beside the lethal waters and persuade him to take him across.

Straightaway Gilgamesh goes in search of Ur-shanabi, and it seems as if there is some kind of affray, but the text is very fragmentary here, and when it resumes, Ur-shanabi has taken up Siduri's refrain:

'Why are your cheeks wasted, your face dejected,
Your heart so wretched, your appearance worn out . . .'

Gilgamesh replies as he did to Siduri and concludes with the same request for directions to Ut-napishtim. In reply, Ur-shanabi tells Gilgamesh he must cut down three hundred poles, each 100 ft (30 m) long. These are to help them cross the lethal waters. They set off, using one pole at a time, Ur-shanabi warning Gilgamesh on no account to let the lethal water wet his hand. As they approach, Ut-napishtim sees them and begins to soliloquise, but unfortunately there is a break in the text of some twenty lines here. After the gap, Ut-napishtim asks Gilgamesh, in exactly the same words as those already used by Siduri and Ur-shanabi, why his cheeks are wasted and his face dejected. Gilgamesh replies exactly as he did to them, concluding with a passage on his long and difficult journey thus far. Ut-napishtim replies:

'Why do you prolong grief, Gilgamesh?
Since the gods made you from the flesh of gods and mankind,
Since the gods made you like your father and mother,
Death is inevitable at some time . . .'

Ut-napishtim then makes what is probably the most profound speech of the epic in an attempt to explain death to Gilgamesh:

'Nobody sees Death,
Nobody sees the face of Death,
Nobody hears the voice of Death.
Savage Death just cuts mankind down.
Sometimes we build a house, sometimes we make a nest,
But then brothers divide it upon inheritance,
Sometimes there is hostility in the land,
But then the river rises and brings flood-water.
Dragonflies drift on the river,
Their faces look upon the face of the Sun.
But then suddenly there is nothing.
The sleeping and the dead are just like each other,
Death's picture cannot be drawn.'

Tablet XI (the so-called Flood Tablet) begins with Gilgamesh wondering how it is that he and Ut-napishtim look just the same, yet one is mortal and the other immortal. Ut-napishtim's response is to tell him about the Flood and, to anyone familiar with the story of Noah's Ark, the parallels are many.

The gods decide to impose a great flood on mankind. Only Ea breaks rank to warn Ut-napishtim of the approaching doom. He sends a message via a reed hut and a brick wall:

'Man of Shuruppak, son of Ubara-Tutu,
Dismantle your house, build a boat.
Leave possessions, search out living things.
Reject chattels and save lives!
Put aboard the seed of all living things, into the boat.'

The great boat is then constructed, according to very precise measurements, and launched. Ut-napishtim relates to Gilgamesh how:

'I loaded her with everything there was,
Loaded her with all the silver,
Loaded her with all the gold,
Loaded her with all the seed of living things, all of them.
I put on board the boat all my kith and kin.
Put on board cattle from open country, wild beasts from open country, all kinds
    of craftsmen.'

The terrible flood arrives, and:

'For six days and seven nights
The wind blew, flood and tempest overwhelmed the land;
When the seventh day arrived the tempest, flood and onslaught
Which had struggled like a woman in labour, blew themselves out.
The sea became calm, the *imhullu*-wind grew quiet, the flood held back.
I looked at the weather; silence reigned,
For all mankind had returned to clay.
The flood-plain was flat as a roof.
I opened a porthole and light fell on my cheeks.
I bent down, then sat. I wept.'

Ut-napishtim puts out first a dove, then a swallow, and both come back. Finally he sends a raven, which does not return, thereby showing that the waters have receded. (In the Bible, Noah sent out a raven first, then two doves.) He then makes a huge sacrifice to the great gods and, after some quarrelling among themselves, Ellil makes Ut-napishtim and his wife immortal, saying:

'Until now Ut-napištim was mortal,
But henceforth Ut-napištim and his woman shall be as we gods are . . .'

His story ended, Ut-napishtim turns his attention to Gilgamesh's immortality and suggests he begin by a trial – not sleeping for six days and seven nights – the length of time that the flood lasted. But Gilgamesh fails the test; as soon as he is sitting down, 'Sleep breathed over him like a fog'. When Gilgamesh awakes after seven nights, he refuses to believe he has been asleep until he sees seven loaves of bread, some in a distinctly mouldy state, that have been placed by his head at the end of each night's sleep.

Disheartened, Gilgamesh determines to abandon his quest for immortality. Ut-napishtim tells Ur-shanabi to bring Gilgamesh a wash-bowl so that he may wash his hair and body.

'Put a new headband on his head.
Have him wear a robe as a proud garment
Until he comes to his city,
Until he reaches his journey's end,
The garment shall not discolour, but stay absolutely new.'

Ur-shanabi and Gilgamesh set off back across the lethal waters, but Gilgamesh does not leave empty-handed. To the people of the eastern Mediterranean the parting gift to a stranger homeward bound bestowed honour on both giver and receiver. (In Homer's *Odyssey* Menelaus and Helen gave parting gifts to Telemachus, and, in the Egyptian myth The Shipwrecked Sailor, the hero is not allowed to leave the island on which he has been washed up until his departure has been made honourable by the bestowal of lavish presents.) Ut-napishtim's parting gift to Gilgamesh is a 'closely guarded matter', a 'secret of the gods' – a plant of rejuvenation. Gilgamesh finds the plant, as directed, at the bottom of the sea, retrieves it and sets off on his journey to Uruk. But after thirty leagues, while washing one evening in a cool pool, a snake smells the sweet-scented plant and carries it off. 'Then Gilgamesh sat down and wept.' He realises that immortality is not to be his: 'I shall give up.'

Gilgamesh, still accompanied by Ur-shanabi, arrives once again at Uruk, and Gilgamesh proudly points out his true achievement, the magnificent city walls: 'Three square miles and the open ground comprise Uruk.'

There the epic probably ended. The last Tablet seems to have been an after-thought; it does not fit harmoniously with the rest of the epic because in it Enkidu is still alive, when we know he died in Tablet VII. In this final Tablet Gilgamesh makes two wooden objects, a *pukku* and a *mekku* (exactly what these are we do not know), and they fall into the underworld. Enkidu descends into the underworld to retrieve them for Gilgamesh but fails to follow his instructions, and so cannot return to the land of the living (a popular motif). Gilgamesh goes from god to god trying to secure Enkidu's release, which eventually he achieves, whereupon Enkidu is able to tell his friend all about the gloomy conditions in the underworld. Thus the epic ends in a sombre mood, very different from that at the end of Tablet XI, where a reconciled Gilgamesh realises that his perpetual memory is ensured by his magnificent building work.

The myth of Atrahasis

The Flood story is also preserved in another Akkadian myth. Atrahasis, according to one version of the Sumerian king-list, was the son of Ubara-Tutu, king of Shuruppak (modern Tell Fara in middle Mesopotamia), who is mentioned in Tablet XI of the Epic of Gilgamesh as being the father of Ut-napishtim. In fact, Atrahasis ('Extra Wise') and Ut-napishtim ('He Found Life') are both precursors of the biblical 'Noah'; there is also a Sumerian equivalent, Ziusudra ('Long Life'). Atrahasis is thus a universal figure of great antiquity.

The myth begins with the gods (rather than men) having to do all the hard work, digging out canals and clearing channels, and they do not like it. After 3,600 years they decide they have had enough and arm themselves to confront Ellil. Ellil dislikes being threatened in the middle of the night

Sculpture of a recumbent human-headed bull. Massive winged bulls and lions decorated and guarded the entrances to palaces and temples.

and his face goes as yellow as tamarisk. He summons the great gods to hear their case, and they decide that Belet-ili, the womb-goddess, shall create mortals, who will then do all the heavy work instead. This she does, creating seven males and seven females. From this small beginning grew a large population, too large for Ellil:

> 600 years, less than 600, passed,
> And the country became too wide, the people too numerous.
> The country was as noisy as a bellowing bull.
> The God grew restless at their racket,
> Ellil had to listen to their noise.
> He addressed the great gods,
> 'The noise of mankind has become too much,
> I am losing sleep over their racket.'

Ellil tries plague, he tries drought, he tries famine. Atrahasis tries to ensure that they do not work. The Standard and Old Babylonian versions differ, but eventually the effect of each of these three is devastating: after six years, the people are eating their daughters, and they can no longer carry out the hard work for which they were created. Enki and Ellil quarrel over the best course of action. Ellil decides to perform a 'bad deed' (the Flood), and Enki warns Atrahasis, giving him specific instructions for the boat he is to build, and warning him that the Flood will last for seven days.

> The Flood roared like a bull,
> Like a wild ass screaming the winds howled
> The darkness was total, there was no sun.

Unfortunately, at the climax of the action (and just where it would be fascinating to make comparisons with both the Epic of Gilgamesh and the Bible) there is a large gap of about fifty-eight lines, and the story only resumes at a point (similar to the one in the Epic of Gilgamesh) where the gods are gathering over the sacrifice made by Atrahasis, quarrelling as to who is to blame. Enki takes the credit for disclosing to Atrahasis what was in store, but in the very fragmentary ending it seems to be agreed that some sort of curb on man's reproduction is needed. The responsibility for this is to fall upon women, whose fertility is to be restricted, sometimes through barrenness and sometimes deliberately in certain social categories (such as temple prostitutes).

The epic ends with a hymnic summary, probably spoken by Ellil:

> 'How we sent the Flood.
> But a man survived the catastrophe.
> You are the counsellor of the gods;
> On your orders I created conflict.
> Let the Igigi listen to this song
> In order to praise you,
> And let them record your greatness.
> I shall sing of the Flood to all people:
> Listen!'

The Epic of Creation

The Epic of Creation, unlike that of Gilgamesh, appears to have been almost unknown outside Mesopotamia. Tablets have been found at Sultantepe, Nineveh, Kish and Babylon, but (again unlike the Epic of Gilgamesh) they show little variation. It is an epic only in that it deals with cosmological events; there are no mortal heroes and, as we shall see, little drama and no cliff-hanging suspense. It is more in the nature of a sacred book and was recited during the celebrations of the New Year's Festival at Babylon.

The epic begins at the very beginning of time,

When skies above were not yet named
Nor earth below pronounced by name, . . .

and there are just two gods: Apsu, who represents the primordial waters under the earth, and Tiamat, who is the personification of the sea. They beget four generations of gods who, as in the myth of Atrahasis, become extremely noisy and their noise becomes unbearable:

The gods of that generation would meet together
And disturb Tiamat, and their clamour reverberated.
They stirred up Tiamat's belly,
They were annoying her by playing inside Anduruna*.
Apsu could not quell their noise . . .

*a name of the god's dwelling

Apsu confronts Tiamat, who is inclined to be indulgent towards her noisy offspring, and in a loud voice he declares:

'Their ways have become very grievous to me,
By day I cannot rest, by night I cannot sleep.
I shall abolish their ways and disperse them!
Let peace prevail, so that we can sleep.'

Tiamat is enraged, but Apsu plots with his vizier, Mummu, to put an end to their troublesome ways. Before they can put their plot into effect, however, it is discovered by Ea 'who knows everything'. He intervenes, puts Apsu and Mummu into a deep sleep and then slays them. Ea assumes the belt, the crown and the mantle of radiance and, well satisfied, retires to his private quarters.

Ea takes over the dwelling-place of Apsu as his own domain, and there he and his spouse Damkina create Marduk, superlative in every way:

Two ugallu-demons in combat (above), and an impression (below) from a black-and-white speckled diorite seal, showing a god standing on a mušhuššu-dragon. An interceding god presents a worshipper who carries a sacrificial animal.

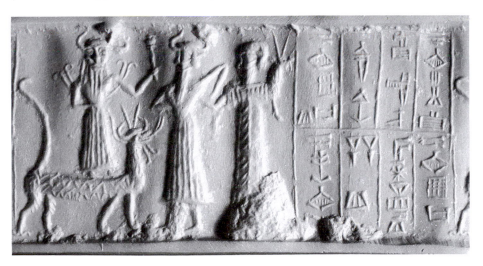

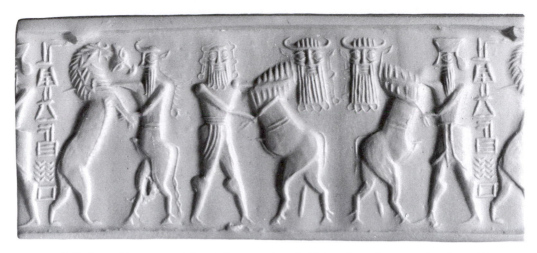

Cylinder seal impression (above) showing a bearded lahmu-hero, hair parted in the middle and curls arranged in three sets either side of the face. He takes part in a contest scene.

Cylinder seal impression (below) showing bull-men in a contest scene.

He suckled the teats of goddesses;
The nurse who reared him filled him with awesomeness.
Proud was his form, piercing his stare,
Mature his emergence, he was powerful from the start.
Anu his father's begetter beheld him,
And rejoiced, beamed; his heart was filled with joy.
He made him so perfect that his godhead was doubled.
Elevated far above them, he was superior in every way.
His limbs were ingeniously made beyond comprehension.
Impossible to understand, too difficult to perceive.
Four were his eyes, four were his ears;
When his lips moved, fire blazed forth.
The four ears were enormous
And likewise the eyes; they perceived everything.
Highest among the gods, his form was outstanding.

Tiamat is disturbed and heaves about restlessly. The gods plot evil in their hearts and persuade Tiamat that she should avenge the death of Apsu.

Tiamat creates a troop of fearsome monsters:

> She stationed a horned serpent, a *mušhuššu*-dragon, and a *lahmu*-hero,
> An *ugallu*-demon, a rabid dog, and a scorpion-man,
> Aggressive *ūmu*-demons, a fish-man, and a bull-man.

Foremost among her monsters is Qingu, on whom she confers leadership of the army. She sets him upon a throne, addresses him as 'her only lover' and gives him the Tablet of Destinies. This ultimate honour bestows on its owner supreme power.

Tablet II begins with Tiamat marshalling her battle force and news of this reaching Ea, who 'was dumbfounded and sat in silence'. To his father Anshar he describes Tiamat's giant snakes, which are:

> 'Sharp of tooth and unsparing of fang.
> She filled their bodies with venom instead of blood.
> She cloaked ferocious dragons with fearsome rays,
> And made them bear mantles of radiance ...'

He then repeats word for word the list of monsters, and the giving of the Tablet of Destinies to Qingu. Anshar is certainly worried: he twists his fingers, bites his lip, his liver is inflamed and his belly will not rest. He roars at Ea, 'You must be the one who declares war!'

In the gap which follows, we can assume that Ea goes forth to do battle with Tiamat, and fails, because then Anshar addresses Anu in similar terms. In another fragmentary part, it is clear that Anu sets forth but he too fails.

> Anshar was speechless, and stared at the ground;
> He gnashed his teeth and shook his head [in despair] at Ea.
> Now the Igigi assembled, all the Anukki.
> They sat silently [for a while], tight-lipped.

Finally they spoke:

> Will no [other] god come forward? Is fate fixed?

This is Marduk's moment. From his secret dwelling, Ea calls out an answer:

> 'The mighty heir who was to be his father's champion,
> Who rushes [fearlessly] into battle: Marduk the Hero!'

Marduk rejoices; he approaches Anshar, whose heart is filled with joy. Setting aside his trepidation, he kisses Marduk on the lips. Marduk is confident:

> 'Father, my creator, rejoice and be glad!
> You shall soon set your foot upon the neck of Tiamat!'

But he lays down one condition: if he is successful in defeating Tiamat and saving their lives, he demands to take over as supreme god:

> 'My own utterance shall fix fate instead of you!
> Whatever I create shall never be altered!
> The decree of my lips shall never be revoked, never changed!'

Anshar convenes a meeting of the gods so that they can be told in repetitive detail about all of Tiamat's doings, of the threat she presents, and of the arrival of Marduk and of the condition he has made. The gods duly assemble at a banquet:

> They became very carefree, they were merry,
> And they decreed destiny for Marduk their champion.

Despite their confidence in him, they first give him a test:

> They set up in their midst one constellation,
> And then they addressed Marduk their son,
> 'May your decree, O lord, impress the gods!
> Command to destroy and to recreate, and let it be so!
> Speak and let the constellation vanish!
> Speak to it again and let the constellation reappear.'
> He spoke, and at his word the constellation vanished.
> He spoke to it again and the constellation was recreated.
> When the gods his fathers saw how effective his utterance was,
> They rejoiced, they proclaimed: 'Marduk is King!'

Marduk fashions his weapons for the great battle: a bow and arrow, a mace in his right hand, lightning before him, and an ever-blazing flame in his body. He also makes a net to encircle Tiamat and marshals seven winds to go behind him to create turmoil inside Tiamat. Then he raises his great flood-weapon and mounts 'the frightful, unfaceable storm-chariot'; its team of four are called 'Slayer', 'Pitiless', 'Racer' and 'Flyer', and their teeth carry poison.

Radiant with terror, Marduk sets out on the road to Tiamat, but at the sight of her his will crumbles and he cannot decide what to do. Although this seems somewhat unrealistic, it is a common mythical device (used also in the Epic of Gilgamesh) to heighten tension, by putting the inevitable victory temporarily in the balance. Tiamat sneers, and Marduk's courage returns. He challenges Tiamat to single combat. Here is the climax, the great battle scene towards which everything has been leading:

> Face to face they came, Tiamat and Marduk, sage of the gods.
> They engaged in combat, they closed for battle.
> The Lord spread his net and made it encircle her,
> To her face he dispatched the *imhullu*-wind, which had been behind:
> Tiamat opened her mouth to swallow it,
> And he forced in the *imhullu*-wind so that she could not close her lips.
> Fierce winds distended her belly;
> Her insides were constipated and she stretched her mouth wide.
> He shot an arrow which pierced her belly,
> Split her down the middle and split her heart,
> Vanquished her and extinguished her life.
> He threw down her corpse and stood on top of her.

The gods who had formed part of Tiamat's terrifying army then panic and turn tail, but they are caught by Marduk and bundled into the net, where they cower:

And as for the dozens of creatures, covered in fearsome rays,
The gang of demons who all marched on her right,
He fixed them with nose-ropes and tied their arms.

Qingu is dispatched and the Tablet of Destinies is wrested from him.
Marduk seals it with his own seal and presses it to his breast. Then he turns
his attention once more to Tiamat:

The Lord trampled the lower part of Tiamat,
With his unsparing mace smashed her skull,
Severed the arteries of her blood. . .

He then slices her in half 'like a fish for drying'; from half of her he makes
a roof for the sky, and from the other half he makes the earth which keeps
out the subterranean waters below. On it he builds the large temple of Esharra
where he founds cult centres for Anu, Ellil and Ea.

Next Marduk proceeds to organise the rest of the universe: naming the
months of the year, apportioning to them three stars each, fashioning stands
for the great gods, making the crescent moon appear and designating it 'the
jewel of night to mark out the days'. From Tiamat's spittle, he makes scudding
clouds, wind and rain. From her poison, he makes billowing fog. From her
eyes, he opens the Euphrates and the Tigris.

*Drawing taken from a cylinder seal
showing Marduk and a subdued
mušhuššu-dragon, one of the monsters
recruited by Tiamat. Here Marduk holds
the rod and ring of kingship in his left
hand. His robe is decorated with
medallions and he wears an elaborate
crown.*

The gods are overcome with gratitude and prepare a reception for Marduk, at which Anu, Ellil and Ea give him presents. They dress him in gorgeous robes and bestow kingship on him. In return, Marduk tells them:

'Over the Apsu, the sea-green dwelling,
In front of Esharra, which I created for you,
[Where] I strengthened the ground beneath it for a shrine,
I shall make a house to be a luxurious dwelling for myself
And shall found his [Marduk's] cult centre within it,
And I shall establish my private quarters, and confirm my kingship.
Whenever you come up from the Apsu for an assembly,
Your night's resting place shall be in it, receiving you all.
Whenever you come down from the sky for an assembly,
Your night's resting place shall be it it, receiving you all.
I hereby name it Babylon, home of the great gods.
We shall make it the centre of religion.'

But Marduk's work is not yet finished. He makes up his mind to perform miracles and tells Ea his plan:

'Let me put blood together, and make bones too.
Let me set up primeval man: Man shall be his name.'

As in the myth of Atrahasis, man is to be created to do the work of the gods so that the gods can be at leisure. Divine revenge is wreaked on Qingu's

Reconstruction of the ziggurat at Babylon, and its ground plan.

corpse and mankind is created from his blood. Then Marduk divides the gods into those of the sky and those of the underworld. In gratitude, the gods offer themselves to build the night's resting place, of which Marduk has already spoken. Marduk is enthusiastic:

> His face lit up greatly, like daylight.
> 'Create Babylon, whose construction you requested!
> Let its mud bricks be moulded, and build high the shrine!'

This is to be the last work the gods will have to perform. For an entire year they manufacture bricks, and by the end of the second year they have built the great shrine and ziggurat of Esagila. To celebrate, Marduk holds a banquet and he is proclaimed king of the gods. The epic then ends with the enumeration of fifty honorific names of Marduk, with esoteric explanations of each one.

Much of the Epic of Creation is concerned with religious matters, which accounts for its rather unexciting style. It is highly repetitive and its message arcane. There is no introductory invitation, as in the Epic of Gilgamesh, for the audience to share the story, and in literary terms it is more heraldic, less narrative, and has a rich vocabulary within the elevated hymnic style. Perhaps it should be viewed primarily as a work to be read and enacted within a religious setting, and less as one intended to entertain.

Shorter myths

The Epic of Creation, described in the previous chapter, told of the rise of Marduk to pre-eminence in the pantheon of gods. The Epic of Erra, probably composed during the ninth to eighth centuries BC, presents a very different picture of Marduk the Hero, here seen as senile, impotent and shambling. Scribes and poets had an awkward time explaining why Babylon, once so glorious, was now abandoned by its god and conquered by enemies, and perhaps for this reason the work is strikingly polemical and rhetorical.

In fact, the epic contains some dramatic descriptive passages about both the effects of war and pestilence, which are the work of Erra, and the blessings of peace and prosperity, which are assured for Babylon when its city-god is returned to his rightful place. Admittedly, the plot is almost non-existent, and the epic makes little attempt to describe events in sequence; instead the three protagonists – Erra, the good vizier Ishum, and Marduk – each take centre stage in turn, and declaim individually at length.

The Epic of Erra

The epic begins with the formula also encountered in the Epic of Anzu: 'I sing of the son of the king of all populated lands . . .', a prologue addressed to Erra and Ishum. Erra, 'warrior of the gods, was stirring at home', his heart urging him to make war. Erra (also known as Nergal) is the god of plague and lord of the underworld. Such was his reputation that extracts of the epic later appeared on amulet-shaped clay tablets; these were hung on the walls of houses to ward off pestilence and protect the inhabitants.

Despite his warlike mood, Erra is assailed by lethargy and cannot make himself act. He tells his weapons to 'Stay propped in the cupboard!'. But these weapons – of whom the Sebitti, seven warrior gods who march at his side, are paramount – take him to task:

'Why do you stay in town like a feeble old man?
How can you stay at home like a lisping child?
Are we to eat women's bread, like one who has never marched on to the battlefield?
Are we to be fearful and nervous as if we had no experience of war?
To go on to the battlefield is as good as a festival for young men!'

They complain that they will soon be unfit for war:

Clay amulet inscribed with the Epic of Erra. Amulets had a magical function, and this particular one would have been hung in a house to protect the family from the plague (personified by Erra). The text is shown the right way up, although the suspension loop is at the bottom.

'And we, who know the mountain passes, we have quite forgotten the road!
Spiders' webs are spun over our campaign gear.
Our trusty bows have rebelled and become too tough for our strength.
The points of our sharp arrows are blunt.
Our daggers are corroded with verdigris for lack of butchery.'

Warrior Erra is inspired by their words, as pleasing to him 'as the best oil'. He tells his vizier Ishum to lead the way. Ishum demurs, but Erra's mind is made up, and he decides to confront Marduk. Entering Esagila, Marduk's temple in Babylon, he tells him without preamble that his finery is dirty and his crown tarnished. This is a ruse to get Marduk out of the way. Marduk explains that the craftsmen needed to restore his insignia to their former glory are now in the domain of sweet water beneath the earth and cannot come back up. Erra persuades Marduk to go down to them, promising that meanwhile he will rule and keep firm control of heaven and earth. Marduk duly sets off.

In Marduk's absence Erra plots to devastate Babylonia, making her cities a wilderness, desecrating her holy shrines, turning her royal palaces into ruins, and sowing conflict within families. Ishum intervenes and twice tries, ineffectually, to make Erra change his mind. On his third attempt, he passionately describes the unnatural effect of the destruction of Babylon:

'He who is ignorant of weapons is unsheathing his dagger,
He who is ignorant of battle is making war,
He who is ignorant of wings is flying like a bird. The weakling covers the master
    of force;
The fatty is overtaking the sprinter.'

Ishum reports that Marduk himself has cried 'Woe!' and clutched at his heart. All over Babylonia, in Sippar, Uruk, and Der, people are at war and the country violated. He concludes:

'O warrior Erra, you have put the just to death,
You have put the unjust to death.
You have put to death the man who sinned against you.
You have put to death the man who did not sin against you.
You have put to death the en-priest who made taklimu-offerings promptly,
You have put to death the courtier who served the king,
You have put old men to death on the porch,
You have put young girls to death in their bedrooms.
Yet you will not rest at all . . .'

Erra is defiant and he addresses all the gods:

'Keep quiet, all of you, and learn what I have to say!
What if I did intend the harm of the wrong I have just done?
When I am enraged, I devastate people!'

Ishum soothes him:

'Warrior, be still and listen to my words!
What if you were to rest now, and we would serve you?
We all know that nobody can stand up to you in your day of wrath!'

Appeased, Erra retires to his temple in Kutha. Ishum gathers the scattered people of Akkad, foretelling victory and prosperity for them as well as a time when they will look back and remember the devastation that once befell them.

'For countless years shall the praises of the great lord Nergal and the warrior Ishum
    [be sung]:
How Erra became angry and set his face towards overwhelming countries and
    destroying their people,
But Ishum his counsellor placated him so that he left a remnant!'

And Erra concludes:

'Let this song endure forever, let it last for eternity!
Let all countries listen to it and praise my valour!
Let settled people see and magnify my name!'

Etana

This myth concerns a very early king of Kish, whose name appears in the Sumerian king-list. A fable about an eagle and a snake who inhabit the same tree is incorporated with a central motif of a childless king who searches for a magical plant to ensure an heir. It is the only Mesopotamian myth

Impression from serpentine cylinder seal showing Etana sitting on the back of the eagle.

for which illustrations have been recognised: cylinder seals of the Akkadian period (2390–2249 BC) depict the episode in which Etana ascends towards heaven on the eagle's back. It is possible that the quarrel between the eagle and the snake was once an animal fable in its own right; the Sumerian story Gilgamesh and the Halub Tree, which tells of a snake and a bird which inhabit a poplar tree, may support this theory.

Tablet I begins with the foundation of the city of Kish, in which the great gods, both the Igigi and the Annunaki, have played a part. Ishtar is searching high and low for a king, and Ellil is looking for a throne-dais. Unfortunately, the last 120 lines are missing, but we can assume that, between them, Ellil and Ishtar ensure that Etana ascends the throne.

Tablet II introduces the eagle and the snake, who live in a poplar within the shade of the throne-dais. The two make a pact not to overstep the limit set by Shamash, and for some time live harmoniousiy, taking it in turns to catch prey which they share between themselves and their young. But once the eagle's young have grown large and flourished:

> The eagle plotted evil in its heart,
> And in its heart it plotted evil,
> And made up its mind to eat its friend's young ones.

Instantly the eagle receives a warning:

> A small fledgling, especially wise, addressed its words to the eagle, its father,
> 'Father, don't eat! The net of Shamash will ensnare you.
> The snares [on which] the oath of Shamash [is sworn] will overturn you and ensnare you.'

But the eagle will not be warned. It waits until evening, then goes down and eats the snake's young ones. The snake comes back, carrying its load of meat, and stares at its nest, 'Stared, for its nest was not there.'

The snake waits all night for the eagle, and in the morning weeps and appeals to Shamash:

'I trusted in you, Shamash the warrior,
And I was helpful to the eagle who lives on the branches.
Now the serpent's nest is grief-stricken.
My own nest is not there, while its nest is safe.
My young ones are scattered and its young ones are safe.
It came down and ate my young ones!
You know the wrong which it has done me, Shamash!
Truly, O Shamash, your net is as wide as earth,
Your snare is as broad as the sky!
The eagle should not escape from your net . . .'

Shamash is not deaf to the appeal, and instructs the serpent to seek a wild bull (which is waiting, bound up), to open its insides and to hide itself within the bull's stomach. Birds of all kinds will come to eat the flesh and the eagle will be among them. When the eagle itself is feeding, the snake is to seize it by the wing, cut its wings, and throw the bird into a bottomless pit where it will be left to die of hunger and thirst.

All goes according to plan, although the exceptionally wise young fledgling again tries to deter its father ('Don't go down, father; perhaps the serpent is lying in wait inside this wild bull!'). Once again it is overruled and soon the eagle, its wings broken, is at the bottom of the pit.

Now it is the eagle's turn to pray to Shamash, which he does every day. Eventually Shamash responds:

'You are wicked, and you have grieved my heart.
You did an unforgivable deed, an abomination to the gods.
You are dying, and I shall not go near you!
But a man, whom I am sending to you, is coming – let him help you.'

The man is Etana, who has also been praying every day to Shamash:

'O Lord, let the word go forth from your mouth
And give me the plant of birth,
Show me the plant of birth!
Remove my shame and provide me with a son!'

Shamash gives Etana precise instructions where to find the abandoned eagle, telling him that the bird will then show him the plant of birth.

Tablet III begins with Etana finding the eagle in the pit and asking the bird to show him the plant of birth. The eagle readily agrees, but first must be helped out of the pit; and so with great patience, Etana teaches the eagle to fly again. One month, two months, three, four, five, six, seven months pass:

In the eighth month he helped it out of its pit.
The eagle, now well fed, was as strong as a fierce lion.
The eagle made its voice heard and spoke to Etana,
'My friend, we really are friends, you and I!
Tell me what you wish from me, that I may give it to you.'

Etana wastes no time in asking the eagle to change his destiny, to find the plant of birth. The eagle hunts around in the mountains but cannot find the plant, so then suggests to Etana that it carry him upwards on its back:

'Put your arms over my sides,
Put your hands over the quills of my wings.'

Etana puts his arms over the eagle's sides, and his hands over the quills of its wings and they soar upwards for one mile. The eagle says to Etana: 'My friend, look at the country! How does it seem?' Etana replies that the wide sea is no bigger than a sheepfold. Up they go a second mile:

'My friend, look at the country! How does it seem?'
'The country has turned into a garden . . .
And the wide sea is no bigger than a bucket!'

A third mile they soar and the eagle asks again. But this time Etana replies that he cannot even see the country, nor pick out the wide sea.

'My friend, I cannot go any further towards heaven.
Retrace the way, and let me go back to my city!'

The eagle takes him back to earth, and there follows a gap of uncertain length in which apparently they return to Kish and Etana has a series of dreams encouraging him to try again to reach heaven. The eagle takes him up once more – one mile, two miles, a third – and they arrive at the heaven of Anu. The eagle and Etana pass through the gate of Sin, Shamash, Adad and Ishtar; they bow down, and there the text breaks off. We do not know what happened in the heaven of Anu, but we may perhaps guess that at some stage they did find the plant of birth for at least in the Sumerian king-list, Etana is succeeded by a son named Balih.

Adapa

Adapa, like Etana and Gilgamesh, is a mortal of divine extraction and, like Gilgamesh, he narrowly misses immortality but receives compensation – in his case, becoming the wisest of men.

Adapa is a priest of Ea in his cult temple at Eridu. Every day Adapa attends to the rites: he bakes bread and sets up offering tables and, as temple fisherman, he goes out in his boat to catch fish. One day his regimented routine is disrupted by South Wind, though we do not know exactly how, since there is a gap of uncertain length. When the text resumes, Adapa is berating South Wind and threatening to break its wing. He then does this and, for seven days, South Wind does not blow towards the land. Anu notices and asks his vizier Ilabrat the reason. Ilabrat tells him that Adapa has broken South Wind's wing, and Anu demands Adapa's presence. Before Adapa sets off, however, Ea warns him:

'When you stand before Anu
They will hold out for you bread of death, so you must not eat.
They will hold out for you water of death, so you must not drink.'

Adapa arrives before Anu and explains what has happened:

'My lord, I was catching fish in the middle of the sea
For the house of my lord [Ea].
But he inflated the sea into a storm
And South Wind blew and sank me!
I was forced to take up residence in the fishes' home
In my fury I cursed South Wind.'

Dumuzi and Gizzida, two door-keeper gods, speak a word in Adapa's favour to Anu. This calms him down, and he instructs food and drink to be given to Adapa.

They fetched him the bread of [eternal] life, but he would not eat.
They fetched him the water of [eternal] life, but he would not drink.

Adapa, remembering Ea's instructions, has rejected the bread and water of immortality. Unfortunately the rest of the epic is lost; we do not know if Ea deliberately tricked Adapa, or whether Ea genuinely believed that Adapa would be offered the bread and water of death.

The Epic of Anzu

With this epic we return to the theme, familiar from the Epic of Creation, of a rebellious contender for supreme power who resorts to trickery and cheating to achieve his ends, whereupon a saviour must be found to defeat

Drawing of a relief from the palace of Ninurta at Nimrud. Ninurta attacks the wicked bird Anzu.

the usurper in heroic combat. In this case we have the evil Anzu, the soaring, bird-shaped son of Anu.

The epic again begins with the formula 'I sing of ...' In the Standard version the hero is the war-god Ninurta. In the Old Babylonian version, the hero is Ningirsu, patron god of the city of Girsu in central Mesopotamia; this version is written in an abbreviated form, and we have only a small part of it.

The story begins with a prologue introducing Ninurta and telling of his powerful feats. Then the gods report to Ellil the birth of Anzu; the full description of him is very fragmentary, but what there is suggests strength, power and fury. At first Ea persuades Ellil to let Anzu serve him as his personal bodyguard, and Ellil appoints Anzu to guard the entrance to his chamber. In Anzu's presence, Ellil often bathes in holy water. Anzu looks on longingly:

> His eyes would gaze at the trappings of Ellil-power:
> His lordly crown, his robe of divinity,
> The Tablet of Destinies in his hands. Anzu gazed,
> And gazed at Duranki's god, father of the gods,
> And fixed his purpose, to usurp the Ellil-power.

Very soon, his wicked plan is made.

> And at the chamber's entrance from which he often gazed, he waited for the start
>   of day.
> When Ellil was bathing in the holy water,
> Stripped and with his crown laid down on the throne,
> He gained the Tablet of Destinies for himself,
> Took away the Ellil-power.

Anzu flies off into hiding with the divine regalia, and Anu immediately calls for Anzu's assassination. First he calls upon his own son Adad to strike Anzu with lightning, his weapon, promising him supremacy in the gods' assembly if he succeeds. But Adad will not go:

> 'Father, who could rush off to the inaccessible mountain?
> Which of the gods your sons will be Anzu's conqueror?
> For he has gained the Tablet of Destinies for himself,
> Has taken away the Ellil-power; rites are abandoned!'

He turns away, saying he will not undertake the expedition. Next, the gods summon Gerra to burn Anzu with fire, his weapon. Gerra replies:

> 'Father, who could rush off to the inaccessible mountain?
> Which of the gods your sons will be Anzu's conqueror?
> For he has gained the Tablet of Destinies for himself,
> Has taken away the Ellil-power; rites are abandoned!'

He also turns away, saying he will not undertake the expedition.

Next they call upon Shara, Ishtar's son to strike (?) Anzu with ..., his weapon (quite what this is we do not know, as the text is broken here). But Shara, too, rejects the chance for glory in identical words. At the third rejection, the gods fall silent, and despair.

Ea, 'the Lord of intelligence', then forms an idea in the depths of his being. He summons Belet-ili, the great mother goddess, to produce broad-chested Ninurta, her 'superb beloved'. This she does, and she makes an inspiring appeal:

'Make a path, fix the hour,
Let light dawn for the gods whom I created.
Muster your devastating battle force,
Make your evil winds flash as they march over him.
Capture soaring Anzu
And inundate the earth, which I created – wreck his dwelling.
Let terror thunder above him,
Let fear your battle force shake in him,
Make the devastating whirlwind rise up against him.
Set your arrow in the bow, coat it with poison'.

Thus inspired, Ninurta marshals the seven evil winds 'who dance in the dust'. He musters a terrifying battle array.

On the mountainside Anzu and Ninurta met.
Anzu looked at him and shook with rage at him,
Bared his teeth like an *ūmu*-demon; his mantle of radiance covered the mountain,
He roared like a lion in sudden rage . . .

A furious battle ensues:

Clouds of death rained down, an arrow flashed lightning,
Whizzed, the battle force roared between them.

Ninurta draws his bow taut and sends another arrow, but Anzu, holding the Tablet of Destinies, easily deflects it. Ninurta sends for advice to Ea. Ea tells the messenger:

'Don't let the battle slacken, press home your victory!
Tire him out so that he sneds his pinions in the clash of tempests.
Take a throw-stick to follow your arrows
And cut off his pinions, detach both right and left . . .'

The messenger returns to Ninurta and repeats Ea's advice word for word. Ninurta marshals once more his seven evil winds and enters the fray again.

At this exciting moment, Tablet II ends. The beginning of Tablet III is very fragmentary, but it seems that devastation reigns; there is blazing heat and confusion during which Ninurta's arrow passes through the heart and lungs of Anzu and he slays the wicked bird. Ninurta regains the Tablet of Destinies and sends the good news winging back to the gods. The epic ends in traditional fashion:

'You captured Anzu, slew him in his powerfulness,
Slew soaring Anzu in his powerfulness.
Because you were so brave and slew the mountain,
You made all foes kneel at the feet of Ellil your father.
Ninurta, because you were so brave and slew the mountain,
You made all foes kneel at the feet of Ellil your father.
You have won complete dominion, every single rite.'

Cylinder seal impression (above) showing Ninurta with his bow and arrow dispatching the Anzu bird.

Terracotta figure (right) of a nude goddess. The bird feet and hanging wings suggest the Queen of the Underworld.

The gods then call him by some twenty honorific names, just as Marduk was named at the end of the Epic of Creation.

The Descent of Ishtar to the Underworld

Unfortunately incomplete, this is a most elegant tale of how (but not why) the goddess Ishtar descended to the underworld, Kurnugi, the land of no return, and how, once there, she was imprisoned until Ea secured her release. The underworld is a dark, dismal and horribly dusty place where Ishtar's sister Ereshkigal is queen.

Ishtar arrives at the gate of Kurnugi, determined to enter.

'Here gatekeeper, open your gate for me,
Open your gate for me to come in!
If you do not open the gate for me to come in,
I shall smash the door and shatter the bolt,
I shall smash the doorpost and overturn the doors,
I shall raise up the dead and they shall eat the living:
The dead shall outnumber the living!'

The gatekeeper goes at once to Ereshkigal:

When Ereshkigal heard this,
Her face grew livid as cut tamarisk,
Her lips grew dark as the rim of a *kuninu*-vessel.*
*The rim of a kuninu-vessel was coated with bitumen, making it black-lipped

She asks herself what can have brought Ishtar to her kingdom, and ominously instructs the gatekeeper:

'Go, gatekeeper, open your gate to her.
Treat her according to the ancient rites.'

There follows a ritualistic and repetitive scene in seven stages, typical of Mesopotamian myth, in which the beautiful and gorgeously attired Ishtar is systematically stripped of her jewellery. At the first gate, Ishtar is stripped of the great crown on her head.

'Gatekeeper, why have you taken away the great crown on my head?'
'Go in, my lady. Such are the rites of the Mistress of Earth.'

At the second gate, Ishtar is stripped of the rings in her ears.

'Gatekeeper, why have you taken away the rings in my ears?'
'Go in, my lady. Such are the rites of the Mistress of Earth.'

At the third gate, Ishtar is stripped of the beads around her neck; at the fourth of the toggle-pins at her breast; at the fifth of the girdle of birth-stones around her waist; at the sixth of the bangles on her wrists and ankles; and at the seventh gate she is stripped of the proud garment of her body. Thus she is naked when she finally comes before her sister, but still it is Ereshkigal who trembles. The queen of the underworld summons her vizier Namtar and instructs him to send out against Ishtar sixty diseases – to her eyes, her arms, her feet, her heart, her head, to every part of her.

Meanwhile, on earth, all sexual activity is at an end.

No bull mounted a cow, no donkey impregnated a jenny,
No young man impregnated a girl in the street,
The young man slept in his private room,
The girl slept in the company of her friends.

Papsukkal, the vizier of the great gods, weeps before Ea, and Ea as usual comes up with a solution. He creates a playboy whose beauty will so gladden Ereshkigal's heart that she will relax; 'her mood will lighten'. He must then ask for a waterskin, possibly under the pretence of drinking from it, and sprinkle Ishtar with its contents so that she may revive.

This ruse fails, however. Initially charmed with his appearance, Ereshkigal suddenly curses him with a great curse:

'Bread gleaned from the city's ploughs shall be your food,
The city drains shall be your only drinking place,
The shade of a city wall your only standing place,
Threshold steps your only sitting place,
The drunkard and the thirsty shall slap your cheek.'

But, in cursing Ea's playboy, she spares Ishtar. She instructs Namtar to sprinkle her with the waters of life and, in a highly satisfactory symmetrical passage reversing her earlier progress, Ishtar is let out of each of the seven gates by which she entered; at each one she repossesses, in strict sequence, the symbols of her divinity, starting with the proud garment of her body and ending with the great crown for her head.

The epic ends with Ishtar paying for her release with Dumuzi, 'the lover

Cylinder seal impression which may portray Dumuzi retained in the underworld, flanked by snakes.

of her youth', who will in future dwell in the underworld. On one day each year he will return to earth at which time rituals will be enacted. This probably refers to the *taklimtu* ritual which took place in the month of Dumuzi (June/July), during which a statue of Dumuzi was bathed, anointed and lay in state in Nineveh.

Nergal and Ereshkigal

This is a myth which has a considerable overlap with Ishtar's Descent to the Underworld, sharing some of the same characters, the same location, and Ea's role in bringing about a solution. As we shall see, there are interesting differences, however, such as the introduction of a ritual chair, the graphic image of a long stairway leading up to and down from the heaven of the gods, and the fact that it is a god, Nergal, who makes the descent and becomes Ereshkigal's husband.

The myth begins with Anu deciding that, since it is impossible for Ereshkigal to come up to them for their annual banquet, or for them to go down to her, her messenger must come to the table and take her portion down to her. Anu sends Kakka, his messenger, to tell Ereshkigal. Kakka goes down the long stairway of heaven, and this time the gatekeeper is welcoming: 'Kakka, come in, and may the gate bless you.'

Seven gates there are, but Kakka is divested of nothing as he passes through them. After the seventh gate Kakka finds himself in Ereshkigal's presence; kneeling down, he kisses the ground in front of her and reports verbatim Anu's message. Ereshkigal and Kakka then exchange pleasantries, and she decides to send her vizier Namtar to fetch her portion.

Unfortunately, the text is somewhat fragmentary at the point when Namtar arrives before the great gods, but it would appear that the god Nergal insults Namtar and is sent by Ea to Ereshkigal. Nergal, however, first equips himself with a special chair which may have had a ritualistic role in warding off evil spirits. He is also forewarned by Ea with the usual cautionary advice: not to sit on any chair they might bring, not to eat bread or meat, not to drink beer, not to wash his feet, and certainly not to succumb to Ereshkigal's charms after she

'. . . has been to the bath,
And dressed herself in a fine dress,
Allowing you to glimpse her body.'

Nergal then sets his face towards Kurnugi, which is described exactly as it was in Ishtar's Descent. When he arrives he is made to wait by the gatekeeper, who goes to Ereshkigal to report his arrival. Meanwhile the vizier Namtar sees Nergal standing in the shadow of the gate.

Namtar's face went as livid as cut tamarisk.
His lips grew dark as the rim of a *kuninu*-vessel.

Namtar tells Ereshkigal of the insult, but she is scornful and tells Namtar to bring Nergal to her. Through seven gates, each with a name, Nergal passes and after the seventh, the gate of Ennugigi, he enters the broad courtyard. There he kneels down, kisses the ground in front of Ereshkigal, and explains that Anu has sent him. They bring him a chair; he will not sit on it. The baker brings him bread; he will not eat it. The butcher brings him meat; he will not eat it. The brewer brings him beer; he will not drink it. They bring him a footbath; he will not wash his feet.

Ereshkigal goes to the bath, dresses herself in fine dress, allowing him to catch a glimpse of her body and 'He resisted his heart's desire to do what men and women do'. Unfortunately his resistance is short-lived; after a short break, Ereshkigal again goes to the bath, again dresses herself in a fine dress and again allows him to catch a glimpse of her body. This time, 'He gave in to his heart's desire to do what men and women do'.

Abandoning all restraint, Ereshkigal and Nergal spend a first and second day, a third and fourth day, a fifth and sixth day, passionately in bed together. When the seventh day comes, Nergal says he must leave and he ascends the long stairway of heaven to stand before Anu, Ellil and Ea.

Meanwhile, in Kurnugi, tears are flowing down Ereshkigal's cheeks:

'Erra [Nergal] the lover of my delight –
I did not have enough delight with him before he left!'

Namtar offers to go to Anu, there to 'arrest' Nergal so that he may kiss her again. Ereshkigal agrees:

'Go, Namtar, you must speak to Anu, Ellil, and Ea!
Set your face towards the gate of Anu, Ellil, and Ea,
To say, ever since I was a child and a daughter,

I have not known the playing of other girls,
I have not known the romping of children.
The god whom you sent to me and who has impregnated me – let him sleep with
     me again!
Send that god to us, and let him spend the night with me as my lover!'

She threatens that if he is not sent back to her, she will raise up the dead so that they outnumber the living – the identical threat made by Ishtar in Kurnugi, and by Ishtar to her father in the Epic of Gilgamesh when she wants the Bull of Heaven.

Namtar ascends the long stairway of heaven and repeats Ereshkigal's speech verbatim, including her threat. Ea then arranges an identity parade of the gods so that Namtar may search out the wrong-doer, but Namtar does not recognise the recreant. He returns to Ereshkigal and tells her that, in the assembly of the gods, there was one 'who sat bareheaded, blinking and cringing'. She instantly tells him to return and fetch that god.

In a somewhat fragmentary passage, Nergal is at last identified and, armed with his magic chair, descends once more the long stairway of heaven. He does not wait for the seven gates to be opened: he strikes down Nedu, the doorman of the first gate, the second doorman, the third, fourth, fifth, sixth and seventh. Entering the wide courtyard, he goes up to Ereshkigal and laughs, and pulls her by her hair from the throne.

Passionately they go to bed, again for a first and second day, a third and fourth, a fifth and a sixth. When the seventh day arrives the text breaks off, and we do not know exactly what happens in the end. But there is a much shorter and earlier version of the same text (called the Amarna Version since is was found at Tell el-Amarna in Egypt), which ends with Ereshkigal saying to Nergal, after she has been unceremoniously pulled from her throne:

'You can be my husband, and I can be your wife.
I will let you seize
Kingship over the wide Earth! I will put the tablet
Of wisdom in your hand! You can be master,
I can be mistress.' Nergal listened to this speech of hers,
And seized her and kissed her. He wiped away her tears.
'What have you asked of me? After so many months,
It shall certainly be so!'

Myth and meaning

Myths can be interpreted in a variety of ways: they can portray cosmic forces personified, as for example when chaos is subdued by order; they can reflect historical events such as military campaigns, the building of city walls and the return of cult statues; they can serve purely cultic purposes, for example, for recitation at the New Year's Festival; and events in them can mirror the cycle of nature, thus reassuring their audience that the national gods are in control. All these interpretations are possible when we consider Mesopotamian myths. We can also identify recurrent themes, such as combat with impossibly over-sized opponents or against hopeless odds, the quest for immortality or eternal youth, and the journey to the underworld. Heroes of myth share universal characteristics: bravery, honour, fidelity and beauty. They often have miraculous births, or divine mothers and/or fathers. The way in which a myth impresses itself upon the community does not differ very much from one civilisation to another, and the myths of Mesopotamia bear hallmarks familiar from other languages and other times.

But in one way they are exceptional. The myths described in this book are among the earliest ever formulated and recorded. Their origins are lost in the sands of time but probably lie as far back as the building of the first cities during the fourth to the third millennium BC, when the features of gods were attributed to real kings and the prestige of particular gods was deliberately enhanced in order to honour cult centres and thereby their inhabitants.

The far-ranging sweep of subject, character and location in these myths makes a strong appeal across the millennia that divide them from their modern audience. We in the West may be so steeped in the literary and religious traditions stemming from classical Greece and the Bible that, from our late and inescapably sophisticated viewpoint, we may be tempted to ascribe to them qualities they did not have for the ancient Mesopotamians. Simply to comprehend a polytheistic viewpoint may be beyond us, and it is also vital to bear in mind that our knowledge is incomplete – we have what may well be only a small number of the pieces in a large jigsaw, with no concept of the overall design. And we must also remember that these tablets were never intended for us to read.

Nevertheless, close study reveals characteristics and patterns which may help us reach more deeply to the heart of these myths. We have seen how the pace of action is always stately and slow-moving, how a change of location

Two winged bulls flanking the main entrance to the throne room of the palace of Sargon II (722–705 BC) at Khorsabad: in their original state (below), and the artist's reconstruction (above).

Ivory mirror handle from Enkomi in Cyprus, about 1200–1100 BC. It shows the climax of a cosmic battle.

73

Limestone plaque surmounted with the head of a demon, used to expel evil spirits, a number of which appear on the other side. The top register portrays symbols of heavenly gods, and demons threaten the sick man in the third register. Hell lies beneath.

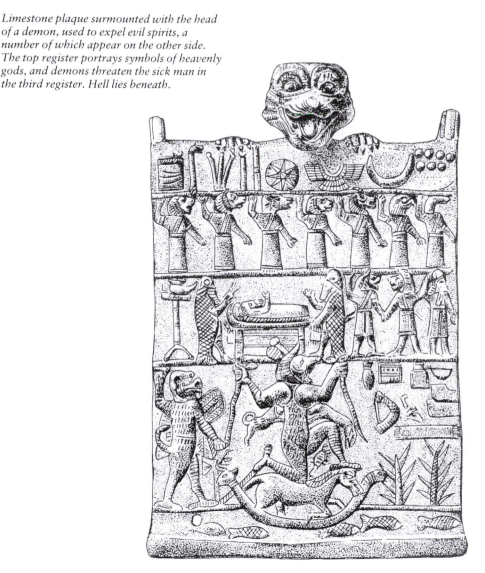

is always effected by the simple expedient of the hero of the myth actually going there. There is no 'meanwhile' device to describe what is happening elsewhere in time or place to other characters involved in the story; only one narrative can develop at a time. The plot is advanced in various simple ways: by dreams which presage future events, by conversations between the main protagonists, by gods giving instructions and advice.

We have seen how repetition is widely used, usually word for word, with no elegant variations of vocabulary. Reality is reinforced by repetition. Some passages in the Epic of Creation are repeated *en bloc* as many as four times, and there is not a single myth which does not contain such repetition. Sometimes this is used to heighten dramatic tension, as for example when

*Sculptured relief of a powerful
Gilgamesh-type hero carrying a
lion cub. From the palace of
Sargon II at Khorsabad.*

the eagle takes Etana up to the heaven of Anu, or when Gilgamesh is making
his way through the dark wasteland. It also serves to emphasise the importance
of certain descriptive passages and to encourage an audience unused to visual
images to use its mind's eye to see what mattered and exactly what was
at stake for the heroes engaged in the action. Thus, when Tiamat's gang
of demons is described over and over again, the audience was meant to see
and feel exactly how terrifying and formidable they were. That is the stuff
of which story-telling is made.

Another epic device is to reach a number and then crown it by moving
on just one higher. Thus there is the crowning of six days by the seventh
after the great Flood, when the mountain Nimush held the boat fast:

Romantic view, published in the early eighteenth century, of the ruins of Persepolis.

> The first and second day the mountain Nimush held the boat fast and did not let
>   it budge.
> The third and fourth day the mountain Nimush held the boat fast and did not
>   let it budge.
> The fifth and sixth day the mountain Nimush held the boat fast and did not let
>   it budge.
> When the seventh day arrived . . .

So also Gilgamesh falls into a deep sleep which lasts six days and six nights. On the seventh day he wakes up. Nergal and Ereshkigal lie passionately in bed for six days and six nights. On the seventh day, real life resumes. In the Epic of Creation, two gods are sent to overcome Tiamat. They fail, and it is the third, Marduk, who succeeds. In the Epic of Anzu, three gods try and fail, and the fourth, Ninurta, succeeds. Numbers are generally significant, particularly three and seven. Dreams tend to come in threes, and winds and weapons in sevens. Tension is increased by cumulative effect.

To attempt to assess the literary merit of these texts is doubtless to undertake a perilous task in which there are endless opportunities for error. The various literary devices must reflect the taste of the original audience, an audience whose tastes lay not so much in nail-biting drama but more in sophisticated complexity and moral purpose. Gods played a far greater part in the life of the ancient world than can easily be comprehended today, when it seems there are scientific explanations for everything. However we ourselves try to evaluate the appeal of these texts, on whatever grounds – their purpose, style or content – we have to realise our own limitations. Perhaps we should let simple enjoyment – of glorious Gilgamesh, ravishing jewel-hung Ishtar, evil Anzu, proud Marduk, wise Ea, shaggy Enkidu, mysterious Ut-napishtim, black-lipped Ereshkigal – be the strongest factor. In the end, the art of recounting myths has one purpose only: to fire the imagination of those who listen or read. The fires of Mesopotamian myth still burn bright.

Suggestions for further reading

Although Akkadian as a written language died out in the first century AD, our modern understanding of it continues to progress. The great Assyrian dictionary produced by the Oriental Institute of the University of Chicago is still being published, and each new volume inevitably generates some new interpretations and ideas concerning the detail of ancient texts, even if the general sense of the whole seldom requires alteration. The most recent works on the whole corpus are *Myths from Mesopotamia* (already referred to in the introduction) by Stephanie Dalley (Oxford, 1989) and two volumes entitled *Before the Muses* by Benjamin R. Foster (Bethesda, 1993). There is a definitive new edition of the Gilgamesh epic, *The Epic of Gilgamesh: A New Translation* by Andrew George (Penguin, 1999), and a highly technical discussion is to be found in *The Evolution of the Gilgamesh Epic* by J. H. Tigay (Philadelphia, 1982). *Atra-hasis: The Babylonian Story of the Flood* by W. G. Lambert and A. R. Millard (Oxford, 1969) is the standard work on the full text of this myth.

For an overview of Mesopotamian texts as a whole, and indeed for comparisons with other ancient texts, look at *Ancient Near Eastern Texts*, edited by James B. Pritchard (Princeton, 1969). Apart from myths, epics and legends, it includes sections on legal and historical texts, rituals, incantations and descriptions of festivals, hymns and prayers, didactic and wisdom literature, lamentations, letters, sacred marriage texts and love songs.

There are many books about the history and civilization of Assyria and Babylonia, among which I would draw attention to *Ancient Mesopotamia* by A. L. Oppenheim (Chicago, 1977), *Babylon* by J. Oates (London, 1986) and *The Might That Was Assyria* by H. W. F. Saggs (London, 1984). The first and second works mentioned have been revised and updated, and all three provide useful background information.

On the rediscovery of this ancient land, Seton Lloyd has recently revised and enlarged his fascinating and well-illustrated book *Foundations in the Dust* (London, 1980). An excellent general picture of the rediscovery of many ancient civilisations is provided by H. V. F. Winstone in *Uncovering the Ancient World* (London, 1985). For the cuneiform script itself, Christopher Walker of the Department of the Ancient Near East in the British Museum has given a thorough survey, including some sample texts, in *Cuneiform* (*Reading the Past* series, London, 1987).

On the general subject of myth, there are of course many hundreds of books and articles which are worth consulting. In the Near Eastern context, I would recommend G. S. Kirk's *Myth: Its Meaning and Functions in Ancient and Other Cultures* (Cambridge, 1971) and, to a lesser extent, *Middle Eastern Mythology* by S. H. Hooke, published by Penguin Books (1963).

PERSIAN
Myths

VESTA SARKHOSH CURTIS

Author's note and acknowledgements

This book is not intended to be a complete and detailed view of all known Persian myths, and undoubtedly many other stories could have been included instead. The choice is personal and subjective, and it has been made primarily to show the importance and continuity of Persian myths from ancient times into the Islamic period.

No standard system of transliteration has been used for personal and place names, but they have been presented in the way most familiar to English readers without using diacritics. Passages quoted in English translation are from J. Darmesteter, *The Zend-Avesta*; E.W. West, *The Pahlavi Texts (Bundahishn)*; A.G. and E. Warner, *The Shahnama of Firdausi*; E.W. Lane, *The Arabian Nights' Entertainments* and E.G. Browne, *A Literary History of Persia* (vol. 1). Shorter translations from the *Shahnameh*, *Vis and Ramin*, *Iskandarnameh* and *Khusrow and Shirin* that appear within the body of the text have been made by the author from the original Persian. More detailed references to published material for further reading can be found on p. 155.

Finally, I am most grateful to the Departments of Ancient Near East and Asia of the British Museum for allowing me to browse through their photographic archives, to Dr Sheila Canby for advice on Persian miniatures, to Miss Ann Searight for drawing the map, and to all those who supported and encouraged me in writing this book; in particular I should like to mention Nina Shandloff, who has edited and seen it through the press. Above all, my sincere thanks go to my family and my husband, John Curtis, for their support.

Picture credits

chapter motif: Vesta Curtis (after BM ANE 124095); *p. 85:* BM ANE 1992-1-25.1; *p. 88:* BM ANE 123267; *p. 91:* BM ANE 124093; *p. 92:* BM GR 1825.6-13.1 (Sculpture 1720); *p. 93:* BM CM R.P. Knight Collection II.A1, p. 202; *p. 94:* Warwick Ball; *p. 96:* BM ANE 135913; *p. 98:* BM ANE 124095; *p. 99:* BM ANE 124092; *p. 101:* British Library Board, Or 371, f. 7r; *p. 103:* BM ANE 134963; *p. 106:* BM Asia 1943.10-9.02; *p. 107:* BL Or 371, f. 8r; *p. 109:* BL Or 371, f. 17r; *p. 111:* (top) BM Asia 1948.12-11.020; (bottom) BL Or 371, f. 24v; *p. 114:* BL Or 371, f. 35r; *p. 115:* BL Or 8761, f. 52v; *p. 116:* BM Asia 1975.5-23.02; *p. 118:* BM Asia 1922.7-11.02; *p. 119:* BM Asia 1948.12-11.025; *p. 121:* BM Asia 1928.12-6.01; *p. 122:* (top) BL Or 371, f. 48r; (bottom) BM Asia 1975.5-23.03; *p. 124:* BL Or 11522, f. 123v; *p. 125:* BL Or 371, f. 178r; *p. 126:* (top) BM Asia 1937.7-10.0327; (bottom) BM Asia 1975.5-23.04; *p. 128:* BM Asia 1920.9-17.051; *p. 131:* BM ANE 90920; *p. 133:* BL Or 2834, f. 266v; *p. 135:* BM CM 1919-8-20-1; *p. 137:* BL Or 2265, f. 77v; *p. 139:* BM ANE 93028; *p. 140:* Hermitage, St Petersburg; *p. 144:* BL Or 2834, f. 70v; *p. 145:* BL Or 2932, f. 110v; *p. 150:* BL Or 8761, f. 115v; *p. 151:* BL Or 371, f. 105v; *p. 154:* Reza Abbasi Museum, Tehran.

Contents

Ancient Iran

Introduction

Persian myths are traditional tales and stories of ancient origin, some involving extraordinary or supernatural beings. Drawn from the legendary past of Iran, they reflect the attitudes of the society to which they first belonged – attitudes towards the confrontation of good and evil, the actions of the gods, and the exploits of heroes and fabulous creatures. Myths play a crucial part in Persian culture and our understanding of them is increased when we consider them within the context of Iranian history.

For this purpose we must ignore modern political boundaries and look at historical developments in greater Iran, a vast area covering parts of Central Asia well beyond the frontiers of present-day Iran. The geography of this region, with its high mountain ranges, plays a significant role in many of the mythological stories. Although the archaeological record shows that civilisation in Iran dates from before 6000 BC, it is only the period from *c.* 2000 BC onwards that is of interest to us here. The second millennium is usually regarded as the age of migration because the emergence in western Iran of a new form of pottery, similar to earlier wares of north-eastern Iran, suggests the arrival of new people. This pottery, light grey to black in colour, appeared around 1400 BC. It is called Early Grey Ware or Iron 1, the latter name indicating the beginning of the Iron Age in this area.

The migration of Iranian-speaking peoples into Iran is a widely discussed issue, and many questions about how the migration took place remain unanswered. Certainly there was a break in tradition at sites on the southern slopes of the Alburz Mountains and in western Iran, where stone tombs were filled with rich grave goods. On the basis of linguistic evidence, these newly arrived peoples are regarded as having originally been among the Indo-Iranians who for a long period shared a common tradition while living as nomads in the Asian steppes of Russia. Eventually the two linguistically related groups separated and migrated southwards. By the middle of the second millennium BC, the Iranian group had moved into the highlands of Iran through the flat passable area south-east of the Caspian Sea, while the Indian tribes had migrated into the Indian sub-continent. Whether the migration was violent and whether the tribes moved in large groups are questions that cannot be answered with certainty. One can only see from the archaeological evidence a break from the previous traditions and the arrival of new pottery types and burial rites. Nor do we know what happened to the language of the indigenous population, which in most parts of the country was replaced by the Iranian languages of the newcomers.

The first definite mention of an Iranian tribe, the Medes, occurs in ninth-century BC Assyrian texts. The Medes became the main threat to the Assyrian empire in the east. Whereas at first the Medes were only a loose confederation of tribes, by the late seventh century BC they had become powerful enough to join forces with the Babylonians and cause the collapse of the Assyrian empire in 612 BC. Another Iranian group, the Persians, had settled in southern Iran, in the area of Fars. It was through the amalgamation of the related tribes of the Medes and the Persians under Cyrus the Great that the Achaemenid empire was formed, emerging as the dominant power in the ancient Near East from *c*. 550 until its conquest by Alexander the Great in 331 BC.

The period of foreign rule by Alexander and his Greek generals, the Seleucids, was brief. Then the Arsacid Parthians, originally an Iranian-speaking nomadic group from the north-east, moved into the area south-east of the Caspian Sea. Under their king Arsaces I, they moved into Seleucid territory and established Parthian rule in 238 BC. By 141 BC the Parthians had conquered Mesopotamia under their great ruler, Mithradates I, and for the next three and a half centuries they remained the major political force in the ancient Near East and the main opponents of the Romans. Under Mithradates II (known as the Great), the Parthian empire stretched from the River Euphrates in the west to eastern Iran and Central Asia.

The dynasty of the Parthians came to an end in AD 224 with the defeat of their last king, Artabanus IV/V, by Ardashir I. The latter was a local prince, from Istakhr near Persepolis, who had received his crown from the Parthian monarch and later successfully challenged him. With his victory, Ardashir established the dynasty of the Sasanians, named after their legendary ancestor Sasan. The eventual collapse of the Sasanians was due to the rise of Islam and the Arab conquest of Iran in AD 642, by which time their army and treasury had been exhausted by numerous wars and the population could no longer endure the high taxes imposed on them. Zoroastrianism, the official state religion of Iran under the Sasanians, was replaced by Islam.

Much of our information about the ancient Iranians, their gods and the creation of their world can be found in the religious texts of the Zoroastrians, whose prophet Zoroaster (Greek for Persian Zarathushtra) may have lived in Khorezmia in Central Asia, or even further north-east. His dates are much debated and far from certain, but linguistic evidence from the *Gatha*, the prophet's hymns, in a part of the *Avesta*, the holy book of the Zoroastrians, suggests a close link with the ancient Indian hymns, the *Rigveda* of *c*. 1700 BC. This is the period prior to the migration of nomadic tribes into Iran and India. The original *Avesta*, written in Avestan, an east-Iranian language, dates from between 1400 and 1200 BC, and Zoroaster himself probably lived around 1000 BC. Some scholars favour a date in the late seventh and early sixth century BC for Zoroaster, but this is less likely.

The holy book of the Zoroastrians was memorised by Zoroastrian priests and passed on by word of mouth over a long period of time. Later sources claim that the *Avesta* was originally written in gold on prepared ox-hides and stored at

Bronze belt plaque of the Parthian period, probably 2nd–early 3rd century AD, showing a bearded rider and his horse. Elaborate belt plaques are common in this period and the rider figure is depicted with the typical bushy hairstyle, headband and outfit of the time, consisting of tunic and trousers.

Istakhr, and that it was destroyed by Alexander. Although parts of the sacred text are assumed to have been written down again during the Parthian period, in the first and second centuries AD, the *Avesta* did not exist in its complete form until perhaps the sixth century AD, under the Sasanians. Unfortunately, this version has not survived. The present *Avesta* dates back to the thirteenth or fourteenth century and contains only a fraction of the original. It is divided into sections: the *Yasna*, which is a collection of prayers and contains the *Gatha* (the hymns of the prophet Zoroaster); the *Visparad*; the *Vendidad* (also known as the *Videvdat*), the 'Law against Demons'; the *Small Avesta* (*Khurdeh Avesta*); and the *Yasht* or hymns, in which many pagan myths of pre-Zoroastrian origin are described.

The *Avesta* was first translated into a Western language in 1771 by a Frenchman, Anquetil du Perron. This much-criticised French version was followed by a series of translations, although the first English edition, by James Darmesteter, was not published until 1887.

The myths which appear in the part of the *Avesta* known as *Yasht* include some tales of very ancient pre-Zoroastrian origin, probably belonging to the pagan Indo-Iranian era. They describe the heroic deeds performed by gods, kings and warriors against both supernatural and human enemies. Many of these myths reappear in the *Shahnameh (Book of Kings)*, an epic in rhyme by the poet Firdowsi, which was completed in AD 1010. Books about the history of the past had previously appeared in the Sasanian period and during the rule of the Abbasid caliphs in the eighth century AD many of these books were translated from Pahlavi (Middle Persian) into Arabic, although in most cases both the original Pahlavi texts and the Arabic translations have been lost. However, writers such as Firdowsi, who were well acquainted with the earlier literature, ensured its survival. Thus written sources, together with a strong oral tradition, have kept the myths and stories of Persia alive down to the present. Their importance and relevance to modern Persian society lies in the fact that most Iranians, whether literate or not, know something about these stories. The *Shahnameh* in particular plays a crucial role in Persian life and culture, not only because of its considerable literary merit but also because of its importance in preserving the myths and history of a very distant past in the Persian language.

The gods and the creation of the ancient Iranian world

Much information about the ancient Iranians, their gods and the creation of their world can be found in the religious texts of the Zoroastrians, which include the *Avesta* and later sources such as the *Bundahishn* and *Denkard*. The *Bundahishn* or 'Creation' consists of Pahlavi (Middle Persian) translations of parts of the *Avesta* that no longer exist and their commentaries (*Zand*). The *Denkard* gives a summary of the *Avesta* in Pahlavi.

Within the *Avesta*, the gods, heroes and fabulous creatures mostly appear in the section known as the *Yasht*. Here, myths of pre-Zoroastrian origin which reflect a pagan ideology are described in hymns dedicated to various gods. For example, *Yasht* 5 (or *Aban Yasht*) is dedicated to the goddess Ardvi Sura Anahita; *Yasht* 14, also known as *Bahram Yasht*, is dedicated to the god Verethragna, and *Yasht* 10, the *Mihr Yasht*, describes the god Mithra. *Yasht* 19 (*Zamyad Yasht*) gives a description of the quest for the Divine Glory. Also informative is the collection of prayers, the *Niyayesh*, which incorporates early Zoroastrian beliefs. These include the *Atash Niyayesh*, a prayer to Fire. The *Vendidad* deals with the creations of Ahura Mazda, the Wise Lord, and the destruction wrought by his opponent, Angra Mainyu, known in later times as Ahriman.

Gods

Ahura Mazda and Angra Mainyu

Ahura Mazda, the Wise Lord, is the ultimate God, the absolute goodness, wisdom and knowledge, creator of the sun, the stars, light and dark, humans and animals and all spiritual and physical activities. He is opposed to all evil and suffering. In opposition to him is Angra Mainyu (Ahriman), the Evil Spirit, who is constantly attempting to destroy the world of truth and to harm men and beasts. Thus life in this world is a reflection of the cosmic struggle between Ahura Mazda and Angra Mainyu. Zoroaster's teaching says that Ahura Mazda personifies goodness and that all human beings must choose between good and evil. The arch-demon Angra Mainyu lives in darkness in the north, the home of all demons, and he is capable of changing his appearance to that of a lizard, a snake or a youth. So disguised, he fights all that is good and attempts to lure all,

Bronze winged demon with lion's body and ferocious head, perhaps representing the Evil Spirit. Allegedly found in Afghanistan. Late Sasanian/early Islamic, 7th–8th century AD.

even Zoroaster himself, into his world of darkness, deceit and lies. In his continuous battle against good, including the creations of Ahura Mazda, he is assisted by a number of other demons. The most important of these is Aeshma, the demon of fury and outrage, and Azhi Dahaka, the monster with three heads, six eyes and three jaws, whose body is full of lizards and scorpions. According to Zoroastrian texts, Angra Mainyu will be defeated at the end of the world.

Ardvi Sura Anahita

Ardvi Sura Anahita is the goddess of all the waters upon the earth and the source of the cosmic ocean. She drives a chariot pulled by four horses: wind, rain, cloud and sleet. She is regarded as the source of life, purifying the seed of all males and the wombs of all females, and cleansing the milk in the breasts of all mothers. Because of her connection with life, warriors in battle prayed to her for survival and victory. The *Aban Yasht* is dedicated to her and describes her descent to the earth thus:

Then Ardvi Sura Anahita came forth, O Zarathustra! down from those stars to the earth made by Mazda . . .
(*Yasht* 5, 88)

When asked by Zoroaster how she should be worshipped, the goddess replies:

O pure, holy Spitama! . . . this is the sacrifice wherewith thou shalt worship and forward me, from the time when the sun is rising to the time when the sun is setting. Of this libation of mine thou shalt drink . . .
(*Yasht* 5, 91)

In a vivid description, Ardvi Sura Anahita is compared to a fair maid with a strong body, tall, pure and

nobly born of a glorious race, wearing ... a mantle fully embroidered with gold; ever holding the baresma [barsom = bundle of consecrated twigs] in her hand, according to the rules, she wears square golden earrings ... and a golden necklace ... Upon her head Ardvi Sura Anahita bound a golden crown, with a hundred stars, with eight rays ... a well-made crown ... with fillets streaming down.
(*Yasht* 5, 126–8)

Anahita is worshipped by heroes and anti-heroes alike in the *Avesta*, who pray to her and offer sacrifices. The important status of this goddess is best seen in the struggle between good and evil and the confrontation between the kings of Iran and the rulers of Turya (Turan), the area to the north-east of Iran.

Verethragna

Verethragna is the warrior god, the aggressive, victorious force against evil. In the *Bahram Yasht*, a hymn dedicated to him, he takes the ten different forms of a strong wind, a bull with yellow ears and golden horns, a white horse with golden trappings, a burden-bearing camel, a male boar, a youth at the ideal age of fifteen, a swift bird (perhaps a raven), a wild ram, a fighting deer, and a man holding a sword with a golden blade. When Zoroaster asks Ahura Mazda what to do if affected by the curse of the enemy, the Wise Lord instructs him to take a feather of Verethragna, incarnated as a bird:

With that feather thou shalt rub thy own body, with that feather thou shalt curse back the enemies. If a man holds a bone of that strong bird, no one can smite or turn to flight that fortunate man. The feather of that bird brings him help.
(*Yasht* 14, 35–6)

There is an interesting parallel here with the story of the Simurgh in the *Shah-nameh*, whose feathers also have a healing effect. Verethragna is also reported to carry

the chariots of the lords ... the chariots of the sovereigns.
(*Yasht* 14, 39)

In a description of the god Mithra, Verethragna is mentioned as the one who

... made by Ahura, runs opposing the foes in the shape of a boar, a sharp-toothed he-boar, a sharp-jawed boar, that kills at one stroke, pursuing, wrathful, with a dripping face; strong, with iron feet, iron fore-paws, iron weapons, an iron tail, and iron jaws.
(*Yasht* 10, 70)

Mithra

Mithra is the best-known divinity of the Iranian pantheon, partly due to the spread and popularity of Mithraism in the Roman empire. The Avestan word *mithra* means 'pact, contract, covenant'. In *Yasht* 10, the *Mihr Yasht*, Mithra appears watching over men and their deeds, agreements and contracts. He is the guide towards the right order (*asha*) and is also responsible for giving protection against attack. As the god who controlled the cosmic order – that is, night and day and the change of seasons – he was associated with fire and the sun, and thus eventually became known as the sun god in both Iran and India. He is described as:

[he] who first of the heavenly gods reaches over the Hara [Alburz Mountains], before the undying, swift-horsed sun; who, foremost in a golden array, takes hold of the beautiful summits, and from thence looks over the abode of the Aryans [Iranian peoples] with a beneficent eye.
(*Yasht* 10, 13)

Among his many other qualities is his sense of justice: he protects the faithful and punishes the unfaithful. In this connection he is associated with warriors, and is described as riding on a chariot pulled by white horses. He carries a silver spear, wears a golden cuirass, and is further armed with golden-shafted arrows, axes, maces and daggers. Mithra is

the lord of wide pastures, who is truth-speaking ... with a thousand ears ... with ten thousand eyes ... strong, sleepless, and ever awake.
(*Yasht* 10, 7)

The mace or club of Mithra is a powerful weapon not only against untruthful humans but also against the Evil Spirit, Angra Mainyu:

... a club with a hundred knots, a hundred edges, that rushes forward and fells men down; a club cast out of red brass ...; the strongest of all weapons, the most victorious of all weapons; from whom Angra Mainyu, who is all death, flees away in fear.
(*Yasht* 10, 96–7)

To this day, new Zoroastrian priests receive the mace of Mithra to help them combat evil. The festival of Mithra, the *Mithrakana* (modern *Mihrigan*) was the celebration of the autumn equinox. The present month of *Mihr* (October) is named after the god Mithra.

One of Mithra's most important duties is to protect the Kingly Fortune or Divine Glory (*khvarnah* or *farr*). Only the legitimate rulers of the Iranians were privileged to possess the Divine Glory, which would abandon a king if he strayed from the righteous path (as will be seen in the case of King Yima). In protecting the *khvarnah*, Mithra is helped by Apam Napat, the god of water.

Perhaps best known to Westerners is the association of the 'Persian God' with the Roman cult of Mithras. The Persian origin of Mithraism is not disputed, but there may be no clear relationship with Zoroastrianism. Scenes depicting the bull-slaying Mithras are no longer seen as the fight of good against evil. Nor are they now interpreted as the killing of the first bull and the creation of the world through the purified seeds of the slaughtered animal. Instead the familiar reliefs decorating Mithraeums all over the Western world are interpreted within an astrological context.

Vayu

Vayu, the god of wind, is also depicted as a warrior god who chases the Evil Spirit with his sharp spear and golden weapons to protect the good creations of Ahura Mazda. He rules between the realms of Ahura Mazda and Angra Mainyu, between light and darkness.

Silver plate of the late 4th century AD, with two investiture scenes in superimposed registers. The central figure holding a diadem (signifying king/divinity) is seated on a bench throne (takht) supported by two Simurgh-type creatures.

Marble sculpture of the god Mithras slaying a bull. From Rome, probably 2nd century AD.

Tishtrya

Tishtrya, the god of rains, is personified as the star Sirius or Canis Major. His opponents are the witch Duzhyairya (Bad Harvest) and, worse still, Apaosha (Drought). He is vividly described as the god who rises from the source of all waters, the Vourukasha Sea, and who divides the waters among the countries. In his battle with Apaosha:

... the bright and glorious Tishtrya goes down to the sea Vouru-Kasha in the shape of a white, beautiful horse, with golden ears and a golden caparison. But there rushes down to meet him the Daeva Apaosha, in the shape of a dark horse, black with black ears, black with a black back, black with a black tail, stamped with brands of terror. They meet together, hoof against hoof, O Spitama Zarathustra! the bright and glorious Tishtrya and the Daeva Apaosha.
(*Yasht* 8, 20–2)

When the demon of drought starts to win, Tishtrya flees from the Vourukasha Sea and complains that if men had worshipped him in the proper fashion,

[he] should have taken ... the strength of ten horses, the strength of ten camels, the strength of ten bulls, the strength of ten mountains, the strength of ten rivers.
(*Yasht* 8, 24)

When finally Zoroaster himself offers a sacrifice to Tishtrya, the god again descends as a white horse to the sea to meet his opponent. Once again they fight hoof against hoof, but this time

the bright and glorious Tishtrya proves stronger than the Daeva Apaosha, and he overcomes him.
(*Yasht* 8, 28)

The god of rains succeeds in making water pour down upon the fields, upon the whole world, and vapour rising from the sea moves forward in the form of clouds, pushed by the wind. The fourth month of the Iranian calendar is called *Tir* after the god Tishtrya, and the festival of *Tiragan* was celebrated as a rain festival.

Atar

Atar (Fire) in Zoroastrianism is regarded as the son of Ahura Mazda, the Wise Lord. Humans were expected to offer meat as a sacrifice to Atar, at the same time holding a bundle of sacred twigs (barsom) in the hand. Every house was expected to have a hearth for making sacrifices, in front of which prayers could be said:

... O Atar, son of Ahura Mazda! Thou art worthy of sacrifice and invocation; mayest thou receive the sacrifice and the invocation in the houses of men.
(*Atash Niyayesh* 7)

Atar is closely associated with the god Mithra: for example, together they succeed in rescuing the Divine Glory from the demon Azhi Dahaka. Atar is described as riding behind Mithra's chariot. Atar's part in the struggle with Azhi Dahaka over the Divine Glory in *Zamyad Yasht* is one of the few surviving myths about Atar:

... But Atar, the son of Ahura Mazda, advanced behind him, speaking in these words: 'There give it to me, thou three-mouthed Azhi Dahaka. If thou seizest that Glory that cannot be forcibly seized, then I will enter thy hinder part, I will blaze up in thy jaws, so that thou mayest never more rush upon the earth made by Mazda and destroy the world of the good principle.' Then Azhi took back his hands, as the instinct of life prevailed, so much had Atar affrighted him.
(*Yasht* 19, 49–51)

Reverse of a coin of the first Sasanian king, Ardashir I (c. AD 224–42). The fire altar is symbolic of Zoroastrianism, which became the official religion of the Sasanian state.

To this day, fire has continued to play a prominent part in Zoroastrian religion and is still worshipped in fire-temples. Fire is a symbol of Zoroastrianism. In Sasanian times the three famous eternal fires, each representing one of the three classes of society, were the Farnabag fire (priests), the Gushnasp fire (warriors) and the Burzin Mihr fire (workers). The Gushnasp fire was probably burning at Takht-i Sulaiman in north-western Iran. To this day the Bahram fire, the most sacred of all fires, is necessary to fight the forces of darkness and evil and is regarded as the symbol of truth.

Haoma

Haoma (Vedic Soma) is the god who gives health and strength, and who provides rich harvests and sons. His name is that of a plant with healing potency, believed to be of the genus *Ephedra*. The juice of the plant gave supernatural powers and had an intoxicating effect. The god was thought to give strength to overcome any enemy. Indeed, when Kavi Haosravah (later Kay Khusrow) defeated the Turanian king Franrasyan (Afrasiyab), he had the physical assistance of Haoma.

The creation of the world

The ancient Iranians, believed that the sky was the first part of the world to be created. It was originally described as a round empty shell made of rock crystal, passing beneath as well as above the earth. Later it was thought to be made of metal. Next to be created was water, followed by the earth. Then came plants and animals. Human beings were the sixth creation, and fire probably the seventh and last.

Mountains were believed to have grown from the surface of the earth, originally a flat disc that encompassed the Western as well as the Eastern world.

View of the peak of Mount Demavand in the Alburz Mountains, north of Tehran.

Certain place names have been linked with the creation of the world. For example, Alburz (Mount Hara or Harburz) is described in the *Avesta* (*Yasht* 19, 1) as the first mountain in the world, which took 800 years to grow, its roots reaching deep into the ground and its peak attached to the sky. It is the most important mountain. The Iranians, like the Indians, believed that the world was divided into seven regions or *karshvar* (*keshvar* in modern Persian, which means country). These regions were created when rain first fell upon the earth. The central region, the Khvanirath, inhabited by humans, was as large as the other six put together. The *Bundahishn* describes it as follows:

On the nature of the earth, it says in revelation, that there are thirty and three kinds of land. On the day when Tistar [god of rain] produced the rain, when its seas arose therefrom, the whole place, half taken up by water, was converted into seven portions; this portion, as much as one-half, is the middle and six portions are around; those six portions are together as much as *Khvaniras*. The name *keshvar* is also applied to them and they existed side by side ... And of these seven regions every benefit was created in Khvaniras ... For the Kayanians and heroes were created in Khvaniras; and the good religion of the Mazdayasnians was created in Khvaniras, and afterwards conveyed to the other regions. (XI, 1–6)

It is in Khvaniras (Khvanirath) that the Peak of Hara (Alburz) was believed to have grown from the roots of the Alburz Mountains; the stars, moon and sun were thought to move around this peak. Alburz is described thus in the *Bundahishn*:

On the nature of mountains, it says in revelation, that, at first, the mountains have grown forth in eighteen years; and Alburz ever grew till the completion of eight hundred years; two hundred years up to the star station, two hundred years to the moon station, two hundred years to the sun station, and two hundred years to the endless light. The other mountains have grown out of Alburz, in number 2244 ... (XII, 1–2)

While Alburz or Mount Hara was the source for both light and water, the Vourukasha Sea is described in the *Avesta* as the gathering point of water. This important sea occupied 'one third of the earth, to the south, on the skirts of the Harburz' (*Vendidad* 21, 16), and was fed by a huge river, the Harahvaiti. Two great rivers flowed out from the sea to the east and the west, thus forming the boundaries of the inhabited world. The rivers were cleansed as they passed around the earth and, when they returned to the Vourukasha, their clean water was taken back up to the Peak of Hara.

In the middle of the Vourukasha grew the mother of all trees, the source of all plants, described in the *Avesta* (*Yasht* 12, 17) as the Saena Tree, Tree of All Remedies or Tree of All Seeds. This first tree held the nest of Saena (Senmurv in Pahlavi, Simurgh in Persian), the legendary bird. It also produced the seeds of all plants. Another important plant growing nearby was the 'mighty Gaokerena', which had healing properties when eaten and gave immortality to the resurrected bodies of the dead.

The first animal in the world was the 'uniquely created bull', white in colour and as bright as the moon. According to Zoroastrian tradition it was

A moulded stucco plaque from Chal Tarkhan, Ray, showing the mythical bird Senmurv (Simurgh). Late Sasanian, 7th–8th century AD.

killed by Angra Mainyu, the Evil Spirit, and its seed was carried up to the moon. Once thoroughly purified, this seed produced many species of animals. It also sprouted into plants when part of it fell to the ground.

The home of the uniquely created bull was on the bank of the River Veh Daiti (Veh Rod), which flowed to the east from the Vourukasha Sea. On the opposite bank lived Gayomartan (Gayomard in Pahlavi, Kiyumars in the *Shahnameh*). In *Yasht* 13, 87 he is described as the first man, as wide as he was tall and as 'bright as the sun'. Gayomartan was slain by Angra Mainyu, but the sun purified his seed and, after forty years, a rhubarb plant sprang from it. This slowly grew into Mashya and Mashyanag, the first mortal man and woman. Beguiled by Angra Mainyu, they turned to him as the creator and thus committed the first sin. Instead of peace and harmony, their world was filled with corruption and evil. Only after fifty years were they able to produce offspring, but the first twins were eaten by their parents. After a long period of childlessness another set of twins was finally born, and from these sprang not only the human race but specifically the Iranian peoples.

On the nature of men, it says in revelation that Gayomard, in passing away, gave forth seed; that seed was thoroughly purified by the motion of the light of the sun . . . and in forty years, with the shape of a one-stemmed Rivas-plant [rhubarb], and the fifteen years of its fifteen leaves, Matro and Matroyao [Mashya and Mashyanag] grew up from the earth in such a manner that their arms rested behind on their shoulders, and one joined to the other they were connected together and both alike . . . And both of them changed from the shape of a plant into the shape of man, and the breath went spiritually into them, which is the soul; . . . Ahura Mazda spoke: . . . 'You are man, you are the ancestry of the world, and you are created in perfect devotion by me; perform devotedly the duty of the law . . . speak good words, do good deeds, and worship no demons . . .' And afterwards antagonism rushed into their minds, and their minds were thoroughly corrupted, and they exclaimed that the Evil Spirit created the water and earth, plants and animals.
(*Bundahishn* xv, 1–9)

Demons, fabulous creatures and heroes

The *Avesta* and other religious texts of the Zoroastrian faith describe demons, fabulous creatures and human heroes who inhabited the world of the ancient Iranians. The most informative source is the *Avesta*, but later texts such as the *Bundahishn* also tell at great length of the ancient heroes and their opponents.

Demons and evil powers

Two types of evil power were common in the early Iranian world: those which attacked the bodies of humans directly and those which moved around them, waiting for an opportunity to harm them and their crops and animals.

Evil beings in general were known as *yatu*, but the word was also used for their opposites: those who were able to combat evil and its power. These were the sorcerers and magicians. (The modern Persian word for magic and sorcery is *jadu*, and *jadugar* is a magician, sorcerer.) The demons were called *div*, a term which had its origin in the ancient word *daeva*, meaning god or false god (cf. Latin *deus*). There was also a group of female evils called *pairaka* (modern Persian *pari*; cf. English fairy) who were most active during the night and had a witch-like personality. *Pairaka* appeared in different guises: for example, they could take the form of a rat or a shooting star. Sometimes they made themselves beautiful in order to seduce and harm men, and in later Persian tradition their beauty is often praised. The most evil demon was the female spirit Naush, who in later Zoroastrian tradition appears as a mottled fly from the north – the source and homeland of all evil. She belongs to the group of evil beings described as *drug* (in modern Persian, *durugh* means lie). One of the opponents of the *div*s and *pairaka* was the god Mithra.

Fabulous creatures

Among the fabulous creatures mentioned in Zoroastrian texts, the legendary bird Saena (Pahlavi Senmurv), a great falcon, enjoys a particular prominence. She sits on top of the Tree of All Seeds, and by beating her wings causes the seeds to scatter. These are then carried away by rain and wind and distributed over the earth. According to later legends she suckles young ones, and although her

Silver gilt plate with a Senmurv, 'the king of birds'. The Senmurv (Simurgh) is a combination of bird and dog or lion. Late Sasanian, 7th–8th century AD.

identification with the later Simurgh is probable but not certain, it is interesting to see how in Firdowsi's *Shahnameh* a similar legendary bird with supernatural powers plays a prominent role in the story of Zal and his son Rustam.

The Tree of All Seeds stands in the middle of the Vourukasha Sea and is protected by a fish, the Kara, which swims around it and is able to keep all harmful creatures away. Particularly dangerous is the frog which tries to gnaw at the sacred tree's roots. Another fabulous creature whose task is to protect the tree is the righteous ass. This white-bodied creature has a golden horn on its head, three legs, six eyes and nine mouths. It too stands in the middle of the Vourukasha Sea and destroys all the harmful beings in the water.

Apart from Saena, other birds mentioned in the *Avesta* are Karshiptar, the 'swiftly flying', which is supposed to have spread the prophet Zoroaster's words, and Ashozushta, the owl, which scares off evil demons by muttering holy words. Then there is the bird Chamrush, whose patriotic task is to peck non-Iranians and who helps to distribute the seeds from the Tree of All Seeds.

Silver gilt plate depicting a king on horseback hunting lions. Sasanian, 5th century AD.
Lions were still present in south-western Iran at the beginning of the 20th century.

The harmful creatures, like demons, were felt to be a constant threat to
mankind, animals, plants and crops. Known as *khrafstra*, they include beasts of
prey, rodents, frogs, lizards, tortoises, spiders and insects such as wasps, ants
and beetles. Cats were disliked because they were regarded as belonging to the
same family as dangerous tigers and lions. Among these unpopular creatures
were also the fabulous monsters which were challenged by human heroes. They
usually took the form of serpents or dragons (*azhi*). The most important of these
was the Azhi Dahaka (modern Persian *azhdaha*), the monster with three heads
who ate humans. The same three-headed, man-devouring monster appears as
Zahhak in Firdowsi's *Shahnameh*. In the *Avesta*, the Azhi Dahaka is described
as:

... the three-mouthed, the three-headed, the six-eyed, who has a thousand senses, that most
powerful, fiendish *Drug*, that demon, baleful to the world, the strongest *Drug* that Angra
Mainyu created against the material world, to destroy the world of the good principle.
(*Yasht* 9, 14)

In another section of the *Avesta*, the *Aban Yasht*, the Azhi Dahaka beseeches Ardvi Sura Anahita, the goddess of water, for assistance in his attempt to seize the Divine Glory:

To her did Azhi Dahaka, the three-mouthed, offer up a sacrifice in the land of Bawri [Babylon?], with a hundred male horses, a thousand oxen, and ten thousand lambs. He begged of her a boon, saying: 'Grant me this boon, O good most beneficent Ardvi Sura Anahita! that I may make all the seven Karshvares [countries] of the earth empty of men.' (*Yasht* 5, 29–30)

This is after the Divine Glory has abandoned the sinful King Yima, two of whose daughters were married to the Azhi Dahaka. This monster is unable to succeed against Atar, the god of fire, who saves the Glory by taking it to the Vourukasha Sea. He is finally defeated by Thraetaona (Fariydun of the *Shahnameh*), who keeps him captive until the end of the world. At this time he will escape only to be slain by Keresaspa (also known as Garshasp).

Other dragons or *azhis* are the horned, yellow-green Azhi Sruvara, which devours horses and men; the golden-heeled Gandareva which terrorises the Vourukasha Sea; and young Snavidhka, which intends to use the spirits of good and evil to pull his chariot when he is fully grown up. There is also a huge evil bird, Kamak; he and the other harmful fabulous creatures are the enemies of mankind, but they themselves fall victim to the heroes. Here is the triumph of good over evil, a struggle central to the Zoroastrian religion.

The first man and heroes

Some of the legendary heroes described in the *Avesta* and later Zoroastrian holy texts probably belong to the pre-Zoroastrian period. At this earlier stage the Indian-speaking and Iranian-speaking peoples, who were related through their language, had not yet separated. With the advent of the prophet Zoroaster and the spread of Zoroastrianism in Iran, some of the ancient pre-Zoroastrian concepts and traditions were incorporated into the *Avesta*, particularly in that part of it known as the *Yasht*. The *Zamyad Yasht* (that is, *Yasht* 19) gives a detailed description of these early heroes, almost all of whom reappear in Firdowsi's *Shahnameh*, written more than two thousand years later. This part of the *Yasht* provides an early short version of the *Shahnameh*.

Gayomartan, whose name means 'Mortal Life', is the mythical first man. Described as 'bright as the sun', he is a large and impressive figure who was created out of earth:

We worship the Fravashi [the deified souls] of Gaya Maretan, who first listened unto the thought and teaching of Ahura Mazda; of whom Ahura formed the face of the Aryan [Iranian] nations, the seed of the Aryan nations. (*Yasht* 13, 87)

Gayomartan falls victim to the Evil Spirit, but his seed is purified by the sun after his death. Forty years after being returned to the earth, his seed becomes a rhubarb plant from which the first mortal man and woman develop.

Illustration from an 18th-century Kashmiri abridged prose Shahnameh, showing the early mythical king Hushang.

The mythological kings of the Iranians begin with the Paradata dynasty (Pishdadian of the *Shahnameh*) and their first king, Haoshanha (Hushang of the *Shahnameh*). In the *Aban Yasht* he appears as Haoshanha, the Paradata, who asks the goddess of water, Ardvi Sura Anahita, for help to overcome the demons and other evil powers.

He is succeeded by Takhma Urupi (Tahmuras of the *Shahnameh*) who ruled over the seven countries, over the evil beings and demons, and who 'rode Angra Mainyu, turned into the shape of horse, all around the earth from one end to the other, for thirty years' (*Yasht* 19, 28–9).

The greatest hero of Iranian mythology was undoubtedly Yima (Jamshid of the *Shahnameh*). As Yima Khshaeta, King Yima, he belongs to the Indo-Iranian traditions. The Indian equivalent, the Vedic Yama, chooses to die and becomes the king of the dead. The Avestan Yima is 'the fair Yima', 'the good shepherd' (*Vendidad* 11, 21). He is highly regarded in the mythical land of Airyaneum Vaejah (Eranvej in Pahlavi), the centre of the world for the ancient Iranians and probably their traditional homeland (that is, Khorezmia). He is described as the king whose rule extended over the entire world; a world where everything was good. He says:

I will nourish, and rule, and watch over thy world. There shall be, while I am king, neither cold wind nor hot wind, neither disease nor death.
(*Vendidad* 11, 5)

101

After three hundred years of his rule, when the world has become over-full of men, animals and birds, Yima enlarges it by one third with his golden stick and whip. Twice more, after six hundred and nine hundred years respectively, he again enlarges the world. Then Yima sins by telling a lie, and the Divine Glory abandons him:

> But when he began to find delight in words of falsehood and untruth, the Glory was seen to flee away from him in the shape of a bird. When his Glory had disappeared, then the great Yima Khshaeta, the good shepherd, trembled and was in sorrow before his foes; he was confounded and laid him down on the ground.
> (*Yasht* 19, 34)

Yima appears once again as the King of Paradise in connection with the birth of the prophet Zoroaster. The description of him in the *Vendidad*, the part of the *Avesta* which probably dates to the second and early third centuries AD, is particularly interesting. Here, a different picture is painted of his character, with no reference to his sin, and he takes part in an epic resembling the Mesopotamian story of the flood. In this version, Yima rules for a thousand years, after which the gods announce that bad times of frost and cold lie ahead and that he should look after one man and woman and specimens of the best animals and plants. Later Zoroastrian legends make Yima immortal, but in Persian folklore and the epic *Shahnameh*, he sins and dies.

Threataona is best remembered for his fight with Azhi Dahaka, whom he does not kill but keeps captive in Mount Demavand until the end of the world (*Bundahishn* XXIX, 9). In the *Avesta* his genealogy is also mentioned:

> Then Thraetaona seized that Glory, he, the heir of the valiant Athwya clan, who was the most victorious of all victorious men next to Zarathustra; who smote Azhi Dahaka . . .
> (*Yasht* 19, 36–7)

Before his encounter with the dragon, Thraetaona asks the water goddess Ardvi Sura Anahita for help and offers her a sacrifice of 'a hundred male horses, a thousand oxen, ten thousand lambs' (*Yasht* 5, 33). He then mentions the two beautiful wives of the Azhi Dahaka, Savanghavak and Erenavak (Shahrnaz and Arnavaz in the *Shahnameh*). In *Farvardin Yasht* (*Yasht* 13, 131), Thraetaona also has the ability to cure certain illnesses and can help 'against itch, hot fever, humours, cold fever, and incontinence' and 'against the evil done by the serpent'. Thraetaona was therefore esteemed as both warrior and physician.

Keresaspa (Garshasp) appears in the *Avesta* as a member of the family of Sam. In the *Shahnameh*, Sam is the grandfather of Rustam, but there does not seem to be a link between the hero of the *Avesta* and Sam of the *Shahnameh*. Keresaspa is described (*Yasht* 13, 136) as curly-haired, very strong, and possessing a club or mace:

> Then the manly-hearted Keresaspa seized that Glory; he who was the sturdiest of men of strength, next to Zarathustra, for his manly courage.
> (*Yasht* 19, 38)

As well as fighting against evil forces, he also engages in battles with dragons, the most famous of these being his encounter with and killing of the horned

Silver bowl showing a figure, probably a king, reclining at a banquet. He has a bushy tripartite hairstyle and wears an elaborate outfit. Parthian, late 2nd–early 3rd century AD.

Sruvara. But once, when Keresaspa is cooking his meal over a fire outside, he does not realise that the dragon is sleeping below the vegetation over which the fire has been made. The monster is woken by the heat, and in moving to run away, causes the pot to fall into the fire. The pollution of the fire is a sin, so Keresaspa is not allowed to enter paradise after his death until Zoroaster himself pleads on the hero's behalf.

The dynasty of the mythical Paradata was succeeded by the Kavi kings of Iran (Kiyanian of the *Shahnameh*) who included Kavi Vishtaspa, the patron of Zoroaster, Kavi Usan, and Kavi Haosravah (Kay Gushtasp, Kay Kavus and Kay Khusrow of the *Shahnameh*). These kings are greatly honoured in the

Avesta, expressed by their possession of the Divine Glory (*khvarnah*). However, also in quest of the Divine Glory is their main opponent, Franrasyan from Turya, the land to the north and east of Iran, which in the *Avesta* counts as one of the five divisions of the Iranians. The name Turya, according to later legends, derives from Tur, son of Thraetaona. According to the *Shahnameh*, King Thraetaona (Fariydun) divided his kingdom between his three sons, Iraj, Salm and Tur. These three appear in the *Bundahishn* (XXXI, 9) as 'Salm, Tug and Airik, the sons of Fredun'. Iraj received the main part (that is, Iran), while Salm was given the western part and Tur the eastern part. It was only after the arrival of Turkish tribes in the areas to the east of the Caspian Sea that a misunderstanding occurred and the ancient Turya of the *Avesta* and its ruler Franrasyan were identified as Turks. In fact, Iranian-speaking peoples occupied Central Asia well before the sixth century AD. *Zamyad Yasht* contains a detailed account of Franrasyan's struggle to obtain the Divine Glory from the Iranian rulers:

He stripped himself naked, wishing to seize that Glory that belongs to the Aryan nations, born and unborn, and to the holy Zarathustra ... Then the most crafty Turanian Franrasyan rushed down into the sea Vouru-Kasha, O Spitama Zarathustra ...
(*Yasht* 19, 56, 58)

Franrasyan is not only the opponent of the Kavis, the Iranian kings, but also a general symbol of evil. He continually attempts to overthrow the Iranian kings in order to obtain their Divine Glory. His evil makes him comparable to a demon:

The Turanian ruffian Franrasyan tried to seize to rule over all the Karshvares [countries]; round about the seven Karshvares did that ruffian Franrasyan rush, trying to seize the Glory of Zarathustra. But that Glory escaped to hidden inlets of the sea.
(*Yasht* 19, 82)

He is finally defeated by Kavi Haosravah, who avenges the brutal murder of his father Siyavarshan (Siyavush of the *Shahnameh*). A large part of the *Shahnameh* is devoted to Prince Siyavush, including his marriage to Afrasiyab's daughter Farangis, and his murder by Afrasiyab and his brother Garsivaz (Keresavazda of the *Avesta*):

To her [Drvaspa, the deity who cares for cattle] did the gallant Husravah, he who united the Aryan nations into one kingdom, offer up a sacrifice, behind the Kaekasta lake, the deep lake of salt waters, with a hundred male horses, a thousand oxen, ten thousand lambs, and an offering of libations: 'Grant me this boon, O good, most beneficent Drvaspa! that I may kill the Turanian murderer, Franrasyan, behind the Kaekasta lake, the deep lake of salt waters, to avenge the murder of my father Syavarshana ...'
(*Yasht* 19, 21–2)

The Book of Kings: Firdowsi's Shahnameh

Written in some 50,000 couplets or double-verses by the poet Firdowsi, the *Shahnameh* or *Book of Kings* is an epic that describes the myths, legends and history of Iran's pre-Islamic past. Firdowsi, who was born in Tus (Khurasan) to a family of landowners (*dihqan*), completed his *Shahnameh* around AD 1010, some three and a half centuries after the Arab conquest of Iran. The *Shahnameh*, which was dedicated to Sultan Mahmud, the Ghaznavid ruler, is regarded not only as a work of great literary importance, but also as a valuable source of information on the traditions, customs and folklore of pre-Islamic Iran.

What were Firdowsi's sources? The poet himself writes that, apart from oral traditions, he had access to written records. Among these are some thousand verses by the poet Daqiqi, who was murdered at the end of the tenth century before he could finish his version of the *Book of Kings*:

> Although he only rhymed the veriest mite
> One thousand couplet full of feast and fight
> He was my pioneer and he alone
> In that he set the Shāhs upon the throne . . .
> To sing the praises of the kings was his
> And crown the princes with his eulogies
> (v, v. 1555)

Many other sources were available to Firdowsi as well, and he is most particular in indicating whether the stories came from a written source or whether they were passed on to him by oral tradition. In the late Sasanian period, the sixth and seventh centuries AD, the mythological past and early history of Iran had been recorded in the official *Khvadaynamak* (*Khudaynameh*), an epic written in Pahlavi (Middle Persian) which no longer exists. This and other Pahlavi books were translated into Arabic in the eighth century, and translations into Persian soon followed. In addition to the Persian translation of the *Khudaynameh* and other Pahlavi sources, Firdowsi's other important written record was the prose *Shahnameh* of Abu Mansur, known as *Shahnameh-yi Abu Mansuri*, of the mid tenth century AD. Unfortunately this *Shahnameh* no longer exists, but Firdowsi's epic is a poetic version of it. His achievement – that of reviving and securing the Persian language as well as Iran's mythological past and early history – thus builds on a long oral and written tradition.

Early 19th-century painting of Kiyumars, the first man and ruler, who dressed in a leopard skin and lived in a cave. Apart from his spotted trousers (indicating the leopard skin), the rest of his outfit and jewelled sword are typical of the Qajar period.

The early myths of the *Shahnameh*

The actual epic of the *Shahnameh* begins with the dynasty of the Pishdadian (the Paradates of the *Avesta*). The first mythological figure described is Kiyumars (the first man, Gayomartan or Gayomard of the *Avesta*). Here he is the ruler who introduces the throne and the crown, the master of the world. He lives in the mountains, ruling over mankind and all creatures, wild and tame. Dressed in a leopard skin which signifies courage and manhood, Kiyumars symbolises the early period in human evolution, a cave dweller who becomes the highest ruler through courage. It is at his court that religion is introduced to people who come from far and wide in search of spiritual and religious values. Kiyumars is the perfect ruler, possessor of all the necessary symbols of kingship – that is, the throne, the crown and the castle. But this perfect harmony comes to an abrupt end when tragedy strikes. As in many of Firdowsi's stories, the tragic event is the death of a beloved son – in this particular story, one who is killed by a *div*, a black demon.

The *Shahnameh* then relates that another mythological ruler, Hushang (Haoshanha of the *Avesta*), the grandson of Kiyumars and son of Siyamak, 'the king of seven countries', was involved in the development of civilisation in the world. His achievements include the discovery of fire, the separation of iron from rock, the smith's craft, tools and weapons, and the irrigation and cultivation of land with the sowing of seeds. In other words, the invention of many important techniques and skills is attributed to this early period. Tahmuras (Takhma Urupi of the *Avesta*), Hushang's son, is described as the one who successfully confronts the demons and, by

Illustration from an 18th-century Kashmiri abridged prose Shahnameh showing Tahmuras, the conqueror of demons, receiving two humble divs, who beseech the king not to kill them.

capturing Ahriman (Angra Mainyu) through magic, rides around the earth on the back of the evil being (there is a parallel story in the *Avesta*). The *divs* beg for mercy and promise to teach Tahmuras the skills of reading and writing.

> The captives bound and stricken begged their lives.
> 'Destroy us not', they said, 'and we will teach thee
> A new and fruitful art' . . .
> (1, v. 22)

The reign of Jamshid

The reign of Jamshid (Yima of the *Avesta*) was an age of invention, partly as a result of the need for more sophisticated weapons of war. In order to protect the ruler and the realm from enemies, a class of warriors is created, marking the beginning of a rigid class structure at an early date in human social development. The epic reveals that there is also a caste of priests, as well as peasants, farmers and artisans. Each of the different groups was kept busy with a specially designed task, and even the so-called unclean demons were given the job of mixing earth with water to make bricks. Using stone and gypsum, they built baths and monumental palaces.

With Jamshid, perhaps the most famous king of Persian mythology, a new and important royal symbol is introduced in the *Shahnameh*: the Divine Glory (*farr-i izadi*) that gave him his famous throne, on which he sat like the shining sun. To celebrate this event, the festival of *Now Ruz*, the new day or the first day of the New Year, was introduced. On this day the world gathered around the king's throne, paid homage to him and celebrated with wine, music and dance. Modern Iranians, as well as Parsees (Zoroastrians in India) and some nations of Central Asia, celebrate this same festival on 21 March, the spring equinox. In Iran, celebrations last up to thirteen days in honour of the beginning of the season of growth. The festival of *Chahar Shanbeh Suri*, which marks the end of winter, is on the eve of the last Wednesday before *Now Ruz*. People gather dried twigs, desert bushes or brush wood, place them in seven bundles in the yard or street, and set them alight at sunset. Then they jump over the fire. Also common at this time and during the *Now Ruz* celebrations is the burning of rue (*isfand*) or frank-incense (*kondor*) against the evil eye and all bad spirits.

The three hundred years of peace and harmony of Jamshid's reign are disrupted through human greed, as so often happens in the *Shahnameh*. Jamshid ceases to believe in a higher power and regards himself as the only and ultimate ruler. His proclamation to this effect upsets the priests and he soon loses his Divine Glory. His army abandons him and the world is thrown into confusion. The way is then open for evil to strike in the form of Ahriman, who gains supremacy over mankind and ushers in a long period of injustice. It is during this era of darkness that Ahriman appears disguised as Zahhak (Azhi Dahaka in the *Avesta*), who through ignorance and greed has sold his soul to the devil.

Zahhak, the serpent-shouldered ruler

It is interesting that Zahhak, who falls into a trap laid by the devil, is described in the *Shahnameh* as the son of a respectable and honest man from the Arabian plains. Because of his association with Mesopotamia in later Zoroastrian texts such as the *Bundahishn*, it is thought that Zahhak's identification as an Arab stems from the Iranians' dislike of the Arab conquest and control of their country. Firdowsi first describes Zahhak as a true hero, a *pahlavan*, brave as his father, who spends most of his time on horseback. But youthful innocence leads him into the arms of the devil, who exploits his unawareness of evil. By disguising himself as a visitor, the devil uses his persuasiveness and charm to capture Zahhak's devotion, finally succeeding in getting the young man to swear allegiance to him. As a result, Zahhak finally agrees, with great reluctance, to murder his father.

It is fascinating to see how this unlawful and evil pact with the devil is marked by a change in Zahhak's appearance. When his benefactor embraces him, two black snakes suddenly grow out of his shoulders. Not only is it impossible for Zahhak to remove the ugly monsters, but he also has to feed them

Illustration from an 18th-century Kashmiri abridged prose Shahnameh showing the enthroned 'snake-shouldered Zahhak' witnessing the execution of King Jamshid.

with the brains of humans every day. Zahhak tries desperately to kill the snakes by cutting their heads off, but they simply grow new heads.

> A marvel followed – from the monarch's shoulders
> Grew two black snakes. Distraught he sought a cure
> And in the end excised them, but they grew
> Again! Oh strange! like branches from a tree ...
> ... At length Iblis [the devil] himself came hurrying
> Tight as a leech. 'This was thy destiny',
> He said, 'cut not the snakes, but let them live.
> Give them men's brains and gorge them till they sleep.'
> (I, v. 32, 33)

Meanwhile Jamshid, whose god-like pretensions have caused him to lose royal power, crown and throne, drives his men into the arms of Zahhak and the devil when they go in search of a new ruler. Zahhak, though an Arab, is hailed as the new king of Iran, after which he marries Jamshid's two daughters, Shahrnaz and Arnavaz (Savanghavak and Erenavak in the *Avesta*). His rule lasts for a thousand years, during which time darkness reigns over the country as young men are sacrificed daily to the serpents rising from his shoulders.

> Zahhāk sat on the throne a thousand years
> Obeyed by all the world. Through that long time
> The customs of the wise were out of vogue ...
> All virtue was despised, black art esteemed,
> Right lost to night, disaster manifest.
> (I, v. 35)

Gradually discontent grows among the population until a group of noblemen plot a revolt, with the aim of offering the crown of Iran to a royal prince of the house of Jamshid. The leader of the noblemen is Kaveh, a blacksmith, who has lost eighteen sons to Zahhak.

The triumph of good over evil

Like many other characters in the *Shahnameh*, Zahhak foresees his own death in a dream, in which a royal offspring appears as tall as a cypress tree, carrying a mace resembling a bull's head. This youth captures him, ties him up and throws him into a well. Zahhak is told by one of his priests that the dream will indeed come true, and that a hero called Fariydun (Thraetaona of the *Avesta*), reaching the moon in height, would look for the royal insignia of belt, crown, throne and tiara. Fariydun's birth is then described in great detail by Firdowsi who, by relating how the baby was fed by a cow, emphasises its physical strength. Fear of being found by Zahhak prompts Fariydun's mother to flee to the Alburz Mountains and take refuge there with her young child. When the day comes for Kaveh to organise the uprising against Zahhak, he leads his followers to Fariydun's hiding-place in the mountains. Wrapped around a spear Kaveh carries the royal banner, the *darafsh-i kaviani*, a piece of leather which the blacksmith had originally worn over his legs. The *Shahnameh* relates that, ever

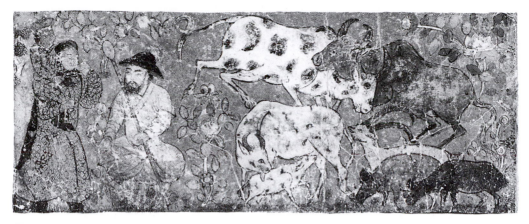

Illustration from a 14th-century Shahnameh showing Fariydun, son of Abtin, carried on his mother's shoulders to the Alburz Mountains, where he is entrusted to a cowherd for protection from the wicked Zahhak.

since that day, the banner had to be covered with jewels each time a new king was chosen.

> ... Thenceforth when any Shāh
> Ascended to the throne, and donned the crown,
> He hung the worthless apron of the smith
> With still more jewels, sumptuous brocade,
> And painted silk of Chin [China] ...
> (I, v. 48)

Before setting off on his campaign, Fariydun orders that a mace be fashioned for him by the blacksmith, which resembles a bull's head. The army, with him at its head and with Kaveh carrying the royal banner, marches towards

Illustration from an 18th-century Kashmiri abridged prose Shahnameh. Fariydun lifts his bull-headed mace and hits Zahhak on the head.

111

Mesopotamia where they have to cross *Arvand Rud* (the River Tigris). The final encounter between good and evil ends in victory for Fariydun, who, on the advice of an angel, takes the trussed-up devil to the mountains and leaves him there with blood pouring out of his heart. Fariydun's long rule of five hundred years marks an era of prosperity, harmony and peace in his realm and among his people.

The division of Fariydun's empire and its consequences

Once again, however, as often happens in the *Shahnameh*, good encounters evil when Fariydun divides his kingdom among his three sons and jealousy breaks out between them. Two of the brothers, Salm and Tur, were born to Jamshid's daughter Shahrnaz, while Iraj is the son of her sister Arnavaz. Fariydun gives his eldest son, Salm, the western part of the kingdom and his second son, Tur, is given Central Asia (Turan). But the most important part, Iran, and Fariydun's golden throne, go to Iraj, their half-brother. Although the youngest, he has proved to be the wisest and bravest of the three.

Soon Salm's discontent and anger over the division become uncontrollable and, together with Tur, he kills Iraj. The murder of one brother by the other two marks the triumph of evil and the beginning of an important episode in Persian mythology: the long and continuous encounters between the kingdoms of Iran and Turan (Airya and Turya of the *Avesta*) and the start of the heroic section of the *Book of Kings*, ushered in by the rule of King Manuchihr (Manushchithra of the *Avesta*), the grandson of Iraj. From this point on, the numerous battles described in the *Shahnameh* result from animosity and rivalry between the two kingdoms, both sides producing a number of famous heroes, but with the Iranians successfully withstanding the attacks and plots of the Turanians and their king, Afrasiyab (Franrasyan of the *Avesta*). The greatest hero of all time, Rustam, spends his life fighting the king of Turan and protecting the boundaries of Iran, as had his father, Zal, and his grandfather, Sam. Zal accompanies Manuchihr on his campaign to Tur to avenge his grandfather's murder. Firdowsi gives a detailed picture of the burial rites and mourning upon the death of Fariydun, describing how the corpse of the late king was placed inside a tomb along with red-coloured gold and lapis lazuli. An ivory throne was put under the body and a crown attached to it, and then the entrance of the tomb was sealed. After this, Manuchihr succeeds his great-grandfather Fariydun, and wears the royal tiara, *kolah*, on his head.

The family of Rustam

Rustam, the son of Zal and grandson of Sam, steps into the limelight at a time when Iran and Turan are continuously in conflict for the supremacy of land and crown. All the heroes on the Iranian side are described as brave, virtuous and deeply attached to the king of kings, for whom they are willing to risk their lives and sacrifice their dearest ones. This is particularly true of Rustam, as shown in the legend of his son Sohrab. Although the name of Rustam's grandfather, Sam, and that of his father Nariman appear in connection with the legendary Keresaspa (Garshasp) in later Zoroastrian texts, neither Rustam nor his son Sohrab is mentioned in the *Avesta*. It seems that the original legends of Rustam did not belong to the same group of stories that were incorporated in the *Avesta*, but were part of an independent cycle. Rustam and his family are described in the *Shahnameh* as kings of Sistan in eastern Iran, and often Rustam is described as Sagzi (Saka). Some scholars believe that Rustam dates from the Parthian period and the time in the first century AD when the Indo-Scythian kings formed an independent kingdom in eastern Iran. Whatever his historical position and origins may have been, Rustam became one of the greatest heroes of Persian mythology, a symbol of great physical strength, spiritual goodness and devotion to his country.

Rustam's father, Zal, is described in detail in the *Shahnameh*, and his birth and upbringing are linked with the legendary guardian bird, the Simurgh (this powerful bird also plays an important part in Rustam's life, coming to his rescue more than once in times of crisis). When Zal is born, to parents who had long awaited a child, his father's joy changes to sorrow and utter helplessness when he sees the newborn baby. The boy's body is described as clean as silver and his face like paradise, but with hair as white as an old man's. Sam is so distressed to see his offspring with such an unusual feature that he becomes disillusioned with the world. In a passionate monologue with God, he questions the reason for his punishment in being given 'the son of Ahriman [the Devil] [with] his black eyes and hair like jasmine [in colour]. When heroes come and ask about this ill-omened child, I shall have to leave Iran with shame. What shall I say, that this is the child of a demon, a two-coloured leopard, or a supernatural being resembling a fairy?'

Sam finally abandons his child in the Alburz Mountains, which are 'near the sun and far from humans', leaving there 'the innocent offspring of a hero, who did not even know the difference between black and white'. But, as so often happens in mythological stories, the little baby survives with the intervention of God the Almighty, who causes Simurgh to discover him while she is flying over her kingdom of the Alburz to look for food for her brood. She takes the abandoned baby to feed to her young ones, but a voice tells her 'to look after this unweaned child, as a man would grow out of this seed'. Thus Zal grows up with Simurgh and her family. Meanwhile, news of a young cypress-like youth living in the mountains has spread to Sam's court, and when Sam tells his wise men about his dream, in which a horseman delivers a happy message about his son being alive, they urge him to go and find his son with the white hair and light-skinned body.

High up in the mountains Sam pleads with God to forgive him and to return his abandoned child, whom he acknowledges is 'not from the sperm of the ill-descended Ahriman'. Simurgh, watching from above, knows immediately why Sam has come to the mountains. She urges Zal to return to his father as her nest is no longer suitable for the son of the greatest of all heroes, the son

Illustration from an 18th-century Kashmiri abridged prose Shahnameh. The mythical bird Simurgh carries the newly born Zal to her nest in the Alburz Mountains. Simurgh's children are shown waiting for her return.

who one day will take over as king. But before returning the sad young hero to his father, Simurgh gives him one of her feathers to light as a signal at times of danger or trouble, and she promises him that she will appear at once.

> . . . Henceforth if men
> Shall hurt or, right or wrong, exclaim against thee,
> Then burn the feather and behold my might,
> For I have cherished thee beneath my plumes
> And brought thee up among my little ones.
> (I, v. 139)

Zal returns to the kingdom of his father in Zabulistan (Sistan). Some time later he meets and marries Rudabeh, the daughter of the king of Kabul, and Rustam, the hero of all heroes, is born to them. Firdowsi recounts that, through her father, Mihrab of Kabul, Rudabeh is related to Zahhak, the usurper of the Iranian throne.

The stories of Rustam

Simurgh's magic power is soon invoked: at the birth of their child, in his desperation to save Rudabeh from the unbearable pains of childbirth, Zal burns Simurgh's feather. The magic bird immediately appears out of a dark sky and soothingly tells Zal that he will soon be the father of a son 'with the height of a

Illustration from an 18th-century Kashmiri abridged prose Shahnameh, showing the birth of Rustam. Sindukht comforts her daughter Rudabeh while Zal and Mihran, the king of Kabul, listen to Simurgh's advice to deliver the baby by Caesarian section.

cypress tree and the strength of an elephant', and that the child is not to be born in the ordinary way but by Caesarian section. The mother recovers fully from her operation with the help of potions prescribed by Simurgh, and by rubbing the feather of the legendary bird on her wound. The boy is named Rustam, of whom it is said that when he was only one day old, you would think he was one year old. Indeed, Rustam develops into a strong lion-like man of such great strength and stature that he has no trouble confronting a roaring elephant and slaying it instantly with his mace. Rustam's heroic deeds and combats are

Page from a 16th-century Shahnameh showing young Rustam, the 'son of a lion',
attacking a white elephant and breaking its neck with his bull-headed mace.

numerous, and his bravery and powers are strengthened by the help of his unusual and equally brave horse, Rakhsh. Together they have a series of adventures, including the seven heroic deeds in which they successfully encounter a lion, pass through a waterless desert, confront a dragon, slay a witch and also finally kill *div*s, one of these being the great white demon who had captured Kay Kavus (Kavi Usan of the *Avesta*), the king of kings. Leading an army of other heroes, they restore the royal power and Kay Kavus returns triumphantly to the land of Iran.

Meanwhile, animosity between Iran and Turan continues with Afrasiyab, the king of Turan, taking every opportunity to attack Iran. But because of the bravery of Rustam, the 'hero of the world', and his dedication to the king of kings, the Iranian army usually withstands the attacks. However, it is just this total dedication to Iran and the king of kings that makes Rustam stumble into traps set by Afrasiyab. One of these even causes him to murder his own son, who has come to enthrone him.

While on a hunting adventure near the plains of Turan, Rustam falls asleep and loses his horse Rakhsh. During his search for the horse, he comes to the town of Samangan in enemy country, where the local king takes him in and promises to find Rakhsh. Rustam meets Tahmineh, the king's beautiful daughter, who has fallen in love with him after hearing all the heroic stories about him. Rustam marries Tahmineh, an event greeted with great joy by the king and inhabitants of Samangan. Just before he departs for Iran, Rustam gives his wife a world-famous amulet seal that he wears on his arm. It is to be given to their future child: if a girl, she should wear it in her hair and, if a boy, he should wear it on his arm like his father.

Nine months later Tahmineh gives birth to a son, who is 'like a shining moon, one would say like the elephant-bodied Rustam, or the lion-like Sam'. Named Sohrab by his mother, at one month the boy resembles a year-old child; when he is three years old, he begins learning the art of combat, and by the time he reaches the age of ten, there is no match for him. He soon realises that he is different from and far advanced over other children of his age, and when he asks his mother about his father, she tells him he is the son of Rustam. This prompts Sohrab not only to set off to find his father, but also to cut his ties with Turan, with the intention of removing Kay Kavus as king of kings of Iran and replacing him with his own father. The news of Sohrab's departure soon reaches the ill-willed Afrasiyab, who immediately plans a deadly plot against both father and son: to prevent Sohrab from meeting and knowing his father and, in turn, to keep Rustam in ignorance of his son's identity, so that they will face each other as enemies. Such a combat between father and son, each unknown to the other, would presumably end in Rustam's death at the hands of his offspring. This devious plot is put into action and, like pieces in a chess game, Rustam and Sohrab are moved against each other by outside forces. The tragic twist in the story is poignantly reinforced by the fact that Sohrab suspects that his adversary might be his father, but when he asks the hero for his name, Rustam hides his true identity. Sohrab then tries to learn the truth from the Turanians, but on

Illustration from a Shahnameh of 1649. Rustam kneels, tearing his shirt in grief, beside the dying Sohrab, having just discovered that his opponent is wearing his amulet and is therefore his son. In the foreground are Rustam's leopard cap, bull-headed mace, sword and shield, and at either side attendants hold the heroes' horses.

Afrasiyab's orders they do not reveal Rustam's identity. Only at their final encounter on the battlefield, when Sohrab receives a deadly blow from his father and Rustam discovers his amulet on Sohrab's arm, does Rustam realise that he has slain his own son.

> . . . The two began
> To wrestle, holding by their leathern belts.
> As for Suhrab thou wouldst have said, 'High heaven
> Hath hampered him' while Rustam reaching clutched
> That warrior-leopard by the head and neck,
> Bent down the body of the gallant youth,
> Whose time was come and all whose strength was gone,
> And like a lion dashed him to the ground;
> Then knowing that Suhrab would not stay under,
> Drew lightly from his waist his trenchant sword
> And gashed the bosom of his gallant son.
> (II, v. 502–3)

From Rustam's very long lifetime, spanning the reigns of many kings, comes another tragic story described in the *Shahnameh*, namely that of Siyavush (Siyavarshan of the *Avesta*).

Siyavush is the son of Kay Kavus and a princess descended from Fariydun and the Turanian royal family. As a young boy he is given into the care of Rustam, who teaches him all the princely arts and skills. When he has grown into a handsome man, one of his father's wives, Sudabeh, falls in love with him. When her temptations cannot lure him to deceive his father, she accuses him of treachery and lies to her husband that Siyavush has declared his love for her. Kay Kavus, who initially believes Sudabeh, forgives his son only after he has proved his innocence by dressing in white and riding through fire on a black horse. Passing through fire was an ancient, probably pre-Zoroastrian practice of proving one's innocence.

Siyavush then moves to the court of Afrasiyab, where he falls in love with the king's daughter, Farangis, marries her and settles in the city named after him, Siyavushgird. Afrasiyab's brother Garsivaz, who is jealous of Siyavush, succeeds in turning Afrasiyab against the young prince of Iran, who is then brutally murdered and has his head cut off. Years later, Kay Khusrow (Kavi Haosravah of the *Avesta*), the son of Siyavush, returns from Turan to Iran. After defeating his rival and half-brother, Fariburz, he is hailed as the legitimate heir to his grandfather Kay Kavus and becomes king. Both Garsivaz and Afrasiyab are killed by Kay Khusrow.

After Rustam's victory over the great hero Isfandiyar, whose murder Simurgh has predicted will have tragic consequences, Rustam is himself killed by his half-brother Shaqad and the king of Zabulistan when he falls, with his horse Rakhsh, into the deadly pit they have dug and filled with knives and daggers. Before Rustam dies, however, he succeeds in lifting himself out of the pit and shooting Shaqad with an arrow, pinning his body to a tree trunk.

Illustration from a 14th-century Shahnameh. Rustam shoots Shaqad as Rakhsh lies in the pit.

Fabulous mythological creatures of the Shahnameh

Evil beings in the form of demons or *div* appear side by side with kings and heroes throughout the *Shahnameh*. Firdowsi refers to these demons as bad humans who have not shown gratitude to God. They are often described as the personification of Ahriman, the devil, but they actually represent a specific group of enemy kings from the areas of Mazandaran and Tabaristan, although their exact geographical location is not clear. While the area south of the Caspian Sea in modern Iran is known as Mazandaran, some scholars believe that the original domain was elsewhere, and only in later times was the name transferred to northern Iran. Nevertheless, both personal and place names in northern Iran show the influence of the *div* in this area. For example, a tribe called Div is known to have inhabited Mazandaran in the sixteenth century.

The encounter with the *div* dates from the reign of the first two mythological kings. Siyamak, the son of Kiyumars, first king of the Pishdadian dynasty, is killed by the Black Demon, the son of Ahriman. Then Hushang, Siyamak's son, goes into battle with the Black Demon and avenges his father's murder, confronting the demon with an army composed of fairies, leopards, tigers, lions, wolves and birds. He puts an end to the demon's life by cutting his throat. As already seen, Hushang's son Tahmuras victoriously challenges the demons, and he rides on the back of Ahriman. It is during his rule that the *div*s are finally forced to beg for mercy.

The heroes of the *Shahnameh* usually have to prove their courage and physical strength as well as their utmost allegiance to the king of kings by confronting *div*s, dragons, wolves and monsters in different disguises. At the same time, there are also stories about heroes being helped or saved by kind and loving supernatural beings. Among these are Simurgh, the legendary bird, and Rustam's horse, Rakhsh.

Rakhsh

Rakhsh is first mentioned towards the beginning of the *Shahnameh*. Before setting off on a major expedition into the mountains to rescue the king of kings, Kay Qubad, Rustam searches for a suitable horse among all the herds of his native Zabulistan, but none that he tests by pressing his hand on its back can

19th-century painting showing Rustam attacking the 'ugly-faced' black div. Wearing his leopard cap, the hero ties the demon's arms with his lasso.

bear the weight, and their stomachs sag to the ground. Suddenly Rustam spots a mare resembling a lion, with ears sticking out like two daggers. Taking short, quick steps, it is followed by a foal resembling the mother in build, with black eyes, a long tail and hooves like steel. Its light-coloured body has red spots shining like the sun in the sky. Its height equals that of a camel and its strength is like that of an Indian elephant. Rustam is about to use his lasso to capture the foal when he is told by the herdsman not to take someone else's horse. When he asks who the owner is, the herdsman replies that he does not know, but that the foal is known as Rustam's Rakhsh.

Rustam then throws his royal lasso over the head of the foal and is immediately attacked by Rakhsh's mother. But Rustam frightens off the mare by roaring like a lion. When he finally captures Rakhsh and tries to push down its back with one hand, the horse does not move, unaware of the immense pressure on its body. After a ride on Rakhsh, Rustam asks the old herdsman the price of the horse. He is told that the price of this horse is equal to the value of the whole of Iran; so, if he is Rustam, he should go and rescue the country of Iran from its enemies and relieve it from sorrow. Rakhsh remains Rustam's faithful servant and companion until eventually both are killed by Rustam's half-brother.

Rakhsh's extraordinary intelligence and dedication to Rustam are beautifully illustrated in the seven adventures or heroic deeds of Rustam (*haft khan*). To stress the importance of this magnificent horse, Firdowsi refers to him affectionately as 'Rakhsh of all Rakhshes' (*Rakhsh-i Rakhshan*), an echo of such titles as 'king of kings' and 'hero of heroes'. In the first adventure, Rustam lays

ABOVE Illustration from an 18th-century Kashmiri abridged prose Shahnameh, showing Rustam using his 'royal lasso' to catch Rakhsh.

Illustration from a 16th-century Shahnameh showing the first stage of Rustam's seven adventures, when Rakhsh kills an attacking lion. The hero, wearing his leopard cap, rests his head on a leopard skin. His bow, quiver and bull-headed mace lie beside him. Rustam is usually described as wearing a babr-i bayan or palangineh, a coat made of leopard skin.

down his sword to take a rest in the reed fields and is unknowingly approached by a lion. 'Boiling like fire', Rakhsh attacks the lion with his forelegs and bites it on the back. When Rustam awakes and sees the dead beast, he reprimands his horse for risking death in the fight, which would have left him without any way of reaching Mazandaran.

In the third of the seven adventures, Rustam has gone to sleep (after an exhausting second adventure, in which thirst has almost killed him and Rakhsh). Before resting, he warns Rakhsh not to fight with lions and dragons. Soon a huge dragon appears, measuring 80 *gaz* (about 80 m) from head to tail. Rakhsh is distressed and tries to awaken his master by pawing the ground with his hooves, but when Rustam opens his eyes, the dragon disappears. Rustam then scolds Rakhsh for disturbing him. The dragon continues with this game, so that each time Rustam is awakened by Rakhsh, he finds only darkness in the wilderness. Finally he threatens to cut off Rakhsh's head. When the dragon reappears once again, breathing fire and smoke, Rakhsh ignores both Rustam's threat and the dragon's disappearing trick and, roaring with excitement and anger, paws the ground until it cracks. This time when the hero awakes, he is able to see the dragon's flames in the darkness. Rakhsh, spellbound until then, attacks the dragon and bites it on the shoulder while Rustam strikes it with his sword and cuts off its head.

Ultimately Rakhsh and Rustam meet their end together, as recounted in the preceding chapter. Even then, when death threatens the great hero, Rakhsh makes a final attempt to rescue his master. Smelling death and danger ahead, he tries in vain to resist bearing Rustam towards the deadly, dagger-filled pits.

Simurgh

The other mythological creature which features throughout the *Shahnameh* as the friend and protector of Rustam and his family is Simurgh, the 'king of birds', who lives at the top of the Alburz Mountains and raises Rustam's father Zal. Zal's Simurgh is also called upon for help when Rustam is fighting Isfandiyar, in the famous encounter between the two equals. Badly injured, Rustam for the first time doubts whether he can withstand Isfandiyar's power, and he asks his father for help. Zal, shocked by the desperate physical condition of both Rustam and Rakhsh, sets alight the feather Simurgh has given him.

Immediately the dark sky turns darker and Simurgh emerges. She listens to Zal's description of the hero's deep wounds. Firdowsi describes how Simurgh first praises Isfandiyar's divine lineage and heroic status and cannot understand why Rustam has confronted him. However, she soon sees to Rustam, pulling eight arrows out of his body and rubbing her feathers over the wounds. She then sees to Rakhsh:

> She in like manner having called for Rakhsh
> Employed her beak on him to make him whole,
> And drew out from his neck six arrow-heads.
> (V, V. 1704)

19th-century Qajar illustration in a 15th-century Shahnameh, showing Rustam shooting Isfandiyar in the eye with his forked arrow.

Simurgh makes it clear that she disapproves of Rustam fighting with Isfandiyar, who is of royal and divine descent,

> a holy man who hath the Grace of God.
> (v, v. 1705)

He is the son of Gushtasp (Vishtaspa of the *Avesta*), the patron of Zoroaster, and he has been made invulnerable by Zoroaster. But despite her disapproval of the fight, Simurgh reveals to Rustam the secret of overcoming Isfandiyar, once again proving her loyalty to Zal and his son. The magic bird tells Rustam to prepare a special shaft with three feathers and two arrow heads, and to aim it towards Isfandiyar's eyes. Rustam follows Simurgh's advice, although before discharging the deadly arrow he suggests to Isfandiyar that they should end their conflict. Isfandiyar, however, still convinced that no one is equal to him, refuses, and thus finally falls victim to Rustam.

It is interesting that, in another story about the hero Isfandiyar (who also has seven adventures), Firdowsi describes how Isfandiyar fights a large monstrous bird, also called Simurgh though obviously not the same one as Zal's protective guardian, and through cunning he defeats her, finally cutting the vicious bird to pieces with his sword. Firdowsi then describes how the earth was covered in feathers from mountain to mountain.

Illustration from an 18th-century Kashmiri abridged prose Shahnameh, depicting Isfandiyar emerging from his ingenious box to kill a vicious bird (also called Simurgh).

Battling with the demons

The last of Rustam's seven heroic deeds in Mazandaran introduces demons such as Arjang and the Div-e Sepid (white demon), the latter being the arch-demon who has captured the king. The *div*s of Mazandaran, who were enemies of the Iranians, looked like demons in that they were large and often furry, but they also possessed human-like qualities. The sorrow of captivity as well as the ugliness and bad temper of the white demon has caused blindness in Kay Qubad, and Rustam is told that the only way to restore the king's eyesight is to kill the white demon and apply three drops of its blood to the king's eyes. As Rustam rides on the wind-like Rakhsh towards the cave of the great *div*, he encounters a whole army of demons asleep in the heat of the sun. When he finally makes his way into the darkness of the cave, he finds the great white demon at rest. Awoken by Rustam's leopard-like roaring, the *div* appears 'like a black mountain', but receives a heavy blow that cuts off an arm and a leg. The white demon continues its struggle with only one leg until, after a long and bloody fight, Rustam lifts it up, throws it to the ground, and cuts out its liver with his dagger. Having witnessed the battle, the other demons flee. The blood of the white demon is applied and the king miraculously regains his sight.

The story of Akvan, one of the most famous demons, is told in great detail by Firdowsi. This demon attacks the royal herd in the shape of a wild ass, but acts like a male lion by breaking the horses' heads. Kay Khusrow, the king of Iran, knows immediately that this unlikely wild ass could only be Akvan, and

Illustration from a late 16th-century Shahnameh showing the seventh and final stage of Rustam's adventures. The hero kills the Div-e Sepid (white demon) and, with the blood from its heart, cures King Kay Kavus' temporary blindness.

BELOW Illustration from a 16th-century Shahnameh. The demon Akvan carries the sleeping Rustam, prior to throwing him into the sea. The fully armed hero is wearing his leopard cap while his bow, quiver and bull-headed mace are lying beside him.

sends for Rustam to come to Zabulistan. On reading the royal command, the hero of heroes hastens to reassure the king that 'whether demon, lion or a male dragon, it will not escape my sharp sword'. Rustam arrives on the scene resembling 'a male lion, holding a lasso in his hand and riding on a dragon' (Rakhsh). He seeks the demon for three days, until on the fourth day he sees it passing by like 'the north wind'. Akvan is described as shining like gold on the outside, but ugly beneath. Protruding like a snake from its skin, its head resembles that of an elephant with long hair. Its mouth is filled with teeth like the tusks of a boar. Its eyes are white and its lips black.

Rustam's attempt to catch the wild ass which is Akvan proves unsuccessful, as every time he throws his lasso, the beast manages to disappear as effortlessly as the wind. Even his arrows do not reach the demon and finally, exhausted by his efforts, Rustam dismounts, unsaddles Rakhsh, takes off his leopard skin, puts down his arrows and lasso, and lies down to rest on the felt underlay of the saddle. It is only then that Akvan, watching from afar, turns into a howling wind, changes the earth into dust, and suddenly lifts Rustam into the sky. When Rustam wakes up, he finds himself trapped, and for once his mighty strength, his sword and mace are powerless, for Akvan is even stronger and more powerful. There then follows an interesting conversation while the demon carries the hero in a flight across the sky. Akvan is planning to drop Rustam either on to the mountains or into the ocean, and he asks the hero which he would prefer. Rustam's sharp intelligence gives him an insight into the character of the demon, so he decides not to tell his true wish, which is for the chance to swim out of the ocean. He therefore beseeches Akvan not to drop him into the ocean, saying souls cannot ascend from its watery depths to heaven, and pleading to be thrown instead on to the mountains among the leopards and the lions. On hearing Rustam's plea, Akvan casts him into the ocean, just as Rustam had divined, and the hero reaches shore safely by fending off the sharks with his right arm, dagger and leg while swimming with his left arm and leg. Rustam then finds Rakhsh and, mounted on his great steed, meets Akvan once again for a final encounter near a water source. This time Akvan asks Rustam whether he has not had enough of battles, he who has escaped the ocean and the jaws of sharks, returning to the plains barely half alive. Rustam replies with a roar like a lion, unties his lasso from his saddle strap, and throws it around the demon's waist. After tying the lasso on to the saddle he turns around, lifts his mace like a blacksmith's hammer, and hits Akvan on the head. Then he hacks off the demon's head with his dagger.

Encounters with dragons

As mentioned above, one of the mythological creatures which Rustam and his horse Rakhsh encounter during their third adventure is a dragon who hides from the hero in the darkness and is finally attacked by Rakhsh before Rustam cuts off its head with his sword. But perhaps one of the most dramatic combats between a human and a dragon appears in the parallel story of Isfandiyar in his

Illustration from an 18th-century Shahnameh showing the fully armed Rustam with his leopard-skin shield attacking the huge dragon while the monster's long tail is coiled around Rakhsh. Trees and mountains indicate the wooded landscape of Mazandaran.

own third adventure. Having already successfully slain wolves and lions and an evil bird, he is faced by a fearsome dragon, described as resembling a black mountain which blots out the sun and the moon. The beast's eyes are said to be like two shining pools of blood, and fire bursts out of its mouth which, when open, looks like a deep dark cave. Before setting out, Isfandiyar devises a most ingenious wooden structure (similar to that used in his battle of wits with the vicious bird). He orders his carpenters to build him a wooden box covered with sharp spikes. This is placed on a wheeled cart pulled by two valuable horses, and Isfandiyar hides inside the box. When the dragon attacks, it swallows the horses and the cart, but the spikes keep the box (with the hero inside) lodged in the monster's throat until a green sea of poison oozes out of the dragon's mouth. Isfandiyar climbs out of the deadly box and sticks a sharp-pointed sword into the dragon's head, splitting open its brain.

> . . . in the dragon's gullet stuck
> The sword blades, and blood poured forth like a sea;
> It could not free its gullet, for the swords
> Were sheathed within it. Tortured by the points
> And chariot the dragon by degrees
> Grew weak, and then the gallant warrior,
> Arising from the box, clutched his keen glaive
> With lion-grip and hacked the dragon's brains
> Till fumes of venom rising from the dust
> O'erpowered him; he tumbled mountain-like
> And swooned away.
> (v, v. 1593)

Stories of Zoroaster, Cyrus and Alexander

Historical figures often enter the world of myths, with legends embroidering the original details of their lives to such an extent that it often becomes difficult to separate fact from fiction.

Zoroaster

Legends surround the birth of the prophet Zoroaster, and later Zoroastrian texts such as the *Denkard* describe how the Divine Glory (*khvarnah*) and the guarding spirit (*fravahr*) were already present inside the prophet's mother. The Divine Glory originated from the world of light of the sun, moon and stars, and found its way from there to the family hearth in the home of Zoroaster's ancestors. Thus Zoroaster's mother, Dughdov, carried inside her body the Divine Glory, which was so bright that it made her shine in the darkness. This illuminating effect was exploited by evil demons to suggest that the girl was a witch, so her father sent her away. She stayed with the head of the Spitama family and later married the son, Purushasp. One day after the two are married, Purushasp is guided by some of the immortals to a special tree. The guarding spirit, having been brought from heaven to earth, has been placed in its branches in the shape of the haoma plant. He takes the plant back to his wife. Zoroaster's physical body (*tan gohr*) actually reaches his mother through the milk of young cows which have been fed on plants nourished in turn by special rainwater made to fall by the lords of waters and plants, Khurdad and Amurdad. Dughdov drinks the mixture of the crushed haoma plant and the milk.

Myths also surround the time after Zoroaster's birth, concerning the demons' continued efforts to show that the Divine Glory is an evil sign. As a result, Zoroaster's father makes several attempts to put an end to his son's life: he tries to burn him in a fire, and he places him in front of stampeding cattle, and then horses. But each time the child is saved: in the first instance, the fire will not start, and in the second and third, a bull and a stallion respectively stand guard over him. He is even abandoned in the wilderness, but a she-wolf rescues him and a ewe suckles the newborn baby.

More legends exist in the *Denkard* and much later stories about the prophet's efforts to convert King Vishtaspa to Zoroastrianism. They describe how the prophet is thrown into prison, but succeeds in gaining his release by curing one of the king's horses. When Vishtaspa finally accepts the new religion, his wish to foresee his fate is granted. By drinking a special mixture containing haoma juice, he falls unconscious and sees himself in heaven. Other wishes are also granted to those nearest to Vishtaspa: one of his sons drinks a cup of milk which makes him immortal; his minister Jamasp gains knowledge by inhaling perfumes; and Vishtaspa's other son, Isfandiyar, eats a pomegranate and thereby becomes invincible.

Cyrus the Great

Cyrus the Great, founder of the Achaemenid empire, came to power after deposing the Median king Astyages in 550 BC. After a series of victories over the Lydian king, Croesus, in 547 or 546 BC, and after his successful campaign against the Babylonians in 539 BC, Cyrus established a large empire stretching from the Mediterranean in the west to eastern Iran, and from the Black Sea in the north to Arabia. He was killed in 530 BC during a campaign in the north-eastern part of his empire.

The legend of Cyrus and the myths surrounding his birth are best described by Herodotus, the Greek historian of the mid-fourth century BC, who lived in Asia Minor. According to him, Astyages was Cyrus' maternal grandfather, who dreamt that his daughter Mandane produced so much water that it overran his city and the whole of Asia. When the holy men (*magi*) hear of the king's dream, they warn him of its consequences. As a result, her father gives Mandane in marriage to a Persian called Cambyses who, although of noble descent, is considered by Astyages to be 'much lower than a Mede of middle estate'. Mandane and Cambyses have not been married a year when Astyages once again has a dream, this time that a vine growing from inside Mandane's womb will spread all over Asia. The *magi* immediately see a bad omen and tell the king that Mandane's son will usurp his throne. The king sends for his pregnant daughter and keeps her under tight guard until the child is born. Royal instructions are given to Harpagus, a Median nobleman and confidant of the king, that he should kill and dispose of the newly born child. But at that moment fate and supernatural forces intervene and Harpagus decides not to kill the baby himself. Instead, he calls for a royal herdsman and orders him to carry out the king's command, adding that he will be severely punished if the child is allowed to live. As it happens, the herdsman's own wife has given birth to a stillborn child during her husband's absence, and she pleads with him to keep the royal baby and regard it as their own. They bury the body of their own dead child and look after the infant Cyrus as their own flesh and blood.

Cyrus soon develops into an outstanding young boy, overshadowing his friends and showing royal qualities of leadership. It is reported that, during a game with other children, Cyrus is chosen to play king. Promptly assuming this role, he metes out harsh punishment to the son of a distinguished Mede who refuses to take orders from him. The father of the badly beaten boy complains to King Astyages, who in turn calls for Cyrus in order to have him punished. When asked why he has behaved in such a savage manner, Cyrus defends his action by

The famous clay cylinder of Cyrus the Great, written in Babylonian cuneiform, recording his capture of Babylon in 539 BC.

explaining that, because he was playing the role of king, he had every reason to punish someone who was not obeying his command. Astyages knows immediately that these are not the words of a herdsman's son and realises that the boy is his own grandson, the son of Mandane. The story is confirmed by the herdsman, albeit with great reluctance. Astyages punishes Harpagus for his disobedience by serving him the cooked remains of his own son's body at a royal dinner. Then, on the advice of the *magi*, the king allows Cyrus to return to Persia to his real parents.

Meanwhile Harpagus burns with feelings of revenge against Astyages and decides to encourage Cyrus to seize his grandfather's throne. Suggesting this plan to Cyrus is not easy, as it has to be sent to him in Persia. Herodotus describes how Harpagus writes his plan on a piece of paper and inserts it into the belly of a slain hare which has not yet been skinned. The skin is sewn up and the hare given to a trusted servant who, posing as a hunter, travels to Persia and presents Cyrus with the hare, telling him to cut open the dead animal. After reading Harpagus' letter, Cyrus begins to play with the idea of seizing power from Astyages. As part of a careful plan, he persuades a number of the Persian tribes to side with him to throw off the yoke of Astyages and the Medes. Cyrus succeeds in overthrowing his grandfather and becomes the ruler of the united Medes and Persians.

This fascinating account by Herodotus is still regarded as the most reliable source on Cyrus' birth and coming to power, although it has a strong mythological flavour. Other descriptions, such as that of Xenophon, the Greek who served more than a hundred years later in the army of Cyrus the Younger, and the accounts of the Greek physician Ctesias in the fourth century BC, are usually considered less reliable. Among the later sources, however, one story is of particular interest. It describes how the baby Cyrus, abandoned in the woods by a shepherd, is fed by a dog until the shepherd returns with his wife and takes the infant into their care. This tale is very much in line with mythological stories surrounding the infancy of other heroes and rulers. For example, Romulus and Remus, the twins who founded Rome, were saved and raised by a wolf, and Zal, Rustam's father, was brought up by the legendary bird Simurgh.

Stories of prophetic dreams like those of Astyages, and of the abandonment of newborn babies, recur consistently in Iranian mythology. Darab, the father of Dara (Darius III), in the *Shahnameh* is said to be abandoned by his mother Humay, only returning to his natural mother when he is grown up. In the story of the birth and upbringing of Kay Khusrow, the Kiyanian king and son of Prince Siyavush, some of the mythological elements are also reminiscent of the story of Cyrus. Kay Khusrow is born in Turan at the court of King Afrasiyab, the opponent of the Iranians. Before being murdered, his father sees in a dream that Kay Khusrow will become the ruler of Iran. When the child is born, he is put in the care of shepherds and his true identity is kept secret. Meanwhile, Gudarz, the great Iranian hero, sees in a dream a cloud full of water ascending from Iran, and an angel informs him of the existence of a new king called Kay Khusrow. Gudarz then sends his son Giv to find Kay Khusrow and bring him back to Iran.

Another story in the *Shahnameh* that has been linked with the legend of Cyrus is that of Ardashir, the founder of the Sasanian dynasty. Ardashir's father, Sasan, is claimed to have been a descendant of the Achaemenid rulers of Iran. The young Sasan works as a shepherd for Babak (Papak), the local king of Fars in south-western Iran. One night Babak has a dream in which Sasan is riding on a huge white elephant with everyone saluting him. He also sees the sacred fires of the Zoroastrians burning in front of Sasan. After consulting his wise men, who tell him that the young man in his dream will become the king, Babak takes in Sasan and gives him his daughter in marriage. The offspring of this union is Ardashir, who defeats the last Parthian king, Ardavan, in AD 224. An almost identical story appears in the *Karnamak-i Artakhshir-i Papakan* (*Deedbook of Ardashir, Son of Babak*), of the Sasanian period dating from the seventh century, which probably was known to Firdowsi. It has been suggested that the idea of the mythological birth of Cyrus the Great was used in stories and legends about other great rulers, and that the resemblance of the Kay Khusrow tale to the Cyrus myth may indicate that Cyrus and Kay Khusrow were the same person.

Alexander the Great

Persian legends were also created around the figure of Alexander the Great, who defeated Dara or Darius III, the last Achaemenid king, in 331 BC. It is surprising, but not impossible to explain, that this foreign conqueror should be hailed as a great man. Although he was a usurper, Alexander entered Persian literature and historical accounts as a great statesman and philosopher, and it is only occasionally that negative aspects of his character or evil deeds are described in the sources. One such instance is in Firdowsi's description of the famous *taqdis*, the mythical throne of the Iranian kings. This says that, until the time of Alexander's conquest, each king had added to the splendour of the throne, but Alexander broke the throne into pieces. It was not until the rule of Khusrow Parviz (Khusrow II, AD 590–628) that the throne was restored. Tabari, the great historian of the tenth century, mentions Alexander in connection with the burning of the *Avesta*, which was considered a most wicked deed. None the less, Alexander has entered national Iranian epics as a hero and the legitimate heir to

Illustration from a late 15th-century Khamseh of Nizami, showing Alexander comforting the dying Dara (Darius III).

the throne. Such legitimacy must have been a political necessity, as only rulers with a genuine right to the Kingly Glory were chosen to rule over Iran. A foreign usurper would have no place in the country's history, and in order to make Alexander qualify, the *Shahnameh* regards him as the half-brother of the last Achaemenid king.

The most important biography of Alexander, the *Pseudo-Callisthenes*, which probably dates from the third century AD, was the original source of information on the Macedonian ruler. Translations into other languages, including Pahlavi and then Arabic, provided the necessary source material for later romances on Alexander. Among these are Firdowsi's description of Alexander in his *Shahnameh* of the early eleventh century and Nizami Ganjavi's *Iskandarnameh* (*Book of Alexander*), also a poetic work but written in the twelfth century.

Firdowsi clearly used two different sources for the character of Alexander in the *Shahnameh*. In the main section on Alexander, the poet describes him as an Iranian prince of the Kiyanian line, with a legitimate claim to the Iranian throne and the Divine Glory. But later, when writing about the Sasanian period and Ardashir, its first ruler, he launches into a fierce attack on Alexander, describing him as an enemy of Iran, as evil and destructive as Zahhak, the usurper of the Iranian throne, and as Afrasiyab, the Turanian. He also accuses Alexander of having destroyed the Iranian throne and condemns him. Nizami, on the other hand, takes a more philosophical approach to Alexander's rule, and his *Iskandarnameh* portrays Alexander as the ultimate and perfect ruler.

133

In the first part of his work, known as the *Sharafnameh*, Nizami describes the birth of Alexander. The poet gives two different versions, but adds that there were others as well. The first story describes Alexander's mother as being from Rum (Greece), and relates that when the devout woman becomes pregnant she leaves her town and her husband in distress. She gives birth to her child alone among some ruins, and then dies, leaving the baby unattended. It so happens that the king, Philphius/Philqus (Philip of Macedon), is hunting in the plains and passes the dead woman. He sees the hungry newborn infant sucking his finger and takes the baby with him, raising him as his own son and making him his crown prince. Here Nizami comments that neither this version nor the one told by Firdowsi, in which Alexander is related to Dara, the Iranian king, is true, and that Alexander was actually the son of Philip. Nizami then gives his second version, in which he describes at great length how Philip falls in love with a beautiful woman of his court, who becomes pregnant by him. The king orders the wise men to read the stars and tell him of any secrets they reveal about the unborn baby. The stars indicate strength, courage, wisdom and the absence of the evil eye, and also show that the baby will be presented with the key to the world. The royal birth is therefore celebrated with much rejoicing. Soon after starting to walk 'gracefully like a pheasant', the young Alexander asks his wetnurse for a bow and arrow and practices target shooting, sometimes at paper and other times at silk. Once grown, he takes up a sword and fights with lions. Then he discovers the joys of riding and follows the path of kingship. Alexander is taught by Aristotle's father and then learns the skills of warfare. After the death of his father, he ascends the Macedonian throne, defeats the Iranian king, Dara, and becomes the ruler of Iran. He then marries Roxana (Rushanak), the daughter of the deposed Dara, and travels across his realm eastwards to India and China. He also visits the Ka'aba, the holy place of the Muslims, and finally returns to Greece, his birthplace.

In the second part of his epic, the *Iqbalnameh*, Nizami elevates Alexander above even the status of world conqueror, to that of philosopher and prophet. Again and again Nizami defends the accuracy of his version, describing at great length Alexander's knowledgeable involvement in philosophy and science. He recounts that, before his death, Alexander divides up his realm among his feudal lords, who thus become independent and need not take orders from each other. This does in fact closely follow the historical facts.

Nizami offers various suggestions as to how Alexander acquired his title of 'the two-horned' (*dhulqarnain*, Persian *zulqarnain*), a title also mentioned in the Qur'an but not necessarily in connection with Alexander. One is that Alexander saw the dawn in both east and west, *qarn* in Arabic meaning the upper edge of the sun. It was also said that in a dream Alexander saw the east and west take the sky away from the sun, or that he lived for two *qarn* (*qarn* also meaning time, a generation). Another suggestion is that he wore his hair in two plaits at the back (*qarn* can also mean a lock of hair in Arabic). Still another, according to a well-known source, has it that in a Greek portrait Alexander was shown flanked by two horned angels, and that one horn (*qarn*) of each angel seemed to be

Obverse of a coin of Lysimachus of Thrace (306–281 BC), showing Alexander with a ram's horn.

protruding from the sides of the ruler's own head, suggesting that Alexander was divine, chosen by God, and that the angels are there to protect him. This portrait was passed around the kingdom, and the Arabs may have believed that the horns belonged to Alexander himself. There is an interesting parallel here with religious beliefs in ancient Mesopotamia, where a divinity was signified by a horned head-dress. But Alexander's title seems to have derived from a connection with the Egyptian god Zeus-Amun, who is often associated with a ram. After conquering Egypt Alexander was declared the son of Zeus-Amun, and on some Hellenistic coins he is shown with a ram's horn on his head.

Nizami then goes on to relate an amusing anecdote on the same subject. The tale is that Alexander had very large ears, which he kept hidden beneath his gold crown. Only the slave who shaved his head knew his secret, but when this slave died he had to be replaced. The new hairdresser arrives and is immediately warned by the king to keep his large ears a secret. If he does not, Alexander threatens to give the slave a good 'ear-rubbing' and kill him. In his fright the poor slave practically loses the power of speech altogether. Carrying the burden of such a great secret finally makes him ill and one day he leaves the palace, driven by despair into the fields. There he sees a deep well and, putting his head into it, he shouts down into the depths that the king of the world has long ears. He then returns in relief to the palace.

Once the slave has gone away, a bamboo stick containing the secret emerges from inside the well. A passing shepherd sees the bamboo stick and takes it to make a flute. One day when Alexander is riding through the fields, he hears a song about his big ears coming out of the shepherd's flute. He questions the shepherd, who recounts how he found the stick and made it into a flute. Alexander realises that his slave has somehow revealed his secret, and accosts the poor man for an explanation. Knowing that he must tell the truth even if it costs him his life, the slave explains that he had been unable to bear the burden of his secret alone and so chose what he thought would be a safe receptacle for it. Alexander forgives the slave, realising that no one can be forced to keep a secret and that, in the end, all secrets will be revealed.

Continuation of an ancient tradition

It is not unusual to find, in many of the written works already mentioned, references to the sources used for ancient stories. These sources were both written and spoken, the latter being part of an ancient oral tradition passed on from generation to generation. The Zoroastrian priests, for example, had to learn religious hymns and prayers by heart and repeat them word for word. The sacred words of the prophet Zoroaster, the *Gatha*, and other parts of the *Avesta*, were preserved by word of mouth until as late as the fourteenth or fifteenth century AD. The fact that the holy book of the Zoroastrians was kept alive in such a manner proves the importance and long history of oral tradition.

In addition to the Zoroastrian priests who kept their religion alive by memorising and repeating the hymns and prayers, there were also minstrels (*ramishgar, khuniyagar*) who performed for the ruler and his court. The existence of such minstrels is mentioned in the works of many poets. The origin of the ancient stories is usually ascribed to the Sasanian period, which began in the third century AD and ended with the advent of Islam. Many of them actually date from an even earlier time, but 'Sasanian' seems to have become a general term for everything pre-Islamic.

Sometimes the figure of a minstrel is built into the story as told by the poet, and the minstrel's songs add to its development. This is certainly the case in the love story of Vis and Ramin, which is of ancient origin. In it Ramin, himself an accomplished minstrel (*gusan*) and harp player, sings about his and Vis' love. The poet Gurgani starts by giving the reader valuable information about the origin of this love story:

A popular story in this country or the world, it was arranged by six wise men ... but its language was Pahlavi [Middle Persian] which is not known and understood by everyone. This was used in this country by those who were studying this language.

This indicates that, at the time of Gurgani in the middle of the eleventh century, a written version in the older language of Pahlavi was available, but a Persian translation must also have existed. The Persian prose version was turned into a romantic poem by Gurgani. He says that, although a myth can be excellent and sweet, it can be improved through rhyme and metre.

The art of storytelling was highly regarded in ancient Iran, and the names of some of the most accomplished and highly acclaimed storytellers have

Illustration from a 16th-century (1539–43) Khamseh of Nizami showing Barbad, the 'king of minstrels', performing on the lute at the court of Khusrow II.

survived in later literature. Often they sang their tales and accompanied themselves on a musical instrument. Bahram Gur (Bahram V, 420–38), the renowned Sasanian king whose bravery, love of hunting, and unrivalled archery skill are widely celebrated in poetry and art, had as his favourite slave a Greek girl, Azadeh, who sang and played the harp. She accompanied him on his hunting expeditions. Bahram once asked the king of India to send him ten thousand male and female minstrels and harpists.

Such references to minstrels are numerous in the *Shahnameh*, the most detailed being the story of Barbad, who is highly praised by both Firdowsi and Nizami. He eventually becomes the king of minstrels at the court of the Sasanian king Khusrow II (AD 590–628), known as Khusrow Parviz. Barbad decides to challenge Sarkash, the reigning court minstrel, but is banned from the royal entourage. Determined to attract the king's attention, Barbad goes to the royal gardens and makes friends with the gardener, who promises to tell him when the king of kings is coming to the gardens. One day Barbad is informed that the king is expected to visit the royal gardens. The minstrel dresses himself in green and dyes his musical instrument green, then hides in a tree. The king arrives and makes himself comfortable. Barbad then begins to sing. The king and his followers are delighted with his beautiful voice and wonder who the singer of such a sweet tune could be. Sarkash faints at the realisation that only Barbad, his rival, could play and sing in such a way. The king orders his entourage to look for the singer, but they are unable to find him in his green camouflage. After another song and another fruitless search, the king manages to lure

Barbad out of hiding by promising to fill his mouth and lap with gems. On hearing these words, Barbad descends from the tree and introduces himself to Khusrow Parviz as his slave, who lives only to sing for him. Barbad is greatly rewarded and replaces Sarkash, the previous court minstrel, becoming the king of minstrels (*shah-i ramishgaran*). When Khusrow Parviz is later murdered, Barbad cuts off his fingers and burns his musical instruments as an expression of devotion.

Minstrels at the courts of kings combined the skills of poets and musicians. It was a privilege to be a minstrel at the royal court, as shown in the story of Barbad. A similarly high status was enjoyed by the first great Persian poet, Rudaki, who lived in the early tenth century. Mentioned in many Islamic sources and hailed as the 'king of poets', the blind Rudaki sang his poems to the accompaniment of harp and lute.

Vis and Ramin

The story of Vis and Ramin dates from the pre-Islamic period. The poet Gurgani used the theme in the mid-eleventh century and claimed a Sasanian origin for it. Now, however, it is regarded as belonging to the Parthian period, probably the first century AD. It has also been suggested that Gurgani's story reflects the traditions and customs of the period immediately before he himself lived. This cannot be ruled out, as stories retold from ancient sources often include elements drawn from the time of their narrator.

The framework of the story is the opposition of two Parthian ruling houses, one in the west and the other in the east. The existence of these small kingdoms and the feudalistic background point to a date in the Parthian period. The popularity of this pre-Islamic story in the Islamic period is mentioned by the poet himself, and shows that there was a demand for ancient themes and traditional lore.

The plot unfolds as a struggle over love and honour between two ruling families. Instead of the Kavi kings of the *Avesta* and the Kiyanian rulers of the *Shahnameh*, one set of protagonists is from the house of Qaren (the Parthian noble family of Karen). In the story their seat of power is the ancient city of Hamadan in Media. Their opponent is Mubad Manikan, the king of Merv (now in Turkmenistan in Central Asia), who rules in the east. The poem begins with Mubad, the old king of Merv, declaring his love for Shahru, the beautiful 'fairy-faced' queen of Mah (Media). Shahru explains to Mubad that she is already married and has a son, Viru, but she has to promise that, if she ever has a daughter, she will give her to Mubad as his wife. Shahru agrees to this because she does not believe she will ever bear another child. The oath is sealed with a handshake and written down on silk. However, it so happens that 'the dried-up tree turned green and came out with a hundred leaves and flowers. In her old age Shahru became pregnant, like a pearl fallen into an oyster'.

The baby is a girl, whom they call Vis. She is immediately given into the care of a wetnurse who takes her to Khuzistan and brings her up with the other child in her care. This is Ramin, younger brother of the king of Merv. When the children grow up, Ramin is called back to Merv and Vis is sent back to her home in Hamadan. Her mother, Shahru, decides that the only man in Iran worthy of such beauty and culture is her son Viru, Vis' own brother. When their stars are consulted and the omens are found positive, a wedding of great splendour takes place. It is during these festivities that Zard, a half-brother of King Mubad, arrives at court to deliver a message reminding Shahru of her promise to give him her daughter's hand. Vis refuses to leave her brother-husband and Mubad in fury determines to go to war with the house of Qaren. He sends messengers to many places and finds much support among their kings, including those of Tabaristan, Gurgan, Dahistan, Khorezmia, Sogdia, Sind, India, Tibet and China. Soon his court is filled with the commanders of armies and the plains of Merv are crowded with people, resembling the Day of Judgement. Meanwhile, Shahru enlists the support of the kings who attended the wedding: those of Azerbaijan, Ray, Gilan, Khuzistan, Istakhr and Isfahan, all in the western part of Iran. The two armies meet on the plains of Nihavand, and Vis' father is killed on the battlefield. Meanwhile, Ramin catches a glimpse of Vis, his childhood friend, and instantly falls in love with her. He tries to persuade his older brother, the king, to give up the idea of marrying Vis, but Mubad's love grows even stronger and he is determined to have her as his wife. Mubad finally succeeds in persuading Shahru to let him marry her daughter by giving her precious gifts, reminding her of their oath, and asking her not to turn her back on the Al-mighty. In fear of God, Shahru opens the gate of the fortress and lets Mubad take Vis away with him.

While celebrations are under way in the city of Merv, Ramin is sick with love for Vis. She, for her part, is determined to use her father's death as an excuse not to allow Mubad to get close to her. At this point, an unexpected character arrives on the scene to control their destiny: the nurse who had

Pottery plaque with a scene of performing acrobats, probably Sasanian.

Silver plate showing a banquet scene. The reclining king wears a crown and diadem and rests on a bench throne (takht). The musician playing a harp is also singing. Late Sasanian, probably 8th century AD.

brought up Vis and Ramin hurries to Merv to be near Vis. Using mysterious powers, she arranges a meeting between her two former charges, which leads to an unfulfilled but passionate love affair. At the same time Mubad, whom Vis has kept distant, pines for his young and beautiful wife. She and Ramin, torn between their love for each other and their feelings of guilt towards Mubad, seem like helpless figures manipulated by destiny. Through the devious plots of the nurse, the two young people finally consummate their love during Mubad's absence from Merv.

Unaware of the affair between his wife and his younger brother, Mubad invites them both to join him in the western highlands and suggests that Vis should visit her family. Mubad then overhears a conversation between the nurse and Vis, revealing her liaison with Ramin. Mad with rage, he threatens to expose Vis and kill Ramin, but Vis manages to turn his rage away, declaring that he means more to her than anyone else. Viru, Vis' brother and first husband, cannot understand her passion for Ramin. He reminds her of her noble lineage and urges her not to shame her ancestors by her infatuation. Vis and Ramin finally flee to Ray, keeping their whereabouts a secret, but when Ramin writes a letter to his mother she betrays him to Mubad. On their return to Merv, the lovers continue their secret meetings, using every opportunity to be together behind the old king's back. He is haunted by the thought of his wife's infidelity and his brother's deception, and he locks her away in an isolated fortress during his absences from court.

By now Vis' and Ramin's liaison is well known in Merv and, during a court banquet, Ramin (himself an accomplished minstrel and harp player) sings of their love. Mubad, infuriated by this openness, threatens to cut Ramin's throat. When Ramin defends himself, the king comes to his senses and stays his hand. Torn between his love for Vis and his loyalty to Mubad, Ramin listens to the advice of a wise man, who tells him that he has come under the spell of a demon and that, if he goes out into the world, he will find many women more truthful and virtuous than Vis. Ramin decides to leave Merv and start a new life, moving westwards after being granted the kingdoms of Ray and Gurgan.

In the west Ramin meets and falls in love with Gul, a Parthian princess, and marries her, finally forgetting his old love. His days of pleasure and love with Gul come to an end, however, when one day he compares her with Vis and suggests that she is like an apple cut in half. Gul, upset to be compared with Ramin's lover, considers this a betrayal. Reminded once again of Vis, Ramin writes her a letter and a long correspondence begins between the two former lovers.

Ramin returns to Merv, where he and Vis are reunited. They escape together, taking with them the king's treasures. Once again, their journey takes them to the west and, after travelling through Qazvin, they settle in Daylaman. When Mubad discovers Vis' and Ramin's flight, he follows them with his army, only to meet a cruel death. Attacked by a wild boar during a night's rest, Mubad chases it on his grey horse and shoots an arrow at the beast, but misses. The boar then throws itself at the king and his horse, dragging them to the ground and tearing the king's body open from chest to navel. With the death of Mubad, Ramin is crowned king of kings. He and Vis happily return to Merv, and they have two sons. When Vis eventually dies, Ramin places her body in an underground tomb and soon joins her there, first handing over the throne and crown to their son Khurshid.

Khusrow and Shirin

The story of Khusrow and Shirin is based on the life of the Sasanian king Khusrow II (Khusrow Parviz). Like the story of Vis and Ramin, the love of Khusrow and Shirin, a Christian princess, has been popular with several poets of later periods. In Firdowsi's *Shahnameh*, however, the love story is a subordinate theme in the life of Khusrow II. By contrast, Nizami makes his late twelfth-century epic revolve around the fortunes and tragedy of the young woman. Nizami wrote his romantic poem one hundred years after the completion of the *Shahnameh*, and his attitude to Firdowsi's work on Khusrow and Shirin is similar to his attitude to the *Iskandarnameh* (*Book of Alexander*). He mentions Firdowsi but regards his account of the two lovers as dry, saying that he will add to the story of their love. And so he does. Nizami's poem is built around the love of Khusrow for Shirin and his struggle to gain her, and Shirin's conflict between her love for Khusrow and her justified fear of being abandoned once he has conquered her. It is interesting that Shirin's mother warns her to remember Vis and not to bring the same degradation and shame upon herself. Other details in Nizami's story, such as Khusrow's passion for another woman followed by his regret and return to Shirin, as well as the long dialogues between the two lovers, are reminiscent of Gurgani's Vis and Ramin, indicating that the poet knew the earlier popular romance but did not regard its story line as morally proper.

Khusrow Parviz, born as son and heir to Hurmuzd IV (AD 579–90), showed remarkable qualities in his early childhood. Not only was his physical beauty striking, but his knowledge and wisdom, courage and power were also unique. He was so skilful with a bow and arrow that he could untie knots and loosen the rings of chain-mail with them. He could bring down lions and make columns fall with his sword. At the age of fourteen he is given into the care of a wise and learned teacher, Buzurg Umid (Buzurg Mihr). Once in a dream his grandfather Anushirvan (Khusrow I Anushirvan) appears to Khusrow and tells the young man that soon he will meet the love of his life; that he will find a new horse called Shabdiz with which not even a storm could keep pace; that he will possess a royal throne; and that he will have a minstrel called Barbad whose art could make even poison taste delicious.

One day Khusrow hears, through his friend Shapur (an accomplished artist), about Mahin Banu and her kingdom near the Caspian Sea. She has a daughter called Shirin (sweet in Persian), whose beauty is like 'a fairy child, a full moonlight'. Her teeth are like pearls, her mouth like ruby. Just hearing about the beauty of the princess makes Khusrow fall in love with her. Shapur plays match-maker by approaching Shirin when he is in Armenia, showing her a picture of Khusrow. She immediately falls in love with him. Shapur gives her a ring of Khusrow's and tells her to ride to Ctesiphon to join him. The following morning Shirin pretends that she is going hunting and asks her mother for permission to ride Shabdiz, a horse which gallops as fast as the wind. She races off, leaving her followers behind, and rides in the direction of Ctesiphon to find Khusrow. Exhausted at one point in her journey, she halts at a lake, 'the source of life', to bathe. So touching is the image of the beautiful Shirin that the 'sky's eyes filled with tears'.

Meanwhile Khusrow has been in trouble at the royal court in Ctesiphon. A rival king, Bahram Chubin (Bahram VI), has issued coins in the name of Khusrow and circulated them within the kingdom. On this evidence, Hurmuzd believes that his own son is attempting to seize power from him. The wise Buzurg Umid advises Khusrow to leave Ctesiphon for a while, but before he does, he tells his harem at the palace to look out for Shirin and to offer her hospitality and friendship if she arrives. He then rides off in great haste to escape the wrath of his angry father.

As it happens, Khusrow's horses stop to rest at the same place where Shirin is bathing. Khusrow catches a glimpse of her and her fabulous horse from behind the bushes, but is unaware of her identity. When she finally notices him, she wonders who he might be, even asking herself whether it might be Khusrow, as only he is able to stir up such emotions in her. However, she discards this possibility because the man is not wearing royal garb, and she cannot know he is in disguise. Shirin then rides off on Shabdiz and, when Khusrow looks for her again, he cannot find her. He weeps, wishing that he had approached her. Sorrowfully he continues his journey to Armenia while Shirin rides to Ctesiphon. Arriving at the court, she presents herself to the women of the royal harem. Although they immediately resent her charm and beauty, they are none the less obliged to welcome her. Shirin soon discovers Khusrow's flight and becomes convinced that the man she saw while bathing was none other than him. Khusrow meanwhile has reached Armenia, where he is warmly welcomed by Mahin Banu. He stays there for a time, drinking wine and lamenting Shirin's absence.

During Khusrow's stay in Armenia, an envoy is sent to him by a group of noblemen who want him to ascend the throne of Iran, as Khusrow's father Hurmuzd has now died and the country needs its legitimate ruler. Khusrow hurries back to Ctesiphon and is surprised to find Shirin gone. He is told by the women of his harem that she has moved to a palace in the mountains, but in fact she has returned to Armenia with Shapur in the hope of joining Khusrow. On arrival Shirin is greeted only by a joyful mother, pleased to see her daughter back, instead of a loving Khusrow.

Now, however, Khusrow's rightful crown is under threat from his old opponent, Bahram Chubin. The rival king has spread rumours that Khusrow is mad with blind love for Shirin, and he has gained enough support to force Khusrow to flee from Ctesiphon via Azerbaijan to Armenia. Here the two lovers finally meet while out hunting, and they at last declare their love for each other. At this point Mahin Banu advises Shirin not to be carried away by her emotions, cautioning her to insist on becoming Khusrow's legal wife so as not to go down the same path as Vis and her lover Ramin. Shirin finally promises to follow her mother's advice, and tactfully turns aside all Khusrow's passionate advances.

Furious at her seeming rejection, Khusrow leaves Shirin, takes Shabdiz and rides off towards Constantinople (Istanbul). There he marries Maryam, the daughter of the Byzantine emperor, and with the help of the Byzantine army he moves against his opponent Bahram. In a bloody battle Khusrow defeats his rival, who abandons his claim to the throne and escapes to China.

Having won his throne, Khusrow begins once again to think about Shirin. He tries to forget his pain over lost love through the songs of his famous minstrel, Barbad, during festivities at court. Meanwhile, after reminding Shirin of her promise to control her passion for Khusrow, Mahin Banu dies and leaves the crown of Armenia to her daughter.

It is at this point in the story that Farhad appears – a great stonemason renowned for his ability to perform the impossible. When introduced to Shirin, he falls hopelessly in love with her. News of his ardent love soon reaches the ears of Khusrow, who tries to get rid of him, first by offering him gold and then by giving him a never-ending task that will keep him away from the court and from Shirin. After an impassioned dialogue between the two contenders for Shirin's love, Khusrow sets him building a passable route through the mountain of Bisitun in order to facilitate the movement of trading caravans. Farhad agrees on condition that, once the work is completed, Khusrow will give up his claim to Shirin. While Farhad is at work Shirin visits him, bringing him a jug of milk to renew his strength. On the way back, her horse gives way under the heavy weight of her jewellery. But just as the horse and its beautiful rider are about to collapse, Farhad rushes up and lifts both of them on to his shoulders, carrying the mounted Shirin majestically to her palace. When Khusrow hears about this incident and also gets news of Farhad's imminent success in tunnelling through the rock of Bisitun, he realises that he will lose Shirin. He therefore sends a messenger to Farhad, informing him that Shirin has died. Not wishing to live without her, Farhad throws himself off the mountain and dies instantly. This is followed soon after by the death of Khusrow's wife, Maryam.

Khusrow travels to Isfahan, where he falls in love with Shakar (meaning sugar), a girl renowned for her beauty and innocence, and he marries her. But once he has gained sugar (Shakar), which he regards as the body, he yearns for

Illustration from a late 15th-century Khamseh of Nizami, showing Farhad and Shirin meeting at Mount Bisitun. Here, she has given him a jug of milk.

Illustration from a 16th-century Khamseh of Nizami. Shiruy (the historical Kavad II) is about to murder his father Khusrow, who lies beside Shirin.

sweetness (Shirin), which he thinks of as the soul. After an exchange of letters, Khusrow and Shirin listen to a beautiful duet sung by the two court singers, Nakisa and Barbad. Nakisa repeats the words of Shirin and Barbad expresses the feelings of Khusrow. This reconciles the two lovers, and Khusrow promises to marry Shirin. Their love is sealed with a royal wedding, but soon darkness clouds their joy. Shiruy, Khusrow's son by Maryam, falls in love with Shirin when he sees her at his father's wedding. Wanting to marry her himself, Shiruy callously murders Khusrow as he sleeps beside Shirin. But on the day of Khusrow's funeral, Shirin locks herself inside her husband's tomb and kills herself. When her body is discovered, she is ceremoniously laid to rest with Khusrow.

Fairy tales and passion plays

Fairy tales involve supernatural beings, the fairies, whose name comes from the Persian word *pari*. Their origin goes back to the witch-like *pairaka* of the *Avesta*, those wicked forces that were most active during the night. Having the power to change their appearance and turn themselves into beauties, they were able to impose their will on men and use them to do evil. *Pari*s, with their great beauty and supernatural powers, play an important role in Persian folklore.

The Thousand and One Nights

One of the most famous collections of ancient tales is *Alf Layla wa Layla*, the Arabic name of *One Thousand Nights and One Night*, commonly known in English as *The Arabian Nights*. These came to Europe during the Middle Ages but were not written down in a European language until the beginning of the eighteenth century, when Antoine Galland translated them into French. Translations into English by Edward Lane and Sir Richard Burton followed in the nineteenth century.

Best known for stories such as *Ali Baba and the Forty Thieves*, *The Adventures of Sinbad* and *Aladdin and the Magic Lamp*, this collection is not a homogenous group but a miscellany with origins in different cultures, some of them very ancient. One of the many lands that has contributed stories to this collection is ancient Persia, and other tales can be traced to India, Greece, Egypt, Arabia, ancient Mesopotamia and Turkey, making the original title of *One Thousand Nights and One Night* more appropriate than simply *The Arabian Nights*.

Sources dating to the tenth century AD which mention this collection allude to the existence of a Persian book called *Hazar afsaneh* (*The Book of a Thousand Tales*), the story of a king, his vizier, and the vizier's daughters Shahrazad and Dinazad. These same characters appear in the story that frames *One Thousand Nights and One Night*, though here the main plot is built around two brothers, the Sasanian kings Shahzaman and Shahriyar, one of whom rules in Samarkand and the other in India and China. Both find out that their wives have been unfaithful, and all the women and slaves involved in their affairs are beheaded. Shahriyar then decides to take a new young bride every night and to have her beheaded in the morning. However, after three years have passed, it is becoming impossible for the king's vizier to find any more young girls for his master. At this point the vizier's own daughter Shahrazad persuades her father to let her go to the king, taking her younger sister Dinazad with her. As part of her plan she instructs Dinazad to ask her for a story every night, and she is then able to make them last for one thousand and one nights by always breaking off at a crucial point, thereby arousing the king's interest in hearing the rest of the story the following night.

During this period Shahrazad gives birth to three male children by the king, and when her storytelling finally ends he offers to grant her a wish. She asks the king to spare her life for the sake of their young children, which he willingly agrees to do, and they live happily ever after.

The names of Shahriyar (holder of a kingdom; prince or king), Shahrazad (Chihrazad, meaning of noble lineage) and Dinazad (exalting the goddess Den) are Iranian, and the name of Shahriyar's brother Shahzaman consists of the Persian *shah* (king) and Arabic *zaman* (time). It is believed that the frame story of *One Thousand Nights and One Night* is of both Persian and Indian origin.

Among the tales in the collection which are believed to be of Persian origin are love stories and fairy tales, which often include *div* and *pari* as well as magical animals and birds. Other stories, such as *The Ebony Horse*, although beginning with a description which fits perfectly into the Persian tradition, are nevertheless believed to be of Indian origin. *The Ebony Horse*, also known as *The Magic Horse*, is about a magical horse presented as a gift to the king of Persia.

There was in ancient times, in the country of the Persians, a mighty King, of great dignity, who had three daughters, like shining full moons and flowery gardens; and he had a male child, like the moon. He observed two annual festivals, that of the New Year's day, and that of the Autumnal Equinox; and it was his custom, on these occasions, to open his palaces, and give his gifts . . . the people of his dominions also used to go in to him and salute him, and congratulate him on the festival, offering him presents and servants . . .

The king's young heir sits on the ebony horse to test the magic and flies into the sky. He visits another country (Yemen), falls in love with a princess, and after a series of adventures returns to his father's court and marries the princess.

The story of Hasan of el-Basra

This story concerns a wealthy merchant of the city of Basra who has two sons. After his death, the brothers divide their father's wealth between them. One opens a copperware shop and the other works as a goldsmith.

Now while the goldsmith was sitting in his shop, one day, lo, a Persian walked along the market-street among the people until he came to the shop of the young goldsmith . . . And the name of the young goldsmith was Hasan . . .

The Persian finds Hasan looking at a mysterious old book. He tells the young goldsmith that he alone in the world knows an art that can bring untold wealth, and he says that he is willing to teach Hasan this art because he has no son of his own. 'To-morrow I will come to thee, and will make for thee, of copper, pure gold in thy presence.'

When Hasan goes home and tells his mother about his visitor she warns him not to trust the Persian, but he takes no notice of her. The next day the Persian magically produces a lump of precious gold from base copper, and Hasan sells it in the market for fifteen thousand pieces of silver. The following day Hasan persuades the Persian to come home with him and teach him the art of alchemy. After some successful experiments, the alchemist tells Hasan that he wants him to marry his daughter and then gives him what looks like a sweet-meat. This causes Hasan to fall unconscious, upon which the alchemist gleefully bundles him and all his family treasures into two trunks and goes out to call a porter. They then sail away on a ship.

The Persian is, in fact, Bahram, the *magian* (Zoroastrian priest) who slaughters a Muslim once a year. During the sea voyage, the *magian* takes Hasan out of the trunk, 'poured some vinegar into his nostrils, and blew a powder into his nose ...' The duped goldsmith regains consciousness and, realising what has happened to him, immediately thinks of his mother's warn-ing. The *magian* tries to convert Hasan to Zoroastrianism, but as a devout Muslim he resists, despite being beaten and suffering greatly. When the sea suddenly becomes rough and the winds howl, the crew know it is the work of God: the *magian* stops torturing Hasan and the stormy weather abates at once. He then regrets what he has done and 'swore to the fire and the light' that he will no longer torture Hasan.

The two are thus reconciled and their voyage continues for three months in the direction of 'the Mountain of the Clouds, on which is the elixir with which we practise alchemy'. Once on land, they mount camels and ride to the top of a high mountain where, according to the *magian*, a special herb necessary to perform alchemy is to be found. There once again he plays a trick on Hasan, abandoning him on the top of the mountain. Hasan plunges into the sea on the other side of the mountain, hoping that God will either put an end to his misfortune or help him. By divine intervention, the waves carry him ashore, and from there he sees a palace, already described to him by the *magian* as the residence of demons and evil creatures. But Hasan does not believe his words and, indeed, when he enters the palace he finds two beautiful young women playing chess. They rejoice greatly to see him alive after they hear his story about the wicked *magian*, the enchanter.

The two princesses and their five sisters have been placed in this isolated palace by their father, a king, and Hasan stays with them for a year. Then one day, while out fishing, he sees the *magian* approaching with a new victim. He and the princesses manage to kill the *magian* and rescue the captive young man.

Later the king comes to take his daughters to a marriage celebration, which will keep them away for two months. They tell Hasan, who has been hidden from the king, to remain in the palace during their absence. They also entrust him with the key to a locked room but warn him never to open it. However, boredom and curiosity overcome him, and one day he opens the forbidden door. After climbing some stairs that lead to a roof, he sees a pool and garden filled with amazing birds and other creatures. There is also a group of beautiful fairy-like girls bathing in the pool and, as he watches them, he loses his senses in complete enchantment.

When the sisters return, one of them finds Hasan hiding in his room, in a state of sorrow and shock, having fallen in love with one of the bewitching bathers. He is told that his beloved is the daughter of a powerful king, and that she comes to the pool once a month at new moon. Hasan waits for the next new moon, goes to the pool and sees the princess arrive with her sisters, disguised in a bird's costume. On leaving the pool, the princess cannot find her costume, which Hasan has hidden, and her weeping sisters must leave her behind. Hasan then takes the princess to his room by force and locks her in, and eventually she agrees to marry him.

One night Hasan has a dream in which he sees his mother weeping, and he decides to return to her with his wife, promising the seven princesses of the palace that he will visit them regularly. After a long journey, they reach his home. His poor mother, who has given up hope of ever seeing her son again, is overjoyed and welcomes his new wife and their two small children. Hasan then decides to move to Baghdad and they set up home there.

When the time comes for him to visit the seven princesses, he entrusts his wife and children to his mother's care, warning her that under no circumstances should she let his young wife leave the house or see the bird's costume which he has hidden in a trunk. Hasan's wife overhears their conversation and, once her husband has left, she begs her mother-in-law to allow her to go to the baths. The old woman finally gives in. While bathing, the beautiful wife is seen by a slave of one of the caliph's wives, who rushes to her mistress to tell her of the fairy-like beauty of Hasan's wife. The slave warns that, if the caliph sees her, he will not be able to suppress his desire to have her. A slave is then sent to Hasan's house to bring his mother and wife to the caliph's palace. Hasan's wife tells the caliph's wife about her extraordinary dress of feathers and how it is being hidden from her. Hasan's mother at first denies it, but then is forced to hand over the dress. Hasan's wife puts it on, enfolds the two children inside it, and fastens it. She then turns into a bird and flies into the air. Hasan's mother, weeping and wailing in desperation, asks what she should tell her son. His wife shouts down to her from above that if he wants her, he will have to follow her to the islands of Wak-Wak. She then disappears in the distance.

When Hasan returns home and finds his wife and children gone, he is heartbroken, but then resolves to return to the palace of the seven sisters and ask for their help. They tell him that their uncle is the only one who can help him, which he does through magic and with the assistance of supernatural beings, and Hasan eventually reaches the islands of Wak-Wak. There he meets an old woman who feels sorry for him after hearing his story, and she leads him to the queen of one of the islands. Hasan is amazed at the queen's resemblance to his missing wife, who is in fact her sister. Angry with her sister for marrying Hasan without asking permission from their father, she has in fact decided to punish her and the two children by putting them all to death. Even this is overcome, however, and again through the intervention of the Almighty and various

Illustration from an 18th-century Kashmiri abridged prose Shahnameh showing the execution of Siyavush. His head is cut off and later a tree springs from his spilled blood.

supernatural forces Hasan manages to escape with his wife (who, incidentally, is overjoyed to see him), their children and the sympathetic old woman. They return to the palace of the seven sisters and from there go back to Baghdad, where they are reunited with Hasan's mother.

The passion plays

The passion plays are written around the martyrdom of holy figures. The best-known ancient saga about the martyrdom of an Iranian prince is that of Siyavush, son of Kay Kavus, who is brutally murdered by Afrasiyab, the king of Turan (described in great detail by Firdowsi in the *Shahnameh*). His death is seen as especially tragic because Siyavush has only gone to live at Afrasiyab's court in order to escape his stepmother's jealousy and his father's suspicion, and because his murder leaves his wife Farangis, daughter of Afrasiyab, five months pregnant (with Kay Khusrow, the future king of Iran). Siyavush foresees his own tragic end in a dream and tells Farangis that he will be beheaded; that there will be no coffin, no grave and no shroud for him; that no one will mourn him.

On hearing the news of Siyavush's death, his father, the king of Iran, weeps and tears his clothes, and heroes such as Tus, Gudarz, Giv, Gurgin and others don black garments. Rustam faints with sorrow and officially mourns for a week. He then swears to avenge Siyavush's murder by destroying Afrasiyab and turning Turan into a river of blood.

The mourning of Siyavush (*sug-i Siyavush*) as described by Firdowsi is thus the mourning of the Iranian people for their beloved young prince, victim of a conspiracy. His loss is turned into an emotional story which has acquired a prominent place in the *Shahnameh*.

The myth of Siyavush is of ancient Iranian origin and his name (Siya-varshan) is frequently mentioned in the *Avesta*. The mourning of Siyavush was already a well-known custom in Central Asia in the tenth century AD, celebrated in song. It is further reported that people in Sogdia mourned Siyavush once a year by striking their faces and offering food and drink to the dead.

The perpetuation in Islamic times of this emotional mourning tradition surrounding the slaying of a martyr is best seen in the passion plays (*ta'ziyeh*) of the Shiite Muslims, in which the murder and martyrdom of Imam Husayn and his family, grandson of the prophet Muhammad, are mourned in the Muslim month of Muharram (first month of the lunar calendar). The historical facts behind this tragedy begin with the death of the prophet Muhammad in AD 632 and the subsequent split in the Muslim community between those who favoured succession by election (the Sunnis) and succession through inheritance from the prophet (the Shiites). Ali, the son-in-law of the prophet and the fourth caliph to succeed him, was seen by the Shiites as the legitimate successor. After both he and his eldest son Imam Hasan were assassinated, the Sunni governor Yezid became the caliph and moved his capital to Damascus. Husayn, Ali's younger son, the legitimate successor in the eyes of the Shiites, was encouraged by the people of Kufa to revolt against the caliphate and to fight for the right of rule by the house of Ali. On his way to Kufa, Husayn and his followers met Yezid and

Illustration from an 18th-century Kashmiri abridged prose Shahnameh. The young prince Kay Khusrow and his mother Farangis (disguised as a man, but without a beard) follow Giv across the River Jayhun (Oxus, Amu Darya) to go from Turan to Iran.

151

his vast army on the plains of Kerbela, south-west of Baghdad. Husayn, his family and his followers survived ten days in the desert without water but were finally brutally murdered by Yezid and his army. The desert ordeal began on the first day of Muharram and the bloody murder took place on the tenth (the *Ashura*).

Mourning processions already existed in the tenth century AD and were common in the city of Baghdad at the time. Under the rule of the Safavids in Iran in the sixteenth century and with the establishment of Shiite Islam as the official state religion, the mourning ceremonies of Muharram officially incorporated the passion plays, the *ta'ziyeh*. The tradition reached its peak at the end of the nineteenth and beginning of the twentieth century, although it is still intact today.

Professional actors, all men, played throughout the year and in particular during Muharram, performing either in the mosque, the *bazar* (covered market) or in a special building, the *takiyeh*. The most famous of these, the *Takiyeh Dowlat*, built in Tehran under the royal patronage of the Qajar king Nasiruddin Shah in 1869, was modelled on the Albert Hall in London. A large audience of several thousand would gather at the *takiyeh*, following the passion plays about Imam Husayn and his family with great excitement. Often, too, there would be stories of the life and deeds of other Shiite martyrs. Once again, the continuation of an ancient tradition, the mourning ritual, has its roots in the traditions of the distant past. The *sug-i Siyavush* was replaced by the mourning of Imam Husayn and other Shiite martyrs.

Edward Browne, one of the great scholars of Iranian studies, described the passion plays as 'heart-moving'. He quotes the *ta'ziyeh* of Bibi Shahrbanu, legendary daughter of the last Sasanian king, Yazdigird III (633–51), who became the wife of the martyred Imam Husayn. Because of the myth of her Iranian ancestry, she is particularly popular among Persians:

Born of the race of Yazdigird the King
From Nushirwan my origin I trace.
What time kind Fortune naught but joy did bring
In Ray's proud city was my home and place.
There in my father's palace once at night
In sleep to me came Fatima 'the Bright';
'O Shahr-banu' – thus the vision cried –
'I give thee to Husayn to be his bride!'
Said I, 'Behold Mada'in is my home,
And how shall I to far Madina roam?
Impossible!' But Fatima cried, 'Nay,
Husayn shall hither come in war's array
And bear thee hence, a prisoner of war,
From this Mada'in to Madina far,
Where, joined in wedlock with Husayn, my boy,
Thou shalt bear children who will be my joy.
For nine Imams to thee shall owe their birth,
The like of whom hath not been seen on earth!'

Conclusion

The myths and legends of Iran, the Persian myths, reflect the survival of an ancient tradition in the culture as well as the language of a large geographical area extending beyond the political boundaries of modern Iran. Neither nomadic movements, invasions nor internal political changes and upheavals have succeeded in destroying the ancient sagas; on the contrary, these legends have survived for millennia. Their preservation has kept alive the traditions and social concepts of a distant past and at the same time helped the Persian language and literature to survive and develop.

Persian myths were primarily passed on through oral transmission and it was only in later periods, mainly under the Parthians and Sasanians, that many of the stories were written down. These myths, some of pagan and others of Zoroastrian origin, survived the Arab conquest in the seventh century and the adoption of the new faith of Islam. The works of such great poets as Daqiqi and Firdowsi enabled people to read or listen to these stories in their own language and not merely through Arabic translations. There is an abundance of such books (*nameh*s) in Persian literature, but Firdowsi's *Shahnameh* occupies a special and unique position because of the beauty and clarity of its language. The heroes of the *Shahnameh*, Rustam, Sohrab and Isfandiyar, are part of the life of every Iranian, and to this day it is common practice to read and recite their stories.

Shahnameh khani, reading the *Book of Kings*, is a special art performed by professional storytellers (*naqqal*) in towns and villages. The *naqqal* puts on a one-man act, reciting tragic and heroic stories. Rustam, the hero of all heroes, is a particular favourite, and his adventures and combats are performed for appreciative audiences of all ages. Through gesticulation and a combination of poetry recitation and singing, the *naqqal* carries his listeners with him from battle-field to royal court, making them laugh with his mimicry and reducing them to tears with moving descriptions of poignant and brutal murders. These stories are often interrupted at crucial points and continued the following day, thus stretching one story over several days.

Persian myths have not only played an important role in Persian literature, but mythological scenes depicting heroes and anti-heroes have also entered the world of visual art. Since at least the fourteenth century, illustrated manuscripts of the *Shahnameh* have included such myths and legends. The snake-shouldered Zahhak, Fariydun and his bull-headed mace, the invincible Isfandiyar, the lion-like Rustam, the guardian bird Simurgh and the *div* have all become familiar

'Coffee house' painting of Rustam holding his dying son Sohrab in his arms. The amulet that once belonged to Rustam is visible under Sohrab's torn sleeve. The armies of Iran and Turan face each other in the background, as do the horses of the heroes. Beside Rakhsh lies Rustam's bull-headed mace. This large oil painting dates from the middle of this century.

figures in Persian paintings. Stories from the Rustam saga were popular for the decoration of tiles. By the end of the nineteenth and the beginning of the twentieth century a genre of paintings by folk artists, the so-called *qahveh khaneh* (coffee house) paintings, were also reproducing scenes from the *Shah-nameh*. In all these ways, Persian myths continue to prove their relevance to the beliefs, social attitudes and tastes of the Iranian people today.

Suggestions for further reading

Perhaps one of the most fascinating aspects of Persian myths is the fact that they have survived into modern Persian literature and language. There is therefore a very wide range of sources, covering several millennia, and the myths are closely related to the history and archaeology of ancient Iran.

The most valuable and informative source for the religion of the ancient Iranians is Mary Boyce, *A History of Zoroastrianism* in three volumes (Leiden, Köln, 1975, 1982, 1991). English translations of Zoroastrian sacred texts appear in the series *Sacred Books of the East*, edited by Max Müller, and they include J. Darmesteter, *The Zend-Avesta* in three volumes (Delhi, 1974, 1975) and E. W. West, *The Pahlavi Texts* (Delhi, 1970). *Persian Mythology* by John R. Hinnells (New York, 1985) examines in detail Zoroastrian and pre-Zoroastrian myths and their significance in modern Zoroastrianism. Ehsan Yarshater, in an article on 'Iranian Historical Tradition' in the *Cambridge History of Iran*, III, 1 (Cambridge, 1983), pp. 343ff, analyses the beliefs of the ancient Iranians and provides a detailed bibliography of ancient and modern sources. This is supplemented by entries in the invaluable *Encyclopedia Iranica* (also edited by E. Yarshater), published in New York since 1985. For an overview of different aspects of Zoroastrianism, see Pheroza J. Godrej and Firoza Puntakey Mistree, *A Zoroastrian Tapestry: Art, Religion and Culture* (Bombay, 2002).

English translations of the *Shahnameh* include the version in verse by Arthur George and Edmund Warner, *The Shahnama of Firdausi* in ten volumes (London, 1905–25). For prose translations see Reuben Levy, *The Epic of the Kings* (London, Boston, 1977) and Jerome F. Clinton, *The Tragedy of Sohrab and Rostam* (Seattle, London, 1987). Important articles on the *Shahnameh* and related topics have been published in the periodical *Iranshenasi* in Persian, but with an English resumé. Also informative are articles in the *Encyclopaedia of Islam* (Leiden, new edition 1960–), and a recent bibliography of Firdowsi has been prepared by A. Shapur Shahbazi, *Firdowsi: A Critical Bibliography* (Costa Mesa, California, 1991).

The original Persian sources themselves exist in a large number of editions which cannot be listed here. It is worth noting, however, that a recent edition of *The Shahnameh* by Djalal Khaleghi Motlagh was published in 1988 and 1990 in New York. The edition used in the present volume was published in Tehran in 1975/6. Other Persian works that have been consulted include Nizami's *Khusrow o Shirin* and *Iskandarnameh in Kulliyat-e Khamseh-ye Hakim Nizami Ganjavi* (Tehran, 1991/2) and Gurgani, *Vis o Ramin* (Tehran, 1971). Publications by Iranian scholars on Persian mythology in Persian include S. Safa, *Hamaseh sara-yi dar Iran* (Tehran, 1984/5) and M. Bahar, *Asatir-e Iran* (Tehran, 1973/4). For the importance and position of storytellers and particularly minstrels in the Iranian tradition, see Mary Boyce, 'The Parthian gosan and Iranian minstrel tradition', in *Journal of the Royal Asiatic Society* (1957), pp. 10ff. E. W. Lane gives an English translation of *1001 Nights* in *The Arabian Nights' Entertainments* (London, 1898), and a detailed examination of the stories appears in Mia Gerhardt, *The Art of Story Telling* (Leiden, 1963). The tradition and development of the *ta'ziyeh*, the passion plays, are dealt with in Peter J. Chelkowski (ed.), *Ta'ziyeh: Ritual and Drama in Iran* (New York, 1979). A useful and informative overview of Persian literature can be found in Edward G. Browne, *A Literary History of Persia* (London, 1909).

For the history and archaeology of Iran in the pre-Islamic period, see Richard N. Frye, *History of Ancient Iran* (Munich, 1984), Georgina Herrmann, *The Iranian Revival* (Oxford, 1977), John Curtis, *Ancient Persia* (2nd edn, London, 2000) and Josef Wiesehöfer, *Ancient Persia* (London, 2001).

CHINESE

Myths

ANNE BIRRELL

Contents

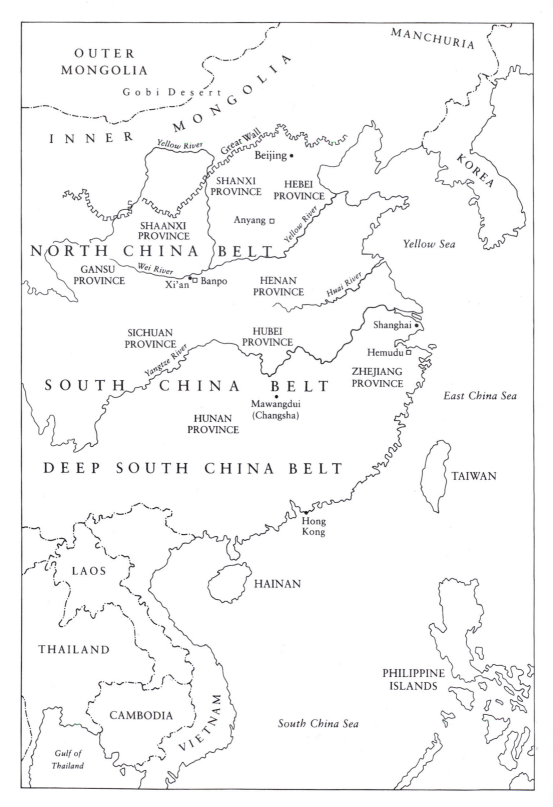

OUTER MONGOLIA

Gobi Desert

MANCHURIA

INNER MONGOLIA

Yellow River

Great Wall

Beijing •

SHANXI PROVINCE

HEBEI PROVINCE

Yellow River

KOREA

SHAANXI PROVINCE

NORTH CHINA BELT

Anyang □

Yellow Sea

GANSU PROVINCE

Wei River

Xi'an •□ Banpo

HENAN PROVINCE

Huai River

SICHUAN PROVINCE

HUBEI PROVINCE

Shanghai •

Hemudu □

SOUTH CHINA BELT

Yangtze River

ZHEJIANG PROVINCE

East China Sea

Mawangdui (Changsha) •

HUNAN PROVINCE

DEEP SOUTH CHINA BELT

TAIWAN

Hong Kong

LAOS

HAINAN

THAILAND

PHILIPPINE ISLANDS

VIETNAM

CAMBODIA

South China Sea

Gulf of Thailand

Introduction

The mythology of Chinese culture and civilization is contained in a variety of sacred narratives which tell how the world and human society were created in their present form. They are sacred narratives because they relate acts of the deities in addition to other episodes, and they embody the most deeply felt spiritual values of a nation. A generally accepted Western definition of myth as 'sacred narrative' reflects the meaning of the Chinese term for myth, *shen-hua*: *shen* means 'divine, deity, holy'; *hua* means 'speech, tale, oral narrative'. The concerns of myth also extend beyond the accounts of the deities, including stories about world catastrophes of flood, fire, drought, famine, of eating, exile and migration, besides leadership qualities, human government, the hero figure and the foundation of dynasties, peoples and clans.

The modern study of mythology combines the disciplines of anthropology, the classics, comparative religion, history, folklore, literature, art and psychology. This broader line of inquiry into the nature of myth contrasts with the study of myth in the nineteenth century, which centred more narrowly on questions of origins and the idea of myth as an explanation of primitive science and primitive society. Compared with the study of Western mythologies, especially those of Greece and Rome, the study of Chinese myth is still in its infancy. Initially, the study of Chinese myth was heavily influenced by the origins and explanations, or 'etiological', approach. But it is now opening up to more contemporary theories of comparative mythology and the worldwide study of mythology, so Chinese mythology is proving to be a valuable and exciting treasure trove of mythic themes, motifs and archetypes.

The subjects and concerns of Chinese mythology can be traced back to the cultural and environmental factors which shaped the earliest form of Chinese civilization in antiquity. The beginnings of this civilization are inextricably linked to its favourable environment. Three zones of ecogeographical systems developed in the land mass of China. There is the temperate North China belt with its fertile plains alluviated by the Yellow River. Its seed culture of millet and hemp, mulberry and fruit trees, and grasslands were conducive to the evolution of wild and domestic plants and animals, and to human habitation. But this region was also prone to harsh winters, severe droughts and catastrophic floods. The South China belt forms a second zone, with a stable, mild and humid climate, the region being alluviated by the Yangtze River. Its vegetative propagation culture benefits from an all-year growing season. It is an aquatic agricultural system that is favourable to rice, beans, lotus, bamboo, fish and turtles. The third zone is the Deep South China belt with rich coastal fishing grounds and a tropical ecosystem.

The different but equally favourable environments of north and south contributed to the dual origin of human culture in China, and led to the emergence of numerous communities of similar economic levels but with varying cultural systems. The earliest known sites of human habitation are the Neolithic settlements at Banpo in the Wei River valley in the north (near modern Xi'an, Shaanxi province) and Hemudu in the Yangtze River valley in the south-east (Zhejiang province). These centres of village farming are datable to around 5000 BC for Banpo and (by radiocarbon techniques) 3718 BC for Hemudu.

The environmental factors of climate, terrain, vegetation, animal life, mineral resources and topology contributed to the gradual evolution of diverse food-producing communities in the major river valleys of the Yellow (Huang) River, the Wei and Han Rivers in the north, the Huai River in the central region, and the Yangtze River in the south.

The development of Chinese civilization must also be viewed from the perspective of its ancient borders and its neighbouring countries in antiquity. China was to some extent protected by natural barriers. It was bounded to the north by the Gobi desert, to the west by the Kunlun and Himalayan mountains, to the east and south-east by the sea. This geographic cordon ensured that embryonic Chinese settlements were neither systematically eliminated nor repeatedly invaded by neighbouring peoples. On the other hand, the geographic disposition of its borders allowed for corridors and routes of communication which facilitated cultural diffusion. Modern research is still in the process of determining which cultural inventions are indigenous to China and which were the result of cultural diffusion. It is believed that millet, the staple crop of north China, arrived from fertile oases in Central Asia, and that rice originated in India and arrived in China by a land route of transfusion through south-east Asia. The cultural innovations of a writing system and metallurgy that were successfully exploited by the rulers of the earliest Chinese state may have been transmitted from non-Chinese peoples rather than independently invented by the ancient Chinese. Other cultural influences are discernible from Siberia in the north, Melanesia in the south-east, Tibet in the south-west, and most crucially from Central Asia in the west through the Tarim Basin, whose peoples formed points of contact with the Middle East and Near East.

The ambiguous relationship between the relative insularity of the Chinese land mass and the proximity of neighbouring ethnic peoples raises the question of the origins of the Chinese people. Considering the size and importance of the region, firm evidence is remarkably poor for their physical origin. The major discovery of skeletal remains in a cave at Zhoukoutian near Beijing, which has been radiocarbon-dated to 16,922 BC, were initially classified as Peking Man hominids but are now believed to be related to American Plains Indians rather than Asiatic or Mongoloid types. The earliest Mongoloid skeleton was found in south China, in Guangxi province, though its date and identification are indefinite. Identification is insecure for an incomplete skull from Sichuan province dated at 5535 BC. One authoritative view is that the origins of the Chinese derive from Mongoloids who represent a mixture of racial populations of great antiquity, which are as diverse as Polynesians and American Indians. But the evidence for the ancestry of the people inhabiting the land mass of China between 10,000 and 5000 BC awaits further archaeological research.

Coming to the Neolithic period, skeletal remains from village cemeteries

Shang dynasty bronze axe decorated with the gaping mouth of a monstrous demon.

of north China dating from around 5000 BC show Mongoloid features with no significant ethnic diversity. For the later period of antiquity, the Late Shang era *c.* 1200 BC, data from sacrificial pits show a great diversity of racial origin, including Melanesian, Eskimo and Caucasoid types. But the ethnic origins of people buried in sacrificial pits, who were presumably non-Chinese prisoners of war, may be separated from the ethnic identity of the emergent civilization in China during the late second to early first millennia BC. Current scholarly findings lead to some firm conclusions. First, the Neolithic northern population shows a considerable physical homogeneity. Second, the population of north China has remained surprisingly homogeneous since the Neolithic era (*c.* 5550–*c.* 2000 BC). Third, the data point to the lack of any significant migration to or foreign invasion of the region during and since around 5000 BC.

Of the three ecogeographical systems in the land mass of China, the North China belt proved to be the most favourable for the development of China's first state and for the beginnings of Chinese civilization. Early on, its culture expanded to take the form of numerous ethnic communities distributed along the main river valleys of the Yellow, Wei, Han, Huai and Yangtze rivers. Their traits were equally developed by the Neolithic era. One of these ethnic groups emerged by about 1700 BC as the dominant power in the Yellow River region of the Central Plains. It progressed to become the first Chinese dynasty, the Shang, with a major site of power in Anyang city (modern Henan province). Two separate Neolithic northern cultures have been

Bronze vessel, gui, *of the late 11th century* BC.

identified by their pottery styles: the Yangshao culture of painted pottery developed along the Central Plains region of the Yellow River, while the Longshan culture of unpainted black pottery was distributed over a large area to the south and east. The Shang state took its genesis from the Longshan culture of Henan province. It rose to prominence in an era of unprecedented cultural and technological innovation. The success of the Shang was due to its superior system of military organization, control of food production, urban settlements, institutions of kinship and the priesthood, methods of transport and communication, and its distinctively robust artistic expression. The Shang state had the power and authority to organize the construction of impressive buildings and to attract specialists such as record-keepers, soldiers, retainers and artisans to maintain the state apparatus and to conduct large-scale ritual ceremonies, including human sacrifice in the burial rite of the ruling elite.

Two factors played a crucial role in the rise of the Shang state and the beginnings of Chinese civilization. Technological expertise in bronze metallurgy meant supremacy in war and material culture. The invention of a usable writing system consisting of graphs or characters by around 1200 BC led to improved methods of social organization through the bureaucratic and administrative control of commerce, calendrical regulation of agriculture, foreign affairs, alliances and religious practices.

Central to the identity and function of the state was the Shang concept of a priestly king. The king's functions were to make divination to the royal

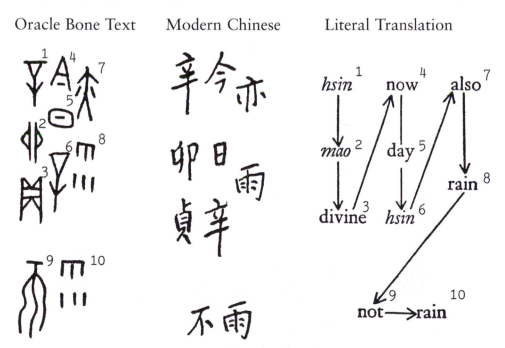

Translation of an oracle bone inscription: 'On this xin-mao *day we divine whether today,* xin (hsin), *it will rain or will not rain'.*

ancestors, to conduct rituals in honour of the ancestors, to make a sacred and symbolic progress through Shang territory, to hold audience, to bestow honours, to lead in war, and to lead the royal hunt. The king's was an itinerant power, as there was no fixed Shang capital. Instead there were several sites that served as ritual, technological and funerary centres. The king ruled through the intercession of the great god Di (pronounced Dee).

One of the north-west regions visited by Shang kings was the Wei River valley west of the Yellow River, which was inhabited by the Zhou people. The Zhou belonged to a different ethnic group from the Shang, but they absorbed Shang cultural influences. They were a warrior people and in time they conquered their Shang overlords and established the Zhou dynasty *c.* 1123 BC. Zhou society was organized into strictly defined social classes and functions, with a dual emphasis on warfare and agricultural productivity. The Zhou kings embarked on a military strategy to unite the diverse communities of the north and south, extending their power into what is now Manchuria and Inner Mongolia, and to the regions north and south of the Yangtze River. They reorganized these settlements into a loose federation of kingdoms (*guo*) to form the Zhou state. Military expansion was reinforced by a hierarchy of aristocratic warriors and a food-producing peasantry who supplied conscript service and forced labour.

The Zhou introduced moral rigour to their political and social system, echoes of which are to be found in China's first literary work, the Zhou *Classic of Poetry* of around 600 BC. The Zhou abandoned the great god Di of the Shang, and instead they worshipped the sky god Tian, with the Zhou king designated as Son of the Sky God (Tian Zi). Zhou divination methods included the use of milfoil or yarrow stalks, culminating in the Zhou text *Classic of Change* (*Yi jing*, pronounced E jing).

The Zhou political system flourished for several centuries but by the fourth century BC it had begun to disintegrate. As early as the year 771 BC Zhou power was effectively diminished, and the capital was moved east from Xi'an to Luoyang, but the king retained nominal control over the federation of kingdoms. These kingdoms gradually formed independent centres of political, military and economic power. They began to merge into larger polities that in the Warring States era of the fifth to third centuries BC contended for supremacy over a reunited state. The most militaristic of these kingdoms, the Qin of Shaanxi province in the north-west, successfully unified the residual Zhou kingdoms into the first Chinese empire. Though short-lived (only sixteen years of rule), it was followed by the four-centuries-long Han empire, which continued Qin socio-economic policies and consolidated imperial power.

Although the Shang had developed a writing system, its main function was divination by the priesthood and later by the king alone. Thousands of inscriptions found at Anyang city consist of oracle bones. The Shang script was not used to record their origins, myths or sacred history. The disintegration of the Zhou empire in the fourth century BC led to cultural fragmentation and the dispersal of older value-systems. Hence the perceived need for classical writers to record and preserve for posterity the remembered heritage

▤ Qian   Heaven   ▦ Kan   Water, Moon

▦ Kun   Earth   ▤ Li   Fire, Sun

▤ Zhen   Thunder   ▦ Gen   Mountain

▤ Sun   Wood, Rain   ▤ Dui   Marsh

The great god Fu Xi invents the hexagrams of the Yi jing.

of their sacred history. Since their different versions of the myths are relatively consistent, it must be assumed that these writers were drawing on a communal fund of oral traditions that date from before the first recorded myths in China's earliest text, the *Classic of Poetry*. Very few recognizably Shang or Zhou myths survive. Most recorded myth is undatable and takes its ancestry from the date of the written texts that were themselves based on an archaic oral tradition.

    The myths of ancient China that emerged from the oral tradition were preserved in classical texts during the Age of the Philosophers with the advent of literary texts in the sixth to third centuries BC. The decline of the Zhou coincided with the emergence of great thinkers and writers, such as Confucius and Mencius of the Confucian school and Zhuang Zhou of the Daoist school. Ancient China had no Hesiod, Homer or Ovid to retell the mythic oral tales at length. Instead, Chinese writers introduced fragmentary passages of mythic stories into their works of philosophy and history to illustrate their arguments and give authority to their statements. Chinese myth thus exists as an amorphous, diffuse variety of anonymous archaic expression that is preserved in the contexts of philosophical, literary and historical writings. They are brief, disjointed and enigmatic. These mythic fragments incorporated into miscellaneous classical texts vary in their narration, and authors often adapted myth according to their own point of view. The result is that Chinese myth survives in numerous versions, the content of which is broadly consistent, but which shows significant variation in the details. Whereas the reshaping of archaic oral Greek and Roman myths into an artistic form of narrative literature implies the loss of the authentic oral voice, the Chinese method of recording mythic fragments in a wealth of untidy, variable stories is a rare survival of primitive authenticity.

The themes of Chinese myths have significant parallels with those of other world mythologies. Where they diverge is in their central concern and cultural distinctiveness. Major mythic themes are narrated in several versions, such as the six story lines of the creation of the world and the four flood myth stories. The world picture of one Chinese creation myth shows similarities with ancient Egyptian cosmology. Other creation myths in the Chinese tradition contrast with the Biblical and other versions in their lack of a divine cause or a creator. One major creation myth, the myth of the cosmological human body, has features similar to ancient Iranian mythology. Chinese flood myths are unique for the absence of the motif of divine retribution and of divine intervention in halting the deluge. Instead, the central concern of the major Chinese flood myth focuses on the concept of human control of the catastrophe through the moral qualities of the warrior hero. Drought myth, probably deriving from the arid conditions of parts of north China, finds frequent and eloquent expression.

Myths of cultural benefits resemble those of other mythologies in two respects: deities are the divine originators of these benefits, and deities are the first to teach humans how to use them. Chinese culture deities are mostly masculine figures. Female deities often figure in cosmological myths, but their mythic narratives have been obscured for us by later scribal prejudice. Modern gender theory has rediscovered vestiges of their myths, such as the creator goddess and maker of humankind, and the mother goddesses of the sun and moon. Myths of dynastic foundation give a unique emphasis to female ancestors, followed by male founding figures, as with the Shang and Zhou origin myths. The theme of love is rare and is narrated in a sexually non-explicit manner, which may suggest early prudish editing. Divine birth is expressed through animalian agency, such as a bird or a bird's egg, or through parthenogenesis, for example from the belly of a male corpse, or an old woman's ear, or a hollow tree. Metamorphosis colours the stories, with objects turning into trees of brilliant and symbolic foliage, or figures becoming a bear, a bird or a star. The foundation motif becomes more frequent in later classical texts as dynastic rulers, ethnic peoples and major families claimed divine descent through populous and conflicting genealogical lines.

Themes of divine warfare and cosmic destruction are significant. There are also the important themes of a second beginning of the world after a hero has saved humankind from a major catastrophe, and of a Golden Age of wise kings who are ideal rulers and inaugurate the first human government. Less strong are themes to do with agriculture, the pastoral life, migration, exodus and exile, odyssey and the epic, and gender conflict. A major theme is the perception of foreigners in myths of the self and the cultural 'other'. Recurring themes of the warrior and the moral hero are represented in numerous episodes. Chinese heroic myth differs from other mythologies in its early emphasis on the moral virtue of the warrior hero.

Many figures depicted in mythical episodes represent cultural archetypes. The saviour figure occurs in myths that feature the creator goddess and the first human giant whose body becomes the universe. The archetype of the nurturing deity is represented by female cosmological and calendrical figures, such as the mothers of the sun and moon, and by the numerous male culture gods. Divine vengeance is symbolized by the myths of Woman Droughtghoul and Responding Dragon, who execute other deities on the command of a great god. There also appears the archetype of the failed hero, and the archetypal trickster figure, though these are not fully delineated in the myths. The stereotype of the successful hero figure is represented in several myths, for example the grain deity Sovereign Millet and the queller of the deluge, Reptilian-Pawprint. The moral hero Hibiscus is the archetypal hero and the leader of his people. These themes, archetypes, symbols and motifs will be developed and explored in the following chapters.

Origins

The creation of the world

China has a rich tradition of creation myth. There are six separate narratives in which different figures have a major role and function. One of the earliest creation myths centres on the archaic goddess named Woman Gua (Nu Gua). The name 'Gua' means a snail-like creature; insects and reptiles that cast off their shell or skin were believed to have the power of regeneration. Her myths are partly obscured by the gender bias of medieval commentators, yet they are present, although elusively in the earliest texts. It is related that Woman Gua made seventy transformations from which the cosmos and all living things took shape. Her divinity was so potent that her guts metamorphosed into ten deities called the Guts of Woman Gua.

Another creation myth is told by the Daoist author, the philosopher Zhuang Zi of the fourth century BC. He used ancient myth to illustrate several philosophical views, such as the danger of political intervention and mis-

The archaic goddess Woman Gua (Nu Gua).

The deity Muddle Thick (Hundun).

guided charity. The creation myth told in his book *Zhuang zi* concerns the myth of the dying god of chaos, whose destruction is necessary for the universe to take shape. It centres on Muddle Thick (Hundun), who had no face or facial apertures. The god Hundun ruled the centre of the world, with the gods of the southern and northern waters ruling on each side. These two sea gods visited Hundun often, and in return for his hospitality they decided that since he had no face they would give him seven openings so he could see, hear, eat and breathe. They chiselled an opening each day, but on the seventh day Hundun died. In another text this god of chaos is described as looking like a yellow sack and as red as cinnabar flame, with six feet and four wings, but without a face or eyes.

A third creation myth represents a vivid world picture. It relates that out of primeval vapour the two cosmic forces of Yin and Yang emerged. Through their interaction the cosmos took shape. The sky appeared as a round canopy that covered the four-sided flat earth, with the sky and the earth held together by massive mountains (or in a variant, pillars) fastened by cords. The world picture of this creation myth is so similar to ancient Egyptian cosmology that it may reflect a cultural transmission from Egypt through Central Asia.

A fourth myth gives more details about the cosmic forces of Yin and Yang. It relates that before the world began there was only a formless expanse of vapour. From this primeval element were produced the Yin force, which is dark, cold, shaded, heavy, feminine and passive, and the Yang force, which is light, hot, sunny, ethereal, masculine and active. The interaction between Yin and Yang created the four seasons and the natural world. Yang gave birth to fire and the sun; Yin gave birth to water and the moon, and then the stars.

The myth of the separation of the sky and the earth belongs to creation narratives. It tells of a monstrously deformed sky god called Fond Care (Zhuan Xu) who rules the pivot of the sky. He commanded his grandson

The giant Coiled Antiquity (Pan Gu).

Chong to prop up the sky for eternity, and his other grandson Li to press the earth down forever. It was believed in antiquity that if the two elements of sky and earth were not kept separate, the cosmos would return to chaos.

The most colourful creation myth centres on the giant Coiled Antiquity (Pan Gu), the first-born, semi-divine human being. It tells how he lay dying and as his life ebbed away his breath became the winds and clouds, his voice thunder, his eyes the sun and moon, and his limbs mountains. His bodily fluids turned into rain and rivers, his flesh into the soil. His head hair became the stars, his body hair became vegetation. His teeth, bones and marrow turned into minerals. The insects on his body became human beings. This myth is made up of a series of metamorphoses in which the various parts of the body became analogous parts of the universe. It is one of many myths of the cosmological human body from around the world, and it contains the important myths of the dying god and the nurturing god, who gave his body for the benefit of humankind.

Another version of the Coiled Antiquity myth relates that at the beginning of time all matter was like a chicken's egg. After eighteen thousand years it separated into the Yang ethereal matter that rose to form the sky and the

The Three Sovereign Deities.

173

Yin heavy matter that sank to form the earth. Coiled Antiquity was born between these sacred primordial elements as they unfolded. The giant went through nine metamorphoses and became as divine and wise as the sky and earth. Eighteen thousand years later the sky, the earth and the first human reached their maximum size and formed a trinity of Heaven, Earth and Humankind. Later on, Three Sovereign Deities emerged (their names vary). The narrative goes on to tell how numbers were created and cosmic distances were fixed, and it provides the etiological myth of the science of mathematics.

The two creation myths of Coiled Antiquity are the latest in textual terms among the six narratives, and they derive from a minority ethnic group of south-western China. Recorded in around the third century AD, they were probably transmitted from Central Asia. Of the two, the first, the myth of the cosmological human body, became the orthodox account of the creation of the world in China.

The creation of humankind

Myths of the creation of human beings are told in three stories. The earliest story is found in the creation myths of Yin and Yang, who produced all living things out of primeval vapour, including crawling creatures and human beings. The story of the death of Coiled Antiquity relates that the insects on his body turned into the first humans. A third myth of the origin of humans is told in a dramatic and colourful way. It centres on the creator goddess Woman Gua and the story begins after the creation of the world. It tells how Woman Gua kneaded yellow clay like a potter and made images of humans which then came to life. She wanted to create more but could not, so she made a furrow in the mud with her builder's cord and lifted the cord in and out of the mud, the falling mud turning into human form. Woman Gua's divine emblems are a knotted cord and a compass.

The myth goes on to explain the origin of social hierarchy. The yellow clay humans became the ruling class of rich and noble people, while the mud produced the mass of the poor and servile underclass. The colour motif of yellow resonates through Chinese culture. The deity called the Great God Yellow (Huang Di) became the supreme god of philosophical and religious Daoism. Yellow also symbolizes the divine Earth, and the centre of the human world. It became the emblematic colour of some dynasties.

The origins of culture and human society

China has numerous myths of the origins of culture and human society. These are etiological myths which contain the statement that a certain deity 'was the first to' grant a gift of culture, or that a deity 'taught humans how to use' the divine gift. It is emphasized that it was the deities who invented and discovered cultural benefits rather than humans, and this conveys the idea of divine control over human life.

Most of the cultural benefits are granted by male deities. The myth of

The Farmer God (Shen Nong) with his forked plough. The inscription reads: 'The Farmer God taught agriculture based on land use; he opened up the land and planted millet to encourage the myriad people'.

神農氏因鳳教田辟土種穀以振萬民

the Farmer God (Shen Nong) relates how he taught humans the uses of medicine and the benefits of agriculture. The god took pity on humans who were suffering illnesses from eating toxic plants and drinking contaminated water. The Farmer God tasted all the plants and taught humans the difference between the poisonous and the edible. His method was to thrash plants with his rust-coloured whip and to judge their value by their taste and smell. He organized plants into four categories: the bland, the toxic, the cool and the hot. This taxonomy forms the basis of traditional Chinese medicine, and the deity became the divine patron of medicine. The Farmer God also showed humans how to distinguish between types of soil and land. He created a wooden plough and taught humans how to till the soil and sow the five grains: hemp, wheat (or barley), leguminous crops and two types of millet. His agricultural function overlaps with that of the grain deity Sovereign Millet (Hou Ji). The emblem of the Farmer God is a forked plough.

The culture myth of the grain deity features the important figure Sovereign Millet. The name of this deity may refer to a male or female figure. In other mythologies, the grain or cereal deity and the earth deity are usually represented as female figures because they symbolize fertility and birth. A long narrative poem from the Zhou *Classic of Poetry* relates how Sovereign Millet taught humans how to sow grain, cook it, and offer it in sacrifice as the first food of thanksgiving from humans. This deity also features in the myth of the origins of the early Chinese and the second historical dynasty, the Zhou.

A god who appears later in the mythological tradition is Fu Xi, whose name means Prostrate (Sacrificial) Victim. The myths of his invention of writing, divination and hunting weapons is told through the device of mimesis – that is, the imitation of an observed act and its application to an analogous method. The narrative relates that at the time when Prostrate Victim ruled the cosmos he looked at the sky and the earth and observed the markings of birds and beasts, and he contemplated their images and patterns. With this knowledge, which was based on the natural order of things, the god created the first written symbols of the Eight Trigrams for humans to make divination. Eight Trigrams (*Ba Gua*) originally referred to a set of eight combinations of three broken and unbroken lines (broken denotes Yin female, unbroken denotes Yang male); these eight were multiplied to make a set of sixty-four, and the three lines were doubled to make six; the sixty-four variations of six lines formed the basis of a system of divination; they were given titles, and explanations were attached to them, which were recorded in the *Classic of Change* (Yi jing). Prostrate Victim also watched a spider weaving its web, and he fashioned knotted cords into nets and taught humans how to use them for hunting and fishing. This god is represented in art with his emblem of a carpenter's square; he has a human form with a snake's tail. In the late classical era, around the first century BC, he was linked to the primeval creator goddess Woman Gua as the first divine married couple, with their tails intertwined to symbolize mating.

The mythical figure of Chi You, whose name translates as Jest Much, has the function of the war god and the inventor of metal weapons. His myth presents the etiology of metal, the art of metallurgy and the invention of weapons. It relates that two mountains burst open and poured out water and metal. The god gathered the metal and made weapons and armour from it. He formed a powerful group with his seventy-two brothers, who all had bronze heads and ate stone pebbles. Jest Much is represented as an ox with horns and hooves. Through his discovery of metallurgy he achieved supremacy among the gods.

Woman Gua (left) holding her compass and Prostrate Victim (Fu Xi) holding his carpenter's square. Their tails are intertwined to symbolize mating.

左右三

The Qin emperor attempts to retrieve a sacred cauldron that flew into the Si River.

The myth of the origin of metal and metal-working is told also through the important figure of the semi-divine hero Yu, whose name means Reptilian-Pawprint. It tells how Reptilian-Pawprint forged nine sacred bronze cauldrons which were engraved with the knowledge of the world. He showed humans how to distinguish between monsters and benign beings in their passage through life. These bronze cauldrons were endowed with the sacred power of judging moral worth and were handed down from dynasty to dynasty. If the ruler was virtuous and governed the people kindly, the cauldrons were heavy with moral power and remained with the ruler and his dynasty. If the ruler was evil and mistreated the people, the cauldrons became light and flew away. These sacred vessels served as a symbol of legitimate dynastic rule and as emblems of wealth, ritual and state control over the strategic production of metal weapons and goods.

The origin myth of sericulture, the preparation of silk, is a distinctively Chinese story. It is told that the god Silkworm Cluster (Can Cong) was a divine silkworm who produced prolific amounts of silk. He ruled the people of Shu in the south-west (modern Sichuan province). He taught his people about silkworms and the mulberry tree leaves which were their food. Silkworm Cluster made several thousand golden silkworms and gave one each to his people. These multiplied and produced huge cocoons, and the people were able to return the gift of their produce to the god-king. On his divine progress around Shu, people would gather at his stopping places, and these became the first markets.

The discovery of harmony and musical instruments is related in numerous myths, and different deities are said to have granted these gifts to humans. Among them are Prostrate Victim (Fu Xi), who created music patterned on the divine harmony of the cosmos and handed it down to humankind, and the Great God Tellswift (Ku), who commanded two deities, one of whom was You Chui (or Skill Weights), to compose tunes and make drums, bells and pipes for humans to play. The most extended narrative of the myth of the origin of music centres on the son of the hero Yu whose name was Open, Lord of the Summer. Open is described as wearing green snakes through his ears and riding a pair of dragons. He was carried into the sky and there he received the gift of the music of Heaven. The titles of this music are reflected in the second early poetry anthology of China, *Songs of Chu*, such as the hymns to river goddesses among 'The Nine Songs', dating from around the fourth century BC. The *Songs of Chu* belongs to the ancient culture of the Huai and Yangtze River region in south China.

The ancient text, the *Classic of Mountains and Seas*, is a treasure trove of classical myth, and it features episodes of more than two hundred mythical figures. Among them are numerous culture deities, such as Turncorner (Fan Yu) who invented boats, Lucky Glare (Ji Guang) who invented wooden carts, Turnabout (Ban) who made bows and arrows, Reap Even (Shu Jun) who made the first ox-drawn plough, and Skill Weights (You Chui or Qiao Chui), who was the first god to come down to earth and bring humans all the arts of skilled craftsmanship.

It is a characteristic of myth that some figures are so potent they inspire cycles of myth stories in which their earliest recorded roles may change and even become diminished. This is evident in the myth of the first marriage in human society. The story tells how Woman Gua and her unnamed brother wanted to make love but were ashamed, so they decided to ask god for permission. God performed a miracle to show his approval, and so the first humans made love. But they hid their shamed faces behind a grass fan. This rare account of an incestuous marriage may contain a rationale for breaking the taboo against marriage between close relatives in times of dire need, such as floods, famine, war or epidemics which destroy populations and threaten the survival of the human race. This myth may be compared with that of the divine marriage of Woman Gua the creator goddess to the god Prostrate Victim. The myth of Woman Gua's marriage to her brother was first recorded in the medieval period, by Li Rong (fl. AD 846–74), when attitudes to women were prejudiced and the position of women was devalued. It reveals how the potent goddess, who created the world and humankind and was the saviour of the world in the catastrophe of fire and flood, became demoted during the period between the classical and medieval eras from a divinity to a human being.

The myth of the first government

The myth of the first human government is narrated by an anonymous classical writer in the *Classic of History* (also known as *Ancient History*). The mythic story he tells illustrates the way a writer uses old myths and interprets them to create a completely new myth, a process called mythopoeia. The author starts his story at the beginning of time: not in the age of the deities, but when the first ideal rulers named Yao and Shun governed the world. When Yao became very old he wanted to abdicate, but he refused to bequeath the throne to his son. Instead, he passed it on to his worthy minister Hibiscus (Shun), to whom he also gave his two daughters in marriage. Shun then formed the first government. He made the hero Reptilian-Pawprint (Yu) the Superintendent of Flood Control Works, and Kui the Director of Music. He made Breath and Blend (Xi and He), two male officials, responsible for regulating the agricultural calendar in the Board of Astronomy. He made Sovereign Millet the Minister of Agriculture. It has already been seen that Sovereign Millet was the primeval grain deity. Similarly, we will see (in later chapters) that Reptilian-Pawprint was a semi-divine hero who brought the world flood under control, and that Kui was a one-legged thunder god. Also, Breath Blend was one deity, the omnipotent sun goddess who was the mother of the ten suns. It is clear that the anonymous writer of the *Classic of History* used familiar figures in the old myth narratives to invent a new story which would tell how the first human government came to be formed. In his story, the ideal rulers Yao and Shun are succeeded by the virtuous Yu to become a triumvirate in the Golden Age of Antiquity, when government was founded on moral values.

Origin myths of the first historical dynasties

Fragments of myth in the Zhou *Classic of Poetry* relate the myths of the divine origins of the Shang and the Zhou dynasties. The Shang origin myth tells how the sky god commanded a divine dark bird to come down from Heaven to earth and give birth to the Shang. Another version appears in the much later first history of China, written by Sima Qian *c.* 100 BC, *Records of the Grand Historian (Shi ji)*. He narrates that a lovely girl called Bamboo-slip Maid (Jian Di) went to bathe. She saw a black bird drop its egg and picked it up and swallowed it. She became pregnant and gave birth to a boy named Xie (pronounced Shieh, also known as Qi, pronounced Chee). Jian Di became the divine ancestress of the Shang people, and her son by virgin or miraculous birth became the male founder of the Shang dynasty.

The myth of the divine origin of the Zhou is told in the same texts. This relates that the girl Jiang Yuan (Jiang the Originator) trod in the big toeprint of a great god and became pregnant. She gave birth to a child called Sovereign Millet. But Jiang Yuan thought her child was unlucky, so she tried to abandon it. She left it in a narrow lane where cattle went, but the cattle suckled the child and protected it. She then left it in some woods, but people from the plains who went to cut wood found the child and rescued it. She then laid her child on ice, but birds raised it on their feathers and kept it warm. Her divinely born child was destined to achieve great things, and despite enduring these three trials the child hero survived. Then Jiang Yuan nurtured her baby, who grew up to possess a divine knowledge of seed culture, especially of millet, and also the vegetal culture of beans. The young hero taught humans these arts. This divinely born person became the grain deity who also taught humans how to cook millet and offer it in sacrifice to Sovereign Millet, the grain deity and the founder of the Zhou people and the Zhou dynasty.

Divine cosmos

Several hundred mythical figures and deities crowd the pages of classical texts. One text alone, the *Classic of Mountains and Seas*, features 204 individual deities and mythical figures, with a total of 237 if several groups of divinities are included. The texts divide into two broad categories: those which present a large number of figures, male and female, with diverse functions and significance, and those which project a distinctively masculine pantheon with a limited number of divine functions. The former, more comprehensive category of texts contains material which belongs to a mythological tradition that has parallels with myths from other cultures. The second category of texts includes those which use mythical figures in a new, inventive way, such as the *Classic of History*, and this category of texts broadly speaking formed the orthodox canon in China. Modern studies of Chinese myth now explore those other texts which fall outside the textual boundary of orthodoxy and are rediscovering much that has previously been overlooked or neglected in Chinese mythology.

The pantheon of the deities and their functions

There is no fixed pantheon in Chinese mythology. The category of orthodox texts which focus on masculine figures generally mentions a limited sequence of about ten major deities and mythical figures which forms a loosely structured pantheon. The following sequence is typical: Prostrate Victim (Fu Xi), the Farmer God, the fire god Flame (Yan Di), the Great God Yellow (Huang Di), the god of light Young Brightsky (Shao Hao), the sky god Fond Care (Zhuan Xu), the Great God Tellswift (Ku), and the semi-divine ideal rulers Lofty, Hibiscus and Reptilian-Pawprint (Yao, Shun and Yu).

In contrast, the more comprehensively mythological texts are teeming with deities. The supreme gods mentioned in the *Classic of Mountains and Seas* are the god Foremost (Jun), and then Fond Care, but the major deity of the masculine tradition, Prostrate Victim, does not even appear in that book. Its other major deities include Queen Mother of the West, the sun-mother

Breath Blend (Xi He) and the moon-mother Ever Breath (Chang Xi), and it is true to say that this text gives greater emphasis to the feminine.

The divine functions of male deities relate to cultural benefits, such as agriculture through the Farmer God, Sovereign Millet and Sovereign Earth (Hou Tu), fire through the great god Flame, writing and divination through Prostrate Victim, the hunt through Yi the Archer and war through Jest Much, besides the benefits of weaponry, musical instruments, transport and craftsmanship which are all gifts of male gods.

The divine functions of female deities involve cosmogony, calendrical systems, nurturing roles, paradisial bliss and sacred violence. The goddess Breath Blend (Xi He) gave birth to the ten suns of the archaic calendrical week and nurtured them. The goddess Ever Breath (Chang Xi) gave birth to the twelve moons and nurtured them. Woman Gua created the cosmos (in one version of the creation myth), rescued the world from the catastrophes of fire and flood in her role as the divine smith and the saviour of humankind, and she created humankind. The Queen Mother of the West (Xi Wang Mu) has two functions: she sends plagues and punishments down to earth, but she also presides over the western mountain paradise.

Male and female deities are theroanthropic, that is, having animalian features, such as serpentine tails, tiger fangs, bovine horns and avian wings, which are emblems respectively of fertility, ferocity, aggression and aerial flight. Queen Mother of the West is represented with wild hair, the fangs of a tigress, and a panther's tail. Three bluebirds bring her food. In the later tradition she is accompanied by a nine-tailed fox and guarded by a leopard. Many deities are represented with snakes in their ears and riding dragons through the sky. The deities and mythical figures in the orthodox, masculine tradition, especially in classical Confucian texts, are represented as humanized beings who bear functional emblems, such as the human figure of the Farmer God with his plough and Reptilian-Pawprint the flood-queller with his dredger.

The names of many deities indicate their rank in a divine hierarchy and also show their function and gender. The term *Di* (pronounced Dee) is generally attached to male deities, such as Huang Di or Di Ku, and has the meaning of 'great god', giving the Great God Yellow and the Great God Ku (translated as Tellswift). Frequently the term *Di* appears without a name: this does not refer to a God Almighty, but to some unknown great god. The names of great goddesses often include 'stopgap' titles such as *Nu* (Woman), *Huang* (Grace), and *E* (Sublime), as with Nu Gua and Sublime Grace (E Huang). Otherwise they are known by their function, such as Breath Blend, the sun goddess, and Woman Droughtghoul (Nu Ba), the female bringer of drought. Lesser divinities are known as *Shen* (Divine or Holy Being, or god). *Ling* means divine power. *Gui* refers to a ghostly divinity. *Shi* with a name is used for a corpse deity, such as the Corpse of Prince Night and the Corpse of the Yellow Giantess. Then there are motley demons, imps and bogies that live in the mountains and streams or guard the gates of Heaven.

Miraculous birth

There are many differences between the gods and goddesses of other mythologies and those of Chinese myths, but none is so striking as the treatment of divine sexuality and procreation. Chinese myths do not include episodes of savage lust inspired by demonic energy. Instead they either refer to sex in a minor way or relate no sexual episodes at all. For example, the Great God Tellswift was the consort of two major goddesses who bore divine sons, but Tellswift was not their father. One of his goddess wives was Bamboo-slip Maid (Jian Di), who (as we have seen) swallowed the divine egg of the dark bird and was miraculously fertilized, giving birth to the male founder of the Shang dynasty. The other wife of Tellswift was Jiang Yuan who (as already mentioned) stepped in the big toeprint of a great god and was miraculously impregnated, giving birth to the founder of the Zhou dynasty. The myth of the divine birth of Reptilian-Pawprint (Yu), the flood hero, relates that he was born from the belly of the corpse of his father Gun, who had been executed by God. The story of the birth of Reptilian-Pawprint's own son is equally miraculous. Yu mated with the daughter of a mountain people, but one day he revealed himself in his divine aspect of a bear. His pregnant wife fled in terror and turned into a stone. Yu followed her and commanded the stone mother to give forth his son. The stone split open and Yu's son Open was born.

The children of virgin birth are usually male. It is possible that by the time the archaic oral tradition of myths was set down in writing they were often told in the idiom of a patriarchal culture. The myth of the Country of Women is the only one that narrates the survival of female infants; the males are left to die before they reach their third year. In this myth the fertilization of virginal women comes from bathing in a miraculous yellow pool.

Many myths of miraculous birth narrate stories of a virgin birth through the egg of a divine bird. This has been seen in the myth of the origin of the Shang people and their dynasty. Besides this form of ornithomorphous hierogamy, birth also occurs through other similar means. The semi-divine founder of a southern ethnic people, the Yao, was born as a worm in the ear of an old palace lady. The worm grew into a dog and became a hero in a time of war.

Although many myths relate narratives of virgin birth from divine goddesses or semi-divine female figures, in the later tradition it is the male gods who give birth through parthenogenesis, without female agency. Many such myths are genealogical foundation myths that relate the lineage of a country, a people or a notable family.

Divine warfare

The wars of the deities are narrated in several myths. There is the struggle for power between the god of war, Jest Much (Chi You), and the Great God Yellow. When the god of war discovered metal and invented metal weapons he threatened the supremacy of other deities. The Great God Yellow fought

183

The god of war, Jest Much (Chi You), inventor of metal weapons.

The god of war is executed by Responding Dragon (Ying Long).

with the god of war and defeated him through his two allies, his daughter the drought goddess named Woman Droughtghoul (Nu Ba) who dried up the war god's weapon of rain, and Responding Dragon (Ying Long) who killed him at Cruelplough Earthmound. Another myth relates that the rebellious worker god Common Work (Gong Gong) challenged the sky god Fond Care (Zhuan Xu) for divine supremacy. In his fury Common Work butted against one of the world mountains called Not Round that propped up the sky. This caused a flaw in the cosmos, so that the sky, sun, moon and stars tilted towards the north-west and the rivers and silt on earth flowed in a south-eastern direction. This narrative forms the etiological myth of the tilt of the earth.

A tragic conflict is told in one of the myths of Hugefish (Gun). He tries to save the world from the deluge by stealing god's divine cosmos-repairing soil called breathing-earth. But before he can use it, god commands his executioner, the fire god Pray Steam (Zhu Rong), to kill Hugefish on Feather Mountain. Hugefish's body does not decompose, however, and his son, the hero Reptilian-Pawprint (Yu), is born from his belly. Then Hugefish metamorphoses into a yellow bear (in variants, a turtle or dragon).

Heaven Punished (Xing Tian).

Another divine figure, named Boast Father (Kua Fu), is executed for an act of hubris. He challenged the divine power of the sun to race with him to the place where the sun sets. But Boast Father became parched with thirst, and even though he drank from a great river it was not enough. Before he could reach the next river he died of thirst, and his abandoned stick turned into a grove of trees. In another myth of a doomed hero, the warrior god named Heaven Punished (Xing Tian) challenges god for supremacy. God decapitates him and buries his head on a mountain, but the warrior god uses his nipples to make eyes and his navel for a mouth, brandishing his shield and battleaxe in a war dance.

Death of the gods

The myth of the dying god is expressed through several figures. Muddle Thick (Hundun), the god of chaos, has to die in order for the cosmos to be created. Hugefish must die because he committed the crime of theft from god. Boast Father is killed for his hubris. Jest Much is executed after his defeat by the Great God Yellow in a titanic struggle. Although it is related that the gods and goddesses die, they continue to live in another form through metamorphosis. Woman Lovely (Nu Wa) drowned in the East Sea, perhaps because she was trespassing or because, as the daughter of the Great God Flame, her own divine power became extinguished. She was transformed into a bird and renamed Sprite Guard (Jing Wei), and for the rest of eternity she tries to dam up the East Sea in revenge.

The myth of the fearsome god called Notch Flaw (Ya Yu) relates a rare rite of resuscitation by shamans. Notch Flaw was killed by two warriors, Twain Load (Er Fu) and Peril (Wei). Six shamans nurtured his corpse and held the drug of immortality over it. The myth does not say whether Notch Flaw was revived and turned into another shape, but it does go on to tell how his murderers were executed by god for their crime. God had them manacled with their own hair and strung up on a tree on the top of a mountain, and left them exposed for birds and beasts to eat. Two other gods who killed another deity were also executed, and they turned into ominous birds of prey which foretold the coming of a great war and drought.

Divine paradise

Several myths relate how deities descend to earth and create paradises in which to enjoy the human world. These paradises have names like God's Bedroom or God's Secret City on Earth. The most famous of these is the four-sided plateau on Kunlun Mountain. This mighty range stretches from north-west China across northern Tibet and ends in northern Afghanistan. It is the most vivid representation of the mythic motif of the celestial archetype. This western mountain paradise, guarded by the ferocious Openbright (Kai-ming) animal, has wells that are always full of fresh water, a precious jewel tree, and fabulous flora and fauna. The goddess Queen Mother of the West reigns on one of its peaks.

Another paradise myth tells of five mountain islands in the eastern sea where deities and immortals live. One day these Isles of the Blest start to drift towards the western ends of the world and are close to destruction. So god commands the giant god of the northern sea, Ape Strong (Yu Jiang), to secure the islands by making fifteen gigantic turtles hold the island paradises on their heads, taking it in turns to bear the load.

Catastrophe myths

Classical writers were keenly aware of the catastrophes which affected human society. It is recorded in a book of the third century BC that the statesman and philosopher Guan Zi, who lived in the seventh century BC, made this assessment of perennial disasters: 'Floods are one, droughts another, wind, fog, hail and frost are another; pestilence is one and insects another . . . Of the five types of disaster, floods are the most serious.' This chapter deals with myths of flood, drought and fire.

The flood myth

The most enduring and widespread of the catastrophe myths worldwide is the flood myth. In classical China the myth is told in four stories. The myth of the rebellious worker-god Common Work (Gong Gong) relates how he stirred the waters of the whole world so that they crashed against the barrier of the sky and threatened the world with chaos. This flood myth is the only one which gives the cause of the flood and the figure who started it. In this version the god Common Work plays the role of the marplot, one who seeks to destroy the design of the cosmos. In this respect, it is linked to the myth which tells how Common Work challenged the supreme sky god, Fond Care (Zhuan Xu), and in his fury butted against the world mountain that held up the sky.

Another flood story tells how the goddess Woman Gua saved the world from raging fires and a deluge. In her role as the divine smith, Woman Gua smelted the cosmic five-coloured stone and restored the sky. Then she cut the legs off a giant turtle and propped up the four corners of the earth and sky. She also dammed the flooding waters with the ashes of burnt reeds.

A third story features the heroic Hugefish (Gun), who is described in one text as the first-born son of god. Unfortunately, this flood myth is narrated in a passage that is garbled. The text itself, 'Questions of Heaven' of the fourth century BC, is presented as a series of questions or riddles about the early myths and legends of China. Piecing the story together, the following account emerges. A group of lesser gods urge god to choose Hugefish to deal with the crisis afflicting the world when there is a great deluge. Although god commands Hugefish to control the flood waters, he is uneasy about this choice of hero. Two divine creatures, the owl (which knows the mystery of the sky) and the turtle (which knows the secrets of the waters), come to the hero's aid. But Hugefish can control the flood only by stealing god's miraculous breathing-earth, the cosmic soil which can repair the world. For this sacrilege of theft, god condemns Hugefish to death before he can use the magic soil. Hugefish is executed on Feather Mountain by the fire god Pray Steam, and left to rot from exposure. But his body does not decompose, and his son Yu is born from his belly. Then Hugefish is revived by shamans, and he turns into a yellow bear. In this myth Hugefish plays several roles: saviour, heroic victim, failed hero and dying god. His mythic function is to try to mediate between god and humankind to ensure the continuation of the world and the human race.

The fourth flood story proved to be the most potent and became the orthodox version of the classical Chinese flood myth. One narrative appears in the same passage of 'Questions of Heaven' which gives the flood myth of Hugefish. It is told that Reptilian-Pawprint (Yu) was favoured by god and was permitted to use the breathing-earth to repair the cosmos and control the flood. Another narrative appears in the philosophical writings of Mencius of the fourth century BC, who was an eloquent spokesman for the moral concepts of the Confucian school. As with other Confucian texts, the narrative of the Yu flood myth as told in *Mencius* is set in the mythical or pseudo-historical era of the beginning of human time, when Lofty (Yao) and Hibiscus (Shun) ruled the world. The story tells how a vast deluge threatened the world when the waters of all the rivers flowed out of their channels and flooded the Middle Kingdom (China). Snakes and dragons overran the land and the people had nowhere to live, so they made shelters in nests on the low

Reptilian-Pawprint (Yu) with his dredger. The inscription reads: 'Yu of the Hsia was skilled in charting the earth; he explored water sources and he understood the Yin [cosmic principle]; according to the seasons he constructed high dikes; then he retired and created the physical punishments.'

ground and lived in caves on the high ground. The ruler Hibiscus ordered Reptilian-Pawprint to control the flood water. Reptilian-Pawprint dug channels to conduct the water out to sea, and he drove out the snakes and dragons and expelled the rapacious birds and beasts. Humans were then able to return to their homes in the plains and resettle there. This narrative contains a number of important mythic motifs. The flood introduces the theme of a return to primeval chaos. The myth of the hero is exemplified by Reptilian-Pawprint's great labours as he struggles to restore order. There are also the themes of a second beginning of the world, of human survival, and the restoration of human society to its dominant position over the animal kingdom. The most significant motif is that the flood is finally ended not by divine intervention but through the agency of the moral hero, who puts his sense of public duty before private concerns and who performs his tasks with courage, obedience and virtue.

The myth of the world catastrophe by fire

The primary myth of a world conflagration features the hunter god, Yi the Archer. The Chinese graph or character for the name Yi shows joined hands and a pair of feathers. This myth provides a cause for the fiery inferno that threatens to extinguish the world. The solar myth of the sun goddess relates that she gave birth to ten suns, which she allowed to rise in turn each day. The myth tells how one day all ten suns rose together and threatened to parch the crops and scorch human beings. The hunter god Yi the Archer felt pity for humankind and asked a sky god, the Great God Foremost (Jun), if he would lend his divine aid to the world. The god gave Yi the Archer a divine vermilion bow and plain arrows with silk cords. The hunter god aimed at the suns and shot them down.

Another mythic narrative relates that nine searingly hot suns fell to earth and landed on a rock that was later named Whirlpool Furnace (Wu Jiao). This name combines the infinite power of the sea which extinguished the suns and the fiery furnace created by their molten remains. Yi the Archer features in several episodes and is linked to one of the moon goddesses and myths of monsters. These stories form a cycle of Yi the Archer myths.

Drought myths

The disaster of drought is told through several different myths. One relates that a drought lasted for five (in a variant, seven) years in the reign of one of the mythical founders of the Shang dynasty, the king named Tang the Conqueror. The king's people were reduced to starvation and thirst, and the royal diviners wanted to offer up human sacrifice to placate the gods and ancestral spirits. But the king chose a more selfless, heroic way to relieve the drought. He went to the sacred grove of Mulberry Forest and prayed to god to forgive human error by accepting himself as a sacrificial victim and removing the punishment of the drought. He said, 'If I, the One Man, have sinned, do not punish the people. If the people have sinned, let me alone take the

The hunter god Yi the Archer shoots down the suns, symbolized by birds in the world tree.

blame.' The king then prepared himself as if he were a sacrificial animal. He cut off his hair and fingernails, rubbed his hands smooth, and sprinkled water on himself. Then he was tightly bound with white rushes and driven to an open-air altar by white horses. (White was the emblematic colour of death.) He was placed on the woodpile, and just as the fire took hold a great downpour of rain fell. In this drought myth, unlike the flood myth stories, the reason for the disaster is given, that is, divine retribution for human error, and in this motif the myth parallels Biblical catastrophe myth and other myths worldwide. The drought myth reflects the semi-arid, drought-prone environment of the northern region of Shang culture, but it is not recorded in Shang writings.

Another drought story exists in fragmentary form. It features a corpse deity named Woman Deuce (Nu Chou). In this myth she plays the role of the victim, but the narrative does not say whether she chose this role or was compelled to do so. It tells how Woman Deuce was born a corpse goddess. At the time when the ten suns all rose at once, she stayed high up on a mountain to expiate human error. She tried to screen her face with her green sleeve or to hide her deformed, scorched face. But she was burned to death on the mountain by the merciless heat of the suns and she died again, to be reborn a goddess. Her green clothes are an emblem of vegetal renewal and the revitalizing power of rain. In another fragment it is related that the goddess Woman Deuce lived in the sea, and she is represented holding her emblematic crab. According to ancient belief the crab waxes and wanes with the moon and is also a creature that knows the sources of life-giving water.

Another narrative tells how the daughter of the Great God Yellow had the power of sending down drought to the human world. Her name was Woman Droughtghoul (Nu Ba). In the cosmic battle between the two gods, Yellow and the war god Jest Much, the war god chose rain as one of his weapons in the form of the rain god. But the Great God Yellow sent his daughter Woman Droughtghoul to dry up the source of rain and also sent his avenging ally Responding Dragon (Ying Long) to execute the god of war. This divine creature had the power to withhold rain or to make rain fall. A narrative also relates that after this war of the gods Woman Droughtghoul's divine power was diminished and she could not rise back into the sky. She remained on earth and caused havoc by drying up water ditches and irrigation channels. The people therefore learned to perform a rite to exorcise the baneful goddess, calling out: 'Goddess, go north!' This would send the goddess back to her place of exile.

Mythic heroes and heroines

The mythical figure of the hero appears in the different roles of the saviour, culture bearer, warrior and founder of a new race, tribe or dynasty. Of over twenty stereotypical features of the hero worldwide, the most frequent and widely distributed among myths of the hero are miraculous birth, the three trials or tests, the labours in performing the tasks, and divine aid from the natural or supernatural world. By hero both male and female figures are intended. Heroism is also characterized by acts of military courage, idealism, devotion to a cause, nobility of spirit, hubris, revenge and patriotism. These include both positive and negative traits, but a unique feature of the archetypal Chinese hero is his moral valour.

Three mythical figures exemplify the stereotypical features of the hero in Chinese mythology. They are Sovereign Millet, Hibiscus and Reptilian-Pawprint.

Sovereign Millet (Hou Ji)

Heroic features are clearly evident in myths of the grain deity Hou Ji, or Sovereign Millet. The earliest and most colourful myth of this figure appears in China's earliest poetry anthology, the *Classic of Poetry*. A long narrative poem tells how this deity was conceived after the goddess Jiang Yuan 'trod in the big toe of God's footprint'. After the birth of her child, Jiang Yuan wanted to get rid of it because she thought it was unlucky. The narrative relates the three trials of the child hero. First, as we have seen, she exposed it in a narrow country lane used by cattle, but the animals suckled the infant. Then the mother left her baby in a wood to die of exposure or to be eaten by wild animals. But woodcutters from the plains found and rescued it. Finally, she put her infant on freezing ice to die of cold, but birds warmed the child with their soft feathers and protected it with their large wings. The baby wailed so lustily that it was found, and its mother decided in the end to raise and nurture it. The child grew up to possess divine knowledge of cultivating beans and millet, and taught humans these arts. Sovereign Millet also taught people how to cook these crops and offer them in sacrifice in an act of

Jiang Yuan leaves her son Sovereign Millet (Hou Ji), the grain god, to die of cold on freezing ice, in the third trial of the child hero.

thanksgiving. The child hero became the grain deity and the founder of this people, the Zhou, from whom the ancient kings took the name of the Zhou dynasty.

Hibiscus (Shun)

The mythical figure of Hibiscus (Shun) centres primarily on his qualities as a moral hero and leader of people. His heroism is especially expressed through his sense of filial piety. His myths relate stories of how his family tried to destroy him, but in each of his trials or tests he responds with acts of filial duty, so that in the end he converts his family's murderous hatred into virtuous conduct. In the first episode of the three trials of Hibiscus, his father, who is called the Blind Man (Gu Sou), and his half-brother Elephant (Xiang) plot to kill him. They order him to repair the family grain store. Hibiscus is obedient, but his two resourceful wives warn him that his father and half-brother plan to set fire to the grain store and burn him alive. His wives tell him to wear his bird-patterned coat. When he goes up into the granary the Blind Man and Elephant remove the ladder and set fire to the building, but Hibiscus has already turned into a bird and flown away.

The second episode relates that the evil pair order Hibiscus to dig a well. Shun is obedient, but his two wives warn him of the plot and tell him to wear his dragon-patterned coat. The Blind Man and Elephant keep watch and, when Hibiscus has dug deep down, they start to fill in the well with the soil to bury him alive. But Hibiscus has already turned into a dragon and disappeared through the watery underworld.

The third trial of the hero Hibiscus tells how the Blind Man plots to kill him by plying him with strong alcohol. His two wives tell him to bathe himself with a magic lotion (in a variant, dog's mess). Hibiscus rubs it all over his body, and obediently drinks all the liquor his father gives him. But however much he drinks, he does not become intoxicated and remains sober throughout his ordeal.

Meanwhile, thinking that Hibiscus will die of alcohol poisoning, his family are busy dividing up his possessions between themselves. His half-brother has taken up residence in the home of Hibiscus and is playing on his lute when Hibiscus walks in. Full of amazement and shame, his half-brother Elephant makes excuses and denies any involvement in the plots. The story of the trials of Hibiscus ends with the words, 'Hibiscus once again served under the Blind Man and he loved his younger brother Elephant, and looked after him devotedly.'

This myth has several motifs that parallel myths of other cultures. The symbolism of the name, the Blind Man, signifies not just physical blindness but, in this story, moral ignorance as well. The barely sketched figure of the Blind Man's second wife, the stepmother of Hibiscus, reveals familiar character traits – cruelty to a young man, preference for her own child, and greed for her stepson's property – which occur in many fairy tales.

One of the earliest books to record the myth of Hibiscus, the filial son, was the *Mencius* of the fourth century BC. The philosopher Mencius was a major exponent of the humanistic doctrines of the Confucian school, and it was he in particular who first emphasized the ethical principle of filial piety. Through his teachings and especially through his narrative of the ordeals of Hibiscus (Shun), Mencius was instrumental in elevating this principle to an ideal standard in Confucian moral philosophy. Besides being endowed with the virtue of filiality, Hibiscus is one of the great heroes of the Golden Age of Antiquity, in the ideal rule of first Lofty (Yao), then Hibiscus (Shun), and finally the hero Reptilian-Pawprint (Yu).

Reptilian-Pawprint (Yu)

The mythical figure of Reptilian-Pawprint (Yu) shows most of the stereotypical features of the hero. He is born miraculously from the belly of his father's corpse. He is favoured by god, who aids him with the divine cosmic soil and the help of divine creatures to control the world flood. The labours of this hero were so great that it is told that his body shrivelled down one side and 'no nails grew on his hands and no hair grew on his lower legs'. He is the model of the successful hero in his role as queller of the world deluge. He also displays leadership qualities in the divine world when he calls the first assembly of the gods. He demonstrates his warrior spirit when he slays the nine-headed monster, Aide Willow (Xiang Liu), who was polluting the soil with his drool so that crops were spoiled. Reptilian-Pawprint stands as the saviour figure for these two heroic feats of calming the deluge and ridding the land of pollution. He also performs the superhuman task of measuring the whole world (in a variant, he deputes another god to do this). Moreover, to help humans make their way through a hostile world, he forges (in a variant, was presented with) nine sacred metal cauldrons which bore images of the good and bad knowledge of the cosmos. This hero is also the third of the three ideal rulers of the Golden Age, following Lofty and Hibiscus. It is related that Reptilian-Pawprint founded the mythical dynasty of the Xia (Summer), which traditional historians until recently have believed to be the first historical dynasty of China, before the historically verifiable Shang and Zhou dynasties.

Although the myth of the trials of the hero is not so clearly told among the many stories about Reptilian-Pawprint, the motif of the labours of the hero is emphatically expressed. The narratives of his labours tell of his physical powers of endurance, his power of survival, and his supernatural strength in restoring the world to the natural order. They also tell of his traits of character, how obedient he was to the command to undertake his superhuman tasks, and with what patience, self-sacrifice and bravery he pursued his goal to the finish. Among the traits of character that he displays, there is the singularly Chinese mythic motif of moral grandeur and moral integrity in his dutiful and devoted performance of the seemingly impossible tasks that are set for him.

The failed hero

The motif of the failed hero complements the dynamic function of the successful hero figure. The two types of hero are well represented by Hugefish (Gun) and his son Reptilian-Pawprint. There are many other examples of the failed hero in Chinese myth, who may be a deity or a semi-divine being, who struggles in a fair contest for supremacy but loses to a more formidable rival. Sometimes failure is caused by an all too recognizable human flaw, such as trickery or hubris. Yet the failed hero is sympathetically treated in Chinese myths. Examples of this motif include the figures of Hugefish, Jest Much the war god, Boast Father who raced with the sun, and the goddess Woman Lovely, who turned into the divine bird Sprite Guard.

These are deities and semi-divine figures whom the communal memory stubbornly refused to vilify or delete from early mythic narratives and later legend and folktale.

The archetypal saviour figure

The archetypal saviour figure is most clearly seen in catastrophe myth. Examples of the saviour figure include the creator goddess Woman Gua, who used her regenerative powers and her skill as the divine smith to repair the cosmos after it was damaged by the world fire and the world flood, and who rescued humankind from these catastrophes. Another example is the hunter god Yi the Archer, who saved the world from incineration when the ten suns rose together. Hugefish and Reptilian-Pawprint are both saviour figures but, whereas Hugefish failed because of his sacrilege of theft from god, Reptilian-Pawprint succeeded. The mythical Shang king Tang the Conqueror was also a heroic saviour, who offered himself up as a human sacrifice to placate the god who had sent down the punishment of a severe drought to the human world. Hugefish is the saviour figure who makes the ultimate sacrifice by giving his own life in his attempt to save the world from the flood.

Other mythic themes represent the archetype of the saviour figure. For example, the theme of the deities who bring benefits to humankind contains the motif of the divine wish to save human beings from a harsh environment and ensure their survival. The myth of the Farmer God, in particular, illustrates this motif. It narrates how the god suffered the pain and torment of tasting noxious plants so that he could show humans which plants were harmful and which were beneficial. Calendrical myths also feature a saviour figure who seeks to relieve the human world of deprivation and hardship. The deity Torch Dragon (Zhu Long), for example, shines his divine light in the north-western region where, it was believed, the sunlight did not reach. This deity is portrayed as scarlet, with a snake's body and a human head. When he shuts his vertical eyes it grows dark, and when he opens them it grows bright over the 'nine darknesses'. Torch Dragon has such care for the well-being of humans that he neither eats, sleeps nor rests.

The hero as slayer of monsters

A narrative of the solar catastrophe myth tells how the hunter god Yi the Archer shot down the nine extra suns in the sky, and at the same time killed monsters that were ravaging the land and plaguing the people. He slew six monsters: the human-devouring monster with a dragon's head called Notch Flaw (Ya Yu), the rapacious monster called Chisel Tusk, the voracious monster called Nine Gullets and the destructive bird Giant Gale, as well as the Giant Boar and the massive serpent Gianthead Snake. Yi the Archer was successful in his tasks of saving mortals. He shot down some monsters, executed others, beheaded the serpent at the numinous lake of Gushcourt, and captured the boar in the sacred grove of Mulberry Forest. In one version of this myth it is god who permits Yi the Archer to perform these saving acts, in others it is the ideal ruler Lofty (Yao) who commands the hero to do these tasks, and Lofty is rewarded by being made sovereign ruler by popular choice.

The hero Reptilian-Pawprint has many mythical functions, and one of these is as the warrior who slays a monster. During his labours to control the world flood, he has to destroy a giant creature that was polluting the people's land so that they could not grow their crops. As we have seen, this monster was called Aide Willow (Xiang Liu). He was the officer of the rebel worker-god Common Work. Aide Willow had a snake's body, coloured green, and nine heads with human faces. Each of his nine heads fed from different parts of the countryside at the same time, and everything the monster

Aide Willow (Xiang Liu).

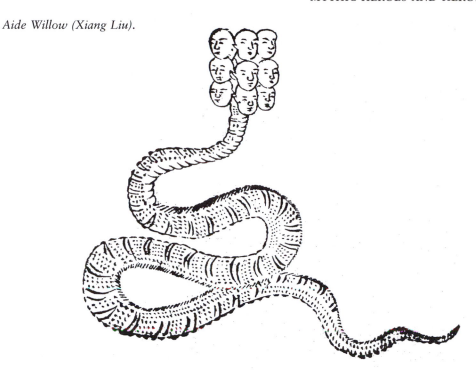

bumped into or his drool dripped on turned rancid and the soil was pollut-
ed. Reptilian-Pawprint slaughtered Aide Willow, but its blood flowed out
copiously and it stank, polluting the earth even more. So the hero dug out
the vile-smelling soil and let the monster's blood flow into these pits. But
each time he dug, the pits overflowed with blood. In the end he used the soil
that he had dug out to make a high terrace, where he worshipped the gods
in thanksgiving for accomplishing his task of slaying the monster and sub-
duing the flood.

The warrior hero

To the first historian of China, Sima Qian (*c.* 145–*c.* 186 BC), the mythical
figure of the Great God Yellow (Huang Di) symbolized the fountainhead of
Chinese culture and civilization. In the mythic narratives this deity is presented as a peace-loving culture bearer, and a warrior god who engages in
purposeful battles with a series of enemies. His battles are not described in
the rich detail of other mythologies, with their frenzy of fury and demonic
anarchy. Of the Great God Yellow it is said in the narratives that he 'took no
pleasure in war or aggression'. In one of the stories it is told how he fought
with his brother, the Great God Flame. Each had ruled half the world with
dual sovereignty, but then they contended for total supremacy. The two
brothers fought with elemental weapons. Flame used the weapon of fire and
Yellow used the weapon of water. The antithetical elements of fire and water
led to the conquest of Flame by his brother Yellow.

The Great God Yellow (Huang Di). The inscription reads: 'The Yellow Emperor created and changed a great many things; he invented weapons and the wells and fields system; he devised upper and lower garments and established palaces and houses'.

It is also related that the Great God Yellow battled with the god of war and inventor of metal weapons, Jest Much. But again Yellow had the advantage, defeating the war god's weapon of rain with his daughter's weapon of drought. In this narrative the warrior god Yellow is said to have been challenged by the god of war, so that Yellow claimed divine right for his cause.

Another of Yellow's battles was with the thunder god Awestruck (Kui). Awestruck was a god in the form of an ox, with a blue body and only one leg. His radiance shone out like the sun and moon. But the Great God Yellow coveted Awestruck's power to make his thunderous sound heard throughout the cosmos, so he killed the thunder god and used his hide to make a drum. He killed another divine creature and used his bone as a drumstick, and then he beat on his cosmic drum so that 'the sound was heard for five hundred leagues and it made the world stand in awe'.

The fourth story of the battles of the warrior god Yellow relates that he was attacked by the Four Emperors, who were the gods of the four cardinal points. Great Whitelight was the green god of the east. Flame was the scarlet god of the south. Young Brightsky was the white god of the west. Fond Care was the black god of the north. Some of these gods have been mentioned before in narratives where they have different functions and roles. This story of Yellow's battle with the Four Emperors belongs to a somewhat later tradition, when the myths had begun to be altered. In earlier myth Fond Care (Zhuan Xu) is the great sky god, and Flame is the great god who was Yellow's brother and an omnipotent god. This later myth tells how the four gods plotted against Yellow and set up their military camp outside Yellow's city walls. But in the end Yellow defeated them.

It is clear that the early myths and some of the later myths of the Great

*The thunder god
Awestruck (Kui).*

God Yellow depict him first and foremost as a warrior god who is always successful against his enemies. Later Yellow became the supreme god of the philosophical school of Daoism and of the Daoist church. He also attracted a number of minor myths and folkloric tales which, taken together, form a cycle of myths of the Great God Yellow. Most importantly, this god became the ancestral deity of Chinese civilization through the sacred history of the people who were descended from the gods, ideal rulers and great heroes.

The motif of the warrior god also emerges in the mythic narratives of the semi-divine hero Reptilian-Pawprint. He is depicted in the role of a punitive deity who chastises the god Guard Gale (Fang Feng) for arriving late at the god's first assembly of the gods. Another story relates how Reptilian-Pawprint exiled the rebellious god Common Work when the former was given the task of controlling the flood. He also executed Common Work's officer, the nine-headed serpentine god called Aide Willow who had been polluting the farmers' crops.

Another strand of myth linked to the flood story tells how Reptilian-Pawprint had to subdue the turbulent river god of the Huai River of central China. This god looked like an ape, with an upturned snout and a high forehead. He had a green body, a white head and metallic eyes, and his neck was a hundred feet long. The river god was stronger than nine elephants together. So Reptilian-Pawprint asked his own ally Seven Dawn (Geng Chen) to help him capture the rebellious river god. In the end his neck was chained with a huge rope and a metal bell was threaded through his nostril, and he was banished to a distant mountain. After this, the water in the Huai River flowed peacefully out to sea.

Gender in myth

Modern works on the subject of gender have shown that neglected female figures can be rediscovered from accounts in traditional history and literature. Also, they reveal how the role of women can be brought to life from the silence of the ancient records. This new approach to the subject of the role of women in history and culture is particularly valuable for the rediscovery of previously unknown or undervalued female figures in Chinese mythology.

Some major examples include the figure of the great sun goddess Breath Blend (Xi He). Early myth narratives relate that she was the mother of the ten suns and that she nurtured them after their day's journey through the worldly sky. Some accounts say that she was the charioteer of the sun. But her role was gradually weakened and her functions transferred to masculine figures. The singular powerful goddess was made into two males, one called Breath (Xi) and the other called Blend (He), and they were said to be in charge of regulating the agricultural calendar.

In the same way the great primeval goddess Woman Gua, who had many roles and functions as creator and saviour, later became an inferior figure who was linked to the male god Fu Xi (Prostrate Victim), and was even turned into a human rather than a divine being.

When Chinese gender myths are examined closely they yield evidence of a significant number of important female roles. These include those of creator and saviour, cosmological and calendrical regulator, dynastic and genealogical founder, punitive and amorous roles, besides those of the trickster figure and the victim. The myths of Woman Gua show her functions as primeval creator, saviour in time of catastrophe, and inaugurator of the social institution of marriage. The sun goddess has the important functions of mother of the ten suns, purifier and fertilizer of the daily suns, and regulator of daylight and night-time and the yearly calendar with the proper rotatation of her solar children. The moon goddess Ever Breath has similar functions in respect of her twelve lunar children. The other moon goddess, Ever Sublime (Chang E), is linked to the theme of immortality and rebirth as the spirit of the moon. She also plays the role of the trickster figure through her

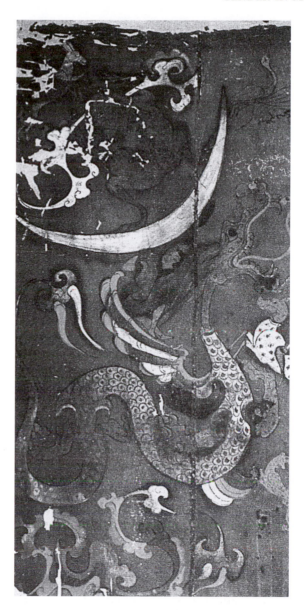

The moon goddess Ever Sublime (Chang E).

theft of the drug of immortality from her consort, the hunter god Yi the Archer.

Two female divinities have the major function of dynastic ancestress. Bamboo-slip Maid (Jian Di) gave birth to the first of the Shang people, the male god who became the divine founder of the Shang dynasty. Jiang the Originator has a similar function as the mother of the first of the Zhou people, the deity called Sovereign Millet who founded the Zhou dynasty.

The *Classic of Mountains and Seas* is a valuable source of female myths, and among the classical texts of ancient China it constitutes one of the most sympathetic in its representation of the female mythical figure. In its last

The Queen Mother of the West seated on her leopard throne, attended by the nine-tailed fox and other figures.

chapters, especially, it relates the myths of numerous female ancestors who founded a genealogical line as a goddess, and who gave birth to deities who inaugurated a people or country. Among these little-known goddesses are Thunder Foremost (Lei Zu) and Hear Omen (Ting Yao).

Another major goddess is Queen Mother of the West. The earliest descriptions portray her as a wild and merciless goddess who punishes the human world with disease and disaster. She has a tangle of hair, the fangs of a savage tigress and a panther's tail. Her guardian animals are ferocious felines. But later writers softened her image, so that she became the goddess who granted immortality to humans and a civilized monarch who grants audience to historical Chinese emperors and conducts a graceful exchange of poems, songs and courtesies with human rulers.

Fragments of mythic narrative tell briefly of goddesses whose names suggest their function as avenging and punitive deities. They include Woman Killer (Nu Qian), Woman Destroyer (Nu Mie), Woman Battleaxe (Nu Qi) and Woman Sacrificer (Nu Ji).

The opposite role of woman as victim is seen in the myth of Woman Lovely (Nu Wa) who drowned and changed into a divine bird called Sprite Guard. The basic graph or character for 'Wa' means a frog. The same role is given to Woman Deuce, who was burned to death by the ten suns and became a corpse deity. As Woman Lovely the frog goddess died and changed into a bird, so too did a figure known as god's daughter, whose full myth is not known, turn into the tree which bears her name, the Silkmulberry-of-Godsdaughter.

The mythical role of divine lover is rare in Chinese mythology compared with other mythologies, especially those of Greece and Rome. But it is told in the stellar myth of Weaver Woman (Zhi Nu) and Oxherd, who were lovers separated by god as a punishment and allowed to meet in the sky just once a year, on the Seventh Night of the Seventh Moon, when Sky River (the Milky Way) could be forded.

Two features relating to gender are significant in Chinese mythology. One is the tendency for those deities which bestow gifts of culture, such as fire or medicine, on humankind to be male. The other is that females are not the only ones to give birth to offspring. Female births already mentioned are the sun-mother, the moon-mother, and the two divine ancestresses of the historical dynasties of the Shang and the Zhou, besides some genealogical goddesses. There is also the myth of virgin birth in the Country of Women, where women bathe in a fertilizing yellow pool and then produce children, allowing only the girls to survive. Many myths relate that birth is through a male parent, as with the birth of Reptilian-Pawprint through his father's belly. Numerous genealogical myths relate that male gods gave birth to other gods, who are usually male.

Weaver Woman
(Zhi Nu) and Oxherd
meeting in the sky.

Female mythical figures are sometimes designated by their names and titles. The clearest example is the 'stopgap' name 'Nu' meaning Woman. The terms Huang and E also denote females, such as Ever Sublime (Chang E) and Sublime Grace (E Huang). The gender of other goddesses is given in their name, such as 'Mu' meaning Mother in Queen Mother of the West. The gender of other figures is recognizable through the story of their myths, such as Bamboo-slip Maid (Jian Di) and Jiang the Originator.

In general, there are fewer female than male deities in the Chinese pantheon. Yet a significant number of female divinities are superior to, or equal to, male divinities in terms of role, function and cult in antiquity. It is in the evolution of the mythological tradition, with the changing social attitudes to male and female roles in the family and in public life, that the female role begins to be displaced by the male. This trend is seen in the latter part of the classical era when myths of female figures are minimally or obscurely narrated, and when the potency of female deities is diminished in various ways by male scribes who recorded and altered the myths. By the medieval period of around AD 1100, when classical texts were being codified and printed, the history of women was being rewritten by a male academic and literary hierarchy who shaped and altered the presentation of ancient myths according to new ideological belief-systems. This anti-female bias led to the disappearance of many significant female mythical figures from the mythological record. It is the task of students of modern Chinese myth to restore them to their true position and to re-evaluate their role in the mythological repertoire.

Metamorphoses

The dividing line between immortality and mortality in Chinese mythology is blurred, and the two states of being often merge. Although the primeval deities are by nature immortal, some die a death, whether by execution, mishap or other causes. Yet the transformational powers of divinities are so mysterious and their nebulous existence is so indefinable that even after death they live on, or parts of them live on in a changed state. Metamorphosis is the final destiny of mythical figures who are said to have been killed or have died.

Many are changed into plants, birds, animals or objects. When the god of war, Jest Much, was executed, his fetters turned into a grove of maple trees. When Boast Father died of thirst, his abandoned stick became Climbton Forest (Deng Lin). The mother of a hero and statesman named Officer Govern (Yi Yin) turned into a hollow mulberry trunk floating on a swollen river when she disobeyed an order in her dream not to look back at her flooded city.

Some mythical figures became metamorphosed into stars. Assistant Counsel (Fu Yueh) was the exemplary minister of the historical Shang dynasty king Wu Ding (c. 1200–1181 BC), and he was rewarded for his wisdom and humane administration by being immortalized as a star. There is also the myth of the two quarrelling brothers, Blocking Lord (Yan Bo) and Solid Sink (Shi Chen), who were punished by being turned into stars which were always apart and never met in the sky. The story of how the two stellar lovers Weaver Woman and Oxherd became stars is not known, but their unhappy love was such a popular theme that the story was told and retold in many versions.

Major myths relate how some figures turned into animals. When the divine hero Hugefish (Gun) failed in his task of quelling the flood and was executed for stealing god's magic soil, he turned into a yellow bear (in variants, turtle or dragon). His ursinity was passed on to his miraculously born son Reptilian-Pawprint, as we have seen. When his son had grown up and begun his task of controlling the flood, he met a girl from a mountain tribe and mated with her. One day he appeared to her by mistake in his bear shape. She fled from him and turned into a stone. He pursued her and commanded her to give him their son. The stone split open and his son was born. He was named Open.

The myth of one of the lunar goddesses, Ever Sublime (Chang E), tells how she turned into a toad when she stole her consort's drug of immortality and was wafted up to the moon. Other versions of her myth relate that the toad and the hare, symbols of regeneration and ingenuity, already lived on the moon, or that the hare (in a variant, the rabbit) was the goddess's pet.

Birds are the most frequent form of metamorphosis, perhaps because their winged flight images aerial divinity. The goddess Woman Lovely, who was the daughter of the great fire god Flame, turned into a bird named Sprite Guard after she drowned. Several fragmentary myths relate that the semi-divine ideal ruler Lofty (Yao) had a son named Cinnabar Crimson (Dan Zhu) of whom he disapproved. When Lofty decided to abdicate, he passed over his own son and gave the rulership of the world to his minister Hibiscus (Shun). The myth relates that Lofty exiled his son Cinnabar Crimson (in a variant, killed him), who turned into the bird of the hot fiery south named Crimsonowl (Zhu). This is a bird of omen that foretells the banishment of officials in the district where it appears. A similar destiny is recounted in the story of Mount Drum (Gu Shan) and Awe Osprey (Qin Pei). They were two mythical beings who murdered the god Lush River (Bao Jiang) and were hacked to death by a great god for this sacrilege. They metamorphosed into birds of prey. Awe Osprey became a giant osprey with black markings, a scarlet beak and tiger claws. It is an omen of war. Mount Drum became a bird like a kite, with scarlet feet and yellow markings. It is an omen of drought. Avian metamorphosis is also related in the myth of a king of the south-western region of Shu (modern Sichuan province). His tragic story tells how this ruler, named King Watch (Wang), heard of a man who had been found as a corpse floating in the river and who had come to life again. King Watch made him his minister. Later there was a flood in his kingdom and the king could not control it. So he sent this minister to the outlying region of his kingdom to deal with the flood water. While the minister was away, the king committed adultery with his wife. But afterwards he was so full of shame that he abdicated in favour of his minister and went into self-imposed exile. The king turned into a nightjar. When people hear the call of the nightjar they say it is the soul of King Watch.

The mythic motif of metamorphosis was used by the Daoist philosopher Zhuang Zi to explain difficult ideas of relative perspective, subjectivity and objective reality. In one of his vivid explanations of these themes he narrates the myth of the fish called Fishroe (Kun) which is thousands of miles large. It changes into a bird with a wingspan measuring thousands of miles across called the Friendlybird (Peng). When Friendlybird flies, it rises three thousand miles up in the sky and it looks like clouds. As it flies it churns up the waters of the ocean for a thousand miles. It can soar for six months without resting. When it gazes down at the human world, earthly figures look like specks of dust so that a crowd of humans appears the same as a herd of wild animals.

The most majestic and lyrical narrative of metamorphosis is the myth of the semi-divine first human being named Coiled Antiquity (Pan Gu). As this giant lay dying, his human form was divinely transformed into the parts of the cosmos. His breath became the wind and clouds, his eyes became the sun and moon, his bodily fluids became rivers and rains, and his flesh the soil. From the insects on his dying body were born the first human beings, who were called 'the black-haired people', an ancient name for the Chinese people.

Metamorphosis occurs also in the myth of the primeval goddess Woman Gua. First it is told that she made seventy transformations and created all things in the world. It is also told that her guts were divinely changed and became the composite deity of ten gods called the Guts of Woman Gua. Her power was so great that her bodily parts retained their divine nature and were immortalized in another form.

There is often a symbolic relationship between the deity or mythical figure who is transformed and the newly metamorphosed state. For example, the criminals who murdered a god turned into rapacious birds of evil omen, the osprey and the kite. Similarly, the maple trees into which the god of war's fetters changed symbolize bloodshed through their brilliant red foliage. The toad into which the moon goddess changed was believed to represent regeneration because it sloughs off its old skin and appears to be reborn. In Chinese mythology the state of immortality means the state of eternal youth, and that is what the moon goddess achieved when she ate some of her consort's stolen elixir. Moreover, the moon of which she became a goddess is also a symbol of regeneration because of its cyclical waxing and waning, which appears to be a cycle of birth, full life and death, and then rebirth. The hollow mulberry trunk into which the mother of Officer Govern (Yi Yin) turned is a symbol of the womb, and the river that the mother-mulberry log floated on is an emblem of life and the waters of birth. Her son grew up and became the hero who was a loyal minister of the mythical Shang king, Tang the Conqueror.

The theme of punishment appears in many stories of metamorphosis. The god of war was punished for challenging the Great God Yellow, and Hugefish was executed for the sacrilege of theft, the same crime for which the moon goddess was turned into an ugly if immortal toad. The transformed states of Cinnabar Crimson, Awe Osprey, Mount Drum, Sprite Guard and King Watch in avian myth all fit this pattern of punitive metamorphosis.

Fabled flora and fauna

Stories relating to nature myth are an early form of unnatural natural history. The mythical bestiary and vegetal myths include divine creatures and plants that express concepts of primitive allegory. The real or imaginary features of animals and plants are shown to possess moral significance. For example, it is related that a mythical judge called Esteemed Potter (Gao Yao), whose complexion was like a peeled melon and who had a horse's muzzle, owned a sacred ram with one horn. When the judge was hearing a case, he would order his ram to butt the guilty person. The innocent were never butted by the divine creature. In the same way three marvellous plants helped the ideal ruler Lofty (Yao) during his administration of the first human government. One plant grew a new petal each day for fifteen days and then shed one petal for the next fifteen days, so that it served Lofty as a natural calendar. Another plant could not only predict an omen, but when it was placed in a hot kitchen it could cool the air by fanning its huge leaves. The third plant possessed the power of knowing who was a flatterer. When a flatterer came to Lofty's court, the plant would bend towards the imposter and point him out. It was called the Point-the-Flatterer plant.

The fabulous calendar plant of Lofty (Yao), the ideal ruler.

Great Meet (Tai Feng), the god of luck.

The most valuable source of bestial and vegetal myths is the *Classic of Mountains and Seas*. Many myths relate to birds of omen, such as the bird like a cock with a human face whose song calls its own name, 'Fu-shee!' When it appears war will break out. Another relates to a mountain animal that looks human but is covered with pig's bristles. It lives in a cave and makes a sound like chopped wood. When it appears this is an omen of military conscription.

This classic is also a valuable source for descriptions of deities. They are depicted in a great variety of ways, with pig's ears, antlers, a reptilian body, a monkey's snout, wings, horns, a bovine body, tiger claws, panther tail, and human-faced or owl-faced. Many deities are represented as hybrid beings having the physical attributes of several real or imaginary creatures. The god of chaos, Muddle Thick (Hundun), for example, has a pig-like body, feline paws and four wings, but no head or face. The god of luck, Great Meet (Tai Feng), has a human shape but is covered in fur and has a tiger's tail. The divine minister of the rebel god Common Work has a snake's body and nine human heads. The deity called Land My (Lu Wu) has the body of a tiger with nine tails, feline claws and nine human heads. The deity Sky God (Tian Shen) looks like an ox; it has eight feet, two heads and a horse's tail, and it drones

The god Land My (Lu Wu).

The god Mount Drum (Gu Shan).

like a beetle. When this god appears it is an omen of war. The god Mount Drum (Gu Shan) has a dragon's body and a human face. But after it was hacked to death in retribution for the murder of another god, it changed into a kite-like mountain pheasant with scarlet and yellow markings. When it appears this is an omen of severe drought.

The potency of these and other deities is manifested in their domination and control of the natural world and the elements. They preside over mountains and rivers, and they make their appearance known by a flash of light or a rumbling sound like thunder. Many deities are generative, and they produce fields, fertile soil and bumper harvests. They also create sunlight and rain, without which plants cannot grow. The deity Torch Shade (Zhu Yin), who lives on Mount Bell, is a calendrical figure. When his eyes open it is daylight, and when they shut darkness falls. When he blows it is winter, and when he calls out it is summer. This deity never drinks, eats or breathes, but if he does breathe there are severe gales. He is portrayed with a scarlet serpentine body which is over three hundred miles long, and he has a human face.

Emblems and attributes

Mythical creatures serve as divine emblems. Three bluebirds and felines are emblems of the goddess of plague and punishment, Queen Mother of the West, who is herself depicted with the features of a tigress and a panther's tail. Her later emblem was the nine-tailed fox. Other emblematic animals are the ram of divine intelligence associated with the mythical judge Gao Yao, the soulful nightjar of the exiled King Watch, the bear associated with the myths of Hugefish (Gun) and Reptilian-Pawprint (Yu), and the toad and hare

*The nine-tailed fox, a divine emblem
of the Queen Mother of the West.*

with the moon goddess Ever Sublime
(Chang E).

    Other natural emblems are
linked to the myths of certain deities,
such as millet with the grain deity
Sovereign Millet, red maple with Jest
Much the god of war, the owl and
turtle with the failed flood-queller
Hugefish (Gun), and the divine
avenger and bringer of rain
Responding Dragon with the Great
God Yellow. Snakes of different
colours are the attribute of many
deities. They are held in the hand,
trodden underfoot, worn in the ears
or on the head, and chewed by deities and mythical beings. Snakes also have
the function of guarding the tombs of deities and heroes who have changed
into another form.

*Responding Dragon
(Ying Long), divine
avenger and bringer
of rain.*

The world tree

The myth of the world tree is narrated in several passages of classical texts. The world tree is represented as an *axis mundi*, that is, the point where the sky and the earth meet in a vision of the perfect centre of the cosmos. The Building Tree (Jian Mu) is said to grow at the centre of the world, and it casts no shadow and releases no echo. It has green leaves, a purple trunk, black blossom and yellow fruit. It grows a thousand feet high without bearing branches, and then at its crown its branches grow into nine tanglewoods, while its roots form nine intertwining knots. Another world tree described in mythic narratives is the giant Peach Tree (Da Tao Mu) which forms a ladder to the sky. On its crown are celestial gates guarded by stern gods of punishment with their ferocious beasts who banish evil mortals trying to enter paradise. There are also the Trinity Mulberry Tree, the Seeker Tree, Accord Tree and Leaning Mulberry, which all form an *axis mundi*.

Leaning Mulberry (Fu Sang) is the most important of these mythological trees. It grows in the east and stands near Boiling Water Valley (in a variant, Warm Springs Valley). Its trunk is described as being a hundred miles

Leaning Mulberry (Fu Sang), the world tree, bearing the ten suns in its branches. Each new sun is carried to the crown of the tree by a bird in this detail of a unique funerary silk painting from Mawangdui.

high. It has the unique function of bearing the ten suns in its branches after each disc has journeyed through the sky and been rinsed and purified by its sun-mother, Breath Blend (Xi He). When the new sun for the day has been dried and revitalized, it is carried to the crown of Leaning Mulberry by a bird before it departs for its worldly passage.

The world mountain

Another form of the *axis mundi* is the world mountain. The most celebrated is the mountain range of Kunlun in the west. One of its peaks is the home of deities descending from heaven. The peak called Mount Jade (in a variant, Mount Flamingfire) is the kingdom of Queen Mother of the West. The world mountain range of Kunlun is also visited by shamans who make their ascent to the sky from its vertiginous summit and who gather the herbs of immortality from its highest slopes. This earthly paradise is full of mythical animals and plants. It is guarded by the feline beast Openbright (Kai-ming), which has nine heads with human faces that all face the east. There are also serpents, a dragon, ferocious felines and birds of prey, such as the six-headed hawk. The divine creature the Lookflesh (Shi Rou) lives there. It is a mass of flesh like an ox's liver with two eyes. When it has been eaten it grows again into the same shape. Three birds of paradise watch over Kunlun's paradise. They wear a serpent on their heads and tread a snake underfoot, and they have a scarlet snake on their breasts. They also wear armour on their heads. There are twelve marvellous trees on Kunlun, such as the Neverdie Tree of immortality, the precious Jade Tree that is guarded by a three-headed man, the Wise Man tree and the Sweet Water tree. It was on this mountain paradise that six shamans tended the corpse of the murdered god Notch Flaw and held the drug of immortality over him to revive him.

The world mountain has an important function in cosmology. In one of the Chinese creation myths the world picture is represented as a domed sky fastened to the flat earth by vast mountains, four in all. One of them, Mount Not Round, features in the catastrophe myth of the marplot Common Work. He rebelled against the power of the sky god, fought with him for supremacy and butted against the prop supporting the sky in the north, Mount Not Round. Other names for these sky props are Mount Notroundborechild, Mount Notstraight and Mount Notwhole. Their significance is not so much as an *axis mundi*, but as natural rocky blocks which keep the sky separate from the earth and so maintain the primeval process of creation.

Besides the earthly paradise of Kunlun in the mountainous west there are other utopian landscapes in descriptive mythic narratives, which are full of mythic flora and fauna. The sites of the burial places of gods and heroes are utopias. They are represented with typical mythic motifs, such as the cosmic number nine signifying the divine sky and the colour scarlet which is the emblem of life-giving power. Utopian motifs include idealized concepts of gigantic size, infinite space and vast distances. These representations create vivid pictorial images of the celestial archetype.

Strange lands and peoples

The inspiration for early Chinese writings on geography was the myth of Reptilian-Pawprint (Yu) and the flood. Some narratives describe his progress through the mythological world known as the Nine Provinces within the Four Seas. According to these accounts, as he travelled over rivers and mountains in his task of controlling the flood, he charted the land and listed the names of local tribes and customs. Early Chinese books mention numerous peoples living near the borders of the territory of the first Shang state, and then that of the Zhou, and also the greater political entity of the Han empire, the three dynasties covering the period between *c.* 1700 BC and AD 200. These peoples just beyond the borders were non-Chinese ethnic groups. They included the Tibeto-Burman Qiang of the north-west, who were probably related to the ancient Rong people from whom the Zhou evolved, and the Miao-Yao along the Yangtze River, including the Ba of Sichuan and the Man tribe of Hunan. The Tai were from the deep south, and the Yi were part of an Austro-Asiatic language group of east China. The Di were a northern people, and the Xiongnu of the north may have been linked to the ancient Scythians.

It was in the Han dynasty, around 100 BC, that the first official Chinese envoys went to foreign lands and recorded their experiences. These accounts were incorporated into the earliest historical records. Han historians maintained a reasonably unbiased viewpoint when they wrote of the customs, appearance, language and names of foreign peoples.

But travel writers of an imaginative mind set down quite different accounts of the peoples they encountered or heard of beyond the pale of Chinese civilization. Their impressions belong to mythology rather than history. They viewed foreigners negatively and often chose abusive characters or graphs with which to represent the names of foreign peoples, suggesting they were bestial or deformed. Foreigners were seen as oddly coloured, misshapen people, and this mythological expression is reflected in the names of their countries. For example, writers invented the names of Forkedtongue, Threehead, Hairy Folk, White Folk, Loppyears, Nogut, One-eyed, Oddarm and Onefoot.

But these mythological depictions may sometimes contain useful socio-logical data about an unfamiliar tribe. Names which indicate a physical deformity such as One-eyed may be explained by the social practice of inflict-ing mutilation as a punishment or as a means of tribal identification. The name Forkedtongue suggests the practice of slitting the tongue in the initia-tion rite of a shaman. Other names, such as Deepseteyes or White Folk, describe non-Chinese features. Peoples described as having two heads or dual bodies may refer to what we know as Siamese twins.

While negative representations convey deep-seated anxieties on the part of classical authors about the nature of the Chinese self in relation to the cul-tural 'other', many narratives about foreign peoples also seek to explain their origin and customs through the medium of myth. For example, there is the myth of how Piercedchest Country acquired its physical characteristic and its name. It relates that when the semi-divine Reptilian-Pawprint (Yu) convened the first assembly of the gods, one deity arrived late, so he slew him. But when he went on to control the world flood, he came to the land of the slain deity where two of the dead god's officers attacked Reptilian-Pawprint in revenge and pierced him. But he was lifted up into the sky by two dragons. The two officers realized that he had been saved by a miracle and that he was a god, so they stabbed themselves in the heart from remorse. But Reptilian-Pawprint took pity on them and revived them with the drug of immortality. Ever afterwards this people bore the mark of this episode in the form of a hole or hollow in the chest.

The myth of Oddarm Country bears the mark of a migration myth. It is told that the people of this country have only one arm, but they have three eyes which serve for daylight and darkness. They ride on piebald horses with a two-headed, brightly coloured bird perched beside them. They are good fowlers and are ingenious at finding ways to carry difficult loads on their shoulders. These people are also inventors. One of their most famous inven-

People of Piercedchest Country.

A traveller from Oddarm Country.

tions was a flying machine which used the currents of the wind. It is told that once a west wind blew their flying machines into Shang territory in the reign of Tang the Conqueror. The king feared their invention and destroyed their machines so that his people would not know about this means of travel. Later the Oddarm travellers made more flying machines and in the end the king allowed them to return home on them.

Ornithological narratives are frequent in the repertoire of Chinese myths. They tell of the Feathered Folk (Yu Min) who are hatched from eggs and are born with feathers. They are said to have a bird's beak, scarlet eyes and a white head. Several myths tell how divine birds taught humans how to survive by eating bird's eggs. The myth of human–avian hybrids called the Chief Xi (Meng Xi) relates mythic themes of the domestication of animals, of eating (sitiogony) and migration. The people of Chief Xi have a human head and a bird's body. In the beginning of their story, their founders tamed and domesticated all birds and beasts and were the first to eat eggs. When the people wanted to migrate to a better land, divine birds led them to the land of Chief Xi and showed them where to settle in the mountains, which had a plentiful supply of magnificent bamboos eight thousand feet high. The divine birds also showed them how to eat parts of the bamboo, and the people made that place their country.

The myth of the Country of Women embodies myths of gender competition, gender roles, matriarchy, virgin birth and the fertilizing power of bathing. As we have seen, it is told that the Country of Women lies north of the land of a shaman who knew the secret art of reviving a corpse. Their country was surrounded by water and beside a yellow pool. When the women bathe in this pool they become pregnant. If their child is male, the mothers do not nurture it and let it die before it reaches the age of three. Only female babies are allowed to survive. The mythic motif of the fertilizing bathe is evident also in the origin myth of the ancestress of the Shang dynasty. The motif of the colour yellow also occurs in the myth of the creation of humankind by the goddess Woman Gua who made humans out of yellow clay.

The most valuable source for myths of foreign countries and peoples is the *Classic of Mountains and Seas*. The last chapters of that book relate numerous genealogical myths, which tell how various deities gave birth to tribes and peoples and founded countries for them. For example, the Great God Foremost founded Blacktooth Country in the east, and a deity called Loppy Ears gave his name to his descendants in their own country. The hero

Reptilian-Pawprint (Yu) is said to have brought about the creation of the Hairy Folk. When one of his descendants killed a deity called Tender Human, a great god took pity on the people of Tender Human and created a country for them, and they became the Hairy Folk.

Chinese geography gradually became less mythological and more of a scientific study as speculation about the old world of gods, goddesses and heroic figures gave way to a real knowledge of the new Chinese empire of the Han and its neighbouring lands and peoples. Despite this, myths which emphasized the difference between Chinese and foreign peoples took root in the national consciousness and have endured for two millennia. These myths established the idea of a cultural hierarchy in which China enjoyed a superior status, while other countries either were given grudging approval or were relegated to the nadir of barbarism.

Continuities in the mythic tradition

Chinese writers and scholars through the centuries transmitted the mythological repertoire in much the same form as it had first been recorded in antiquity. That is, the classical books which contained the mythic narratives were preserved for the most part, and so the myths became part of the written record. That they were preserved is mainly due to Chinese scholarly reverence for the sacred canon of antiquity. Yet no individual writer or editor felt inspired to gather the mythological passages from the books of the classics and shape them into an artistic whole.

That mythic texts were preserved does not mean they stagnated once they had entered the canon and later were printed in the first published books of around AD 1000. Nor does it mean that classical myths experienced no outward change. On the contrary, later writers influenced myth in two major ways. Some writers transmitted myth by quoting it in their works, while at the same time interpreting the myth in a completely different sense from its original meaning, altering myth according to the spirit of the customs and values of their own times. This is particularly evident in the case of the first author to write a commentary to the ancient *Classic of Mountains and Seas*. He was Guo Pu (276–324), a learned scholar and a poet who was influenced by the new vogue of mysticism and alchemy in the early fourth century. He was separated from the earliest myths recorded in the classic by at least five hundred years. By his time, the old myths were no longer believed and often were not even understood. In trying to interpret them, Guo sometimes changed their basic meaning.

Other writers consciously rejected the content and meaning of the myths of antiquity and wrote critical works with the intention of disproving the acts of the gods and the superhuman feats of past heroes. The late classical writer Wang Chong (27–100) was such an author. In his essays he goes to great lengths to prove that mythic events could not have occurred. To the modern reader his arguments sometimes sound comical, since Wang supported them with occasional superstitious beliefs which are now self-evidently mistaken. Nevertheless, despite the bias and incomprehension of such authors, they preserved the myths, which became a valued part of the cultural tradition.

Although in one sense a mythic narrative becomes fixed once it is written down, it remains a flexible force in the sacred beliefs of a nation. The potency of ancient myth is expressed in many forms of Chinese culture – the arts, religion, state ritual, education, social mores, historical writing, in politics, and in the expression of national identity.

The clearest example of this is seen in literature. The nature poet Tao Yuanming (365–427) lived a little later than the interpreter of myth Guo Pu. Guo had access to a set of illustrations to the myths recorded in the *Classic of Mountains and Seas*, and he wrote a set of verses on them. Tao Yuanming wrote a famous series of thirteen poems called 'On Reading the *Classic of Mountains and Seas*', in which he described his reaction to reading the old book and looking at the illustrations to it in the form of a narrative scroll. The myths that Tao singles out for admiration are about Boast Father who raced with the sun, the doomed bird Sprite Guard who was transformed from the goddess Woman Lovely, and the warrior Heaven Punished who carried on fighting even when he had been decapitated. An interesting feature of Tao's selection of myths is that most of his figures were heroic failures. The poet was himself writing in a time of political unrest, when the Chinese court had been driven out of the ancestral heartland of the Central Plains and forced into exile south of the Yangtze River. The message the poet conveyed through his use of these myths is that it does not matter whether one wins or loses so long as one has high aspirations and is dedicated to one's cause.

The Tang poet Li He (790–816) wrote within the mythological tradition, conjuring up visions of goddesses, shamans and mystical figures. He also lived in a period of unrest, when the Tang empire (618–906) was threatened by rebellious militia. His creative spirit was revitalized by the divine world of antiquity. He describes, for example, Mount Wu with the line, 'Its emerald rocky clusters pierce high heaven', evoking the numinous haunt of goddesses and female shamans of the old culture of the Yangtze River.

The stellar myth of the unhappy love of Weaver Woman and Oxherd became a popular theme in love poetry during the Period of Disunity between the Han and the Tang (220–618). Southern poets in exile focused on the mythical figure of Weaver Woman as she waits for her one night of love and fulfilment on the Seventh Night of the Seventh Month. Her frustrated desire may be read as an allegory of political disenchantment among Southern courtier poets who longed for a return to their ancestral heartland in the north.

The myth of the goddess of the northern Luo River is commemorated in literature and in art. First represented in a rhapsody by the royal poet Cao Zhi (192–232), the river goddess is a capricious and flirtatious figure who denies the amorous desire of mortal men. Later, the painter Gu Kaizhi (c. 344–406) painted a famous narrative silk scroll telling of the doomed love between the prince and the goddess. This artistic evocation of the river goddess is based on mythic fragments, such as that presented by an early com-

Goddess of the Luo River as painted on a handscroll in the 12th century, based on the style of Gu Kaizhi (c. 344–c. 406).

mentator who related that the hunter god Yi the Archer dreamed that he had an affair with this goddess, named Fu Fei, the spirit of Luo River.

A unique silk painting has recently been discovered in the tomb of a noblewoman known as Lady Dai (Xin Chui) who died *c.* 168 BC. The site is south of the Yangtze River, at Mawangdui near Changsha in Hunan province. It is a narrative painting which tells the story of the dead woman's journey from the human world of her funeral to her eternal life in the western mountain paradise. The climax of the picture shows her immortal soul in her human form, complete with her walking stick, asking the way to the gates of heaven. Beyond the gates are the world tree of the east, with nine of its daily suns hanging out to dry, and the crescent moon in the western sky with its hare and toad and the moon goddess Ever Sublime (Chang E). The figure of a goddess reigns supreme over the cosmos, represented in the painting on three planes: a watery underworld, the human world on earth and the celestial sphere. The goddess is depicted with a serpentine tail and long flowing hair, and she glows with a divine crimson light. Around her the birds of paradise sing in heavenly harmony. The anonymous painter of this superb

Funerary silk painting from the early Han dynasty tomb of Lady Dai (Xin Chui) at Mawangdui. It relates a narrative of nine episodes (see overleaf).

EPISODE 9
(left) Above the
crescent moon
are the hare and
toad, holding
the drug of
immortality.
Below is the
figure of a young
girl, either the
moon goddess or
the immortalized
Lady Dai.
(centre below)
The bell of destiny.

EPISODE 8
Guardians of the
Gates of Heaven.

EPISODE 6
Either the owl,
symbol of death,
or the bat, symbol
of happiness.

EPISODE 4
Feline beasts
guard the sacred
chart of the skies.

EPISODE 2
The human world,
showing the
funeral feast of
Lady Dai.

*Diagram of the narrative
episodes in the funerary silk
painting (see previous page).*

EPISODE 9
(centre top)
Serpentine
female deity,
sovereign of tl
cosmos. Below
her, two birds
collect the
aroma from tl
cooked funera
feast.
(right) The
rising sun, wit
symbolic bird,
at the top of
the world tree
which holds tl
other suns.

EPISODE 7
The canopy o
the sky with
two divine
birds.

EPISODE 5
Lady Dai asks the way to
paradise, accompanied by
her three ladies-in-waiting.

EPISODE 3
The aerial sphere, symboliz
by the round jade (*bi*).

EPISODE 1
The watery underworld
where the mortal soul will
perish; a giant holds the fla
surface of the earth.

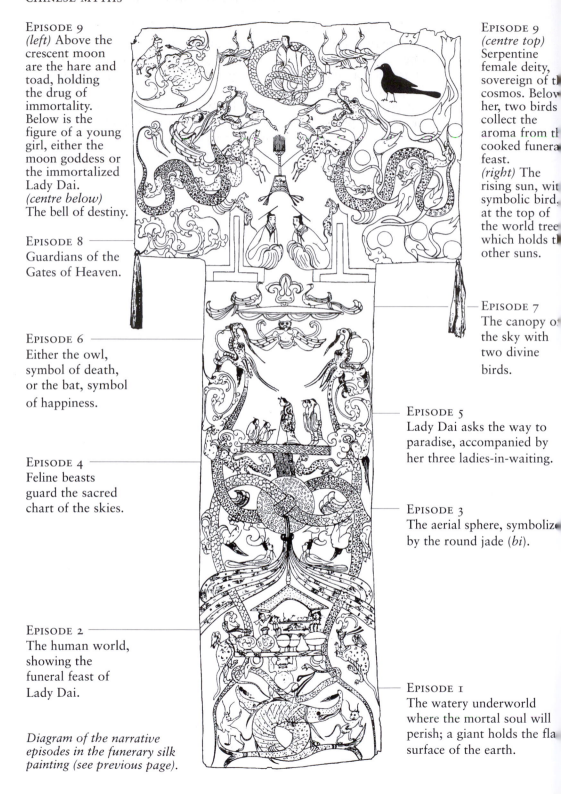

silk funeral banner has made creative use of early myth to depict the dead woman's rite of passage to paradise. For example, the figure wafted up to the moon appears to be the moon goddess, but she might also suggest the rejuvenated figure of Lady Dai as she was as a young girl. The presiding goddess at the centre of the picture appears to be the powerful creator deity Woman Gua, but she might also be Queen Mother of the West as she looks in welcome at the direction of the female figure ascending to the clouds around the moon. Since it was the custom in traditional China for tombs, coffins and funereal objects to be prepared before the death of the occupant of the tomb, it is likely that Lady Dai watched the painting taking shape and directed the painter to represent her favourite mythic stories on the banner that was eventually laid to rest on her coffin.

The ethnic myths contained in the *Classic of Mountains and Seas* originally expressed Chinese fears of the unknown lands and peoples beyond their borders. The structure of the classic is based on a mythological journey around China and to all its outlying regions in the four cardinal directions. This structure and the plot of visiting strange countries and peoples were inventively used by a late-eighteenth-century novelist named Li Ruzhen (1763–c. 1830). He translated the ancient myths into an original and amusing novel in which he satirized not foreigners but his own Chinese people. His novel, *Flowers in the Mirror*, tells how the hero travels around imaginary countries with similar or the same names as those in the ancient classic. In describing grotesque customs, manners and appearance among various peoples the hero meets, the author criticizes some of the negative national characteristics of China as he saw them, such as hypocrisy in the Country of Two-faced People, greed in the Country of Long-armed People, and excessive seriousness in the Country of Scholars. He used the Country of Women to denounce the Chinese custom of footbinding, presenting the women of that country as men and vice versa, so that it is the men who have to endure the agony of having their feet squashed into the sexually attractive shape of

The result of footbinding was a shape called the 'Golden Lotus'.

The Monkey King (Mei Hou Wang), the most familiar figure in Chinese opera.

'Golden Lotuses'. Li's reversal of gender roles was effective social satire and a fine example of the enduring power of myth to challenge traditional customs and beliefs.

Myths of divine creatures and animalian deities are vividly transmitted in Chinese culture through art and the performing arts. The most familiar figure is that of the Monkey King (Mei Hou Wang) in Chinese opera. The opera of the *Monkey King* was itself based on the sixteenth-century novel *Journey to the West*, attributed to Wu Chengen (*c.* 1506–82). The novel tells the story of a monk's pilgrimage from China to India to collect Buddhist scriptures. He is accompanied by Monkey, the main character of the novel, who is known as 'The Monkey Who is Enlightened about the State of Emptiness', and also by Pig, Sand Monk and White Horse. The opera focuses on Monkey's divine playfulness and his godlike power of metamorphosis and magical travel.

The flood myths of the classics became less important in the modern era than the stories of the world flood that were preserved in the oral traditions of minority groups in south China. Forty-nine versions of this minority flood tradition exist, which all follow a similar plot. Their myth tells of a world flood in which the human race perished except for a brother and his sister, who survived by getting into a giant gourd which floated on the surging waters. When the flood subsided the gourd came to rest on land. The couple went on to marry and found a new race of humans. The theme of sibling marriage occurs also in one of the late myths of the foundation of the institution of marriage which features an unnamed brother and his sister Woman Gua. It is not known how old the minority flood myth is, since it was recorded in writing only in the twentieth century. It is representative of the many myths of ethnic peoples absorbed into the Chinese political system over the centuries which have co-existed with the more orthodox myths of the educated elite.

Some myths became perpetuated through the potent symbolism of historical personages. For example, the tomb of the great sky god Young

The tomb of the sky god, Young Brightsky (Shao Hao).

Brightsky (Shao Hao) is located near the modern shrine to Confucius (c. 551–479 BC) at Qufu in Shandong province, near the shrine to Mencius. In the flexible way of myth, the god's tomb is placed in the east although he was an ancient god of the west.

One of the primary teachings of the Confucian school of moral philosophy was the precept of filial piety. This family ethic was first dramatized by Mencius (c. 372–c. 289 BC) in the retelling of the myth of the three trials of Hibiscus (Shun) the dutiful son. Later, passages extolling the virtue of filial piety were gathered together and produced as the book, the *Classic of Filial*

The modern shrine to Confucius.

Piety. It became a basic text for the elementary education of boys, not only in China but throughout East Asia. Its most famous teaching that is still observed in the region states, 'The greatest rule of filial piety is to honour one's parents. The second is not to disgrace one's parents.' The archaic myth of filial Hibiscus (Shun) was preserved through the writings of Mencius, encapsulated in the precept of filial piety, incorporated into the Confucian classics, and revitalized through the writings of the famous medieval scholar Zhu Xi (1130–1200) and the late medieval philosopher Wang Yangming (1472–1529).

    The flexibility and vitality of myth are seen in the way the precept of filial piety was adopted by the Taiping rebels in their revolutionary ideology in the nineteenth century. Although the xenophobic and anarchic followers of their leader, Hong Xinquan, destroyed images and temples dedicated to Confucian, Daoist and Buddhist deities and worthies, they honoured as their second moral precept (after a reverence for God, Jesus and their leader Hong) the ancient ideal of filial piety. The movement began as a violent ethnic revolt against the Manchus who had conquered China with their superior military power in 1644. The rebellion took root in the south-east and centred on the Hakka ethnic group of south China. It burnt itself out in the lower Yangtze region and was finally put down in 1860.

One of the major ways myth is perpetuated is through ritual. This process is exemplified in the magnificent imperial rite to the Altar of Heaven which began in the Han dynasty and continued into the early twentieth century. The late imperial celebration of this rite took place at the Temple of Heaven, a four-mile-square religious complex south-east of the Imperial Palace in Beijing. The temple consists of three buildings set in wooded grounds, the Altar of Heaven, the Imperial Vault of Heaven and the Hall of Prayer for Good Harvests. The rite of worship of Heaven took place at dusk on the eve of the winter solstice in December. The emperor was the celebrant as the priestly king. Clothed in the twelve-symbol dragon robe of embroidered golden silk, the emperor was carried in silence on a golden throne among a retinue of two thousand males along a yellow path symbolizing the earth. At dawn, to the sound of sacred music, he went up the three round white terraces of the Altar of Heaven, symbolizing the round dome of the sky, and worshipped the sky as his predecessors had done for two thousand years. The emperor's robe was decorated with twelve sacrificial emblems: the cosmic emblems of the sun and moon on the shoulders, the stars on the chest; and the world mountain, dragon and pheasant, the symbol of excellence, the

Part of the complex of the Temple of Heaven in Beijing.

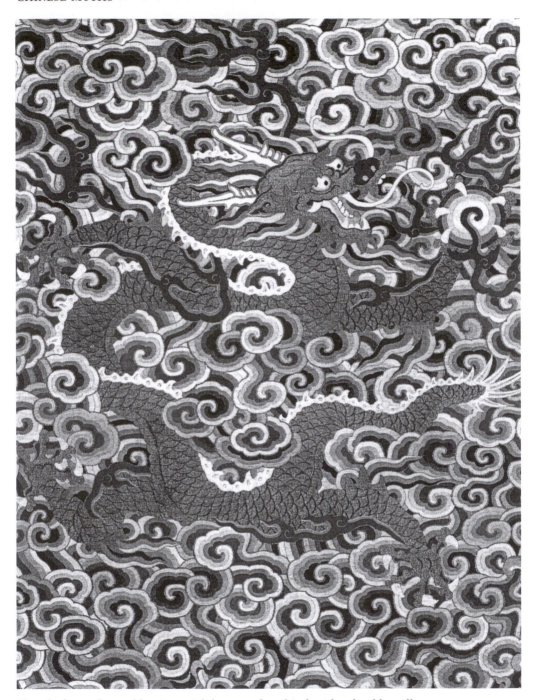

Detail of a twelve-emblem imperial dragon robe of embroidered golden silk.

punitive axe-head symbolizing justice, as well as waterweed, two chalices, fire and grains of rice, were embroidered on the body of the robe. Most of these were emblems that originated in the Han dynasty.

The mythic symbolism of the earth, the archaic idea of the four-sided world of humans beneath the sacred cupola of the sky, has remained deeply embedded in the Chinese cultural consciousness. This mythic square of earth represented China in antiquity. As people in ancient China came to learn of other countries and peoples on their borders, so Chinese writers began to develop the idea of this mythic space that was their land as surrounded by four seas and four outer wildernesses bounded by the ends of the earth. This central mythic space they called 'The Central Kingdom' or 'The Middle Kingdom'. To them this space, the Middle Kingdom (Zhong Guo), was the universe, the real world, and everything that lay outside it was beyond the pale of civilization. For the sixty million Chinese living outside China today, in other parts of Asia and in Europe and America, the idea of the homeland that is the centre of the universe is an immense source of pride, and it is one that irresistibly draws them to 'return' (*gui*), to go home to die when their lives are drawing to an end.

Resonating through Chinese culture from antiquity to the twentieth century is the powerful mythical symbolism of the Golden Age of the ideal rulers Lofty (Yao), Hibiscus (Shun) and Reptilian-Pawprint (Yu). It is manifested in politics and history. Early in China's political history the myth of

Lofty (Yao). The inscription reads: 'The God Yao, Fang Hsun, was humane like Heaven itself, and wise like a divine being; to be near him was like approaching the sun, to look at him was like gazing into clouds'.

Hibiscus (Shun). The inscription reads: 'The God Shun, Chung Hua, ploughed beyond Mount Li; in three years he had developed it'.

Lofty's abdication in favour of his unrelated worthy minister Hibiscus, passing over his hereditary son, was exploited by successful military leaders who challenged the legitimate dynasty. To war lords such as General Cao Cao (d. AD 220), the Lofty abdication myth signified the supremacy of the political doctrine of abdication over hereditary succession, even if 'abdication' in fact meant the removal of the rightful emperor from the throne by force. General Cao Cao was a usurper, and his model of appropriating the throne from the Han emperor who 'abdicated' was one that later usurpers adopted as a political and legal precedent.

The myth of the Golden Age of Lofty, Hibiscus and Reptilian-Pawprint was also appropriated by China's first historian, Sima Qian (*c.* 145–*c.* 86 BC), who traced in his *Records of the Grand Historian* the beginnings of Chinese civilization from the Age of the Gods to the Golden Age of the Ideal Rulers. So potent was his reworking of the ancient myth that the archetype of the Golden Age of the Ideal Rulers became the archetype of the first human government. For centuries thereafter historians transformed the mythical figures of Lofty, Hibiscus and Reptilian-Pawprint into real historical personages who stood at the fountainhead of Chinese culture and civilization. This archetype has endured into the modern era. Its mythological inspiration rather than its historical authenticity reflects the power of myth to affirm and re-enact the sacred history of a nation.

Suggestions for further reading

Birrell, Anne. *Chinese Mythology: An Introduction*. (1993) Baltimore: Johns Hopkins University Press, 1999.

Birrell, Anne. *The Classic of Mountains and Seas*. Penguin Classics. London: Penguin Books, 1999.

Birrell, Anne. 'Gendered Power: The Discourse on Female-Gendered Myth in the *Classic of Mountains and Seas*'. *Sino-Platonic Papers*, no. 120, July 2002, pp. 1–47.

Birrell, Anne. 'Return to the Cosmic Eternal: The Representation of a Soul's Journey to Paradise in a Chinese Funerary Painting *c*.168 BC'. *Cosmos*, vol. 13, no. 1, June 1997, pp. 3–20.

De Bary, William Theodore, Wing-tsit Chan and Burton Watson, eds. *Sources of Chinese Tradition*. 2 vols. Introduction to Oriental Civilizations. New York and London: Columbia University Press, 1964.

Hawkes, David. *The Songs of the South: An Anthology of Ancient Chinese Poems by Qu Yuan and Other Poets*. (1959). rev. edn. Penguin Classics. Harmondsworth: Penguin Books, 1985.

Karlgren, Bernhard. *The Book of Odes*, Stockholm: Museum of Far Eastern Antiquities, 1974 (poem nos 245 and 303).

Keightley, David N., ed. *The Origin of Chinese Civilization*. Studies on China, 1. Berkeley, Los Angeles and London: University of California Press, 1983.

Rawson, Jessica. *Ancient China: Art and Archaeology*. London: British Museum Publications, 1980.

Watson, Burton. *The Complete Works of Chuang Tzu*. New York: Columbia University Press, 1968.

Watson, Burton. *Records of the Grand Historian of China*. Translated from the *Shih chi of Ssu-ma Ch'ien* [*Shi ji*, Sima Qian], 2 vols. New York: Columbia University Press, 1961.

Wu Hung. *The Wu Liang Shrine*. Stanford: Stanford University Press, 1989.

Picture credits

The author and publisher acknowledge with thanks permission granted to reproduce the following illustrations, including those previously published or printed elsewhere. Every effort has been made to trace copyright holders, but if any have inadvertently been overlooked, the publisher will endeavour to make necessary corrections at the first opportunity.

p. 160: John Gilkes; *pp. 161, 170, 181, 187, 192, 200, 205, 208, 214, 218:* adapted from Noel Barnard, *Studies on the Ch'u Silk Manuscript,* 2 vols, Canberra: Australian National University, Dept of Far Eastern History, 1973, vol. 1, pp. 2–3; *pp. 163, 164, 220:* © The Trustees of the British Museum (Asia 1947.7-12.413; 1936.11-18.2; 1930.10-15.02 Add 71); *p. 165:* adapted from Edwin O. Reischauer and John K. Fairbank, *East Asia: The Great Tradition,* 2 vols, Boston: Houghton Mifflin, 1960, vol. 1, p. 46; *pp. 167, 170, 175, 176, 177, 184, 188, 190, 198, 208, 229:* after Feng Yunpeng and Feng Yunyuan, *Shi suo [Research on Stone Carvings],* Part 2, *Jin Shi suo [Research on Bronze and Stone Carvings],* 12 ch., 1821, reprinted Shanghai: Shangwu, 1934, by permission of the Syndics of Cambridge University Library; *pp. 171, 197, 199, 209, 210, 211:* after Hu Wen-huan, ed. (1596), *Shan hai jing tu [Illustrations to the Classic of Mountains and Seas],* photolithic reprint of the Ming edn of Hu, 1596, in the series Zhongguo gudai banhua zong, Shanghai: Guji, 1944, by permission of the Syndics of Cambridge University Library; *p. 172:* after Yuan Ke, *Shen hua xuan yi bai ti [One Hundred Myths: An Anthology with Translations and Annotations],* Shanghai: Cuji chubanshe, 1980, p. 2; *pp. 173, 193, 203:* after Yuan Ke, *Zhongguo shen hua chuanshuo cidian [Dictionary of Chinese Myths and Legends],* Shanghai: Cishu chubanshe, 1985, p. 20 and unnumbered front pages [16a, 20b]; *pp. 185, 215, 216:* after Yuan Ke, *Shan hai jing jiaozhu [Collated Notes to the Classic of Mountains and Seas],* Shanghai: Guji chubanshe, 1980, pp. 214, 195, 213; *pp. 201, 212, 221:* after Wenwu, eds, *Xi Han bohua [The Western Han Silk Painting],* Beijing: Wenwu, 1972, by permission of the Syndics of Cambridge University Library; *p. 202:* after Shi Yan, *Zhongguo diaosu shi tu lu [Record of Historical Chinese Carvings and Brick Illustrations],* in the series Zhongguo meishu shi tu lucongshu, Shanghai: Renmin meishu, 1983, vol. 1, p. 248, by permission of the Syndics of Cambridge University Library; *p. 222:* after An Zhimin, *Changsha xin faxian di Xi Han bohua shi tan [An Investigation into the Western Han Silk Painting Recently Discovered at Changsha],* Kaogu 1 (1973), 43–53, p. 44 (narrative explanations by Anne Birrell); *p. 223:* after Howard S. Levy, *Chinese Footbinding: The History of a Curious Erotic Custom,* New York: Bell Publishing Co., 1967, ch. 4, p. 69; *p. 224:* after 'The Monkey King', National Chinese Opera Theater [Chung-hua min-kuo kuo-chü t'uan], First North American Tour Program, Taipei: National Chinese Opera Theater, 1973–4, back cover; *pp. 225–7:* CITS (China International Tourist Service); *p. 228:* The Metropolitan Museum of Art, New York, Rogers Fund, 1932.(32.23).

Eras

Antiquity   *c.* 2000 BC–AD 300
Medieval era   *c.* AD 300–1600
Pre-modern era   *c.* 1600–1800
Modern era   *c.* 1850–

Chronology of ancient China

Late Palaeolithic 16,922 BC
Neolithic   *c.* 5500–2000 BC
Shang   ?1766–?1123 BC
Zhou   ?1123–221 BC
Han   221 BC–AD 220

Note on pronunciation

For the transliteration of Chinese names and terms the pinyin system has been used throughout, except for the familiar spelling of the Yangtze River (Yangzi in pinyin) and some original illustration captions.

Mostly the sounds of the pinyin transliteration are the same as for English, but the following differences should be noted:

Can is pronounced Tsan			Si	:	Sser
Ce	:	Tser	Xie	:	Shieh
Di	:	Dee	Xu	:	Shu
E	:	Er	Yi	:	Ee
He	:	Her	You	:	Yo
Qi	:	Chee	Yu	:	You
Qun	:	Chyun	Zhuan	:	Juan
Shi	:	Sher	Zi	:	Dzer

AZTEC and MAYA
Myths

KARL TAUBE

Acknowledgements

I am grateful to Dr Stephen Houston of Vanderbilt University, Dr Mary Ellen Miller of Yale University and Nina Shandloff, Senior Editor of the British Museum Press, for their perceptive comments and suggestions during the preparation of this book. I am indebted to Justin Kerr for generously providing the original cover photograph, and I also want to give special thanks to the Akademische Druck-und Verlagsanstalt, Graz, for granting permission to publish photographs from their fine facsimiles of Mesoamerican codices. Dr Iain Mackay of the British Museum provided much appreciated assistance with the photographic archive of the Department of Ethnography. I wish particularly to thank and credit Dr Emily Umberger of the University of Arizona, Tempe, for providing her line drawing of the Aztec Calendar Stone, and my late grandmother, Alice Wesche, for her drawing of the Maya death god ballplayer figurine. Sources for all the illustrations are cited in the picture credits on p. 311.

The direct quotes from particular colonial texts are drawn from the works of Miguel León-Portilla, Arthur J.O. Anderson and Charles E. Dibble, Dennis Tedlock, Alfred M. Tozzer, Ralph L. Roys, and Munro S. Edmonson. At times, their original text has been altered slightly in order to be consistent with the spelling and punctuation used in the present volume. Details of each of these sources are given in the suggestions for further reading on pp. 310–11.

Contents

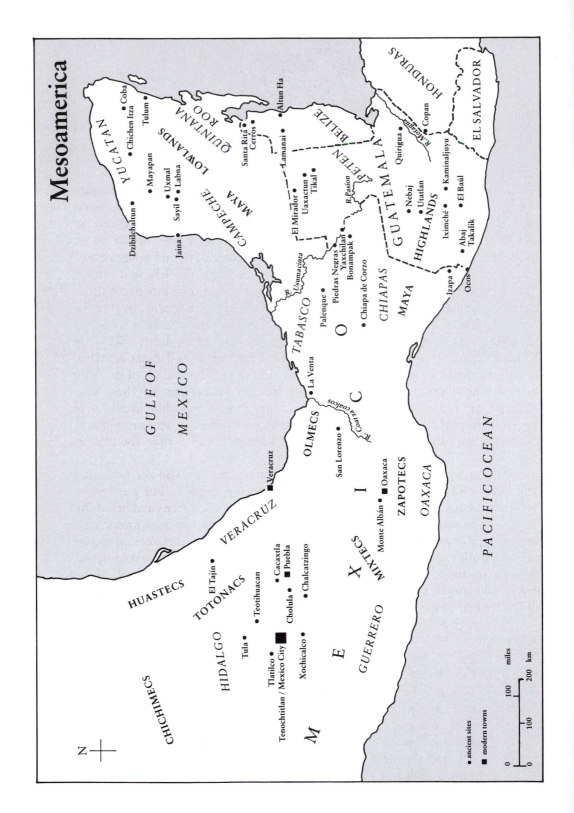

Mesoamerica

GULF OF MEXICO

PACIFIC OCEAN

CHICHIMECS

HIDALGO

HUASTECS

TOTONACS

VERACRUZ

Veracruz

Tula

Tlatilco

Tenochtitlan / Mexico City

Xochicalco

El Tajín

Teotihuacan

Cacaxtla

Cholula

Puebla

Chalcatzingo

GUERRERO

MIXTECS

Monte Albán

Oaxaca

ZAPOTECS

OAXACA

OLMECS

San Lorenzo

La Venta

R. Coatzacoalcos

TABASCO

Usumacinta

Palenque

Piedras Negras

Yaxchilán

Bonampak

Chiapa de Corzo

CHIAPAS

MAYA

Izapa

Ocós

CAMPECHE

YUCATAN

MAYA LOWLANDS

QUINTANA ROO

Dzibilchaltun

Jaina

Mayapan

Uxmal

Sayil

Labna

Chichen Itza

Tulum

Coba

Santa Rita

Cerros

Lamanai

Altun Ha

BELIZE

PETÉN

El Mirador

Uaxactun

Tikal

R. Pasión

GUATEMALA

HIGHLANDS

Nebaj

Utatlan

Iximché

Abaj Takalik

Kaminaljuyu

El Baúl

HONDURAS

R. Motagua

Quirigua

Copan

Kaminaljuyu

EL SALVADOR

ancient sites ●

modern towns ■

0   100   200 km

0   100   miles

N

238

Introduction

Although 1492 marked the initial contact between New World peoples and Renaissance Europe, it was not until the early sixteenth century that Spanish explorers first encountered major native civilisations in southern Mexico and neighbouring Central America. The peoples of this region inhabited great cities with complex forms of administration and government, employed intricate systems of writing and calendrics, and celebrated refined poetry, music, dance and art. Unfortunately, it was not sophisticated culture but the promise of gold and riches which drew the first Europeans. In 1521 the Aztec capital of Tenochtitlan was conquered and looted, and only a minute fraction of its treasures were preserved or recorded for posterity. While in Brussels in 1520, the German artist Albrecht Dürer examined Aztec material previously sent by Hernán Cortés to King Charles v: 'All the days of my life I have seen nothing that rejoiced my heart so much as these things, for I have seen among them beautiful works of art, and I marvelled at the subtle intellects of men in foreign places.' Although little understood by Dürer, these same works of art portrayed complex modes of thought no less refined than the objects themselves.

It is easy to lament the massive destruction of screenfold books, sculpture and other native works at the time of the Spanish conquest, but a far more profound cultural loss was the destruction of indigenous customs and beliefs by death and disease, slavery and mass conversion. However, although a great deal of the mythology presented in this book derives from those few precious works now carefully preserved in major museums and libraries around the world, this is by no means a description of dead gods of a vanished people; much of the mythology survives to this day in the beliefs and speech of the living descendants of the Aztecs, Maya and other native peoples of Mexico and Central America.

The region occupied by the ancient Aztec and Maya, now commonly referred to as Mesoamerica, is an area encompassing southern and eastern Mexico, all of Guatemala, Belize and El Salvador, western and southern Honduras, and the Pacific side of Central America as far south as the Nicoya Peninsula of Costa Rica. Ancient Mesoamerican peoples shared a series of cultural traits; among the most striking are two calendars of 260 and 365 days that permutate in a great cycle approximating fifty-two years, hieroglyphic writing, screenfold books and masonry ballcourts with rings. Although the peoples inhabiting this area were of many distinct cultures, often speaking mutually unintelligible languages, none the less there was widespread contact over millennia through migration, trade, conquest and pilgrimage. It is there-fore not surprising that many themes are shared between the mythologies of the Aztec, Maya and other peoples of ancient Mesoamerica.

Certain gods, symbols and mythical episodes described in this book may appear strikingly similar to Old World examples, yet they derive from indepen-dent development, and no evidence exists of any exchange between Old and New World civilisations prior to the sixteenth century. Along with all other native New World peoples, the inhabitants of Mesoamerica arrived by crossing the Bering Strait between Siberia and Alaska near the end of the Ice Age. Indeed, certain Mesoamerican beliefs, such as shamanic transformation, a lunar rabbit, and the importance of world directions and trees, do suggest a link to eastern Asia and may well have been introduced by these first immigrants, perhaps as early as the tenth millennium BC.

Ancient Mesoamerican history

In comparison with Sumer, Egypt and other early civilisations of the Old World, those of Mesoamerica are of relatively recent origin. The Olmec, the first great culture of the region, and perhaps the first to warrant the term civilisation, developed in the tropical lowlands of southern Veracruz and neigh-bouring Tabasco. By the twelfth century BC the Olmec were constructing ceremonial architecture and monumental sculpture representing a complex iconography of cosmology, gods and symbols of rulership. Like later Meso-american societies the Olmec economy depended on farming, especially maize – still the most important crop in Mesoamerica today. Another early civilisation, that of the Zapotec of highland Oaxaca, inscribed the earliest known instances of calendrics and writing in the region, and by 600 BC they were recording calendrical information of historical significance. The mountain city of Monte Albán served as the Zapotec capital for well over a thousand years. Whereas Olmec culture ended by 400 BC, the Zapotec remain one of the major native groups of contemporary Oaxaca.

The Protoclassic period (100 BC–AD 300) marks the development of com-plex urban cultures over much of ancient Mesoamerica. In the Maya region of eastern Mesoamerica, the lords of such sites as Izapa, Abaj Takalik, Kaminal-juyu, El Mirador, Uaxactun and Tikal began erecting impressive monumental art and architecture. At Izapa, in particular, many stone monuments clearly portray mythological episodes.

Although known to the Protoclassic Maya, writing achieved an especially high level of complexity and importance during the following Classic period (AD 300–900). As a result of deciphering Maya glyphs, one can today voice the actual Mayan names of gods, cities and kings. In addition, abundant texts and art graphically portray many aspects of Classic Maya mythology. Because of the artistic and architectural achievements at such sites as Palenque, Yaxchilan, Tikal and Copan, the Classic period is commonly regarded as the apex of Maya civilisation. The inhabitants of these and other sites clearly shared similar

Olmec celt figure, ground stone axe head (Museum of Mankind, London), Middle Formative period, c. 600 BC.

beliefs, although there is no evidence that the Classic Maya were ever unified in a single empire or confederation. Instead, the picture appears to be one of competing city states, and by the end of the Classic period many Maya sites had been abandoned. However, this was not the end of Maya civilisation; its greatest known epic, the *Popol Vuh*, came from the pen of a sixteenth-century Quiché Maya. Indeed, sacred narrative continues to be a vigorous tradition among modern Maya peoples, although the main focus of this book is pre-Hispanic Maya mythology.

One site in particular, which rose to prominence during the Protoclassic period in central Mexico, was known by the later Aztec as Teotihuacan, meaning 'place of those who became gods'. This is where the sun and moon were created according to the mythology of the Aztec, who named its two greatest pyramids after the sun and the moon. The largest of these, the Pyramid of the Sun, was constructed about the beginning of the Christian era. This massive structure directly overlies a natural cave – a possible reference to the emergence of people out of the earth, a well-known creation episode in later Mesoamerica. At its height in the Classic period, Teotihuacan covered over 20 square kilometres (some 8 square miles) and contained a population of perhaps 200,000. The city's plastered walls were covered with brilliant mural paintings, many of which depict gods known to the subsequent Toltec and Aztec cultures of central Mexico.

By the beginning of the Early Postclassic period (AD 900–1250), Teotihuacan, Monte Albán and many Maya sites were virtually abandoned. The central Mexican site of Tula, which dates from this period, is now known to be the legendary Tollan, the capital of the Toltecs ruled by Topiltzin Quetzalcoatl – human counterpart of the great god Quetzalcoatl. According to both central Mexican and Yucatec Mayan texts, Quetzalcoatl moved his capital to the red lands of the east, quite probably Yucatan. The site of Chichen Itza, in Yucatan, exhibits strong and specific Toltec traits, and clearly this site shared a very special relationship with Tula during the Early Postclassic period.

The Late Postclassic period (AD 1250–1521) corresponds to the cultures encountered by the Spanish in the sixteenth century, and virtually all of the

The rain god Tlaloc carrying maize. Detail of Teotihuacan mural, Classic period.

Tula, Hidalgo, the legendary Toltec city of Tollan. Early Postclassic period, c. AD 900–1250.

known surviving pre-Hispanic screenfold books date from this time. Moreover, early colonial works composed by both Spanish and native scholars provide a wealth of documentary material on Late Postclassic customs and beliefs. Whereas the Maya are best known for the Classic era, the Aztec epoch is wholly within the Late Postclassic period. The Aztec, or Culhua–Mexica as they preferred to call themselves, were relative newcomers to central Mexico. Their great island capital of Tenochtitlan – future site of Mexico City – was not founded until approximately 1345. None the less, by the time of the Spanish conquest, less than two centuries later, the Aztec had created the greatest empire known in ancient Mesoamerica.

The origins and growth of the Aztec state are strongly reflected in Aztec religion. As a means of legitimisation, the Aztec aggressively adopted the beliefs and iconography of earlier peoples. For instance, the site of Tula, the legendary Toltec capital, was accorded special prominence, and certain Aztec gods can be traced back to Tula and still earlier Teotihuacan. The Aztec also incorporated religious practices from contemporaries, including peoples of Puebla, the Gulf Coast Huastec and the Mixtec of Oaxaca. The conscious adoption of foreign customs both solidified conquest and offered cultural unification; the Aztec even had a special temple, the Coateocalli, which contained the captured images of foreign gods. Although Aztec mythology thus has many deities and themes derived from other Mesoamerican cultures, certain myths are wholly Aztec – particularly the mythic origins of Huitzilopochtli at Mount Coatepec, which served as a sacred charter for the expansion of the Aztec state.

The founding of the Aztec capital of Tenochtitlan. Codex Mendoza, f. 2r, early colonial period. In the centre stands an eagle on a flowering nopal cactus and a rock (the place-name of Tenochtitlan). According to Aztec migration accounts, the eagle and cactus served as a sign and omen for the future capital of the Aztecs.

244

The day Ce Cipactli, or 1 Caiman. As the first day of the 260-day calendar, 1 Caiman is widely associated with beginnings and creation in Mesoamerican mythology. Detail from stone box, Aztec, Late Postclassic period.

Ancient Mesoamerican religion

Calendrics

In pre-Hispanic Mesoamerica, calendrics played an essential role in mythology as well as in daily life. One of the most important cycles was the calendar of 260 days, composed of twenty consecutive day-names combined with the numerals one to thirteen. For example, a given day such as 1 Caiman was formed of two parts: the numeral 1 with the day-name Caiman. A particular day would not repeat until all 260 combinations of day-names and numerals were played out. In ancient Mesoamerica individuals, gods and even world epochs were often named by this calendrical cycle. Thus the legendary ruler of Tollan, Topiltzin Quetzalcoatl, was also named by the day 1 Reed, or Ce Acatl in the Aztec Nahuatl language. In a similar vein, many of the gods mentioned in the Maya *Popol Vuh* creation epic possess names drawn from the 260-day calendar. Although of less importance in native mythology, Mesoamericans also tracked a vague-year calendar of 365 days composed of eighteen twenty-day months with a final period of five days. The 365-day vague year ran concurrently with the 260-day cycle, with each vague year being named by a specific 260-day date. Due to the permutations of these two cycles, a particular named vague year, such as 2 Reed, would not recur until the completion of fifty-two vague years.

Still another calendrical system was favoured by the Maya and neighbouring peoples of south-eastern Mesoamerica. Known as the Long Count, this vigesimal system (based on the number twenty) consisted of a constant count of days from a mythical event in 3114 BC. Although first known among non-Maya peoples in the first century BC, this system was developed to its highest level of complexity and popularity by the Classic Maya. An abridged form of the Long Count continued in use well into the colonial period among Yucatecan-speaking peoples of the northern Maya lowlands.

In Mesoamerican thought, the calendar concerned the definition and ordering of space as well as time. Each of the twenty day-names of the 260-day calendar was oriented to a particular direction, passing in continuous counter-clockwise succession from east to north, west and finally south. Similarly, the

245

A Mesoamerican model of time and space. Gods, day-names, trees and birds are oriented to the four directions, with Xiuhtecuhtli in the centre. Codex Fejérváry-Mayer, p. 1, Late Postclassic period.

365-day years also moved in a counter-clockwise succession from year to year. Page one of the Fejérváry-Mayer Codex depicts the 260-day calendar oriented to the four directions with associated birds and trees. The central Mexican god of fire and time, Xiuhtecuhtli, stands in the centre of the scene as a warrior backed by four streams of blood. The source of this blood appears near the four birds at the outer corners of the page: it originates from the severed arm, leg, torso and head of Tezcatlipoca, one of the greatest gods of central Mexico. Although this precise mythic episode is not known from other sources, the scene suggests that the casting of Tezcatlipoca's dismembered body to the four quarters by Xiuhtecuhtli was tantamount to the creation of the calendar and directions – that is, the delineation of time and space.

Mesoamerican calendrical systems were not simply used to delineate thirteen-day weeks, twenty-day months, vague years and other periods of daily reality. They also distinguished intervals that were especially charged with sacred and often dangerous powers. The peoples of ancient Mesoamerica keenly observed the sky and used the calendar to predict solar and lunar eclipses, the cycles of the planet Venus, the apparent movements of constellations and other celestial events. To them, these occurrences were not the mechanical movements of innate celestial bodies but constituted the activities of gods, the actual recapitulation of mythical events from the time of creation. In central Mexico, the first appearance of Venus as the Morning Star was Tlahuizcalpantecuhtli, Lord of the Dawn, who battled the rising sun at the first dawning at Teotihuacan. The calendrical cycles themselves also delineated sacred moments of time. The vast majority of Classic Maya stone monuments celebrated the completion of major Long Count calendrical periods. Among the Postclassic Maya of Yucatan, the end of the 365-day vague year was an especially dangerous time and, according to the colonial *Cantares de Dzitbalché*, was equivalent to the destruction and re-creation of the world. Thus much of the imagery in the Yucatec new year rites also appears in Maya creation mythology. Similarly, the completion of the Aztec fifty-two year cycle was marked by an anxious vigil: if new fire was not successfully drilled, the terrifying star demons of darkness, the *tzitzimime*, would reassert their control over the world.

Day versus night

The contrast of night and day constitutes one of the most basic oppositions of Mesoamerican thought. Native accounts of the first dawn describe this event as the origin of the legendary and historical time of mortals, in contrast to the mythical period of creation. Thus in the Quiché Maya *Popol Vuh*, the gods and fierce beasts become stone at the first appearance of the sun. Similarly, according to one Aztec account, Tlahuizcalpantecuhtli turns into the god of stone and

The Venus god Tlahuizcalpantecuhtli attacking a watery mountain or altepetl, the Aztec term for town. Detail of Venus pages, Codex Cospi, p. 10.

cold at the first dawning at Teotihuacan. In Aztec myth, the gods were sacrificed during the dawning at Teotihuacan and, according to one version, sacred bundles were made from their remains. Both the Aztec and Maya accounts explain the origins of the later condition and appearance of the gods, who in reality were represented in inert stone sculpture or wrapped in sacred bundles.

Whereas dawn marks the daylight period of stability and order of daily mortal existence, the night corresponds to the mythic time when gods and demons come alive. According to modern peoples of Veracruz, once the sun sets, only the night stars keep rocks from turning into jaguars. In Mesoamerican belief, the night is when form-changers and other demons prowl. The dark nocturnal hours are also a special time when mortals communicate with the supernatural. During dreams, one's spirit familiar performs hazardous journeys to meet ancestors, gods and other supernatural beings. The night is also the preferred time for consuming psilocybin mushrooms, peyote, morning glory seeds and other hallucinogens in order to communicate with the spirit world. Above, in the night sky, the sacred episodes of creation are continually played out in the apparent movements of constellations and planets. Solar eclipses are especially feared, since they constitute the violent reassertion of the stars and other night beings over the day.

Although there is a contrast between the chaotic nocturnal hours and those of the day, it is by no means a simple distinction between good and evil. In Mesoamerican thought, such dualistic principles tend to be considered in complementary opposition: both are required for existence. Just as sleep is a necessary revitalising counterpart of daytime activity, the night and sacred time infuse daily reality with renewed power and force. The junctures noted in calendrical periods correspond to those times of rejuvenation when the forces of creation recur. This sacred mythic time can penetrate into daily existence through ritual and omens, and even by the presence of actual living individuals such as kings, priests and shamans, curers and twins.

Twins

Twins are commonly regarded with a certain apprehension in Mesoamerica where, much like monster births, they are feared as strange and abnormal portents of religious significance. In central Mexico the canine god Xolotl was god of both twins and deformities. According to the Dominican Fray Bartolomé de las Casas, Aztec twins posed a mortal threat to their parents and for this reason one of the pair would be slain at birth. However, the fear of twins involves more than parental well-being, for they also embody the mythic time of creation. Twins are widely found in the creation mythology of the Aztec, Maya and other Mesoamerican peoples. Quite commonly they serve as monster-slayers and culture heroes who create the environment and materials necessary for human life. But just as they are the creators of order, they are also the embodiment of conflict and change.

The Quiché Maya *Popol Vuh* contains a detailed account of the hero twins Xbalanque and Hunahpu, who descend to the underworld to avenge the deaths of their father and uncle (also twins). In central Mexico, the culture hero Quetzalcoatl is identified with twins, and the concept is even contained in his name since in Nahuatl the term *coatl* signifies both 'twin' and snake. Quetzalcoatl is often paired with Xolotl or Tezcatlipoca in Aztec creation mythology. Although not as explicit as the Quichean Hunahpu and Xbalanque, these pairings also allude to the concept of hero twins. The motif is clearly of great antiquity in the New World; aside from Mesoamerica, hero twins are commonly found in the creation mythology of neighbouring Central America, lowland South America and the American Southwest.

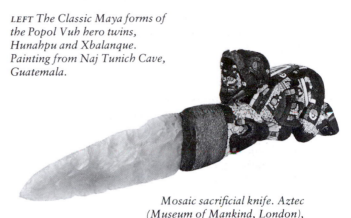

LEFT *The Classic Maya forms of the Popol Vuh hero twins, Hunahpu and Xbalanque. Painting from Naj Tunich Cave, Guatemala.*

Mosaic sacrificial knife. Aztec (Museum of Mankind, London), Late Postclassic period.

Role models and social conduct

Mesoamerican myths are more than sacred accounts of the origins of the world; they also contain profound lessons for proper behaviour. Among the most commonly mentioned vices to bring disaster or defeat are arrogance and greed. In Aztec mythology it is not the vain and wealthy Tecuciztecatl but rather the humble yet brave Nanahuatzin who eventually becomes the sun. In the *Popol Vuh*, the hero twins slay the monster bird Vucub Caquix because of his excessive pride and bragging. Arrogance and avarice are vices common to high office, and a great deal of the preserved mythology provided models for royal conduct. However, Aztec and Maya mythology also address broader and more profound matters, such as the meaning of human existence. According to the *Popol Vuh*, the gods create the present race of humans, the people of maize, to supply sustenance to the gods in the form of prayer and sacrifice. Similarly, the accounts of sacrifice of the gods at Teotihuacan and the killing of Coyolxauhqui and her brothers describe the necessity of human sacrifice for the continuity of the world. Although this continues to be the most vilified aspect of ancient Mesoamerican religion, human sacrifice arose out of a basic premise, a recognition of the active role and responsibility of people for the maintenance of cosmic balance.

Major sources and the history of research

L ike other peoples of ancient Mesoamerica, the Aztec and Maya were
literate and recorded their mythologies in a wide variety of media, including screenfold books, painted vases, carved wood and bone, and
monumental stone carving. But equally important are the accompanying images, which illustrate mythical episodes and the attributes of particular gods.

The pre-Hispanic screenfold books, commonly referred to as codices,
have been essential for the study of native religion. Sadly, only some eighteen
books in pure native style have survived. Just four Postclassic screenfold books
exist for the Maya: the Dresden, Madrid and Paris codices, and a fourth recently discovered book, the Codex Grolier. For central Mexico, there is an
especially important series of five manuscripts: the Borgia, Vaticanus B, Cospi,
Laud and Fejérváry-Mayer codices. Named after the most impressive of these
screenfold books, the Borgia Group is painted in a style typical of Late Postclassic central Mexico. However, the precise provenance of this group is unknown, and it is unlikely that they derive from a single locality. Whereas the
Codex Borgia itself may well have come from the state of Puebla, Veracruz has
been suggested for the Laud and Fejérváry-Mayer. Although these manuscripts
may have originated in regions under Aztec control, body proportions and
other conventions indicate that they were probably not painted at the Aztec
capital of Tenochtitlan. None the less, the religious meanings and content of the
Borgia Group confirm and amplify what is known for the Aztec.

The nine extant Maya and Borgia Group of codices are primarily divinatory manuscripts used with the sacred calendar. The gods usually appear in
relation to specific auguries and rarely in sequential narratives. For this reason,
these pre-Hispanic codices usually contain only tangential references to mythological episodes, with the one noteworthy exception being the poorly known
middle pages of the Codex Borgia, portions of which correspond to recorded
Aztec myths. Although these nine codices are divinatory, other pre-Hispanic
books concern mythology. An example is the obverse of the Codex Vindobonensis, which describes creation events including the origins and history of
9 Wind, the Mixtec form of Quetzalcoatl. Unfortunately, no such pre-Hispanic
manuscript survives for the Aztec or Maya. However, some colonial mythological accounts written in Latin characters seem to have been transcribed from
pre-Columbian books. According to the early colonial Quiché writer of the

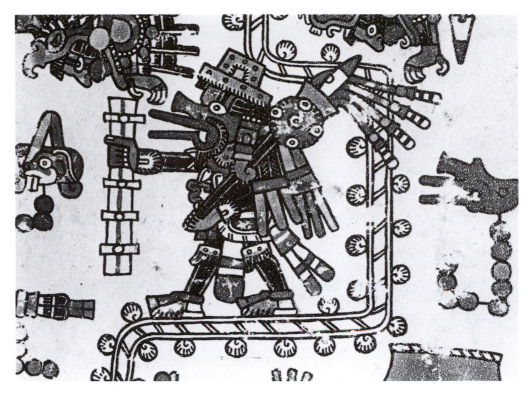

God 9 Wind, the Mixtec form of the wind god Ehecatl-Quetzalcoatl. Codex Vindobonensis, p. 48 (detail), Late Postclassic period.

Popol Vuh, this Maya manuscript derived from a lost ancient book, and certain mythological accounts pertaining to the Aztec were also transcribed from now-lost pre-Hispanic codices.

The most important sources for Aztec mythology derive not from the pre-Hispanic era, but from the early colonial period. Whereas many Spanish colonists considered the native population primarily as a source of brute labour and tribute, the Franciscan, Augustinian and Dominican religious orders saw these peoples as a utopian opportunity to create a new and better world. Rather than denigrating the ancient achievements of the Aztec, they saw these works as proof of an innate ability to achieve greatness. As humans possessing rational souls and the capacity for civilised life, the natives thus merited the attention and protection of the Church. In the writings of Bernardino de Sahagún, Juan de Torquemada, Bartolomé de las Casas and other sixteenth-century friars one can frequently discern admiration for the complexity and sophistication of pre-Hispanic civilisation. Of course, not all aspects of native culture were appreciated, and native religion in particular was considered evil and barbaric, anathema to successful conversion and the construction of the new utopian world.

Of the religious orders in sixteenth-century Mexico, or New Spain as it was then called, the Franciscans were the most prolific recorders of native customs and beliefs. The acknowledged favourites of both the Spanish Crown and Hernán Cortés, the Franciscans founded the first mission in Mexico City in 1524. Like the other religious orders, the Franciscans sought the true conversion of the natives, something that could not be achieved without a thorough knowledge of their language, customs and beliefs. Among the first successfully to study Aztec language and culture was Fray Andrés de Olmos, and he is probably the author of one of the most important accounts of Aztec creation mythology, the *Historia de los mexicanos por sus pinturas*. Still another major mythological source, the *Histoyre du Mechique*, a French copy of a lost Spanish original, may derive at least in part from the work of Olmos.

By far the most renowned chronicler of Aztec society and religion was Fray Bernardino de Sahagún. Arriving in Mexico in 1529, Sahagún devoted most of his life to the study of Aztec language and culture. Like his contemporaries, he considered many Aztec traditions evil and pernicious. In an oft-cited passage, Sahagún compares himself to a physician who must understand the origins and symptoms of a disease in order to effect a cure. However, he also wanted to record a fascinating, unique world that was rapidly disintegrating before his eyes. Along with other chroniclers of his time, Sahagún not only had access to learned old men who had spent much of their lives in pre-Hispanic Aztec society, but with the assistance of native scholars he was able to consult ancient codices. Sahagún describes with some admiration these books and their relevance for his studies:

The books they had about them were painted with figures and images in such a way that they knew and had memory of the things their ancestors had done and had left in their annals, more than a thousand years back before the arrival of the Spanish in this land.

Most of these books and writings were burned at the time of the destruction of the other idolatries, but many hidden ones which we have now seen did survive and are still kept, from which we have understood their antiquities.

Although Sahagún was a prolific scholar with many contributions to his name, his most important surviving work is the *Historia general de las cosas de Nueva España*. A massive encyclopaedia of Aztec culture accompanied by more than 1850 illustrations, this is the most comprehensive and detailed treatise on any pre-Hispanic culture. Written in both Nahuatl and Spanish, the bilingual text is composed of twelve books, each with a particular subject matter. For the study of Aztec mythology, three books are of special importance. Book One provides detailed descriptions and illustrations of the major gods, while Book Three contains some of the more important myths, including the birth of Huitzilopochtli, and the quasi-historical account of Quetzalcoatl at Tula. Although Book Three contains a tangential reference to the creation of the sun at Teotihuacan, this is described in far greater detail in Book Seven, which describes celestial phenomena and the celebrations pertaining to the end of the fifty-two-year cycle.

Not everyone in New Spain applauded the work of Sahagún. By the 1570s a growing anti-native attitude was shared by both the crown and the Franciscans. The great experiment had failed; there was no New World utopia. The native populations were being decimated by disease, forced labour and over-taxation. At least as disturbing were the growing indications that true conversion was not being achieved, and that many were returning to their idolatrous ways, often with unholy blendings of Catholic and native beliefs. In this light, religious works written in native languages were increasingly considered threats to conversion and even political stability. In 1577, Philip II presented a royal decree to confiscate the bilingual works of Sahagún. Although the first version of the *Historia general* was lost, a second copy was sent to Spain in late 1579 or early 1580. It is doubtful that Sahagún ever knew what became of his life's work,

Tezcatlipoca deity impersonator to be sacrificed during the twenty-day month of Toxcatl. Illustration from Book Two of the Florentine Codex, early colonial period.

which was suppressed and forgotten until its rediscovery in 1779. Now commonly known as the Florentine Codex, this manuscript is in the Mediceo-Laurentian Library in Florence.

Aside from the Florentine Codex there are many other central Mexican pictorial manuscripts created under Spanish patronage, and quite frequently these books were illustrated by artists familiar with pre-Hispanic conventions. The magnificent Codex Borbonicus, rendered in almost pure Aztec style, was probably painted shortly after the Spanish conquest, possibly as a guide to native calendrics and religion. Along with providing important texts describing native gods and ritual, such manuscripts as the Magliabechiano, Telleriano-Remensis and Vaticanus A codices also present detailed illustrations of costume and other attributes of major Aztec gods. The Vaticanus A, also known as the Codex Ríos, contains a unique section illustrating the levels of the sky and underworld, a version of the five suns myth, and the mythical battle between Quetzalcoatl and Tezcatlipoca at Tollan.

Although containing little illustrative material, the closest surviving equivalent to the Florentine Codex in the Maya region is the *Relación de las cosas de Yucatan*. Written by the Franciscan Fray Diego de Landa about 1566, this study also offers an encyclopaedic survey of native culture, in this case the lowland Maya of Yucatan. However, in terms of quality, content and scope this manuscript in no way approaches the work of Sahagún. A self-acknowledged book burner, Landa wrote his *Relación* in Spain during his trial for instigating the notorious 1562 *auto de fé* at Mani, during which thousands of Yucatec Maya were tortured under suspicion of idolatry. Clearly, Landa was no unbiased or sympathetic chronicler of native traditions. Although he provides valuable information concerning Yucatec Maya history, calendrics and ritual, there is virtually no reference to Maya mythology. The only noteworthy exception is a somewhat garbled reference to the flood. Unlike those of central Mexico, there are no major extant colonial Spanish texts devoted to Maya mythology.

For the Maya region, the important colonial mythological sources were written by the Maya themselves. As an aid to conversion in New Spain, the religious orders adapted the Latin alphabet to record native languages. Almost all of the god names and sacred places mentioned in this book derive from these colonial spellings. The alphabetical systems were frequently taught to youths culled from the native élite, who would then serve as teachers of church doctrine. However, it was not long before native people were recording their own traditions with the new Latin-based orthographies (spelling systems). Such is the case for the most outstanding document of Maya religion known, the *Popol Vuh* of the Quiché of highland Guatemala. For sixteenth-century central Mexico, no extant mythological account approaches the *Popol Vuh* in either complexity or scope. The original manuscript, now lost, was evidently transcribed into colonial Quiché spelling during the later half of the sixteenth century. The *Popol Vuh* probably derived from a pre-Hispanic book or series of books, augmented by Quiché oral traditions. The surviving copy of the *Popol Vuh* derives from the work of the Dominican Fray Francisco Ximénez, who between 1701 and 1703 copied and translated the manuscript into Spanish while in his parish town of Chichicastenango. Ximénez graphically describes his efforts at recording ancient Quichean culture:

It was with great reserve that these manuscripts were kept among them, with such secrecy, that neither the ancient ministers knew of it, and investigating this point, while I was in the parish of Santo Tomás Chichicastenango, I found that it was the doctrine which they first imbibed with their mother's milk, and that all of them knew of it almost by heart, and I found that they had many of these books among them.

The original Ximénez transcription and accompanying Spanish translation is now housed in the Newberry Library in Chicago.

The *Popol Vuh* is thematically divided into three major sections: the first concerns the primordial origins of the world: the second, the mythical doings of

Market day at Chichicastenango, Guatemala. In the background is the church of Santo Tomás, the parish church of Francisco Ximénez, the Dominican scholar who copied and translated the Popol Vuh.

two sets of twins and the origins of modern humans and maize; and the third, the legendary history of the Quiché, ending with a list of kings extending to 1550. The following discussion of Maya mythology describes major episodes from the first and especially second sections. In recent years, it has become increasingly apparent that the *Popol Vuh* episode of the hero twins and their descent to the underworld was present among the Classic Maya, well over six hundred years before the Spanish conquest. Thus the *Popol Vuh* serves as an essential document for understanding not only the Postclassic Quiché, but Classic Maya religion as well.

Aside from the Quichean *Popol Vuh* of highland Guatemala, another major body of early Maya mythology is known for the lowland Maya of the Yucatan Peninsula. Like their Quichean contemporaries, the colonial Yucatec Maya also began recording their traditions in a Latin-based alphabet. The most important corpus of native writings survives in a series of community books named after the native priest Chilam Balam, who prophesied the coming of the Spanish. Along with the name of the ancient prophet, each book is called by the town from which it derives. Among the most famous of these manuscripts are the Book of the Chilam Balam of Chumayel and the Book of the Chilam Balam of Tizimin, both bearing the names of communities which still exist in Yucatan.

To this day, forms of the Chilam Balam books are still being written by traditional scribes in remote communities of Quintana Roo in Mexico.

Although none of the colonial Chilam Balam manuscripts predate the eighteenth century, they often contain references to ancient myth and history probably copied from earlier colonial texts and still older screenfold books. A great many of the texts describe auguries concerned with repeating cycles of time. The repetitive nature of these cycles frequently makes for a telescoping or overlapping of time, so that a single passage can contain events pertaining to colonial, pre-Hispanic and even mythical eras. Given the strongly divinatory nature of many of these texts, it is not surprising that they are often arcane and difficult to interpret. None the less, three of the texts, found in the community books of Chumayel, Tizimin and Mani, share closely related accounts of the mythical flood and the re-creation of the world.

The early colonial Aztec also continued to create books for their own uses. Don Baltasar, a native leader of Culhuacan, was tried in 1539 for hiring a native artist to illustrate his genealogy, beginning with the emergence of his ancestors and certain gods from a sacred cave. Although this seems to have been primarily a pictorial document, the Aztec also composed Nahuatl accounts written in the new Latin-based spelling. This may have been the case with the remarkable document known as the *Leyenda de los soles*. Writing in a formal and archaic Nahuatl, the author seems to have been an Aztec trained by Franciscan schooling. Like the *Historia de los mexicanos por sus pinturas* and the *Popol Vuh*, this manuscript was probably transcribed from one or several pre-Hispanic documents. After narrating the origins of the world, people and maize, the account continues with the legend of Quetzalcoatl and Tollan, and ends with actual Aztec history. Since the final historical section is incomplete, it is unknown whether the document ended with early colonial genealogies. As in the *Popol Vuh*, the linking of such genealogies to myth was commonly used to validate lineages and ancestral rights.

The colonial recording and documentation of native traditions diminished rapidly after the sixteenth century. Many of the manuscripts mentioned were either forgotten or suppressed, and not until the mid-eighteenth century was there a renewed interest in native customs and beliefs, beginning an important period for the rediscovery of pre-Hispanic and early colonial manuscripts. The Italian Lorenzo Boturini journeyed through Mexico amassing a major collection of pre-Hispanic and sixteenth-century documents. In 1744, Spanish colonial authorities expelled Boturini and confiscated his library. Although Boturini was eventually exonerated of all charges in Spain, his precious collection remained in Mexico where it was eventually dismantled.

Following the independence of Mexico and Guatemala from Spain in the early nineteenth century, the search for manuscripts continued at an even more vigorous pace. While in Mexico from 1830 to 1840, the French physicist J. M. A. Aubin amassed a large number of early documents, many from the former Boturini collection. Taken to France, they eventually became part of the Bibliothèque Nationale in Paris. But another Frenchman, the eccentric Abbé

Charles Etienne Brasseur de Bourbourg, ranks as the most famous discoverer of colonial manuscripts. With his clerical title and charming manner, Brasseur de Bourbourg gained access to many unpublished manuscripts in Mexico, Guatemala and Spain. Although Carl Scherzer first published a Spanish version of the *Popol Vuh* in 1857, this was soon eclipsed by the 1861 Brasseur de Bourbourg edition in Quiché and French. In fact, the now widely used title *Popol Vuh* derives from the French edition. While in Spain in 1863, Brasseur de Bourbourg had the good fortune to discover the *Relación de las cosas de Yucatan* by Diego de Landa. A few years later, in 1866, he also found a major portion of the pre-Hispanic Maya Codex Madrid. Although Brasseur de Bourbourg was himself most proud of discovering the Codex Chimalpopoca, which contains the *Leyenda de los soles*, this work was previously part of the Boturini collection and had already been copied and translated by Aubin.

Brasseur de Bourbourg has been justly praised for his tireless efforts in searching out rare manuscripts, but his often fanciful interpretations were poorly received by his contemporaries and subsequent researchers. He was convinced that the pre-Hispanic and colonial documents contained hidden references to Atlantis and cataclysmic geological events. The noted nineteenth-century linguist Daniel Garrison Brinton had this to say concerning the abbé's commentary to the Troano fragment of the Codex Madrid:

It is painful not to be able to say a single word in favor of his views . . . They are so utterly wild that we are almost afraid to state them.

Although few of his interpretations have stood the test of time, Brasseur de Bourbourg deserves lasting credit for calling attention to and publishing some of the major documents pertaining to ancient Mesoamerica.

The systematic publication of the screenfold books constituted another major development in nineteenth-century studies of ancient Mesoamerican religion. From 1831 to 1846 the Irishman Edward King, Viscount Kingsborough, published his famed series *Antiquities of Mexico* at a cost of £32,000. The nine massive volumes contained colour copies by the artist Agostino Aglio of codices from England and continental Europe, including the Borgia, Dresden and the Vindobonensis. For his efforts, Lord Kingsborough died of typhus in 1837 in a debtor's prison.

Along with pre-Hispanic and colonial manuscripts, ancient sculpture and ceramics are major sources for interpreting Aztec and Maya mythology. In the early colonial period of the sixteenth century, pre-Hispanic stone sculptures were considered potent satanic threats to successful conversion. Writing in 1531, the bishop of New Spain, Juan de Zumárraga, reported destroying 20,000 idols. None the less, many sculptures survived, whether hidden in caves, on mountain tops, or even buried under the foundations of Mexico City. In 1790 two major monuments were discovered buried in the central plaza of Mexico City. After over 250 years of conversion and colonial rule, these monuments were no longer viewed as a threat. Rather than being destroyed, the newly discovered Calendar Stone and Coatlicue sculptures were treated as objects of

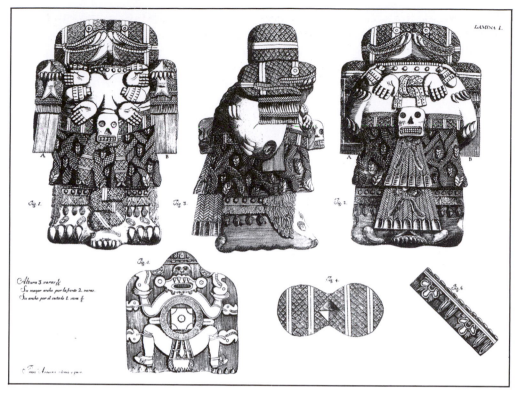

Illustration of the Coatlicue sculpture by León y Gama, first published in 1792.

curiosity and study. In 1792 Antonio de León y Gama published a detailed analysis of the two monuments, both now cornerstones of the Museo Nacional de Antropología in Mexico City.

In the Maya region, the most prolific period for the creation of monuments was not at the time of the Spanish conquest but long before, during the Classic period. The great majority of Classic Maya cities lay abandoned in forest bush, far from centres of colonial occupation. For this reason, they were largely ignored until active exploration developed near the end of the colonial period. In 1784 José Antonio Calderón reported on the Classic site of Palenque, which was subsequently visited by Antonio del Río, Guillermo Dupaix and other late colonial explorers. However, it was John Lloyd Stephens and Frederick Catherwood who first brought worldwide attention to Classic Maya antiquities. Between 1839 and 1842 Stephens and Catherwood traversed much of the Maya region and published two accounts of their journeys. Combining the engaging and vivid accounts written by Stephens and the fine illustrations of Catherwood, the volumes were extremely popular and gave rise to a future generation of explorers and researchers.

For the later half of the nineteenth century, Alfred P. Maudslay and Teobert Maler deserve special mention for their efforts in discovering and recording Maya monuments. A century later, the publications of Maudslay and

Maler continue to be indispensable sources for the study of Maya writing and religion. Inspired by the writings of Stephens, the Englishman Alfred Maudslay first visited the Maya region in 1881. During the ensuing years until 1894, Maudslay travelled to Copan, Quirigua, Palenque, Chichen Itza and other Maya sites, recording stone monuments with photographs and plaster casts. Publication of his photographs with fine drawings by Annie Hunter began in 1889, and the final work appeared in 1902 under the title *Archaeology: Biologia Centrali-Americana*. Teobert Maler, a naturalised Austrian citizen, first came to Mexico in 1865 as a soldier in the army of the ill-fated emperor Maximilian. Beginning in the 1880s, Maler recorded Maya ruins and sculpture with notes, figures, maps and, most notably, excellent photographs, labouring for months at a time through thorny brush and jungle under the most trying and difficult conditions. The only institutional support he received was from the Peabody Museum of Harvard University, which from 1901 to 1911 published a series of monographs describing his explorations in the southern Maya lowlands. Unfortunately, much of Maler's work never has been published. He died in 1917, angry, embittered and largely ignored by the new generation of Maya scholars.

With the publication of stone monuments and other remains, late-nineteenth-century scholars began to incorporate archaeological finds into the study of pre-Hispanic codices and colonial texts. Among the most brilliant was Ernst Förstemann, then chief librarian of the Royal Public Library at Dresden and caretaker of the Maya Codex Dresden. His ground-breaking research on this codex and other manuscripts provided fundamental insights into the nature of ancient Maya calendrics, mathematics and writing, including the all-important base date of 4 Ahau 8 Cumku for the great Maya Long Count, clearly an event of vast mythological importance for the ancient Maya. Förstemann's pioneering work made it possible for Joseph Goodman and others to determine the base date of 3114 BC for the present Long Count cycle. The delineation of the Long Count system also demonstrated that the majority of Maya sites and monuments dated well before the Late Postclassic period of Spanish contact.

A contemporary of Förstemann, Eduard Georg Seler was born in 1849 in what was then Prussia. Seler was one of the most brilliant and prolific scholars to work with the manuscripts and art of ancient Mexico. Along with an encyclopaedic understanding of native sources and culture, Seler possessed a keen visual eye and made many important identifications in the ancient codices and sculpture. Although Seler worked successfully with ancient Maya religion and art, he is best known for his studies of central Mexican codices, most notably the Borgia Group. Seler was generously assisted in his research by the wealthy American Joseph Florimond, who bore the papal title of Duc du Loubat. Wishing to finance not only the publication of accurate facsimiles of ancient and early colonial pictorial manuscripts but also their interpretation, Florimond founded a chair for Seler at the University of Berlin in 1899. Thanks to his support, Seler published major commentaries to four screenfold codices, the Aubin Tonalamatl, the Fejérváry-Mayer, the Vaticanus B and finally the Codex

Borgia, the last and greatest of the Seler commentaries. Many of Seler's articles appear in his five-volume collected works, the *Gesammelte Abhandlungen zur Amerikanischen Sprach-und Altertumskunde*.

The late nineteenth- and early twentieth-century regime of Porfirio Diaz marked an important period for the study of Aztec language and culture in Mexico. Many carefully edited and sumptuous volumes pertaining to Aztec history and culture derive from this epoch, including the many works of Joaquín García Icazbalceta. One of the most renowned Mexican scholars was Francisco del Paso y Troncoso, a skilled translator of Classical Nahuatl who published many important texts on Aztec religion. In 1899 he produced a facsimile edition and commentary to the most important Aztec screenfold, the Codex Borbonicus. But his major interest was the massive corpus of Sahaguntine material. Paso y Troncoso scoured the libraries of Europe in search of sixteenth-century Aztec documents. He worked in Madrid and Florence from 1892 to 1916, never once returning to Mexico. Unfortunately, a combination of factors, including the Mexican Revolution, First World War, and his own compulsive insistence on detailed notes, prevented much of his work from being adequately published.

The study of Aztec religion continued to thrive during the first half of the twentieth century, with former Seler students among the more prominent scholars, including Walter Lehmann and Walter Krickeberg. Another German, Hermann Beyer, was also strongly influenced by the approach and findings of Seler. One of Beyer's students was the Mexican Alfonso Caso, one of the greatest Mesoamerican archaeologists of the twentieth century and an expert in highland Mexican writing, calendrics and religion.

By the end of the Porfiriato, archaeological excavations were underway in many areas of Mexico. Some of the first controlled excavations in Mexico were begun in 1909 by Manuel Gamio, a student of the famed American anthropologist Franz Boas. In 1922 Gamio published a massive work on the site and present community of Teotihuacan, including his excavations at the famed Temple of Quetzalcoatl. However, the chronological relationship of the Aztecs, Toltecs and Teotihuacan was still poorly understood, and for many years Teotihuacan was considered the great Tollan of Aztec legend. In 1941 the ethnohistorian Wigberto Jiménez Moreno established that Tula was the real Tollan of the Toltecs, and it then became possible to determine the development of central Mexican culture from Teotihuacan to Tula and finally to the Aztecs.

In 1978 a massive stone monument was discovered in Mexico City at the heart of the former Aztec capital of Tenochtitlan. A representation of the slain goddess Coyolxauhqui, this monument marked the base of the most sacred Aztec structure, the great Templo Mayor, situated at the symbolic hub of the Aztec universe. From 1978 to 1982, excavations directed by Eduardo Matos Moctezuma uncovered the foundations of the Templo Mayor. The sculpture and many rich offerings found in the excavations confirmed colonial accounts that the north side of the dual temple structure was dedicated to Tlaloc, the god of rain and lightning, while the southern temple marked the shrine of Huitzilopochtli, the cult god of the Aztec. Whereas the Tlaloc half symbolised a watery mountain of sustenance, the southern half represented Coatepec, the mountain where the newly born Huitzilopochtli slew Coyolxauhqui and her four hundred brothers. In all of Mesoamerica, no archaeological project has pertained so directly to known native mythology. The Templo Mayor project constituted the dramatic excavation of Aztec myth as well as of artefacts.

During the first half of the twentieth century, the Carnegie Institution of Washington played a prominent role in Maya archaeology. With its support, major investigations were performed at Kaminaljuyu, Uaxactun, Chichen Itza and other sites in the Maya region. Sir J. Eric S. Thompson was among the prominent archaeologists affiliated with the Carnegie Institution, and for much of this century he dominated the fields of ancient Maya writing and religion. Like Seler, Thompson used his extensive knowledge of central Mexican religion to interpret Maya writing and art, and recognised the importance of recent Maya ethnography for studying pre-Hispanic Maya religion.

In their decipherment of Maya hieroglyphic writing, Thompson and his contemporaries relied heavily on the epigraphic insights of Ernst Förstemann. Ancient Maya writing was thought to deal primarily with calendrics and astronomical lore, with little concern for historical or mythological events. However, this view changed dramatically in the early 1960s with epigraphic breakthroughs by Heinrich Berlin and Tatiana Proskouriakoff, who established that Classic Maya script was not just calendrical but contained historical references to birth, accession, marriage, warfare and other human events. These episodes were not limited to humans but were also recorded for the gods in distant antiquity.

At about the same time as the discoveries of Berlin and Proskouriakoff, yet another fundamental change occurred in the study of Maya writing. The Russian epigrapher Yuri Knorozov had argued since the 1950s that ancient Maya writing was a phonetic syllabic script. Although Thompson was sharply critical of this phonetic approach, other scholars began expanding on the findings of Knorozov, and it is now widely recognised that Maya writing is strongly phonetic. The decipherment of Maya writing is continuing at a rapid pace, and each year there are new readings that shed more light on deity names, mythical events and other aspects of Maya religion.

Although Classic Maya monuments do contain references to gods and mythology, the most important source of Classic Maya myths appears on another medium – finely carved or painted ceramic vessels. Over the years these vessels have been found in controlled excavations of royal tombs, but by the 1960s vast numbers of Maya pots began appearing on the art market as the result of unfortunate aggressive looting. Suddenly there was a major but little understood corpus of elaborate narrative scenes. In 1973, archaeologist Michael D. Coe suggested that much of the vessel imagery concerns an ancestral version of the Quichean *Popol Vuh*, a detailed account of two sets of twins through their underworld journeys. Although there have been some minor modifications in the ensuing years, it is now clear that a form of the *Popol Vuh* creation epic

Late Classic Maya vase illustrating supernatural figures (Museum of Mankind, London), c. 7th century AD.

was present among the Classic Maya, with many episodes appearing on contemporaneous Maya vases.

Thanks to Sahagún and other sixteenth-century chroniclers we have excellent documentation of Aztec myth and ritual, and quite frequently a single myth can be found in several sources. The central Mexican material has also been studied intensively by trained Aztec specialists for over a century in a tradition that continues unabated to this day. However, the study of ancient Maya mythology is still in its infancy. Aside from the *Popol Vuh* there are relatively few contact-period texts pertaining to Maya myths. Moreover, ancient Maya writing and art are still being deciphered, and new texts and scenes continue to be discovered at a rapid pace. However, even at this stage of research, pre-Hispanic Maya texts and art can tell us a great deal about ancient Maya mythology, including myths not documented in the colonial record. The intricate, highly developed nature of Classic Maya writing and iconography provides us with a unique opportunity to see into a religious world some thousand years before Spanish contact.

Aztec mythology

In 1524, a scant three years after the conquest of Mexico, a group of Aztec scholars spoke with the first Franciscan missionaries to arrive in the newly founded capital of Mexico City. These were some of the words spoken by the Aztec in defence of their beliefs:

You said that we know not the Lord of the Close Vicinity, to Whom the heavens and earth belong. You said that our gods are not true gods. New words are these that you speak; because of them we are disturbed, because of them we are troubled. For our ancestors before us, who lived upon the earth, were unaccustomed to speak thus. From them we have inherited our pattern of life which in truth did they hold; in reverence they held, they honoured our gods.

This remarkable dialogue, recorded in the works of Fray Bernardino de Sahagún, marks an initial exchange between two worlds of religious thought that had developed entirely independently of one another for thousands of years.

To the Aztec, creation is the result of complementary opposition and conflict. Much like a dialogue between two individuals, the interaction and exchange between opposites constitute a creative act. The concept of inter-dependent opposition is embodied in the great creator god, **Ometeotl**, God of Duality, who resides in the uppermost thirteenth heaven of Omeyocan, Place of Duality. Possessing both the male and female creative principles, Ometeotl was also referred to as the couple **Tonacatecuhtli** and **Tonacacihuatl**, Lord and Lady of Our Sustenance. Although Ometeotl constitutes the ultimate source of all, his and her progeny of lesser but still powerful deities perform the actual deeds of creation. Since humans are the products or offspring of these younger gods, Ometeotl is something akin to our grandparents. Perhaps for this reason, and to indicate his and her primordial origins, Ometeotl is often portrayed as an aged being with a sagging lower jaw. However, old age is by no means synonymous with infirmity; among the Aztec and other Mesoamerican peoples, individuals are thought to accrue more life force in the process of ageing.

Two children of Ometeotl, **Quetzalcoatl** and **Tezcatlipoca**, play a very special role in Aztec creation mythology. Sometimes allies and sometimes adversaries, these two gods create the heavens and earth. Quetzalcoatl, the plumed serpent, is widely identified with water, fertility and, by extension, life itself. One aspect of Quetzalcoatl, Ehecatl, is the god of wind, who appears in the breath of living beings and the breezes that bring the fructifying rain clouds. Whereas Quetzalcoatl is widely portrayed as a benevolent culture hero identified with balance, harmony and life, Tezcatlipoca represents conflict and

Quetzalcoatl, the plumed serpent. The feathered body of the serpent undulates down the back (right). The human face of Quetzalcoatl projects out of a rayed solar ring (left), and it is possible that he is here portrayed as the sun of wind, or Nahui Ehecatl, the second creation in the Aztec cosmogony. Aztec stone sculpture (Museum of Mankind, London), Late Postclassic period.

change. Among the many Aztec epithets for this awesome being are 'the adversary' and 'he whose slaves we are'. The name Tezcatlipoca signifies Smoking Mirror, and this god typically appears with a smoking obsidian mirror at the back of his head and another replacing one of his feet. The smoking quality of the mirror may allude to the black obsidian glass, but it also evokes his mysterious nature, constantly changing through a cloud-like haze.

A great many other deities inhabit the Aztec pantheon, among them gods and goddesses of agriculture and rain, fire, love and pleasure, death, war and celestial bodies. A large number were worshipped over much of Late Postclassic central Mexico, and not only do they appear in Aztec manuscripts and sculpture, but also in the five pre-Hispanic books comprising the Borgia Group. The virtually ubiquitous **Tlaloc**, god of rain and lightning, can be traced back as early as the first century BC in central Mexico. In the Late Postclassic period he typically appears with goggles and a pronounced upper lip containing a set of large, jaguar-like teeth. His consort **Chalchiuhtlicue**, She of the Jade Skirt, is the water goddess of rivers and standing water. The youthful maize god, **Cinteotl**, often displays a broken line running down his face, and maize ears in his headdress. One of the more striking fertility deities is **Xipe Totec**, a deity of springtime rejuvenation and the patron of goldsmiths. He can be readily identified by his mask and suit of flayed human skin. During the Aztec twenty-day month of Tlacaxipehualiztli, men impersonated Xipe Totec by wearing the skins of sacrificial victims. The significance of this is obscure, although some interpret the skin as new spring growth covering the earth.

A number of deities concern fire, of whom the most ancient is **Huehueteotl**, the Old God; he is portrayed on incense burners as early as 500 BC in Puebla. Another important fire deity is **Xiuhtecuhtli**, the Turquoise Lord, god of time and a patron god of rulership.

Other central Mexican gods personify pleasure and lust. **Xochipilli**, the Flower Prince, overlaps considerably with the corn god, and is the patron god of pleasure and the arts. Xochipilli is also closely associated with **Macuilxochitl**, Five Flower, a god of games and gambling. The lovely goddess **Xochiquetzal**, or Flower Quetzal, is frequently distinguished by her flowery headband containing two horn-like tufts of plumes from the emerald quetzal bird. She is a goddess of the arts, physical pleasure and amorous love. The goddess **Tlazolteotl**, Filth Goddess, is associated with the consequences of lust and licentiousness. Another of her names, Tlaelquani, Eater of Excrement, expresses her identification with confession and purification; the blackened region around her mouth probably refers to this unpleasant but necessary duty. The primary god of death was **Mictlantecuhtli**, Lord of Mictlan, the dark and gloomy underworld. Frequently accompanied by his wife, **Mictlancihuatl**, he is depicted as a skeleton wearing a pleated conical cap and other vestments of paper.

A great many central Mexican gods represented the sun, the planet Venus, stars, the Milky Way galaxy and other celestial bodies. Perhaps because their permutations through the sky were viewed as cosmic battles, many were identified with war. One of the fiercest of these celestial gods was **Tlahuizcalpantecuhtli**, Lord of the Dawn, the personification of Venus as Morning Star. The first appearance of Venus as Morning Star was greatly feared in ancient Mesoamerica, since it was believed that its light could inflict great injury. Several codices in the Borgia Group contain complex astronomical tables predicting the cycles of Venus over a span of roughly 104 years. In these scenes, Tlahuizcalpantecuhtli hurls his fiery rays with a spear-thrower. **Mixcoatl**, Cloud Serpent, was another stellar god. His body is usually painted with the red and white stripes associated with captive warriors destined for sacrifice. A god of the Milky Way, Mixcoatl personified the souls of warriors that became stars at death. Among the most prominent of the sky gods is **Tonatiuh**, the sun. First known in the art of the Early Postclassic Toltec, Tonatiuh commonly appears as a weapon-wielding warrior within a rayed solar disc. Although central to the cult of war – much of its underlying ethos was to obtain captives and hearts for the sun – Tonatiuh was not the only Aztec solar war god.

The creation of heaven and earth

Like the Maya and other Mesoamerican peoples, the Aztec believed that other worlds existed before our own. According to the Aztec, there were four previous worlds or 'suns', each named by a date in the 260-day cycle and identified with a particular deity and race of humans. Along with its calendrical name, each sun was linked with earth, wind, fire or water. Each of the four elements relates not only to the nature and composition of its world, but also to its destruction. Thus, for example, the sun of earth, Nahui Ocelotl (4 Jaguar), is destroyed by jaguars, creatures closely identified with the earth and the underworld. Tezcatlipoca and Quetzalcoatl figure prominently in the four suns, as if the multiple creations and destructions are the result of cosmic battle between these two great adversaries. In addition to its representations in ancient Aztec sculpture, more than ten versions of this myth appear in colonial sources. Although the colonial documents are not consistent in the order of the various suns, two of the earliest and most important sources, the *Historia de los mexicanos por sus pinturas* and the *Leyenda de los soles*, share the same order as appears on Aztec monuments. The following version derives from these two major accounts.

Within the thirteenth heaven, the creator couple give birth to four sons. The first is the Red Tezcatlipoca, but it is the second son, the Black Tezcatlipoca, who corresponds to the Tezcatlipoca so prominent in Aztec myth. The third son is Quetzalcoatl and the fourth, Huitzilopochtli, is the patron god of the Aztecs. Together these four brothers make fire, the heavens, earth, sea and underworld, the first human couple, and the sacred calendar. The Black Tezcatlipoca rules over the first world, the sun of earth, peopled by a race of giants. So powerful are these giants that they pull up trees with their bare hands. Wielding a staff, Quetzalcoatl strikes Tezcatlipoca into the sea. Rising out of the ocean, he becomes a great jaguar, still seen today as the constellation Ursa Major, and with his return the race of giants is utterly devoured by fierce jaguars. One early source suggests that the Aztec considered the fossil remains of extinct mammoth and other great creatures found near Tenochtitlan as the bones of this ancient race.

Quetzalcoatl presides over the next creation, the sun of wind. This world is destroyed by Tezcatlipoca, who bests Quetzalcoatl by kicking him down. As a result, Quetzalcoatl and his race of people are carried off by fierce winds. The descendants of this early race can be seen as monkeys who swing and scamper high up in the forest trees. The *Leyenda de los soles* describes this world as follows:

This Sun is known as 4-Wind.
Those who lived under this second Sun were carried away by the wind. It was under the Sun 4-Wind that they all disappeared.
They were carried away by the wind. They became monkeys.
Their homes, their trees – everything was taken away by the wind.
And this sun itself was also swept away by the wind.

The rain god Tlaloc rules over the third creation, the sun of rain. This world is destroyed by Quetzalcoatl in a rain of fire – probably volcanic ash, a relatively common geological occurrence in central Mexico. The fiery rain magically transforms the people of this race into turkeys. The fourth sun, the sun of water, is presided over by the wife of Tlaloc, Chalchiuhtlicue, She of the Jade Skirt, the goddess of streams and standing water. A great flood destroys

The destruction of the sun of wind and the transformation of humans into monkeys. In the upper portion of the scene, Quetzalcoatl appears as the sun of wind encircled by a rayed solar sign. Codex Vaticanus A, f. 6r (detail), early colonial period.

BELOW *Chalchiuhtlicue, the Aztec goddess of standing water and the sun of water, Nahui Atl. Codex Borbonicus, p. 5 (detail), early colonial Aztec.*

this world, and its people are transformed into fish. So massive is the flood that the mountains are washed away, causing the heavens to crash down upon the earth.

The *Leyenda de los soles* mentions a man, Tata, and his wife Nene, who are cared for by Tezcatlipoca. Much like a New World form of Noah and his wife, they escape the flood by hiding in a hollow tree. Told by Tezcatlipoca to eat only one ear of maize apiece, they slowly nibble the grains of corn and watch the waters gradually recede. When it is finally safe to leave the tree, they see a fish – one of their unfortunate brethren, transformed by the deluge. Tempted by the promise of ready food, they create new fire with a fire drill and cook the fish. But the star gods Citlallinicue and Citlallatonac notice the smoke and call out: 'Gods, who has made fire? Who has smoked the heavens?' Immediately Tezcatlipoca descends from the sky and in a fury asks, 'What have you done, Tata? What have you all done?' In an instant he cuts off their heads and places them on their buttocks: thus were the first dogs created.

The restoration of the sky and earth

Although clearly agents in the destruction of the previous four suns, Tezcatlipoca and Quetzalcoatl are also credited with the re-creation of the heavens and earth, not as adversaries, but as allies. The *Historia de los mexicanos por sus pinturas* relates one important version in which, aided by four other deities, the four sons of the creator couple create four roads leading to the centre of the earth. With the earth thus divided into four quadrants, the eight gods raise the heavens. To help support and sustain the sky, Tezcatlipoca and Quetzalcoatl transform themselves into two enormous trees. The tree of Tezcatlipoca is marked by shining mirrors, and that of Quetzalcoatl by the plumes of the emerald quetzal bird. To reward them for their efforts, Tonacatecuhtli makes them lords of the heavens and stars; the Milky Way is their road by which they cross the starry sky.

The Aztec earth deity, Tlaltecuhtli. Detail from stone sculpture, Late Postclassic period.

In another Aztec myth of creation, Quetzalcoatl and Tezcatlipoca fashion the heavens and earth by dismembering the great earth monster, Tlaltecuhtli. Although the name Tlaltecuhtli means Earth Lord, this being is actually dually sexed and is often described as female. Tlaltecuhtli sometimes merges with another earth monster, a great caiman whose spiny crocodilian back forms the mountain ridges of the world. The Tlaltecuhtli myth was widespread in Mesoamerica, and a form was present among the Maya of Yucatan.

In one Aztec version appearing in the *Histoyre du Mechique*, Quetzalcoatl and Tezcatlipoca descend from the sky to observe Tlaltecuhtli striding upon the sea. So fierce is her desire for flesh that not only does she have a great toothy maw, but also gnashing mouths at her elbows, knees and other joints. Quetzalcoatl and Tezcatlipoca agree that creation cannot be completed with such a horrendous beast in their midst. To create the earth, therefore, Quetzalcoatl and Tezcatlipoca transform themselves into two great serpents. One snake seizes the left hand and right foot of Tlaltecuhtli and the other her right hand and left foot, and between them they tear the monster apart. The upper portion of her body then becomes the earth, while the other half is thrown into the sky to create the heavens.

The violent slaying and dismemberment of Tlaltecuhtli angers the other gods. To console the mutilated earth, they decree that all plants needed for human life will derive from her body. From her hair are fashioned trees, flowers and herbs, and from her skin come the grasses and smaller flowers. Her eyes are the source of wells, springs and small caves; her mouth, great rivers and caverns; and her nose, mountain ridges and valleys. At times, the earth goddess can still be heard screaming in the night for the blood and hearts of people. Ultimately, only sacrificial flesh and blood can soothe and quiet Tlaltecuhtli sufficiently to keep her producing the fruits needed for human life.

The origin of people

The gods decide, having refashioned the world, that people are needed to repopulate the earth. A number of colonial accounts describe the creation of the present race of humans; the following version derives from the *Leyenda de los soles* and the *Histoyre du Mechique*. It is agreed that the god of wind, Quetzalcoatl, must go to the underworld to retrieve the human bones of the last creation, the race turned into fish by the flood. The underworld, a dangerous place known as Mictlan, is ruled by the devious skeletal god Mictlantecuhtli, Lord of Mictlan. Once in the underworld, Quetzalcoatl asks Mictlantecuhtli and his wife for the bones of the ancestors:

And then Quetzalcoatl went to Mictlan. He approached Mictlantecuhtli and Mictlancihuatl; at once he spoke to them:
'I come in search of the precious bones in your possession. I have come for them.'
And Mictlantecuhtli asked of him, 'What shall you do with them, Quetzalcoatl?'
And once again Quetzalcoatl said, 'The gods are anxious that someone should inhabit the earth.'

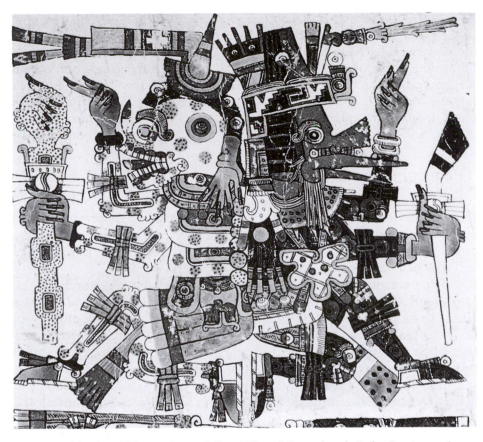

The gods of death and life, Mictlantecuhtli and Ehecatl-Quetzalcoatl. Codex Borgia, p. 56 (detail), Late Postclassic period.

The crafty god of death agrees to give up the bones, provided that Quetzalcoatl can fulfil an apparently simple task. He tells Quetzalcoatl to travel around his underworld realm four times while sounding a conch shell trumpet. However, instead of a shell trumpet, Mictlantecuhtli gives Quetzalcoatl a simple conch with no holes. Not to be outsmarted, Quetzalcoatl calls upon worms to drill holes in the shell and for bees to enter the trumpet and make it roar. (As an emblem of his powers of wind and life, Quetzalcoatl is often depicted wearing the cut conch Wind Jewel on his chest.)

Hearing the conch blast, Mictlantecuhtli first allows Quetzalcoatl to take the bones of the last creation but quickly changes his mind. However, Quetzalcoatl again outwits Mictlantecuhtli and his underworld minions, and escapes with the bones. The enraged Mictlantecuhtli then commands his followers to make a deep pit. As Quetzalcoatl runs towards it, a quail bursts out and startles him, causing him to stumble into the hole.

The pit having been made, Quetzalcoatl fell in it, he stumbled and was frightened by the quail. He fell dead and the precious bones were scattered. The quail chewed and gnawed on them.

Although Quetzalcoatl eventually revives and retrieves the bones, they are now broken, and for this reason people today are of different sizes. Having escaped the underworld, Quetzalcoatl carries the precious load to Tamoanchan, a miraculous place of origin. There the old goddess Cihuacoatl, or Woman Serpent, grinds the bones into a flour-like meal which she places in a special ceramic container. The gods gather around this vessel and shed drops of their blood upon the ground bones, and from the bones of the fish people mixed with the penitential blood of the gods, the present race of humans are born.

The origin of maize

Although people thus returned to the surface of the earth, they still required food to give them sustenance and strength. While there are several distinct myths describing the origins of maize and other cultivated plants, one of the most important appears in the *Leyenda de los soles*. Versions of this myth are still known today in many regions of Mexico and Guatemala.

After creating people at Tamoanchan, all the gods go in search of their future food. Quetzalcoatl spies a red ant carrying a grain of maize, and asks him where he found this wondrous food. The ant refuses to tell, but after much bullying agrees to take Quetzalcoatl to the source, Mount Tonacatepetl, Mountain of Sustenance. Transforming himself into a black ant, Quetzalcoatl squeezes through the narrow opening and follows the red ant deep into the stony mountain to a chamber filled with seed and grain. Taking some kernels of maize, Quetzalcoatl returns to Tamoanchan. The gods chew the maize and place the mash in the mouths of the infant humans to give them strength.

They then ask, 'What are we going to do with Tonacatepetl?' Quetzalcoatl slings a rope around the mountain and tries to carry it off, but the mountain is too large to lift. Then the old diviner couple, Oxomoco and Cipactonal, cast lots to determine how to acquire the seeds of Tonacatepetl. The couple divines that the diseased god Nanahuatzin must break open the rock of sustenance, so, with the help of the four directional gods of rain and lightning, the blue, white, yellow and red Tlalocs, Nanahuatzin splits Tonacatepetl wide open, causing the maize kernels and other seeds to scatter in all directions. The Tlalocs quickly

Tlaloc pouring out water and crops from a precious jade jar. Detail of Aztec stone box (Museum of Mankind, London), Late Postclassic period.

271

snatch up seeds of white, black, yellow and red maize, as well as those of beans and other edible plants. Having obtained the seeds at Tonacatepetl, the Tlalocs are the real dispensers of crops as well as rain.

The origin of pulque

An alcoholic beverage made from the fermented sap of the maguey plant, pulque played a major role in Aztec ceremonial life both as a ritual drink and a sacrificial offering. Pulque was often drunk at banquets and festivals, although public intoxication was strongly condemned, particularly for those of noble birth. The mythic origins of pulque are described in one major source, the *Histoyre du Mechique*, which contains one of the few mythical references to the horrific *tzitzimime* (singular *tzitzimitl*), celestial demons of darkness that continually threaten to destroy the world. These night demons, often female, are

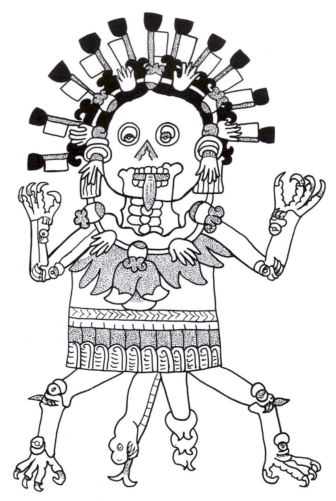

A female tzitzimitl demon. Codex Magliabechiano, p. 76r, early colonial Aztec.

the stars that do battle against the sun at every dusk and dawn.

Although humans had been provided with seeds from which to make food, there was little in their lives to inspire pleasure or joy. The gods conclude that something is needed to make people sing and dance. Quetzalcoatl decides that intoxicating drink will bring pleasure to people's lives, and he recalls Mayahuel, the lovely young goddess of maguey, who lives in the sky with her fearsome *tzitzimitl* grandmother. Finding the virgin Mayahuel asleep, Quetzalcoatl wakes her and persuades the goddess to descend with him to earth. There they join themselves into a great forked tree, with Quetzalcoatl as one branch and Mayahuel the other.

Awakening to find Mayahuel missing, the enraged grandmother calls upon her fellow *tzitzimime* star demons to find her errant granddaughter. The furious *tzitzimime* dive headlong from the sky to the tree where Quetzalcoatl and Mayahuel are hidden. Just as they arrive, the tree splits in half and the two branches crash to the ground. The grandmother *tzitzimitl* recognises the branch of Mayahuel and, savagely tearing it apart, she passes parts of her granddaughter to all the other *tzitzimime* to devour. But the branch of Quetzalcoatl is left untouched and unharmed, and once the *tzitzimime* return to the sky, Quetzalcoatl turns back into his actual form. Sadly gathering the gnawed bones of Mayahuel, Quetzalcoatl buries them in the earth, and from this simple grave grew the first maguey plant, the miraculous source of pulque.

The creation of the fifth sun

The creation of the fifth sun, Nahui Ollin, comprises the climactic end to the epic of creation. For the Aztecs, this occurred at the ancient city of Teotihuacan, located some 40 kilometres (25 miles) north-east of Mexico City, and they considered this the place where time began. The following account derives from two principal sources, the Florentine Codex and the *Leyenda de los soles*.

After the creation of the earth, people, and their food and drink, the gods convened in darkness at Teotihuacan to decide who will be the new sun to light the world:

It is told that when yet all was in darkness, when yet no sun had shone and no dawn had broken – it is said – the gods gathered themselves together and took counsel among themselves there at Teotihuacan. They spoke; they said among themselves:
'Come hither, O gods! Who will carry the burden? Who will take it upon himself to be the sun, to bring the dawn?'

A haughty god named Tecuciztecatl quickly volunteers, but the other gods elect the humble and diseased Nanahuatzin (who had split the rock of sustenance to get maize) as a second contender. Like a warrior, he stoically accepts this as his duty and debt to the other gods. Two hills are made for Tecuciztecatl and Nanahuatzin to fast and do penance while the sacrificial pyre is prepared, and these can still be seen today as the Pyramids of the Sun and Moon. The offerings that Tecuciztecatl presents during his fast and vigil are of the finest and most costly materials. Instead of fir boughs he has quetzal plumes, and gold balls serve as his bundles of bound grass. In place of maguey spines spotted with his own blood, he offers awls of jade tipped with red coral. The incense burned by Tecuciztecatl is also of the rarest and finest quality. The offerings of Nanahuatzin, however, are of little material value. For his fir branches and grass balls he uses bundles of reeds, and he offers real maguey spines with his own blood. For his incense, he burns scabs picked from his body.

At midnight after four days of penance, the gods dress the two and whereas Tecuciztecatl is richly adorned, Nanahuatzin wears only simple vestments of paper. The gods then encircle the great sacrificial pyre, which has been burning for four days and is now fiercely hot. Standing along both sides of the fire, the gods call for Tecuciztecatl to jump into the flames. Tecuciztecatl runs towards the pyre, but the heat and searing flames terrify him and he falters. Once more he tries, and once again he is halted by the fire. Four times he runs towards the fire, but every time he wavers and stops. Finally, the gods call out for Nanahuatzin, and in an instant he runs and jumps into the fire:

And Nanahuatzin, daring all at once, determined – resolved – hardened his heart, and shut firmly his eyes. He had no fear; he did not stop short; he did not falter in fright; he did not turn back. All at once he quickly threw and cast himself into the fire; once and for all he went. Thereupon he burned; his body crackled and sizzled.

Seeing the heroic death of Nanahuatzin, Tecuciztecatl follows him into the flames and dies, and after him, the eagle and jaguar also dive into the pyre. The tips of the eagle's feathers are scorched black, and the jaguar's pelt is smudged with black spots. Because of their bravery at Teotihuacan, the eagle and jaguar became the two great military orders of Aztec warriors.

After the fiery deaths of Nanahuatzin and Tecuciztecatl, the gods wait and look to see where they might reappear. Gradually, the sky begins to redden in all directions. The gods peer and turn their heads, craning to see where brave Nanahuatzin will first emerge. Some rightly guess that Nanahuatzin will appear in the east, and pointing in that direction, they are the first to witness him emerge. No longer sickly and humble, Nanahuatzin returns rising as Tonatiuh, the fiery sun god whose rays shoot out in all directions:

And when the sun came to rise, when he burst forth, he appeared to be red; he kept swaying from side to side. It was impossible to look into his face; he blinded one with his light.

Soon after, Tecuciztecatl also rises in the east, just as brightly as Tonatiuh. So similar are the two that the other gods worry that the world will be too bright. One of the gods runs out and throws a rabbit in the face of Tecuciztecatl. Thus wounded, the face of the moon is dimmer than the sun, and during full moons, the rabbit can be seen seated in the face of the moon.

Although the sun and moon thus appear, they do not follow their paths but instead hover motionless in the sky. Tonatiuh demands the fealty and blood of the other gods before he will move. Infuriated by this arrogance, the god of the morning star known as Tlahuizcalpantecuhtli, Lord of the Dawn, shoots a dart at the sun. However, the dart misses its mark, and the sun throws his own

ABOVE *The Aztec Calendar Stone. The centre contains the date Nahui Ollin, the current sun of motion created at the site of Teotihuacan. The calendric names of the four previous creations appear within the four flanges of the Ollin sign. Aztec (Museo Nacional de Antropología, Mexico City), Late Postclassic period.*

Itztlacoliuhqui with a dart piercing his forehead. The morning star, Lord of the Dawn, is transformed into the god of stone and cold by the sun's dart. Codex Telleriano-Remensis, f. 16, early colonial Aztec.

275

back at the morning star, piercing Tlahuizcalpantecuhtli through the head. At this moment, the Lord of the Dawn is transformed into the god of stone and coldness, Itztlacoliuhqui, and for this reason it is always cold at the time of the dawn. The gods finally agree that they must sacrifice themselves to make the sun move. Methodically, one by one, Quetzalcoatl cuts the hearts out of each god with a sacrificial blade. The mantles and finery of the dead gods are wrapped up in sacred bundles, the form in which they are then worshipped by people. From the slaying of the gods at Teotihuacan, the Sun of Motion, Nahui Ollin, is created. Just as the gods had to sacrifice themselves, so humans must supply their own hearts and blood to ensure that the fifth sun continues to move in its path.

Mythology of the Aztec state

The Aztec myths of the five suns and of the creation of the present world, humans, maize and pulque were surely known over much of Postclassic central Mexico. Much of this mythology is very old, and probably developed out of earlier Classic period traditions. For example, a Late Classic period version of the creation of people from the remains of the last creation is represented at the Late Classic site of El Tajín, in Veracruz. In this scene, Tlaloc bleeds his member upon a dead fish-man, a reference to the race of people turned into fish by the flood.

Although the Late Postclassic creation mythology of central Mexico bears many similarities to other myths of ancient and contemporary Mesoamerica, there is another creation epic that is wholly Aztec, essentially serving as the state

Tlaloc letting blood upon a fish-man. This scene may illustrate an early version of the creation of people. Detail of bas-relief from South Ballcourt, El Tajín, Veracruz, Late Classic period.

Huitzilopochtli letting blood from his ear. A hummingbird headdress projects up from behind his right hand. Detail from colossal jaguar sculpture, Aztec (Museo Nacional de Antropología, Mexico City), Late Postclassic period.

mythology of the developing Aztec empire. This concerns the origins of **Huitzilopochtli**, Hummingbird on the Left, cult god of the Aztec people. Like the mythology that surrounds him, Huitzilopochtli seems to be an entirely Aztec innovation. Possessing attributes of Tezcatlipoca, the star god Mixcoatl and the fire god Xiuhtecuhtli, Huitzilopochtli is a solar deity whose symbolic domain overlaps considerably with that of Tonatiuh. Although of central importance to the Aztec, it is unlikely that Huitzilopochtli enjoyed a widespread and enthusiastic following outside the Valley of Mexico. Indeed, representations of him are notably rare in the art of ancient Mesoamerica.

The birth of Huitzilopochtli

Colonial accounts describing the origin of Huitzilopochtli are numerous and varied but in many versions his birth occurred at Coatepec, Serpent Mountain, a hill located near the ancient city of Tula. According to the *Historia de los mexicanos por sus pinturas* the Aztecs returned to Coatepec every year to celebrate a feast in honour of Huitzilopochtli. All the major deities in this creation epic are specific to the Aztec pantheon, and are not found among other peoples of Late Postclassic central Mexico. The mother of Huitzilopochtli, **Coatlicue**, She of the Serpent Skirt, is readily identified by her skirt of woven snakes. **Coyolxauhqui**, the half-sister of Huitzilopochtli, is partly derived from **Chantico**, an obscure central Mexican fire goddess. The name Coyolxauhqui means Painted with Bells, and she typically displays a pair of metal bells on her

Coatlicue, She of the Serpent Skirt, the mother of Huitzilopochtli. Snakes representing blood emerge from the severed stumps of her arms and throat, indicating that she has been slain. Aztec (Museo Nacional de Antropología, Mexico City), Late Postclassic period.

cheeks. She is accompanied by a multitude of brothers known as the **Centzon Huitznahua,** the Four Hundred (or innumerable) Southerners, who are thematically related to the four hundred pulque gods of Aztec belief. The most thorough accounts of the birth of Huitzilopochtli at Coatepec appear in the works of Sahagún. The following account derives from Book Three of the Florentine Codex.

One day while performing penance and sweeping at Coatepec, the chaste and pious Coatlicue discovers a ball of feathers. Wanting to save the precious feathers, Coatlicue places them in her waistband. However, when she later looks for the ball of feathers, it is gone. Unknown to her at the time, the feathers had impregnated her with the seed of Huitzilopochtli. Gradually Coatlicue grows in size until her sons, the Centzon Huitznahua, notice that she is with child.

Enraged and shamed, they furiously demand to know the father. Their elder sister, Coyolxauhqui, decides that they must slay their mother:

And their elder sister, Coyolxauhqui, said to them:
    'My elder brothers, she hath dishonored us. We can only kill our mother, the wicked one who is already with child. Who is the cause of what is in her womb?'

The news of her children's intentions terrifies the pregnant goddess, but the child within her womb consoles Coatlicue, assuring her that he is already aware and ready. Dressed in the raiment of warriors, the Centzon Huitznahua follow Coyolxauhqui to Coatepec. When her raging children reach the crest of the mountain, Coatlicue gives birth to Huitzilopochtli fully armed. Wielding his burning weapon, known as the Xiuhcoatl or Turquoise Serpent, he slays Coyolxauhqui and, cut to pieces, her body tumbles to the base of Coatepec.

Then he pierced Coyolxauhqui, and then quickly struck off her head. It stopped there at the edge of Coatepetl [Coatepec]. And her body came falling below; it fell breaking to pieces; in various places her arms, her legs, her body each fell.

Having killed Coyolxauhqui, Huitzilopochtli chases the Centzon Huitznahua around Coatepec and slays vast numbers of his half-brothers, with only a few escaping to the south.

Eduard Seler suggested at the turn of this century that the birth of Huitzilopochtli at Coatepec represents the dawning sun fighting off the gods of darkness. With his Xiuhcoatl fire serpent, Huitzilopochtli is the newly born sun shooting out burning rays and, clearly enough, the Centzon Huitznahua are the stars who at every dawn are vanquished by the rising sun. However, the precise cosmological identity of Coyolxauhqui is still unknown. Although Seler suggested that she is the moon, she bears no obvious lunar attributes, and according to Carmen Aguilera, she may represent another astronomical body of the night sky: the Milky Way.

As well as having cosmological significance, the birth of Huitzilopochtli also symbolises the Aztec ascendance over competing peoples of central Mexico. Huitzilopochtli was the supernatural embodiment of both the Aztec people and their empire. The birth of this god provided the mythic charter for

Scenes from Book Three of the Florentine Codex. The illustrations portray the birth of Huitzilopochtli (top) and the defeat of his enemies at Coatepec. Early colonial period.

*The Coyolxauhqui stone
discovered at the base of the
Huitzilopochtli side of the
Templo Mayor. Aztec (Museo
Templo Mayor, Mexico City),
Late Postclassic period.*

the political expansion of the Aztec and their right to rule over their defeated enemies. As relative newcomers to the Valley of Mexico, the Aztecs conquered and eclipsed the existing inhabitants of the already occupied region, much as Huitzilopochtli vanquished his elder half-sister and half-brothers.

The great Templo Mayor dominated the landscape of the Aztec capital, continually reminding its citizens of Huitzilopochtli and his miraculous origins. Whereas the north side of this dual temple was dedicated to Tlaloc, the rain god, the southern half was the principal temple of Huitzilopochtli. According to native and Spanish acccounts, captive warriors were frequently sacrificed here. Stretched over a sacrificial stone, their hearts were removed and the lifeless bodies were then thrown to the base of the temple steps. Sixteenth-century sources also report that the southern side of the Templo Mayor symbolised the mythical mountain of Coatepec, the birthplace of Huitzilopochtli.

Remarkable physical proof of this appeared on 21 February 1978, when excavations by an electrical company accidently uncovered a massive stone monument of Coyolxauhqui at what was the ancient centre of Tenochtitlan. A masterful portrayal of humiliation and defeat, the monument portrays Coyol-xauhqui naked and brutally dismembered. Although her head and limbs are severed from her bleeding torso, she appears in a dynamic and almost running pose, as if portrayed in the instant of tumbling down Coatepec. Excavations soon revealed that the Coyolxauhqui stone lay at the base of the stairway on the Huitzilopochtli side of the Templo Mayor. In other words, each sacrificed human prisoner thrown down the temple stairs in Aztec rituals re-enacted the killing of Coyolxauhqui at Coatepec.

Monument fragment portraying the segmented body of the Xiuhcoatl serpent penetrating the chest of Coyolxauhqui. Aztec (Museo Templo Mayor, Mexico City), Late Postclassic period.

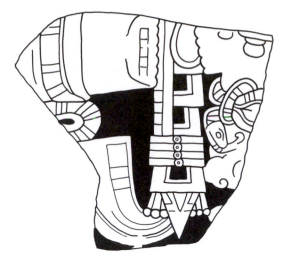

The Templo Mayor excavations uncovered another stone monument of Coyolxauhqui. Although fragmentary, this piece clearly portrays the Xiuhcoatl fire serpent penetrating her chest and probably illustrates the mythical origins of Aztec heart sacrifice. Just as the Xiuhcoatl serpent pierces Coyolxauhqui, the sacrificial knife would tear the heart from the human captive's chest.

Against a majestic background of aeons of world creations and cataclysmic destructions, the myth of the five suns presents sacrifice as an essential means for maintaining human life and cosmic balance. Through the penitential offering of their own blood, the gods create the present race of mankind. An even greater sacrifice occurs at Teotihuacan, where the gods slay themselves so that the sun can follow its course. In their own acts of bloodletting and sacrifice, humans are simply following a tradition set down by the gods at the time of creation. Although the five suns myth provides a rationale for some of the most important and profound rites of Postclassic central Mexico, this was not enough for the Aztec, who were interested not only in explaining their origin and role in the cosmos, but also in validating their unique status as a chosen people. For this reason, the Aztecs developed their own special mythology for their patron god Huitzilopochtli, in whose origins warfare is an explicit and central motif. The rout and utter defeat of Coyolxauhqui and the Centzon Huitznahua by Huitzilopochtli portrays in sacred myth the Aztecs' victories over their enemies, providing a mythic charter for the heart sacrifice performed on such a massive scale at the Templo Mayor.

Like the five suns episode at Teotihuacan, the vanquishing of Coyolxauhqui and her brothers describes the origins of the sun and human sacrifice. However, the Aztec imperial myth does not concern the sun god Tonatiuh, but rather the solar-related Huitzilopochtli. The fifth sun and Huitzilopochtli episodes are overlapping and probably competing myths. It is quite possible that, were it not for the Spanish conquest, the Huitzilopochtli myth might eventually have eclipsed the solar Teotihuacan myth – much as the Aztec were increasing their domain over the peoples of ancient Mesoamerica.

Maya mythology

At the time of Spanish contact, the Maya were neither politically nor culturally a single unified people. Some thirty distinct Mayan languages were present in the sixteenth century, and most are still spoken today. The languages may be as similar as modern Spanish is to Portuguese, although the differences can also be far greater, as for example between English and French. Aside from language, there are other cultural differences between the Yucatecan Mayan speakers of the northern Maya lowlands and such highland Maya peoples as the Tzotzil, Tojolabal, Mam, Quiché, Kekchi and Chorti, who occupy the dramatic mountainous region of Chiapas, southern Guatemala and neighbouring Honduras.

In the sixteenth century, notable differences in calendrics and religion also existed between the lowland Maya of Yucatan and the Maya peoples of the southern highlands. Although an abbreviated version of the Classic Maya Long Count continued to play an essential part in the ritual, mythology and history of the Yucatan Peninsula, this calendrical system was no longer observed by the Postclassic peoples of the Maya highlands. Although widespread in Postclassic and colonial Yucatan, the concept of trees, colours and other features oriented to the four directions was little developed among the highland Maya. In addition, many of the sixteenth century gods recorded for the Quiché and other highland Mayan peoples cannot easily be identified in the writing and art of Postclassic and early colonial Yucatan.

In addition to having distinct customs and language, the Postclassic Maya were also politically diverse. At the time of the Spanish conquest there was no single great empire, as in the case of the Aztec, but many competing Maya states. Although the neighbouring Quiché and Cakchiquel spoke very similar languages, they were fierce enemies, and during the 1524 conquest of the Guatemalan highlands by Pedro de Alvarado, the Cakchiquel readily served as Spanish allies against the Quiché. Even the culturally homogeneous region of Yucatan was broken into a complex patchwork of competing city states and provinces at the time of Spanish contact and widespread unified resistance against foreign domination did not occur until well after the various groups had been subsumed under Spanish colonial rule.

Despite this regional diversity, many religious traits were shared between the various Postclassic Maya peoples. Some common elements seem relatively recent introductions from Postclassic central Mexico, which had close political and economic ties to the Maya region. An example is the central Mexican god

283

Quetzalcoatl, the plumed serpent, who was known by the Yucatec equivalent of Kukulcan and as Gucumatz by the highland Maya Quiché and Cakchiquel. Although of considerable importance in Postclassic Maya myth and legend, this god is virtually absent from Maya writing and art of the earlier Classic period. Another probable Postclassic introduction is the legendary western place of origin known as Zuyua by the Yucatec Maya and Tulan Zuiva by the Cakchiquel and Quiché. Clearly the highland Maya term links this place to Tollan of the Toltecs, now known to be the Early Postclassic site of Tula in Hidalgo.

Although certain specific traits found among both lowland and highland Maya peoples are comparatively recent Postclassic introductions from highland Mexico, the majority of shared religious elements derive from a deeper level of Maya culture and appear in the earlier Classic period writing and art of the Maya lowlands. Human sacrifice – often said to have originated in Postclassic central Mexico – is now known to have been widely practised by the Classic Maya. Another common Postclassic Maya form of sacrifice, penitential bloodletting from the tongue, penis and other parts of the body, is now recognised as one of the more common ritual themes in Classic Maya texts and monumental art. In addition to ceremonies, many of the gods and myths of the Postclassic Maya derive from earlier Classic traditions. The vast majority of major Maya deities known from the Postclassic codices of Yucatan, some fifteen in all, were already worshipped among the Classic Maya.

Perhaps the greatest deity of the ancient Maya was **Itzamna**, an old, wizened creator god similar to Tonacatecuhtli of central Mexico. Representations of Itzamna are widespread in both Classic and Postclassic Maya art. His consort seems to have been **Ix Chel**, an aged goddess identified with the roles of midwife and curer. Like Tlaloc, his central Mexican counterpart, the Maya god of rain and lightning, **Chac**, is one of the longest continuously worshipped gods in Mesoamerica. First known in Protoclassic Maya art dating to roughly the first century BC, Chac is still invoked in the mythology and prayers of modern Maya peoples. The ancient Chac wields serpents and axes, symbols of his lightning power.

Another major deity of the Classic and Postclassic Maya was the maize god. Surprisingly, his Postclassic name remains unknown, but there are indications that one important Classic form was named Hun Nal. In both form and

The old creator god, Itzamna, facing a tree with a caiman trunk. Detail of Late Classic Maya vase.

Chac fishing with a net.
Izapa Stela 1,
Protoclassic Maya.

symbolic domain, the ancient Maya death god was very similar to the central Mexican Mictlantecuhtli. One of the modern and Postclassic Maya terms for this skeletal deity is **Cizin**, meaning 'flatulent one', although he was also known as **Yum Cimih**, or Lord of Death. The name of the ancient sun god was **Kinich Ahau**, Sun-Faced Lord, a powerful being closely identified with the jaguar. It seems that this god transformed into a jaguar during his nightly journey through the underworld.

The early colonial *Popol Vuh* is perhaps the most striking example of Maya religious continuity from the Classic period to the sixteenth century. Recent research indicates that much of the creation mythology of the Quichean *Popol Vuh*, particularly the portion concerning the hero twins and their father, was known to the Classic Maya. Moreover, parts of this section can be traced back still earlier, to the Protoclassic site of Izapa. As it now stands, the Classic and Protoclassic scenes pertaining to the *Popol Vuh* constitute the oldest well-documented mythology of the New World.

The *Popol Vuh*: primordial origins

The first portion of the *Popol Vuh* movingly describes the creation of the world and its inhabitants out of the primordial sea and sky. Like the Aztec myth of the five suns, there are multiple creations and destructions, each associated with a particular race of people. Here, however, the series of human creations are fashioned and destroyed for a specific reason. According to the *Popol Vuh*, people are made to provide nourishment for the gods in the form of prayer and sacrifice. The concept of nourishment is taken quite literally in the *Popol Vuh*, and at one point the act of creation is described much like the preparation of a four-sided maize field with a measuring cord:

> The fourfold siding, the fourfold cornering,
> measuring, fourfold staking,
> halving the cord, stretching the cord
> in the sky, on the earth,
> the four sides, the four corners.

It is the people of maize, the product of this cosmic corn field, who finally provide sustenance for the gods.

Although little of the first section of the *Popol Vuh* is represented in the writing and art of the Classic Maya, this may be partly because it tends to deal with general cosmic abstractions rather than easily identified mythical episodes. The colonial Yucatec also conceived of the earth as a four-sided maize field. Many elements described in this beginning section of the *Popol Vuh*, such as multiple creations and the dualistic opposition of sky and earth, are probably among the most basic and ancient features of Mesoamerican religion.

The creation epic of the *Popol Vuh* begins with the vast, still expanse of the sea and sky before the creation of the earth:

There is not yet one person, one animal, bird, fish, crab, tree, rock, hollow, canyon, meadow, forest. Only the sky alone is there; the face of the earth is not clear. Only the sea alone is pooled under all the sky; there is nothing whatever gathered together. It is at rest; not a single thing stirs. It is held back, kept at rest under the sky.

Coiled within the water, surrounded by shimmering green and blue feathers, lies the plumed serpent Gucumatz. In the sky above is Heart of Heaven who, by his other name of Huracan, appears as three forms of lightning. Out of the still silence, Heart of Heaven and Gucumatz begin to speak to one another, discussing the creation, the first dawn and the making of people and their food. By their speech alone, the mountains and earth magically rise from the

The lightning deity God K, or Kauil, a possible aspect of Huracan.
Detail of Late Classic Maya vase.

waters, and forests of cypress and pine instantly blanket the landscape.

To inhabit the newly made earth, the creators fashion birds, deer, jaguars, serpents – all the creatures of the forest mountains. After providing them with shelter, the creators ask the animals to praise and name them in prayer. But the animals are unable to speak:

> They just squawked, they just chattered, they just howled. It wasn't apparent what language they spoke, each one gave a different cry.

Because the animals cannot speak properly and worship the gods, the creators decide that they will not be given dominion over the earth, but instead must remain in the wilds to be food for the people who *will* worship and sustain the gods.

For a second time, the creators try to fashion people, and they model one out of clay. But although it talks, its words make no sense and its body is weak and poorly made and soon begins to crumble and dissolve. Realising that it cannot survive or multiply, they break up the image, and begin yet again to create another form of people.

After their first two unsuccessful attempts, Heart of Heaven and Gucumatz consult the old diviner couple Xpiyacoc and Xmucane. Using maize grain and red seeds, the soothsayers cast lots while counting the days of the sacred calendar. They divine that humans should be made of wood and, upon hearing this, the creators say 'so be it', and instantly the world is populated by a race of wooden people. While the men are made of wood, the women are formed of rushes. Although they look, speak and multiply like people, they are dry, bloodless beings with expressionless faces. The wooden people lack souls and understanding, and do not respect or worship their creators. Concluding that they must be humiliated and destroyed, the gods create a great flood. A rain of resin falls from the sky, and fierce demons gouge and tear apart the wooden people. Even their utensils and animals rise up against them:

> Into their houses came the animals, small and great.
> Their faces were crushed by things of wood and stone.
> Everything spoke: their water jars, their tortilla griddles, their plates, their cooking pots, their dogs, their grinding stones, each and every thing crushed their faces.

The wooden people try to flee but there is no refuge – everywhere they are pushed away and killed. The descendants of the race of wooden beings are the forest monkeys, left as a sign (and perhaps a warning) of this ancient, thoughtless creation.

Following the flood and the destruction of the wooden race, the earth is again devoid of humans. Still the gods lack beings to sustain them with prayer and offerings. Proper humans cannot be produced until the hero twins rid the world of demons and obtain the material from which human flesh is made.

The hero twins and the vanquishing of Xibalba

The second major portion of the *Popol Vuh* concerns the activities of two related sets of twins. The older twins, born of the soothsayers Xpiyacoc and Xmucane, are called by the calendrical dates of **Hun Hunahpu** (One Hunahpu) and **Vucub Hunahpu** (Seven Hunahpu). Hun Hunahpu has a pair of sons named **Hun Batz** and **Hun Chouen**, trained as great artists and performers by their father and uncle. **Xquic**, who is impregnated by Hun Hunahpu, gives birth to another pair of twins, **Xbalanque** and **Hunahpu**, the great hero twins who slay the monster bird **Vucub Caquix**. But their most spectacular victory is the defeat of the death gods and demons of Xibalba, the fearsome underworld.

Hun Hunahpu and Vucub Hunahpu are great gamesters who love to throw dice and play ball in their masonry ballcourt with Hun Hunapuh's sons, Hun Batz and Hun Chouen. Although it is on the earth, this ballcourt is also the path to the gloomy netherworld realm of Xibalba. The principal lords of Xibalba, Hun Came and Vucub Came (One Death and Seven Death), become enraged at the thundering noise from the ballgame above and call together all the gods and demons of death and disease to decide how to defeat and kill the twins. They send four owl messengers up to the surface to invite Hun Hunahpu and Vucub Hunahpu to play ball with them in Xibalba. Although their mother Xmucane tries to persuade them not to go, the two agree to follow the owls into the deadly underworld.

The path to Xibalba is long and treacherous, and the twins must pass obstacles such as fierce rapids, thorny spikes, and a river of blood. All these are successfully overcome until they reach a crossroads with four paths of different colours. They wrongly choose the black path, which marks the beginning of their undoing. When they arrive at Xibalba they greet the underworld lords, but in fact these are only wooden dummies dressed like the gods of death. The denizens of Xibalba roar with laughter, now certain of their victory. They invite Hun Hunahpu and Vucub Hunahpu to sit on a bench, which is no ordinary seat, but rather a searing hot slab of stone:

So now they were burned on the bench; they really jumped around on the bench now, but they got no relief. They really got up fast, having burned their butts. At this the Xibalbans laughed again, they began to shriek with laughter.

As a final test, the lords of Xibalba give the twins cigars and torches that must remain lit as well as intact all night while in the House of Gloom. At dawn, the gods of death find that the twins have failed this impossible task: the cigars and torches have burned away.

Tricked and overpowered by the lords of Xibalba, the twins are sacrificed and buried within the underworld ballcourt. As a token of their victory, the netherworld gods place the head of Hun Hunapuh in a barren tree. Instantly, this tree becomes laden with calabash gourds, with the head becoming one of the many round fruits. The underworld maiden Xquic hears of this miraculous gourd tree, and goes to see it for herself. The young woman asks herself aloud whether she should pick one of the fruits. The head of Hun Hunahpu hears

Xquic and tells her that the fruits are nothing but a crop of skulls. None the less, the maiden asks for the fruit. Spitting into her hand, the skull impregnates Xquic and tells her of his essence:

It is just a sign that I have given you, my saliva, my spittle. This, my head, has nothing on it – just bone, nothing of meat. It's just the same with the head of a great lord: it's just the flesh that makes his face look good. And when he dies, people get frightened by his bones. After that, his son is like his saliva, his spittle, in his being, whether it be the son of a lord or the son of a craftsman and orator. The father does not disappear, but goes on being fulfilled.

Eventually the father of Xquic notices her pregnant condition and demands to know who the father is. Although Xquic steadfastly denies having known a man, it is of no avail, and her father resolves to kill her. The messenger owls then take the maiden away to be sacrificed, but she convinces them to spare her. In place of her bloody heart, they return with a thick mass of resin, the blood of trees. Burning the resin incense, the death lords are entranced by its smell, and take no notice of the owls leading Xquic to the surface of the earth. In this way, the lords of Xibalba are tricked and defeated by the maiden.

Arriving at the home of Xmucane, the mother of the slain twins, Xquic declares herself to be her daughter-in-law, the wife of Hun Hunahpu. But

Death god ballplayer. Jaina style ceramic figurine, Late Classic Maya.

Xmucane, convinced that her sons are dead, wants nothing to do with the pregnant maiden. None the less, as a test, she sends Xquic to gather a netful of maize from the field of Hun Batz and Hun Chouen. Although the field has only a single maize plant, she returns with a great load of corn, and in so doing, proves that she is the wife of Hun Hunahpu.

Xquic gives birth to the hero twins Hunahpu and Xbalanque. Although they are the children of Hun Hunahpu, the twins are not well received by Xmucane, their grandmother, or by Hun Batz and Hun Chouen, who are jealous of their younger half-brothers. While the older brothers dance and make fine music and art, Hunahpu and Xbalanque roam the forest, shooting animals with their blow-guns. The spoiled older brothers snatch away all their game and leave them with only scraps of bone and gristle. One day the twins return with nothing, telling their brothers that the shot birds are caught high in a tree. Hun Batz and Hun Chouen agree to climb the tree but as they go up, the trunk miraculously swells and grows to a great height. The panicked elder brothers call out to Xbalanque and Hunahpu for help, who tell them: 'Untie your loincloths, wrap them around your hips, with the long end hanging like a tail behind you, and then you'll be able to move better.' Upon doing this, Hun Batz and Hun Chouen are turned into forest monkeys, tricked by their younger brothers Xbalanque and Hunahpu. But rather than being forgotten, these two monkeys become the patrons of artists, dancers and musicians.

After the great flood, a host of monstrous beings dwell on the surface of the world. The greatest is Vucub Caquix, Seven Macaw, a vainglorious bird who proclaims himself the sun and moon, lord over all. Angered by this false boasting, Hunahpu and Xbalanque decide to slay the monster bird. Hiding under his favourite fruit tree, the twins wait with their blow-guns, and when Vucub Caquix alights, Hunahpu shoots him in the face. Wounded and enraged, the bird tears off Hunahpu's arm and escapes with this trophy. Enlisting an old couple to pose as healers, the twins tell them to visit Vucub Caquix and offer to cure his aching eyes and teeth. The aged pair tell the monster bird that they must

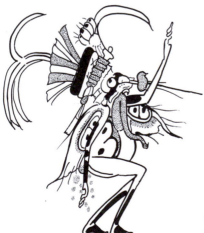

The mosquito, an ally of the hero twins.
Detail from Late Classic Maya vase.

Camazotz, the killer bat. Detail from Chama style Late Classic Maya vase, Guatemala.

replace his teeth and eyes, but in place of his teeth they insert grains of corn. Once his eyes and teeth are gone, Vucub Caquix loses his glory and power, and quickly dies. Placing the severed arm of Hunahpu against the stump, the old couple heal the wound so that his arm is perfectly restored.

Like their father and uncle, the hero twins learn to play ball at the ballcourt. The lords of Xibalba are again infuriated by the incessant pounding above their heads and send their owls to summon the twins to the underworld. In their descent to Xibalba, Hunahpu and Xbalanque successfully pass rivers of pus and blood and other deadly obstacles until they come to the crossroads. Here Hunahpu plucks out a hair from his shin and creates a mosquito to spy ahead and bite the underworld lords. The insect first attacks the enthroned wooden images, but then finds the actual lords, and as they are bitten they cry out each other's names. In this way, the twins learn the names of all the underworld lords.

When Xbalanque and Hunahpu arrive at the palace of the underworld lords, they ignore the wooden statues and the burning hot seat and correctly greet all of the death gods by name. The astonished lords of Xibalba then send them with the cigars and torches to the House of Gloom. The twins cleverly place red macaw feathers on the torches and fireflies on the cigars to make them seem as if they are burning. At dawn the unburned fire brands and cigars are as new. The twins then play ball with the death gods, eventually allowing themselves to be beaten. That night they face another series of tests, but by their cunning they pass safely through the House of Knives, the House of Cold, the House of Jaguars and the House of Fire. Finally, they are sent to the House of Bats, a room filled with fierce knife-nosed bats. To protect themselves the twins hide inside their hollow blow-guns, but Hunahpu peeks out to see if dawn is approaching, and at that moment the killer bat Camazotz snatches off his head.

The head of Hunahpu is taken to the ballcourt and all of the death gods and demons rejoice, since their victory over the twins now seems all but certain.

However, in the late pre-dawn hours, Xbalanque calls on all the animals to bring their various foods. Some creatures present rotten things, others offer leaves and grasses. Finally, the coati (similar to a raccoon) arrives with a large squash, and Xbalanque places it against the severed neck of Hunahpu like a new head. Magically, the squash takes the form of Hunahpu's features, and he can see and speak. At dawn, the twins appear together at the underworld ballcourt as if nothing had happened.

The death gods begin the game by throwing out the real head of Hunahpu to serve as the new ball. Xbalanque strikes the head so hard that it bounces out of the court and into the woods. A rabbit, previously told to wait in the trees, immediately bounds away, confusing the death gods who mistake it for the ball. While their attention is distracted, Xbalanque retrieves Hunahpu's real head and places it back on his body. When the death gods return, the twins throw the squash into the court:

The squash was punted by Xbalanque, the squash was wearing out; it fell on the court, bringing to light its light-coloured seeds, as plain as day right in front of them.

Thus the confused and astonished death gods are truly defeated in their underworld court of sacrifice.

Although Xbalanque and Hunahpu are victorious, they know that the death gods will not rest until they are killed. The lords of Xibalba fashion a great fiery pit and invite the twins to jump over it. However, knowing that the death gods only want their deaths, the twins bravely jump into the pit and die. The gods of Xibalba then grind their charred bones and cast them into the river. The bones do not drift away but instead settle to the bottom, and in five days the twins reappear as fish-men. The following day they return to Xibalba disguised in rags as poor itinerant performers. Hearing of their wonderful dances, the lords of Xibalba command them to perform at their palace. After many dances, the twins are told to sacrifice a dog and then bring it back to life. This they do, and then they sacrifice a man and also bring him back to life. Xbalanque then decapitates Hunahpu and tears out his heart, only to restore him once again. The principal death gods, Hun Came and Vucub Came, are overjoyed and ecstatic at this miraculous dance and, in the throes of their enthusiasm, they ask to be killed. The twins kill one of them but they leave him dead and lifeless.

As soon as they had killed the one lord without bringing him back to life, the other lord had been meek and tearful before the dancers. He didn't consent, he didn't accept it:
'Take pity on me!' he said when he realised. All their vassals took the road to the great canyon, in one single mass they filled up the deep abyss.

Thus, through trickery and cunning, the twins completely vanquish the evil kingdom of Xibalba. Appearing before its defeated inhabitants, they reveal their true identities and threaten to slay everyone. The Xibalbans beg for mercy and tell them where their father and uncle are buried. The twins then agree to spare the people of Xibalba, but tell them that they will never again be powerful:

The Maya maize god. Stone sculpture (Museum of Mankind, London) from Temple 22,
Copan, Honduras, Late Classic period.

All of you listen, you Xibalbans: because of this, your day and your descendants will not be great. Moreover, the gifts you receive will no longer be great, but reduced to scabrous nodules of sap. There will be no clearly blotted blood for you, just griddles, just gourds, just little things broken to pieces.

The twins then recover and speak to the remains of their father and uncle, reassuring them that they will continue to be respected and worshipped. Xbalanque and Hunahpu then rise into the heavens, where they become the sun and moon.

The origin of maize and people

Although the monstrous gods and demons of the earth and underworld had been destroyed, there were still no people to nourish the gods. In the pre-dawn darkness, Gucumatz and Heart of Heaven call on fox, coyote, parrot and crow to bring yellow and white maize from Paxil and Cayala, a mountain filled with seeds and fruits. Old Xmucane grinds the maize and, from the meal, the first four men are fashioned. Unlike the previous wooden race, these people of corn possess great knowledge and understanding and correctly give thanks to their creators. However, Gucumatz and Heart of Heaven are troubled; these corn men can see everywhere – through earth and sky to the limits of the universe. The creators decide that these people are too much like themselves, and that their powers must be diminished. As though they were breathing mist on a mirror, the gods blur the vision of the first people so that they can see clearly only what is near. In place of omniscience, the creators give the first men happiness by providing them with four beautiful wives to be their companions. With these four women, the first lineages of the Quiché are begun.

In darkness, the first tribes of the world journey to Tulan Zuiva, the place of Seven Caves and Seven Canyons. There they receive their various gods, including Tohil, a patron god of the Quiché and the source of fire. When the different peoples finally depart from Tulan with their gods, they no longer speak one language but many. In the dark pre-dawn hours, each group of people sets off in a different direction, with the Quiché going towards the west. While fasting and seeking the dawn, the Quiché look back to the east, the region of Tulan Zuiva. Finally the Quiché arrive at Mount Hacauitz, where they witness the dawn. At the appearance of the morning star, they joyfully offer incense to the east, and soon afterwards the sun appears:

The sun was like a person when he revealed himself. His face was hot, so he dried out the face of the earth. Before the sun came up it was soggy, and the face of the earth was muddy before the sun came up. And when the sun had risen just a short distance he was like a person, and his heat was unbearable.

At this moment the Quiché gods are turned to stone, along with the images of powerful animals such as the puma, jaguar and rattlesnake. Ever since the first dawn, therefore, this is how these images have been seen.

The *Popol Vuh* creation epic in Classic Maya religion

A great many of the characters and events mentioned in the portion of the *Popol Vuh* describing the hero twins are fully present in Classic Maya mythology, over seven hundred years before the sixteenth-century manuscript was written. Finely painted or carved ceramic vessels constitute the most valuable Classic source pertaining to the *Popol Vuh*. Most of the known Classic vessels derive from the lowland jungle Peten of Guatemala, centre of the Classic Maya area. Whereas Classic Maya stone monuments tend to focus upon historical individuals in scenes of personal aggrandisement, the vessel scenes are filled with allusions to mythical events. Although many of the mythical episodes appearing on Classic Maya pottery can be related to the *Popol Vuh*, events are also depicted which are not mentioned in the colonial Quiché text. These Classic episodes sometimes provide insights into the basic underlying meanings of the *Popol Vuh*.

The Classic period counterpart of Hun Hunahpu, the father of the hero twins, is a form of the maize god. This deity is depicted with a flattened and elongated forehead, often accentuated by shaved zones delineating patches of hair on his brow and the top of his head. The elongated and shaved head imitates a ripened ear of corn, with the capping tuft of hair representing the silk at the tip of the cob. The removal of the ear from the stalk at harvest represents his decapitation, the same fate also meted out to Hun Hunahpu. On one Late Classic vessel the head of the maize god appears in a cacao tree; among the cacao pods above, one can discern a human head partially transformed into a cacao

The head of the maize god placed in a cacao tree. A second human head, partly transformed into a cacao pod, can be seen at upper right. Detail from Late Classic Maya vase (Museo Popol Vuh, Guatemala City).

fruit. This scene clearly portrays a version of the *Popol Vuh* incident in which the severed head of Hun Hunahpu is placed in a tree, although in this case the head has become a cacao pod rather than a calabash gourd.

The episodes illustrated for the Classic form of Hun Hunahpu are much more detailed and complex than what is contained in the early colonial *Popol Vuh*. In many cases, he is shown with bodies of standing water; this is probably a reference to Xibalba, since the ancient Maya regarded the underworld as a watery place. In one important episode, he stands in the water while being dressed in his finery by a group of nubile young women. Sometimes this event seems to have erotic overtones, although it is unknown whether these beautiful women are his wives. The women appear to be dressing him for a journey, and in a related episode he is being paddled in a canoe. Although this may be a journey to his death, it probably also refers to his eventual resurrection.

The Classic form of Hun Hunahpu is frequently portrayed as a dancer and artist. However, as in the *Popol Vuh*, it is not Hun Hunahpu but his sons, Hun Batz and Hun Chouen, who serve as the Classic patron gods of scribes. In Classic iconography, Hun Batz and Hun Chouen typically appear as monkeys (transformed by their half-brothers, Hunahpu and Xbalanque) wielding pens and cut-shell inkpots as they paint in screenfold books.

The hero twins Hunahpu and Xbalanque appear commonly in Classic Maya art and writing. Both usually wear the red and white cloth headband associated with Classic Maya rulership, and in fact the face of Hunahpu serves as a glyph for the day-name Ahau, a word meaning king in Mayan languages. Hunahpu is typically marked by large black spots on his cheeks and body. Xbalanque, on the other hand, displays jaguar skin patches around his mouth and on his torso and limbs. As well as appearing with their father and the monkey scribes, the twins are often shown with their blow-guns shooting down the Classic form of the monster bird Vucub Caquix. However, this bird is not a macaw but rather a mythical creature with serpent-faced wings and a long pendulous beak possibly based on the King Vulture.

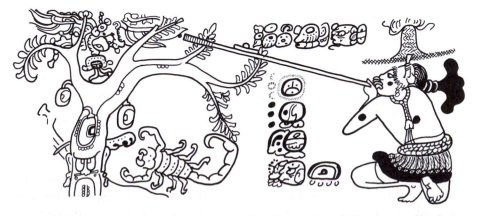

Late Classic Maya vessel scene, illustrating Hunahpu shooting Vucub Caquix out of his fruit tree.

The defeat of Vucub Caquix by the hero twins. Izapa Stela 2, Protoclassic period.

The monster bird slain by the hero twins is very common in Protoclassic Maya art, that is, around the beginning of Maya civilisation. The site of Izapa, situated in the southern coastal region of Chiapas, near the Guatemalan border, reveals that even at this early date the monster bird was clearly related to the *Popol Vuh* character. Dating to approximately the beginning of the Christian era, two Izapan monuments depict an especially early version of the Vucub Caquix episode. On Izapa Stela 2, the great bird descends to his fruit-laden tree; running towards the tree is a pair of human figures, probably the earliest known New World version of the hero twins. The monster bird appears again at the base of the fruit tree, in this case with a fleshless lower jaw and with his wing awkwardly bent under his body. The entire scene graphically represents the defeat of Vucub Caquix as he is struck down from his fruit tree by the hero

A possible representation of Hunahpu with his arm severed. Detail from Izapa Stela 25, Protoclassic period.

twins. The other Izapa monument, Stela 25, depicts the monster bird hovering above a male with only one arm; the other limb is clearly torn off, and blood is pouring from the severed stump. This scene probably concerns the battle in which Vucub Caquix tears off and escapes with the arm of Hunahpu.

As in the *Popol Vuh*, the hero twins are related to the ballgame in Classic Maya art. At the site of Copan, a stone marker from an actual ballcourt represents Hunahpu playing against a death god. On another Late Classic ballcourt marker, discovered near Chinkultic in highland Chiapas, a ballplayer dressed in death symbols strikes the ball with his hips. Lightly incised on the ball is the head of Hunahpu, recalling the *Popol Vuh* episode in which the death gods play with Hunahpu's head after snatching it from the House of Bats. These ballcourt markers reveal that the Classic Maya re-enacted in actual ballcourts the mythical game between the hero twins and the lords of Xibalba.

In one of the most common and important themes of the hero twins on Classic Maya pottery, they appear assisting their father, the maize god. In certain vessel scenes, the twins stand in water with the nude young women and hold the regalia of the maize god, such as his jewellery and a sack bundle. Certain scenes reveal that this sack contains maize grain, the essence of their

Late Classic vessel depiction of the emergence of the maize god out of the earth. On either side of the split turtle shell, a pair of Chac figures wield lightning weapons, including a burning, serpent-footed lightning axe at right.

father. In a related episode, the twins appear with the maize god as he rises out of a turtle shell. Among the ancient Maya, the turtle served as a metaphor for the earth floating upon the sea, and it is quite likely that this scene represents the maize god being resurrected from the earth. In one vessel scene, a pair of Chacs are brandishing lightning weapons as they flank the carapace. This represents the Maya version of the origin of maize from Tonacatepetl (see p. 39). In the Maya myth – still present today in the Maya area – the Chacs split open the maize rock with lightning.

Although it is not mentioned in the early colonial *Popol Vuh*, the resurrection of the maize god by the hero twins and the Chacs adds an important insight into the underlying meaning of the journey of the hero twins in search of their father. In addition to vengeance, their mission is to resurrect him from the underworld and thus bring maize to the surface of the earth. But this episode probably concerns more than just the origin of corn. In the Quichean *Popol Vuh*, the search for maize immediately follows the vanquishing of Xibalba and the partial revival of Hun Hunahpu and Vucub Hunahpu. This maize is the source of the modern race of humans, the people of corn. Thus, for the Classic period, the elaborate underworld journey of the maize god and his sons ultimately concerns the origin of people – the creation of mankind from corn. In both content and meaning it is very similar to the underworld descent of Quetzalcoatl to retrieve the bones from which people will be made. In the Aztec myth these bones were ground into meal by the aged goddess Cihuacoatl, and in the *Popol Vuh* episode old Xmucane grinds the corn from which people are eventually made.

Maya mythology of Yucatan

Unlike the highland Maya Quiché, there is very little mythological material available for the sixteenth-century Maya of the Yucatan Peninsula. Fray Diego de Landa does provide detailed information on Yucatec Maya ritual and calendrics, but regrettably he makes little mention of particular myths. The one exception is a short reference to sky-bearers and the flood (see p. 69). The three pre-Hispanic Yucatec books known as the Dresden, Madrid and Paris codices contain only oblique references to mythological episodes. The poorly understood 'serpent-numbers' section of the Codex Dresden refers to events in remote antiquity, before the present Baktun cycle era which began in 3114 BC. Like similarly ancient Classic period dates, these pre-3114 BC references probably concern such mythological events as the origins of particular gods and the creation of the present world. It is noteworthy that the pre-Hispanic forms of Xbalanque and Hunahpu are represented in the Yucatec codices, frequently in association with the maize god. Thus, although the contact-period form of the *Popol Vuh* epic is only preserved for the Quiché Maya, a version was probably also present among the Postclassic Maya of Yucatan.

The most important sources of ancient Yucatec Maya mythology are the native community manuscripts known as the Books of Chilam Balam. Dating to

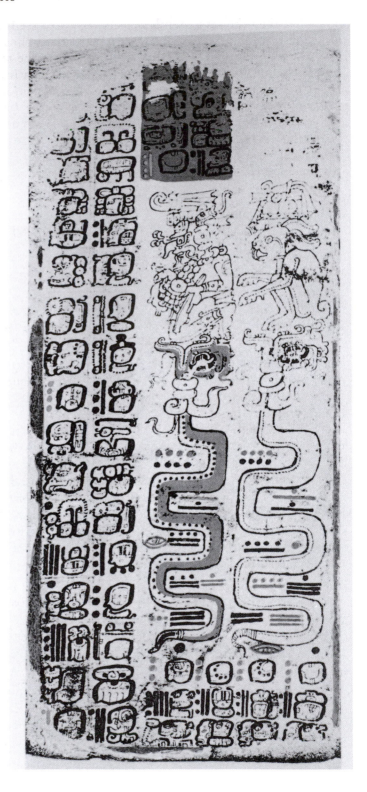

A portion of a serpent-numbers passage. Chac and a rabbit sit in the mouths of serpents marked with numbers denoting vast units of time. Codex Dresden, p. 61.

no earlier than the seventeenth century, the preserved myths are frequently placed in relation to calendrical cycles, particularly those based on the Maya Long Count. Although this may be distracting to the modern reader, it is a traditional lowland Maya convention for sacred narrative and is of respectable antiquity; mythological events in the Dresden serpent-number passages and Classic Maya inscriptions are presented in a similar fashion. Three Chilam Balam books, from the towns of Chumayel, Tizimin and Mani, contain virtually identical references to the flood and the restoration of the world. The passages contained in these Books of Chilam Balam share traits with Aztec creation mythology as well as with Landa's account and with the pre-Hispanic Codex Dresden.

Yucatec creation mythology and the flood

The sixteenth-century *Relación de las cosas de Yucatan* by Diego de Landa alludes to the flood in relation to four sky-bearers, known as Bacabs:

Among the multitude of gods which this nation worshipped they worshipped four, each of whom they called Bacab. They said that they were four brothers whom God placed, when he created the world, at the four points of it, holding up the sky so that it should not fall. They also said of these Bacabs that they escaped when the world was destroyed by the deluge.

These Bacab sky-bearers are probably forms of the ancient Maya god known as Pauahtun. Four-fold in nature, this aged being is frequently represented as a world-bearer in ancient Maya art and may personify sky-supporting mountains at the corners of the Maya world.

The accounts of the flood in the colonial Chilam Balam books can be understood as a creation event, as they lead directly to the origin of the present world. The principal protagonists are Ah Muzencab, possibly a god of bees, and Oxlahun-ti-ku and Bolon-ti-ku, whose names probably refer to the sky and underworld respectively, since the sky was believed to have thirteen (*oxlahun*) levels and the Underworld nine (*bolon*). In this episode, the flood is caused by Ah Muzencab and Bolon-ti-ku attacking Oxlahun-ti-ku and taking his regalia. Like the Landa account, both the Chumayel and Mani versions mention the Bacabs in relation to the flood:

There would be a sudden rush of water when the theft of the insignia of Oxlahun-ti-ku occurred. Then the sky would fall, it would fall down upon the earth, when the four gods, the four Bacabs, were set up, who brought about the destruction of the world.

As in the *Popol Vuh*, the Yucatec flood episode includes the destruction of an earlier, thoughtless race of people; however, the Yucatec texts do not specify the material from which this ancient race was made.

The Mani and Tizimin versions of the flood also mention the killing of a great earth caiman known as Itzam Cab Ain, Giant Fish Earth Caiman, which is identified with the earth as well as the flood. In both accounts, the caiman is slain by Bolon-ti-ku:

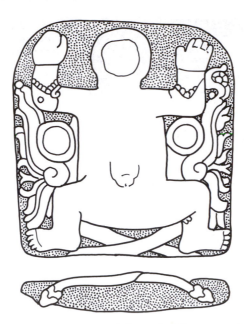

Yucatec Maya sculpture depicting Tlaltecuhtli with a pair of intertwined snakes. Mayapan, Late Postclassic period.

Then occurs the great flooding of the earth. Then arises the great Itzam Cab Ain. The ending of the world, the fold of the *katun*: that is a flood which will be the ending of the world of the *katun*. But they did not agree, the 9 Gods [Bolon-ti-ku]; and then will be cut the throat of Itzam Cab Ain, who bears the country on his back.

This episode is markedly similar to Aztec mythology, in which Tlaltecuhtli or a great caiman is slain to create the earth, and it is possible that this portion of the Maya flood account may have been a Postclassic central Mexican introduction. A sculpture from the Late Postclassic Yucatec site of Mayapan represents a form of the Aztec Tlaltecuhtli in its typical squatting pose. A pair of snakes accompany the figure, recalling the *Histoyre du Mechique* episode in which Tezcatlipoca and Quetzalcoatl dismember Tlaltecuhtli by transforming themselves into two serpents.

Immediately after the flood, five great trees are set up to the four directions and the centre to sustain the sky. In the three accounts, these world trees are associated with colours and birds as well as with directions. The following is the Chumayel description of this event:

After the destruction of the world was completed, they placed a tree to set up in its order the yellow cock oriole. Then the white tree of abundance was set up. A pillar of the sky was set up, a sign of the destruction of the world; that was the white tree of abundance in the north. Then the black tree of abundance was set up in the west for the black-breasted *pidzoy* to sit upon. Then the yellow tree of abundance was set up in the south, as a symbol of the destruction of the world, for the yellow-breasted *pidzoy* to sit upon, for the yellow cock oriole to sit upon, the timid *mut*. Then the green tree of abundance was set up in the centre of the world as a record of the destruction of the world.

In the Mani and Tizimin versions, the first of the trees stands at the east and is red. The Mani also mentions that this first eastern tree, the Chac Imix Che, supports the sky and is a sign of the dawn.

Codex Dresden, p. 74,
a probable representation
of the flood.

Creation mythology and calendrics in Yucatan

It has already been noted that much of the creation mythology found in the Books of Chilam Balam is couched in terms of calendrics. For example, the three cited versions of the flood and the creation of the world occur in Katun 11 Ahau, which is the first of thirteen roughly twenty-year Katuns which repeat in a cycle of approximately 260 years. Individually named by the 260-day date on which they end, the thirteen Katuns invariably end on the day-name Ahau and begin on the day-name Imix (corresponding to the Aztec day-name Cipactli, or caiman). Although they are given varying colour designations, the trees set up after the flood are all termed Imix Che, or Imix trees, probably alluding to the first day in a new Katun cycle.

Not only are creation events described in terms of calendrical cycles, but calendrical rituals frequently express creation episodes. Landa's account of the flood and the Bacab sky-bearers is actually a preface to a detailed discussion of Yucatec Maya new year celebrations marking the completion and renewal of the 365-day vague year. The pre-Hispanic Codex Dresden contains a very similar situation: the scene on Dresden page seventy-four has been widely interpreted as representing world destruction and the flood. A partly reptilian skyband spouting three great channels of water dominates the upper portion of the scene. Below, the aged goddess Chac Chel (Ix Chel) pours water from a jar, and a black god, probably Chac, brandishes weapons. As well as mentioning the names Bacab, Chac and Chac Chel, the accompanying text also refers to black sky and black earth, probably a reference to world destruction.

The new year erection of the world tree of the west.
Codex Dresden, p. 27.

In the original pagination of the Codex Dresden, page seventy-four immediately precedes the pages concerning the installation of the new year as described by Landa. One of the primary events in these four pre-Hispanic new year pages is the erection of four world directional trees, the first being the red tree of the east. Like Landa's account of the flood, page seventy-four introduces the new year ceremony in terms of world destruction and renewal, with the setting up of the trees signifying world renewal. The new year celebrations were annual ritual re-enactments of the destruction and re-creation of the world. The graphic accounts of the flood and the erection of world trees in the three Books of Chilam Balam reveal that the ritual installation of the Katun and other Long Count periods were thought of in very similar terms.

Rather than being unique to the Maya area, the documented mythology of the ancient Quiché and Yucatec shares many traits with Aztec myths. Like the Aztec, the Postclassic Maya of Yucatan and highland Guatemala believed in previous worlds, and that a flood immediately preceded the creation of the present era. The underworld descent of Xbalanque and Hunahpu in search of their father and their defeat of the gods of death recall the netherworld journey of Quetzalcoatl to retrieve the bones of the previous creation. Classic Maya art suggests that the underlying meaning of both the Quiché and Aztec myths is much the same. It seems that, in both cases, the descent to the underworld is a quest for the substance from which mankind is made. Classic Maya depictions of the hero twins' resurrection of their father reveal the considerable antiquity of the Maya version, showing that it was not a relatively recent introduction from central Mexico.

Certain aspects of Maya mythology do derive from Postclassic central Mexico. Thus the *Popol Vuh* mentions the plumed serpent Gucumatz and the city of Tollan. The Yucatec Itzam Cab Ain episode is clearly related to the Aztec myth describing the dismemberment of the earth monster. The previously mentioned Mayapan sculpture of the squatting earth monster suggests that the

A possible Classic representation of the flood caiman, reminiscent of the reptilian skyband which appears on p. 74 of the Codex Dresden. Detail from Late Classic Maya vase.

Maya of Yucatan were aware of Aztec mythology and even iconographic conventions. However, the Classic Maya may well have also conceived of a great earth caiman associated with the flood. One surviving Late Classic Maya vessel depicts a caiman with death and water markings suspended from the sky, recalling the reptilian skyband on page seventy-four of the Codex Dresden. The date associated with this scene is 4 Ahau 8 Cumku, which marks the beginning of the present great Baktun cycle beginning in 3114 BC. Could this Long Count event constitute a Classic version of the flood and the subsequent re-creation of the world? If so, the Classic period setting up of stone stelae at important Long Count intervals could be ritual re-enactments of the erection of world trees at the creation of the present era.

Mesoamerican mythology

In the recorded creation accounts of ancient Mesoamerica, the myths rarely stray far from the natural world. There is frequent mention of gods of wind, lightning, water, celestial bodies and other natural phenomena. Processes related to the agricultural cycle play an especially important role and, according to the *Popol Vuh*, the very flesh of humans was fashioned from maize. It is readily apparent from these sources that humans have an inherent responsibility – literally, a blood debt – to the gods who make existence possible. The repeating series of world creations and destructions is a continual reminder of the consequences of neglecting this obligation.

Calendrics and astrology served as basic templates for organising and observing the processes of the natural world, and thus it is not surprising that they too play a prominent role in ancient Mesoamerican mythology. Myths of world creations and destructions are frequently couched in terms of calendrical events. This is especially true for Late Postclassic Yucatan, where imagery of world destruction and renewal is repeatedly used to express the calendrical completion of the 365-day year and the Katun cycle. But the Mesoamerican relationship between calendrical events and myth is not simply metaphoric: the calendrical cycles were used to predict potential periods when the world might be destroyed. These calendrical period endings were seen as powerful and frightening times of living myth, when the gods and other forces of creation and chaos would again do battle in the world of mortals.

Ancient Mesoamerican calendrics, astrology and mythology were thus integrated into a single compelling system of belief. During the Aztec new fire vigil, marking the completion of a fifty-two-year calendar round cycle, the inhabitants of Tenochtitlan would look anxiously to particular star groups to see if the world would continue or be destroyed. The profound influence on Mesoamerican life of the movements of the sun, stars, planets and other celestial bodies was also reflected in the mythology. Such celestial beings as Tlahuizcalpantecuhtli, Mixcoatl and Tonatiuh appear widely in central Mexican myth. Recent research by Linda Schele and David Freidel suggests that the Classic Maya version of the journey of the hero twins and their father through dark Xibalba was played out every year in the procession of constellations across the ecliptic – that is, the same annual path observed in the Old World zodiac of constellations. In support, they note that in a number of Mayan languages the Milky Way galaxy is referred to as Xibal Be, the road of Xibalba. These ongoing investigations present the intriguing possibility that the apparent movements of the stars and planets may have served as a basic structural model for the development of Mesoamerican mythology.

Compared with the Old World mythologies of Mesopotamia, Egypt or Greece, far less is known of the ancient myths of Mesoamerica. It is clear that we now understand only a fraction of the mythology present at the time of the conquest, and much less of myths of the Classic period. As has been noted, the dismemberment of Tezcatlipoca by Xiuhtecuhtli on page one of the Fejérváry-Mayer is not recorded in the myths of ancient central Mexico, and this is also true of many episodes illustrated in the middle pages of the Codex Borgia. For the Classic Maya, many vessel scenes illustrate obvious mythical episodes that bear no direct relationship to the *Popol Vuh* or other mythologies of the Post-classic, colonial or contemporary Maya. An excellent example, appearing on a number of polychrome vessels, is the theft by a rabbit of an old god's broad hat and other regalia. Not even the Maya name for the aged deity is known, and currently he is simply referred to as God L.

However, it is unlikely that such myths of the Classic Maya are lost forever. Great advances have been made recently in the decipherment of Maya hieroglyphs, and it is at last possible to read the names and deeds of particular gods. For ancient Maya studies, the current situation is much like the nine-teenth-century flood of insights and interpretations that followed the decipher-ment of Egyptian hieroglyphs and Mesopotamian cuneiform. The next few decades therefore promise to be an extremely exciting time for the study of ancient Maya religion.

Late Classic Maya vessel scene, representing a rabbit seizing the clothes and regalia of the old God L.

Scene illustrating the resurrection of the maize god, the Classic form of Hun Hunahpu, out of the earth, symbolised by a turtle shell. His two sons, Hunahpu and Xbalanque, are shown assisting their father, and all three are accompanied by their identifying name glyphs. Interior of a Late Classic Maya ceramic bowl.

Unlike the Old World myths of Mesopotamia, Egypt and Greece, many of the mythic episodes and their protagonists mentioned in this book are still a part of contemporary Mesoamerican mythology. The adventures of Nanahuatzin continue to be invoked by Nahuat-speaking peoples living in the Sierra de Puebla. The myths of the Cora and Huichol of western Mexico share many similarities with known Aztec mythology. Just as the Classic Maya version of the *Popol Vuh* can shed light on the Quichean epic, contemporary myths often provide crucial insights into frequently laconic contact-period texts. Modern myths of the Kekchi, Mopan and other Maya peoples frequently contain episodes and motifs related to the *Popol Vuh*. This is also true for contemporary myths of the Mixe, Popoluca and Totonac of Oaxaca and Veracruz, which provide resonating parallels with the *Popol Vuh*, frequently concerning the origin of the maize god. Although modern Mesoamerican myths do often contain elements that are not pre-Hispanic in origin – such as Catholic saints and relatively recent historical events – these are not indications of a dying or decadent mythical tradition, but rather proof of a thriving oral legacy that continues to respond to a constantly changing world.

Suggestions for further reading

Mesoamerican religion is a vast and complex topic, and there are relatively few works encompassing the entire subject. *Religions of Mesoamerica* by D. Carrasco (San Francisco, 1990) provides a general overview of Mesoamerican religion, including two chapters devoted to Aztec and Maya ritual and belief. Incorporating introductory chapters on Mesoamerican religion, *Gods and Symbols of Ancient Mexico and the Maya* by M. Miller and K. Taube (London, 1993) presents the reader with an illustrated encyclopaedia of relevant religious terminology. The *Flayed God* by R. Markman and P. Markman (San Francisco, 1992) focuses specifically upon Mesoamerican mythology and contains translations of early colonial texts. Yet another text devoted to Mesoamerican mythology, *The Mythology of Mexico and Central America* by J. Bierhorst (New York, 1990), is a valuable synthesis of both ancient and contemporary Mesoamerican mythology.

For Aztec and central Mexican religion, the voluminous contributions of E. Seler remain indispensable. An English version of his massive compilation of studies, the *Gesammelte Abhandlungen zur Amerikanischen Sprach-und Altertumskunde*, is currently being published, with three volumes now available (Culver City, Calif., 1990–2). An excellent discussion of Aztec world view and philosophy is to be found in *Aztec Thought and Culture* by M. León-Portilla (Norman, Okla., 1963). *The Great Temple of the Aztecs* (London, 1988) by Matos Moctezuma provides a thorough discussion of the Huitzilopochtli myth and the recent excavations at the Templo Mayor.

Of the primary colonial sources pertaining to Aztec religion, the Florentine Codex is of central importance. An excellent English translation is provided by A. Anderson and C. Dibble (Santa Fe, New Mex. and Salt Lake City, Utah, 1950–82). A recent translation of the Nahuatl *Leyenda de los soles* is to be found in *History and Mythology of the Aztecs: The Codex Chimalpopoca* by J. Bierhorst (Tucson, Ariz., 1992). The *Historia de los mexicanos por sus pinturas* and the *Histoyre du Mechique* can be found in *Teogonía e historia de los Mexicanos* by A. M. Garibay (Mexico City, 1965).

The decipherment of Maya hieroglyphic writing is essential for the study of ancient Maya religion. Two recent discussions of the history of decipherment and the nature of Maya hieroglyphic writing are to be found in *Maya Glyphs* by S. Houston (London and Berkeley, 1989) and *Breaking the Maya Code* by M. Coe (London, 1992). For an introduction to some of the recent advances in the study of Classic Maya writing and religion, *The Blood of Kings* by L. Schele and M. Miller (Fort Worth, Tex., 1986 and London, 1992) is highly recommended. *The Major Gods of Ancient Yucatan* by K. Taube (Washington, DC, 1992) describes the identities and iconography of ancient Maya deities. An excellent corpus of Maya vase scenes with accompanying essays entitled *The Maya Vase Book* is currently being published by J. Kerr, with three volumes now available (New York, 1989, 1990, 1992).

A number of translations of the *Popol Vuh* are available, and two highly recommended versions are by A. Recinos (Norman, 1950) and D. Tedlock (New York, 1985). *Landa's Relación de las Cosas de Yucatan* by A. Tozzer (Cambridge, Mass., 1941) is not only a useful translation of the Landa document, but also provides a great deal of relevant information regarding Late Postclassic Yucatec religion. Of the colonial Yucatec Books of Chilam Balam, the books of Chumayel, Tizimin and Mani are best known. For the Chumayel, the edition by R. Roys (Norman, 1967) is highly recommended. M. Edmonson (Austin, Tex., 1982) has supplied a complete translation of the Tizimin. An English version of the Mani has been published by E. Craine and R. Reindorp in *The Codex Pérez and the Book of Chilam Balam of Maní* (Norman, 1979).

There are many important studies describing myths and legends of contemporary Mesoamerica, and many of the published accounts can be related to pre-Hispanic mythology. Two valuable publications relating to Nahua mythology of highland Mexico are *Nahuat Myth and Social Structure* by J. Taggart (Austin, 1983) and *Mitos y cuentos Nahuas de la Sierra Madre Occidental*, a compilation of texts collected by K. Preuss in 1907 (Mexico City, 1982). For myths of modern Maya peoples, the Tzotzil of Chiapas are particularly well represented, and *Chamulas in the World of the Sun* by G. Gossen (Cambridge, Mass., 1974) and *Of Cabbages and Kings* by R. Laughlin (Washington, DC, 1977) are two important works. A compilation of Yucatec Maya accounts can be found in *An Epoch of Miracles* by A. Burns (Austin, 1983).

Picture credits

p. 238: Sergio Ransford; *p.241:* © Trustees of the British Museum (BM St.536); *p. 244:* Bodleian Library, Oxford, MS. Arch.Selden.A.1, f. 2r; *pp. 246, 247:* Akademische Druck-und Verlagsanstalt; *p. 253:* Sahagún, *Historia general de las cosas de Nueva España*, 1905–9; *p. 258:* León y Gama, *Descripción histórica y cronológica de las dos piedras que se hallaron en la Plaza Principal de México*, 1832; *p. 262:* BM 1974.AM8; *p. 264:* BM 1825.12-10.11; *pp. 267, 270:* Akademische Druck-und Verlagsanstalt; *p. 275 (top):* Dr Emily Umberger; *p. 278:* photo Irmgard Groth-Kimball; *p. 280:* Sahagún, *Historia general de las cosas de Nueva España*, 1905–9; *p. 289:* Alice Wesche; *p. 293:* BM 321-1886; *p. 300:* American Philosophical Society, Philadelphia; *p. 303:* Akademische Druck-und Verlagsanstalt.

If not otherwise credited, photographs and line drawings are by Karl Taube.

INCA
Myths

GARY URTON

For my mother, Bernice Coslett

Acknowledgements
I would like to express my great appreciation to Frank Salomon, Julia Meyerson, Tony Aveni, Colin McEwan and Nicole Casi, who read and commented on earlier drafts of this work. I alone am responsible for any errors that remain. Colin McEwan was both generous and accommodating in facilitating my work in the British Museum and in the photo archives of the Department of Ethnography. I also thank Clara Bezanilla, who provided invaluable assistance in the British Museum collections. Thanks to Christopher Donnan and Michael Moseley for granting permission to reproduce illustrations. Finally, at British Museum Press, I thank Nina Shandloff, who was both gracious and persistent in getting this project underway, and Coralie Hepburn, who guided the work to its final conclusion with utmost efficiency and congeniality.

Contents

N

COLUMBIA

Quito •
Manta •
ECUADOR

Marañón

BRAZIL

Amazon

Ucayali

Lambayeque •
Chiclayo •
Cajamarca •
Trujillo •
Moche •
Chavín de Huantar •

Huallaga

PERU

Lima •
Pachacamac

Apurímac
Urubamba

Huari •
Cuzco •
• Urcos

• Nazca

Lake Titicaca

BOLIVIA

• La Paz
Tiahuanaco
Cochabamba •

Arica •

Potosí •

CHILE

*Pacific
Ocean*

Antofagasta •

ARGENTINA

Boundary (approx.)
of the Inca Empire

• **Santiago**

316

Introduction:
the settings of Inca myths in
space and time

The land and people of Tahuantinsuyu

The Andes, home of the Incas, are made up of three parallel chains of mountains in western South America which run like a colossal nerve fibre from north-west to south-east, through the centre of the modern nation-states of Ecuador, Peru and Bolivia (see map). The northern boundary of the empire lay near the present-day border between Ecuador and Colombia, while its southern reaches extended nearly halfway down the length of what is now Chile and eastwards into north-western Argentina. The Incas divided this territory into four parts, and they knew this land, and their empire, by the name *Tahuantinsuyu*, 'the four united quarters'.

Although the Inca empire is commonly referred to as an 'Andean civilization', a phrase evoking the image of a society adapted to a rugged, essentially mountainous terrain, this view in fact obscures the great environmental complexity and ecological diversity that existed within the territory controlled by this ancient society. For while the rugged terrain of the Andes mountains did indeed make up the core of Inca territory, it was the relationship between the highlands and two adjacent strips of lowlands which gave Inca civilization its true environmental richness and cultural complexity.

One of these lowland strips is an exceptionally dry coastal desert lying along the western edge of the continental shelf, washed by the frigid waters of the Humboldt Current. Numerous rivers emerge from the foothills of the Andes to flow westward to the Pacific Ocean across this dry coastal plain, forming fertile ribbon-like oases which were the home sites of numerous pre-Columbian civilizations. The other lowland region, stretching along the eastern edge of the Andes, includes the humid tropical forest watersheds of the Amazon and Paraná river basins.

Within Peru, the core of Inca territory, several large intermontane tributaries of the Amazon, such as the Marañón, Huallaga and Ucayali rivers, start out by flowing northwards but then break out of the mountains toward the east, running down through rugged foothills into the tropical forest lowlands. These riverine arteries, connecting the upper Amazon with the eastern Andean foothills, have served for millennia as important routes of travel and communication linking the human populations of these two vast ecological regions.

The environmental setting in which Inca civilization thrived thus incorporated the three major ecological zones of coast, mountains and tropical forest, each of which was home to a seeming myriad local and regional ethnic groups. Through years of archaeological research and the study of early colonial documents, researchers have arrived at a widely shared understanding of how the Incas and their neighbours adapted their social, economic, political and ritual institutions to the land of Tahuantinsuyu. In some cases, this involved reliance on tried-and-true practices inherited from earlier civilizations; in other cases, the Incas were challenged to devise new institutions, adaptive strategies, and principles and practices of rulership. In the broadest terms, we should give special emphasis to one institution in particular and describe its relationship to a widespread strategy of adaptation by means of which at least late pre-Hispanic Andean societies met the challenges of adapting to this particular environmental setting. The institution in question was the *ayllu*, and the strategy was the exploitation of resources in multiple ecological zones.

Ayllus – a Quechua word meaning 'family', 'lineage' or 'part' – of which there were perhaps several tens of thousands spread throughout that part of the Andes incorporated within the Inca empire, were kinship, landholding and ritual-ceremonial groupings. The membership of each ayllu was distributed discontinuously over a wide area. That is, some members of the ayllu would live at a mid-altitudinal setting; others would inhabit the high *puna* (tundra) zone; and still others would occupy settlements in lower-lying areas, including the intermontane valleys and the coastal and/or tropical forest lowlands. The economy of each ayllu was based on the exchange of goods among members who lived in different ecological zones. Such exchanges may have gone on both through the relatively continuous movement of individuals belonging to the group as they travelled (probably in llama caravans) between ayllu settlements, as well as during annual gatherings, or festivals, of ayllu members held at some central settlement. We know that the ayllu maintained ancestral mummies, which were venerated by the group as a whole. Ayllu festivals would have provided the setting both for the veneration of these ancestral mummies, and for the retelling of the origin myths of the ayllus.

In addition to ayllus, researchers often speak of the presence of different 'ethnic groups' in the Inca empire. In the Inca case, this nomenclature refers to groupings of ayllus that recognized a higher-level unity among themselves, often tracing their common origins back to the ancestor(s) of the ancestors of the various ayllus. Such collectivities of ayllus also constituted what are referred to (particularly in the southern Andes) as confederations. Another common, intermediate-level of organization throughout the empire were two-part – so-called 'moiety' – groupings of ayllus. In many cases, the two

Group of Inca polished stone mortars in the shape of llamas.

parts, which were commonly referred to as 'upper' (*hanan*) and 'lower' (*hurin*), derived from a locally important topographic and hydrological division, recognized most clearly in the distribution of water through a network of irrigation canals. In addition, the ancestors of the moieties were often thought to have had different origins and/or specializations (e.g., farmers/herders, or autochthonous peoples/invaders).

The genius of Inca civilization was its successful integration of these many and varied peoples and resources into a single, hierarchically organized society. This was achieved by processes of conquest and alliance, as well as by a high level of bureaucratic organization, which allowed the state not only to co-ordinate and direct the activities of these numerous ayllus, ethnic groups and confederations, but also to integrate and synthesize what I will term below the 'mythic-histories' of these various groups. In this regard, it will be useful to establish from the beginning two important, interrelated distinctions that should be made concerning religious and mythic traditions in the pre-Columbian Andes. One distinction is that between Andean religion and Inca religion, while the other is that between Andean myths and Inca myths.

As it is generally understood by specialists working in the Andes, 'Andean religion' refers to locally based sets of beliefs and practices that identify and pay homage to local earth, mountain, and water spirits and to the deities that were linked to local (i.e., provincial) ayllus and ethnic groups and their ancestors throughout the empire. These beliefs and practices were linked to, and explicated by, cosmic origin myths, myths of primordial relations between humans and animals, and accounts of mythical encounters between the ancestors of different ayllus and ethnic groups within a given area that were retained by the story-tellers within that region.

'Inca religion', on the other hand, encompasses the beliefs, ceremonies and ritual practices that were promoted by the Inca nobility and their priestly and political agents for the benefit of the Inca state. Inca mythology refers to the mythological traditions that contextualized, explained and justified state beliefs and practices to the subjects of the Incas. Although there were numerous similarities and interconnections between the two, the focus of Andean religion and mythology was on the unity and perpetuation of each of the myriad ayllus and ethnic groups, whereas the driving force behind Inca religion and mythology was the unification of all such local groups within the empire in the service, and under the hegemony, of the Incas.

Central to the practice of Inca and Andean religion was the worship of and care for mummies. Reverence for and continuous care of the mummies of the Inca kings, as well as the ancestral mummies, called *mallquis*, of ayllus were important practices in the religion of people throughout the Inca empire. Numerous myths were told by the Incas and their provincial subjects concerning the life and deeds of those individuals whose mummified remains were prominently displayed in public places, or were stored in caves near the towns where their descendants lived. It was believed that caring for, redressing, and offering food and drink to the ancestral mummies were requirements for maintaining cosmic order, as well as the continued fertility of the crops and herd animals. Such beliefs and practices continued to haunt the Spanish priests who struggled for centuries to stamp out such 'idolatrous' practices and to Christianize the descendants of the Incas and their provincial subjects.

The organization of the Inca empire

At the centre of the empire was the capital city, Cusco, located in a fertile valley in the south-central Andes of Peru at an altitude of about 3,400 m (11,000 ft) above sea level. Cusco was home to the royal lineage of the Incas, from which was drawn the dozen kings who ruled the empire from sometime near the beginning of the 1400s until the Spanish conquest of the Andes in 1532. The population of the city, and by extension the empire as a whole, was divided into four ritual and administrative districts, called *suyus* ('part', 'quarter'). Beginning in the north-west and going clockwise, the four quarters were called Chinchaysuyu, Antisuyu, Collasuyu and Cuntisuyu. The quarters were produced by a complicated intersection of two dual divisions within the city of Cusco. The true centre of the city of Cusco and of the four quarters of the city and the empire was the set of a half-dozen or so buildings called the Coricancha ('golden enclosure'), which is sometimes referred to as the Temple of the Sun.

One room of the Coricancha housed the mummies of past kings of the empire. These were taken out of the Coricancha during important ritual celebrations and, riding on litters, were paraded around the central plaza of the city. In other rooms of the Coricancha were images and idols depicting and dedicated to the creator deity (Viracocha), the Sun, the Moon, Venus (of

The four quarters of the Inca empire.

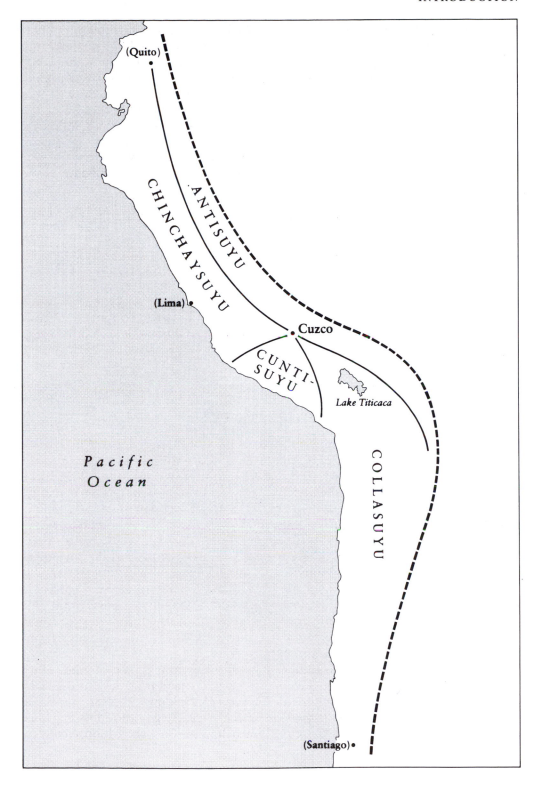

Eastern rooms of the Coricancha in Cusco.

the Morning and Evening), Thunder, the Rainbow, and other lesser objects of worship. While the Coricancha was the focal point of ritual life within the capital, the palaces, shrines and population of Cusco represented the focal point of the empire of Tahuantinsuyu as a whole.

At the top of the imperial hierarchy stood the Inca king, called *sapa* ('unique', 'sole') *Inca*. The ruling Inca was believed to be the direct descendant of the first king, Manco Capac, as well as the earthly manifestation of the sun (*inti*), whose light and warmth made the world of the high Andes habitable. Alongside the king was his primary wife, called the *qoya* ('queen'), who was, at least in late imperial times, also his sister. The queen was considered to be the human embodiment of the moon (*quilla*), the celestial body whose monthly rhythm of waxing and waning established the tempo of ritual life in the capital. Around the Inca king and queen were the nobility – the descendants of the dozen or so royal ayllus, or kin groups (called *panacas*), that occupied the capital. The panaca groupings were ranked hierarchically depending on their closeness to the line(s) of kings descended from Manco Capac.

In addition to his primary wife, the king had numerous secondary wives – different Spanish sources say between forty and a hundred. These women were often the daughters of high-ranking provincial aristocrats whose marriage to the Inca elevated the rank of their natal lineage and ayllu. Children of secondary wives were considered to be lower-ranking nobles, and many became administrative officials of the empire. They were supplemented by accountants, record-keepers, diviners, military commanders and other functionaries who belonged to lineages of panacas or ayllus composing the lesser nobility.

From the capital, administrators went out to the four quarters of the empire to oversee and regulate affairs of state, especially to oversee the performance of state labour. In the Inca empire 'tribute' was assessed in the form of public labour, the local ayllus having the obligation to work the lands, or herd the flocks of camelids, of the king and the gods in their local communities, as well as to perform 'turns of service' (*mit'a*) at state installations. For such purposes, the tribute-payers were organized into decimal groupings (i.e., groupings of 5, 10, 100, 500, 1000, etc. households). The state administration was similarly organized in a decimal fashion, with overseers designated to direct the affairs of different levels of decimal household groupings, keeping records on a device, called a *quipu* ('knot', see p.26), that recorded the information in a decimal-based numeration. Imperial runners (*chaskis*) carried messages between the capital and its provincial administrative centres, located at ecologically and demographically critical nodal points throughout the empire.

Numerous rituals and state ceremonies, such as the daily sacrifice of a hundred llamas in the plaza in Cusco and the celebration of two great festivals of the sun at the times of the solstices in December and June, as well as a festival of the moon in October, sanctified the unity and antiquity of collective life under the stewardship of the Incas.

In the provinces, the majority of the population was made up of commoners, or *hatunruna* ('the great people'), who were organized into a multitude of ayllus. Among the settlements occupying any given region, the highest-ranking lineage(s) among those groups held hereditary lordships, called *curacas*. The curacas acted as local authorities and imperial agents, overseeing affairs of state on behalf of the Incas within their home territories.

One particularly dramatic ceremonial expression of the unity between the Inca in the capital and the people in the countryside was the annual sacrifice of specially designated victims (usually children) called *capacochas*. These individuals were sent from the provinces to Cusco where they were sanctified by the priests of the Incas. The capacochas were then returned to their home territories, marching in sacred procession along straight lines (*ceques*), where they were sacrificed. We learn from colonial documents of capacochas being buried alive in specially constructed shaft-tombs, and recently there have been discoveries of capacochas sacrificed by being clubbed and their bodies left on high mountain tops. In all such cases, the sacrifices sealed bonds of alliance between the home community and the Inca in Cusco. The sacrifice of the capacochas also served to reaffirm the hierarchical relation between the Incas at the centre and high-ranking lineages in the provinces.

The Incas also employed a strategy of population control and economic organization whereby certain ayllus, or segments of them, were moved from their home territories, at the will of the Inca, for purposes such as working on state projects or serving as guards at frontier outposts. These transplanted people were called *mitimaes*. Such movements and the consequent mixing of people in imperial times undoubtedly had a profound impact on notions of origin places and (mythical) histories retained by ethnic groups throughout the empire. Finally, there was a hereditary class of servants known as *yanaconas* ('dark/servant people'). These were retainers of the royalty – people who lived on and worked the lands of the kings and the high nobility.

Like the myths of other ancient civilizations around the world, the cosmic creation myths and the origin myths of the Incas legitimized their rule and validated the hierarchical social, political and economic relations organizing society as a whole. It is important to stress, however, that the Incas drew on a store of knowledge, beliefs and practices that came down to them from earlier civilizations. This is not unusual, as few if any states of the ancient world arose entirely independently of earlier kingdom or chiefdom-level societies.

The archaeological remains of Inca and pre-Inca civilizations from Ecuador southward through Peru, Bolivia and Chile are extensive and extremely varied. For many of these cultures, we possess numerous examples of works of art displaying rich and complex iconographic representations of humans, animals, and human–animal composites that appear to represent supernatural entities. Such images and scenes as those of important personages standing serenely among subordinates, winged figures, and anthropomorphized animals, plants and aquatic creatures that we see painted on ceramics, woven into textiles or hammered from lumps of gold offer modest clues as to the nature of and relations among indigenous deities, spirits and other mythological beings before the time of the Incas. Thus, exercising appropriate caution, we can contextualize, enrich and enlighten our understanding of Inca mythology by surveying the archaeological and iconographic records from pre-Inca civilizations.

Precursors to the Incas

The Incas were not the first Andean civilization to unify the peoples of western South America. In fact, it is evident to archaeologists that the Incas were able to affect unification as rapidly as they did (over a few centuries) by building on pre-existing relations, institutions of state, and habits of empire inherited from earlier peoples. Archaeologists divide Peruvian prehistory into five major periods, primarily on the basis of continuities and changes in ceramic shapes and styles over time and across space. Three of these periods are known as 'horizons', a term that is meant to indicate that these were periods of relative unity in art, architecture, ritualism and economy over broad regions in the central Andes. Intervening between the three horizons were two so-called 'intermediate' periods, which designate times and processes of local and regional (rather than pan-Andean) development.

Period	Approximate Time Range
Early Horizon	900–200 BC
Early Intermediate	200 BC–AD 500
Middle Horizon	AD 500–1000
Late Intermediate	AD 1000–1400
Late Horizon	AD 1400–1532

One of the earliest civilizations ancestral to the Incas is known as Chavín. This culture, whose extension in time and space defines the Early Horizon, takes its name from the site of Chavín de Huantar, which is situated at the point of union of two small rivers near the headwaters of the Marañon and Santa rivers, in the central Peruvian highlands. Chavín de Huantar exhibits all the trappings of Andean ceremonial centres: stone-faced pyramids with internal passageways converging on oracular chambers; open plazas situated between mounds that extend arm-like outward from the pyramids; and a complex arrangement of carved stone stelae and free-standing statuary bearing distinctive iconographic images. The themes of Chavín art are drawn from the animals, plants and aquatic life of the coast, highlands and tropical forest. Similarly, sites displaying this distinctive imagery are located from the upper Amazon westward, through the high intermontane valleys of the Andes mountains to the lush river valleys of the Pacific coastal desert.

Chavín images include animals, especially felines, in human-like poses, as well as harpy eagles, falcons and a profusion of serpents, many of which are rendered with formidable canine teeth. A common element that appears

Façade of the New Temple, Chavín de Huantar.

ubiquitously in Chavín art, and will reappear in art down to the time of the Spanish conquest, is the so-called 'staff deity'. These are standing frontal figures, perhaps representing human-animal composites or masked humans, both male and female, holding staffs or corn stalks in either hand. We do not know the precise meaning or significance of the staff deities for the Chavín peoples themselves. However, given the prominence and ubiquity with which such figures appear during Chavín times in architecture and on portable works of art in sites throughout much of present-day Peru, it is fairly certain that this character represented a supernatural force and personality of exceptional importance, perhaps a creator deity, of sorts. This conclusion is made all the more likely in view of the fact that staff deities of similar posture and with similar accoutrements appear commonly in artistic representations from Chavín until – and including – Inca times.

The Early Horizon was followed by another period of roughly equal length in which a number of regional chiefdoms allied and competed with each other for control of people and resources over the ecologically varied landscape of the Andes. It would be a mistake to think of the period following the Early Horizon, known as the Early Intermediate Period (200 BC–AD 500), as a time of chaos and cultural degeneration, despite the fact that the Incas themselves tended to portray such periods of decentralization and regionalism in precisely these terms. Instead, a number of major social, political and artistic innovations were achieved during this period.

For instance, city-building on the part of the chiefdom- or kingdom-

*Female staff deity
from Chavín-Period
painted textile.*

level societies on the north coast of Peru produced urban centres of astonishing complexity. This occurred in and around such sites as the Huaca del
Sol, in the Moche valley, and Pampa Grande, in the Lambayeque valley. The
recent discovery of the tombs of the lords of Sipan, near present-day
Chiclayo, Peru, display a level of sophistication in metallurgy matched only
by later Andean civilizations. Such works of art, rich in the imagery of feline,
jaguar–human and other animal representations, recall in certain respects
the art of Chavín. The mythology that underlay and gave meaning to
such iconography was undoubtedly shared by (or at least known to) other
contemporary civilizations of the north coast of Peru, as well as by earlier
and later Andean civilizations.

One body of artistic work from north coastal Peru that has been the
focus of a considerable amount of study and speculation by scholars interested in iconographic depictions of Andean mythological traditions is the
modelled and painted imagery of Moche ceramics. Here, particularly in
scenes painted on the bodies of stirrup-spout vessels, we see figures of
humans and anthropomorphized animals, birds and marine creatures, some
of which are thought to have been important characters in north coastal
(Moche) mythology. Several of the figures are shown in postures and
groupings that are so standardized, and are repeated with such regularity,
that scholars have suggested that the scenes depict a fairly limited number
(e.g., a couple of dozen) of widely shared mythic ritual 'themes'. The ritual
circumstances and mythological settings include such scenes as the capture

Mound constructions in the Lambayeque valley.

The Huaca del Sol, Moche valley.

Moche stirrup-spout vessel painted with images of beans and running messenger.

and sacrifice of enemy warriors, the offering of drink – which in some cases seems to represent goblets filled with the blood of sacrificial victims – by subordinates to high lords, or deities, and the passage of a character through the starry sky in a moon-shaped boat.

When we look to the south coast of Peru during the Early Intermediate Period, we find less emphasis on, or at least less evidence for, the development of large, urban centres than is evident at this same time on the north coast. Nonetheless, there were numerous ceremonial centres, such as those in the Pisco, Ica and Nazca river drainages, that probably served as regional pilgrimage centres visited by peoples belonging to different ethnic groups who gathered at these centres for a variety of ritual and economic motives. In addition, there are many cemeteries located within the south coastal Peruvian river valleys dating to the Early Horizon and Early Intermediate Period that are notable for the burial and display of mummies. Many such mummified remains are wrapped in beautifully woven and embroidered textiles displaying a wide array of both natural and supernatural iconographic images. The latter have been interpreted by researchers as having been linked to ritual practices (especially in agriculture and warfare) and mythological traditions of the valley residents.

The next era of cultural unification in the pre-Columbian Andes, a period known as the Middle Horizon (AD 500–1000), saw the emergence of two political and ritual centres. One, called Tiahuanaco, was located on the high Bolivian plateau (*altiplano*) not far inland from the south shore of Lake Titicaca; the other, called Huari, was situated in the south-central Peruvian highlands. The societies represented by these co-existing centres have been named after them.

Paracas weaving.

Gateway of the Sun, Tiahuanaco, showing central staff deity flanked by winged attendants.

While there were certainly numerous characteristics distinguishing Tiahuanaco and Huari societies, there were at the same time a number of notable similarities. Chief among the latter was a rich and complex iconography rendered in diverse media, particularly stone, cloth, ceramics and shell. Many images of religious and mythological significance appear commonly in the art of both Tiahuanaco and Huari. These include staff deities, as well as winged, running falcon-headed figures that are often shown in profile holding clubs and in some cases decapitated heads. The posture and location in architectural and other compositions of Tiahuanaco and Huari staff deities emphasize the centrality of this character in Tiahuanaco and Huari culture and attest to its probable religious, ritual and mythological continuity from similar figures in Chavín times. It is quite likely that, like the so-called creator gods of Inca times, such as Viracocha and Pachacamac, the staff deities of the Tiahuanaco and Huari peoples were considered to be responsible for the origin of humans and the fertility of crops and animals.

The staff deities and numerous free-standing, carved stone images at the site of Tiahuanaco are striking when seen *in situ* by tourists today, just as they were when viewed by travellers and pilgrims in Inca times. Inca informants in the early years following the Spanish invasion told their conquerors that the statues at Tiahuanaco represented an earlier race of giants whose origins were in an era before the appearance of the Inca kings. In fact, as we shall see, a ubiquitous theme in the mythology both of the Incas and of

Stone statue at Tiahuanaco.

their provincial subjects throughout much of present-day Peru was the claim that their ancestors came from Lake Titicaca and the site of Tiahuanaco itself.

The Late Intermediate Period (AD 1000–1400) was a second period of regional development in central Andean prehistory. This period falls between the Middle Horizon societies of Tiahuanaco and Huari and the emergence of Inca civilization, whose widespread distribution in space and time is referred to as the Late Horizon (c. AD 1400–1532). One society that emerged during the Late Intermediate Period and is of particular interest in terms of the study of Andean and Inca myths is that of the Chimu peoples. Chimu was a state-level society of north coastal Peru whose capital was at Chan Chan, in the Moche river valley. At Chan Chan and other sites that were incorporated into the Chimu state, we find the remains of massive, royal compounds containing open plazas, burial mounds and administrative quarters. Such sites display a variety of decorative adobe friezes, including repeated images of marine birds and sea creatures, as well as what has been interpreted as double-headed rainbow serpents.

Chimu, which is often referred to under the geographic–linguistic label *Yunga* ('lowlands'), is especially important in the study of Inca myths for two reasons: first, in the early colonial documentation we possess a number of accounts detailing relations between Chimu and Inca kings in mythic times, as well as encounters between the idols of these respective societies; second, the Chimu state represents perhaps the only other pre-Inca Andean state from which we have extant versions of origin myths. We will discuss the shape and contents of these myths later.

Adobe frieze at site of Chan Chan, Moche valley.

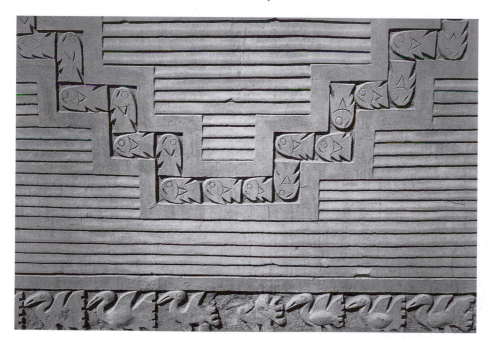

Adobe frieze depicting double-headed serpent, Huaca El Dragon, Moche valley.

The above survey provides a highly schematic overview of the succession of cultures and a periodization of the developmental phases in Andean prehistory that led up to the emergence of the Incas. Cultural developments up to the time of the Incas in the Late Horizon included kingship, a highly centralized and bureaucratic statecraft, local (ayllu-based) and state redistribution of economic resources, a priesthood, ancestor worship, and rich traditions of art and iconography in a variety of media. Although our colonial sources do not speak directly on the matter of long-term continuities of deities and mythic themes uniting one civilization and cultural phase to the next, the persistence of certain iconographic themes (e.g., feline–human hybrids, staff deities, falcon-headed warriors, or 'spirits'), and an archaeological record of the mixing and blending of cultures over time, rather than the wholesale replacement of one culture by another, lend strong support to the notion that Inca mythological traditions were the products of a long and complex process of innovation, borrowing and reworking of myths among a succession of Andean societies.

In the next chapter, we will review the early colonial sources that detail the results of these continuing Andean traditions of cosmic, state and local myths.

Sources for the study of Inca myths

How do we know about the myths the Incas told about themselves and the world around them? The first thing to note in regard to this question is that, in fact, none of what we now refer to as 'Inca myths' has come down to us from documents that were originally written by native Andean peoples in their own language(s) before the arrival of the Spaniards. This is because the Incas did not develop a system of writing – or if they did, we have not yet succeeded in identifying or deciphering it. Thus all accounts of Inca myths available to us were recorded by Spanish chroniclers or scribes, or by Spanish-trained native Andeans, all of whom wrote with pen or quill on paper or parchment. The majority of these myths were written in Spanish. However, a few early sources, such as those of the native chronicler Felipe Guaman Poma de Ayala, or of another native, Juan de Santacruz Pachacuti Yamqui Salcamaygua, are written in a Spanish liberally sprinkled with words, phrases and grammatical structures deriving either from the Inca lingua franca – a language known as Quechua – or from another widespread though unrelated language, Aymara, which was, and still is, commonly spoken around Lake Titicaca and southward, throughout much of present-day Bolivia.

At the same time as noting the absence of native written accounts of Inca myths, it is important to appreciate the role played by one indigenous recording device in particular, the *quipu*, in the collection and recording of Inca myths and histories in early colonial times. Quipus, from the Quechua word for 'knot', were linked bundles of dyed and knotted strings, which were used by the Incas to record both statistical information, such as census accounts and tribute records, as well as information that could be interpreted – in some manner that we do not yet fully understand – by experts called *quipucamayoqs* ('knot-makers or keepers') in narrating stories about the Inca past.

Before the arrival of the Spaniards, the narratives retained on the quipus were recounted by the quipucamayoqs in public settings on important ceremonial occasions. The tasks of remembering and recounting the past were also the duties of the court poet-philosophers, called *amautas*. These people were responsible for putting accounts of the genealogies and deeds of the Inca kings and queens, as well as reports of coronations, battles and so on, into song form and for performing them, on demand, before the king and the

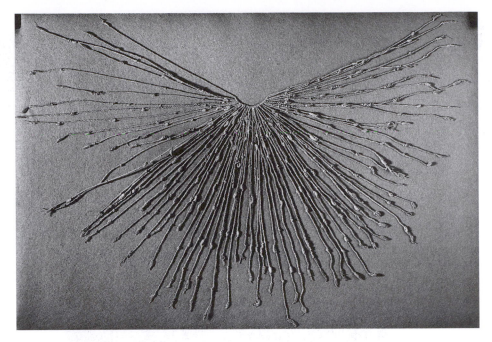

Quipu – Inca knotted-string recording device.

court. Following the Spanish conquest, these same native officials were the principal sources from whom the Spaniards heard accounts of myths, dynastic genealogies and histories, and other stories of the Inca past. In this process, the quipu accounts were 'read', or interpreted, by the quipucamayoqs in their native language, translated into Spanish by a bilingual translator (*lengua*), and written down by a Spanish scribe.

The fact that so much of the information pertaining to the Inca past collected by the Spaniards in the early years following the conquest came from (primarily male) informants in Cusco who were members of the Inca nobility gives a decidedly élitist, masculine and Cusco-centric cast to the corpus of myths available to us. It is only as we encounter documents produced during the early to mid-seventeenth century that we begin to read accounts pertaining to the lives of commoners (both women and men) in the provinces.

We must also remember that the process described above of quipu reading, translation and transcription was fraught with opportunities for both groups of people involved – natives and Spaniards – to twist, elide, embellish, or otherwise amend stories to suit their own personal or political motives. This could involve, for instance, the careful crafting of a genealogical history by a native Andean who wanted to put his or her lineage in a better light in testimony before the Spaniards. In addition, it is clear that some of the Spaniards were bent on portraying the Incas as tyrants and illegitimate rulers. This latter kind of manipulation of the past became an integral part of the Spanish strategy of justifying their own conquest of, and rule over, Andean peoples.

Qero – colonial drinking mug with Hispanicized images of Inca and queen.

There is, unfortunately, no magical or easy way to 'read between the lines' of mythic accounts to know what elements are indigenous and which are imposed, or imported, by natives or Europeans for some particular, political end(s). It is only by coupling a study of the colonial documents with archaeological investigations of Inca sites that we can begin to separate out myth from history in the chroniclers' accounts of Inca 'history'. Thus careful

337

and critical study of the sources are required in order for us to arrive at what may be, in all likelihood, relevant and culturally meaningful constructions of Inca myths.

An additional point that should be borne in mind in order to appreciate fully the nature and limitations of the information on myths contained in our sources is that since the accounts available to us were all written down from informants' testimony taken after 1532, this body of myths does not possess an undisputed absolute chronology. While we can obviously follow the storyline within a given myth, noting that one event is said to have happened after another, we cannot sensibly assign an absolute date during the period before the onset of recorded history in 1532 to any one of these events solely on the basis of what the post-conquest accounts tell us.

Numerous attempts have indeed been made since the beginning of the colonial era to devise a scheme of fixed dates as a temporal framework for interpreting the possible historical significance of certain events recounted in Inca myths. These range from Spanish efforts on the one hand to correlate events mentioned in the Inca origin myths (e.g., a universal deluge, the supposed appearance of the disciples of Christ) with biblical 'history', to contemporary endeavours to impose a kind of Western, linear logic, including absolute dates, on the succession of kings said to have ruled in the Andes in late pre-Hispanic times. All such chronologies rest on shaky ground and none has been confirmed even in the most general of terms by independent, scientific archaeological investigations. It is only through the science of archaeology, with its radiocarbon and other dating techniques, that we can securely assign dates to events in the pre-Hispanic era and, thereby, begin to build up a chronological framework for evaluating the historicity of some elements of the Inca myths.

Principal chroniclers of Inca myths

The works of a couple of dozen chroniclers who wrote during the first century following the conquest provide us with material for the study of Inca mythology. Among these the following sources, discussed generally in chronological order, are some of the most interesting, useful and/or reliable.

Cieza de León was a Spanish soldier who travelled throughout much of western South America, beginning in the earliest days of Spanish penetration into the continent. Having entered Peru in about 1547, he travelled over the next several years from the far north coast, near Tumbes, southward through the former heartland of the empire and as far south as Charcas, in south-central Bolivia. Cieza was a careful observer who talked to numerous informants and took copious notes during his travels. There is much of value for the study of Inca myths in the first two parts of his *Crónica del Peru*. The first part of this work, published in 1553, contains Cieza's geographical descriptions; the second part, which carries the title *El Señorío de los Incas*, was published in 1554 and is one of our earliest sources on the history and the mythology of the Inca empire.

Juan de Betanzos was born in Spain but spent his adult life in Peru.

Around 1541, Betanzos married an Inca princess, a niece of the last undisputed king, Huayna Capac. Betanzos lived in Cusco, became fluent in the Quechua language, and was on intimate terms with numerous descendants of Inca nobility in the former capital city. In 1551 Betanzos was ordered by the Viceroy of Peru, Antonio de Mendoza, to write a history of the Incas. His account, which has recently appeared in its first English translation under the title *Narrative of the Incas* (tr. R. Hamilton and D. Buchanan, 1996), was completed in 1557. This is one of our best sources on Inca myths as told from the point of view of the Inca nobility in Cusco during the first few decades following the conquest.

Polo de Ondegardo served as the top colonial administrator (*corregidor*) of Cusco from 1558 to 1561 and again from 1571 to 1572. A jurist with a real interest in the religion, customs and 'superstitions' of the Inca peoples and their descendants, Polo carried out investigations on these and other matters – including attempts, mostly successful, to locate and dispose of the mummies of the Inca kings – during the 1550s and 1560s. These investigations resulted in the publication of a number of reports, including a treatise entitled *Los Errores y supersticiones de los indios* (1567), as well as a report on the religion and government of the Incas (1571). These provide useful background material for contextualizing our early accounts of Inca myths; material from them were digested and incorporated into a number of later works, including the chronicles by Acosta and Cobo (see below).

Polo de Ondegardo was a precursor and early proponent of a late sixteenth-century genre or tradition of interpretation and writing about the Incas and their history that developed in relation to the reorganization of the colonial state under the fourth viceroy of Peru, Francisco de Toledo (1569–81). Toledo undertook a programme of investigating Inca history, including the organization and structure of the Inca empire, as a basis for instituting reforms of virtually every aspect of life in the colony – from the operation of the colonial bureaucracy to the location and layout of native villages. Toledo also ordered the writing of several histories of the empire, based on interviews with former Inca nobility and quipucamayoqs.

The chronicles produced during or soon after the Toledan viceroyalty included such works as Sarmiento de Gamboa's *Historia de los Incas* (1572), the Cusqueñan Cristobal de Molina's *Las Fabulas y Ritos de los Incas* (1575), and José de Acosta's *Historia natural y moral de las Indias* (1590). In addition, Cabello de Balboa's *Miscelánea Antártica* (1586), an excellent source on myths of the north coast of Peru (in the area of the Chimu peoples), also incorporated materials on Inca mythology taken from the chronicle of Sarmiento de Gamboa.

A theme uniting various of these histories was the view that the Inca dynasty represented a tyrannical regime that had essentially gained power by fraudulent means. According to the Toledan interpretation, Inca rule was not only abusive, it was also illegitimate. Such assertions cleared the way for the Europeans to claim that the Spanish conquest of the Incas was a justifiable enterprise, replacing as it did the rule of a bogus nobility (that of the Incas) by the legitimate rule of the Spanish crown. Thus while the Toledan chronicles represent some of our earliest, most comprehensive and best-informed sources for the study of Inca myths, it is necessary to read them critically, with a recognition of their ideological and political underpinnings.

Another important yet somewhat problematic source on Inca mythology is the chronicle written by the *mestizo* (Spanish/Quechua mixed-blood) Garcilaso de la Vega. Garcilaso was born in Cusco in 1539, the son of an Inca princess, Isabell Chimpu Ocllo, and a Spanish *conquistador*, whose name Garcilaso bore. Garcilaso lived in Cusco until the age of twenty-one and then, in 1560, travelled to Spain, where he remained for the rest of his life. In 1602 he began writing his great history of the Inca empire, entitled *Comentarios Reales de los Incas* (1609–17). Part memoir and part compilation of earlier, especially Toledan, sources, Garcilaso's text contains numerous myths, some of which are attested to by other authors (especially Blas Valera and José de Acosta), but an equal number of which are either not found in other sources, or are indeed recounted by other authors but with notable variations from the versions remembered by Garcilaso.

At about the same time that the first part of Garcilaso's chronicle appeared, an exceptionally important text on the mythology of local peoples in the region of Huarochirí, in the central highlands of Peru, was produced. This work, which was written in the Quechua language, has been published in several languages under various titles, such as a Spanish version entitled *Dioses y Hombres de Huarochirí* and, most recently in an English translation, *The Huarochirí Manuscript* (tr. F. Salomon and G.L. Urioste, 1991). The work appears to have been composed under the direction of the local priest of this region, Francisco de Avila, although its author(s) was (were) clearly native to the area of Huarochirí. This work represents one of our best sources on the pre-Hispanic and early colonial mythological traditions of peoples in one of the former provinces of the Inca empire.

At approximately the same time that the Huarochirí manuscript was written down, a work was composed in Spain, which is known as the *Relación de los Quipucamayoqs* (1608/1542). It appears to have been assembled on behalf of a late pretender to the Inca throne, a man named Melchior Carlos Inca, in 1608. In what was an apparent attempt to add weight and legitimacy to his claims to the throne, Melchior had incorporated into the early section of his manuscript mythic materials concerning the foundation of the Inca dynasty that derived from an inquest undertaken in Cusco, in 1542, before the Licenciado Vaca de Castro. The informants at that inquest were four elderly quipucamayoqs who had served the Inca as historians before the time of the conquest. These materials represent some of the earliest origin myths of the Inca state that we have.

We should take note here of another Spanish chronicler, Antonio de la Calancha, whose *Coronica moralizada del Orden de San Augustín en el Perú* (1638) contains valuable information on the religion, customs and myths of peoples of the north coast of Peru.

An important development in the recording of myths from outside Cusco that occurred during the early seventeenth century was the appearance of chronicles written by native, Quechua-speaking authors. The most notable authors to mention in this regard are Felipe Guaman Poma de Ayala and Juan de Santacruz Pachacuti Yamqui Salcamaygua.

Guaman Poma was born in Huamanga, in the central Peruvian Andes. He claimed that his father had been a provincial nobleman who served as an emissary of the Inca Guascar to Francisco Pizarro at Cajamarca. Guaman Poma received intensive ecclesiastical training from priests in and around Huamanga, and he even participated in the 'extirpation' of native idolatries during the late sixteenth and early seventeenth centuries. In 1613 Guaman Poma completed his monumental work, entitled *Nueva Corónica y Buen Gobierno* (1583–1613). This document contains, in its approximately 1,000 pages, a description of life in Peru before, during and after the Spanish conquest. In addition to its text, the work also contains almost 400 drawings, which constitute one of our best sources of information on Inca dress, agricultural implements, and other features of everyday life, as well as depicting scenes of ritual and worship at places mentioned in some of the origin myths, such as the mountain and cave of origin of the first Inca king. While Guaman Poma was an early and ardent convert to Christianity, who believed that it was the Inca kings who had led their Andean subjects into idolatry, his chronicle contains much information of value for a study of Inca myths.

Juan de Santacruz Pachacuti Yamqui Salcamaygua was another important native author, from the area of Canas and Canchis, midway between Cusco and Lake Titicaca. Although he also wrote from the perspective of a Christian convert, he was somewhat more sympathetic to the Incas than was Guaman Poma. In his work, entitled *Relación de Antiguedades deste Reyno del Pirú* (c. 1613), Pachacuti Yamqui recounts myths, as well as a substantial body of quasi-mythic/historical data that can be linked to myths recounted by other authors. His work is decidedly idiosyncratic and challenging in its composition, given its frequent use of Quechua words and grammatical structures, yet it contains much of interest and value for the study of Inca myths.

Bernabé Cobo was a Jesuit priest who was born in Spain, entered Peru in 1599, and remained there for all but a few years of the rest of his life. Cobo travelled from Lima to Cusco in 1609, and spent much of the next twenty years undertaking missionary work and travelling in southern Peru and northern Bolivia. In 1653 he completed his great work, *Historia del Nuevo Mundo*. To date, the translator Roland Hamilton has prepared two excellent English translations of different parts of Cobo's *Historia*, under the titles, *History of the Inca Empire* (1983; books 11 and 12 of *Historia*), and *Inca Religion and Customs* (1990; books 13 and 14 of *Historia*). Cobo drew extensively on previous chronicles, including the works of Polo de Ondegardo, Cristobal de Molina, José de Acosta and Garcilaso de la Vega. He is considered by many Andeanists to be one of our most reliable sources on Inca history. Certainly the myths, descriptions of state ceremonies, and accounts of Inca religious beliefs and practices which he synthesized from earlier sources resulted in the production of our most comprehensive and balanced chronicle of life in the Inca empire.

A final set of documents that are important for the study of Inca myths are the so-called *idolatrías* ('idolatries'). These documents were produced primarily during the first half of the seventeenth century as a result of investigations by Catholic priests into what the church took to be the continuing idolatry practised by peoples in the Andean countryside. Investigators queried local authorities (*curacas*), as well as curers, 'witches', and other diviners and religious specialists concerning the persistence of the worship of ancestral mummies and sacred places in the landscape, such as mountains, caves, and springs. These documents are rich sources of information for contextualizing accounts of myths, as well as descriptions of similar beliefs and practices among the Incas, as recounted in earlier sources. In addition, the idolatrías provide testimony of the continuing religious persecution of native men and women in the Andean countryside during the colonial era.

Paqcha – painted wooden device used in performing divinations (Colonial Period).

The local, state and cosmic themes uniting Inca myths

One of the most salient facts of life in the pre-Columbian Andes was the great ethnic diversity characterizing the subjects of the Incas. Such diversity seems to have had at least two important consequences for the shape and substance of myths in the empire. One was that this diversity itself needed an explanation. Why were people so different in terms of their language, dress and other customs and habits? Did near, or even distant, neighbours who seemed so fundamentally different from one another have different origins? Or did all people in the empire have a single origin?

Answers to questions such as these, which are represented in the contents of the myths themselves, lead us to distinguish two quite distinct bodies of origin myths. On one level, peoples in different parts of the empire appear to have insisted on the distinctiveness of their individual origins, and the myths resulting from these locally based myths and ideologies of origin display a multiplicity of creator deities and places and times of origin. We have a few dozen such origin myths from various parts of the empire, including the Lake Titicaca region, the north coast of Peru, and the central and northern highlands of Peru. What is important to recognize is that such myths exist in sufficient numbers to assure us that peoples in different parts of the empire promoted their individual origin myth, and their unique place of origin in the landscape, as components of ayllu or ethnic group identity and unity.

The Spanish priests and chroniclers had little patience with this notion of multiple places of origin. For instance, Bernabé Cobo was clearly frustrated by the different ideas about creator deities and the many versions of origin myths which he encountered in Peru. He concluded that the reason these 'blind people' accepted all these different ideas and beliefs was that they never knew about the one, true God. Furthermore, he continued, 'another contributing factor was their lack of any kind of writing. If they had had a system of writing, they might not have made such dim-witted errors.'

Juan de Betanzos, writing a century before Cobo, concluded that the 'confusion' was due to a more sinister cause, namely, the devil. As he put the matter, 'sometimes they [the Indians] hold the Sun up as the creator, and other times they say it is Viracocha. Generally, in all the land and in each of its provinces, the devil has them confused. Everywhere that the devil showed up, he told them a thousand lies and delusions. Thus he had them deceived and blind.'

On another level, the high degree of ethnic diversity that existed throughout the empire seems to have provided a powerful stimulus for the development of myths portraying the diverse ayllus and ethnic groups as descendants of a single event of origin in ancestral times. That is, in order for the diverse peoples within the empire to begin to think of themselves as citizens of a single society, it was essential that there be a powerful story and image linking them together, projecting their histories from a common past towards a united future. This latter tendency, which was motivated by the political interests of the Inca state bureaucracy in promoting unity throughout the empire, is reflected in myths depicting an intimate connection between the origins of the Inca kings and certain basic characteristics of the imperial organization, such as the hierarchical ranking of kin groups. To support their claims that imperial structures were foreordained and sanctioned by supernatural force(s), the Inca mythographers and story-tellers linked the origin of the Inca kings to two powerful deities – a creator deity (for instance, Viracocha or Pachacamac) and the sun – as well as to a place of origin located near to Cusco, called Pacaritambo.

Finally, at the most general, inclusive level, peoples throughout the Andes, including the Incas, commonly identified Lake Titicaca and the site of Tiahuanaco as the principal place where the cosmos, including the sun, moon, stars and the ancestors of humans, was first brought into being. We will see these various aspects of Inca origin myths – the local, the state, and the cosmic – in the myths that follow.

Cosmic origin myths

Cosmic origins

The story of the origin of the world that was apparently most commonly told by Inca informants, especially in Cusco, centred on Lake Titicaca. Most versions of this origin myth start by asserting that, in the beginning of time, all was in darkness, as the sun, moon and stars had not yet been created. Into this primeval darkness there emerged the creator Viracocha, whose name may be glossed as 'sea fat', or 'sea foam'. In various versions the creator is called Con Ticci Viracocha, Thunupa Viracocha, and Viracocha Pachayachachic. Later, in our discussion of myths from the Inca

Lake Titicaca.

provinces, we will also recount certain coastal myths that identify the creator as Pachacamac ('maker of earth/time').

In this time and space of darkness, Viracocha, who is described by Betanzos as a lord who emerged from Lake Titicaca, came forth and created the first race of humanity. These first beings, whom some chroniclers identify as a race of giants, lived in the darkness for a period of time but then, for some unspecified reason, they angered Viracocha. Because of his anger and his disappointment with them, the creator brought the first age to an end by a flood and transformed these beings into stone. Remnants of this first age were present for all to see in Inca times, and today, in the stone sculptures at the site of Tiahuanaco, near Lake Titicaca.

Viracocha next set about creating another race of humanity. He began this second act of creation by first calling the sun, the moon and the stars to come forth from an island in Lake Titicaca. The Incas maintained an important shrine, the focus of an annual pilgrimage, on an island in Lake Titicaca that they recognized as the Island of the Sun. After creating the celestial luminaries and setting them in motion, Viracocha fashioned the second race of humanity. In one telling of this creation story (Betanzos), Viracocha began by moulding individuals out of the stone along the shores of the lake, which was still malleable

Stone statue at Tiahuanaco.

345

at that time. He made figures of men, women (both pregnant and without child) and children.

Cobo, in his version of this myth, says that after Viracocha made these people, who would come to represent the different nations of Tahuantinsuyu, 'he painted each one with the clothing to be used by that nation, and he also gave each nation the language they were to speak, the songs they were to sing, as well as the foods, seeds and vegetables with which they were to sustain themselves.'

In the version of the origin myth recounted by Cristobal de Molina, we read a slightly different account of the nature of events at the beginning of time. Molina begins when the world was already populated. Then there came a great flood, the waters of which covered even the highest mountains. The only survivors of this deluge were a man and a woman who, as the waters subsided, were thrown up onto the land at Tiahuanaco. Viracocha appeared and commanded the couple to remain there as *mitimaes*, the name given to groups of people who were moved by the Inca from their home territory to some other place in the empire.

Molina then says that after the flood subsided, the creator set about repopulating the land, fashioning the ancestors of the different nations of Tahuantinsuyu out of clay and painting them in the manner of the dress they were to wear. At the same time as Viracocha created this second race of humans at Tiahuanaco, he also created there all the animals and birds, making a male and a female of each, indicating where the various creatures were to live and what they would eat, and giving to each type of bird its distinctive song.

Keeping two of his creations with him in Lake Titicaca, Viracocha sent the others away, underground. According to Cristobal de Molina, the two individuals that Viracocha kept with him, who in some accounts are said to have been his sons, were named Imaymana Viracocha and Tocapo Viracocha. The repetition of the name 'Viracocha' has been interpreted as a kind of classifier indicating that the deity or supernatural force named was recognized as a creator. We will meet these two sons of Con Ticci Viracocha again later.

Viracocha's act of sending the new, stone-made humans of the second age away from the origin place at Lake Titicaca was done in such a way as to accommodate their coming-into-being (which will occur later) at the particular places within the territory of Tahuantinsuyu that the different 'nations' who were descended from these ancestral beings would later recognize as their unique place(s) of origin. This matching of ancestors to places of origin was accomplished by sending these beings underground to await the call of the creator to come up out of springs, caves, or other places.

Having in this way 'seeded' the land with the future ancestors of the different nations of the empire, Viracocha then turned for help to his two sons whom he had created (and kept with him) earlier. He instructed the elder brother, Imaymana Viracocha, to travel north-westward from Lake Titicaca along the road bordering the forest and the mountains; the younger brother, Tocapo Viracocha, he sent along the coastal highway. Con Ticci

Viracocha himself travelled north-westward along the road through the central highlands, between his sons.

As the three creators passed through the land on this primordial journey of creation, they called on the ancestors of the local peoples to come up out of the springs, caves and mountain-tops. In addition, as the three Viracochas moved across the land, they named all the trees and plants in their particular places and said when each was to flower and give fruit. Viracocha and his sons travelled to the north-western edge of the empire, finally coming to Manta, along the coast of Ecuador. From there they continued in the same direction and passed out to sea, walking across the water until they disappeared.

An Andean triadism? Or the Christian trinity?

The fact that most versions of the myth of origin from Lake Titicaca identify the creator as a trinity (i.e., the three Viracochas) has led some scholars to suggest that this Andean myth of creation, as well as the very idea of a creator deity itself, was taken over by Andean peoples from Spanish Catholicism. This notion receives support from several of the descriptions in the chronicles of the appearance of the creator as a tall, bearded and light-skinned man. The native chronicler Pachacuti Yamqui strongly averred that the creator, known to him by the names Thunupa, Tarapaca and Thunupa Viracocha, was the apostle St Thomas, whereas the native chronicler Guaman Poma identified Viracocha as St Bartholomew.

There are, in fact, strong arguments to be made for the interpretation of triadic elements in Inca myths as Spanish introductions. For example, it is clear that many of the chroniclers who recorded Inca myths would have been pleased to see a reflection of their own beliefs in the Andes, and may have been inclined to read such references into their informants' accounts. Certain native writers who adopted Christian beliefs, such as Guaman Poma de Ayala and Pachacuti Yamqui, were themselves intent on demonstrating to their Spanish overlords (and readers) that they were believers in the one true God. In addition, these two native chroniclers also consistently argued that Andean peoples had known the God of Christianity, and therefore had been practising Christians – except for those who were led astray by the Inca kings, who preached idolatry and the worship of ancestral mummies – before the arrival of the Spanish.

Despite the fact that there were at the time a number of converging interests and motives that might lead us to conclude that triadism and creator deities in the Andes were products of Spanish Catholic influence, it is important to bear in mind that 'triadism' is a very general concept, one which is found in numerous cultures around the world. In addition, the particular manifestation of triadism that we are confronted with here, that of a creator/father who is assisted by his two sons, seems quite distant from the peculiar characteristics attached to trinitarianism in Christianity. In any case, given the absence of records indicating how creator deities were conceptualized in

Inca society before the time of the Spanish conquest, we may never be able to resolve this question with any degree of certainty.

Works of the creator in and around Cusco

In the versions of this origin myth recorded in the 1550s by Cieza de León and Juan de Betanzos, there is considerably more attention given to events that transpired in the central highlands as Con Ticci Viracocha travelled north-westward from Lake Titicaca. For instance, Cieza says that the creator, who had the appearance of a tall white man, travelled along the highland route healing the sick and restoring sight to the blind by his words alone. However, when Viracocha approached a village called Cacha, in the district of Canas (south-east of Cusco), the people came out of the town in a threatening manner, saying they were going to stone him. Betanzos says the people rushed at Viracocha with weapons.

Viracocha dropped to his knees and raised his hands toward the sky, as if seeking aid. The sky immediately filled with fire, and the terrified people of Cacha approached Viracocha, asking him to forgive and save them. The fire was then extinguished (Betanzos says that the creator gave the fire three strokes with his staff), but not before it had burned the rocks around there- so that large blocks were consumed and became as light as cork. Betanzos says that he himself travelled to Cacha to investigate this mythic incident and clearly saw the scorched earth resulting from this cataclysmic event.

Betanzos elaborates on the repercussions of the creator's acts in and around this town, noting that the people of Cacha began to recognize the place where this event occurred as a *huaca*, or sacred place. They built a large stone sculpture in the shape of a man at the site where Viracocha appeared, and offered gold and silver to the huaca and statue. Betanzos is quite detailed and specific in describing the physical appearance of the creator, as this topic was apparently of considerable interest to him. That is, he not only tells us that he actually saw the statue of Viracocha himself, but also that he talked to people thereabouts, asking them what Viracocha looked like. Betanzos was told that 'he [Viracocha] was a tall man dressed in a white garment that reached to his ankles and was belted at the waist. His hair was short and he had a tonsure like a priest. He went bareheaded and carried in his hands something that seemed to them to resemble the breviaries that priests of today carry.' Betanzos says that the people around Cacha told him that the creator's name was Contiti Viracocha Pachayachachic, which he translates as 'God, maker of the world'.

Continuing his description of the events that transpired during Viracocha's travels north-westward, in the direction of Cusco from Lake Titicaca, Betanzos says that the creator next went to the site of Urcos, located six leagues (*c.* 33 km) from Cusco. Arriving there, Viracocha climbed to the top of a high mountain, sat down on the summit, and called the ancestors of the peoples who were native to that region in Betanzos' time to come out of the mountain-top. In homage to the time when the creator sat atop this mountain, the people of Urcos built a bench of gold there and placed a statue of Viracocha upon it. Molina tells us that the image of Viracocha at Urcos was called *Atun-Viracocha* ('great creator') and that the statue was in the form of a man with a white robe hanging down to his feet.

From Urcos, Viracocha passed on to Cusco. Here, in the place that would become the Inca capital, he created, or called up out of the earth, a great lord, whom he named Alcavicça. This name will reappear later as the name of the indigenous nation of people who were living in the valley of Cusco when the Incas first arrived there. In fact, Viracocha's last act upon leaving the valley of Cusco was to order that the so-called *orejones* – meaning 'big ears', the name given to the Inca nobility from their practice of piercing their earlobes and inserting golden spools in the holes – should emerge from the earth after he left. This final act in Cusco provides the link (in Betanzos' account) between the origin myth beginning at Lake Titicaca and the origin myth of the Inca kings.

The origin myth centring on Lake Titicaca contains several features which suggest strongly that its point of orientation was Cusco and its focus of validation was the hierarchical structures underlying the Inca state. For instance, the space traversed by characters in the myth begins at the lake and proceeds north-westward to the coast of Ecuador. The more detailed narration of encounters between the creator and people – those occurring in Cacha and Urcos – centre on the Vilcanota, or Urubamba river valley, which courses north-westward near Cusco and within the Cusco valley itself. Thus the myths of the origins of the world told by informants in the Inca capital project a vital connection between Lake Titicaca, the site of one of the principal highland civilizations of pre-Inca times (Tiahuanaco), and Cusco, the successor capital.

The origin myths we have discussed thus far pay curiously little attention to what would become the major geographic, demographic and political division defining the Inca world, that of *Tahuantinsuyu*, 'the four united quarters'. An especially puzzling omission in the origin myths concerns the quadrant of Collasuyu. This quarter of the empire, which included the territory south-east of Cusco, extended not only from the capital to Lake Titicaca but also much farther to the south-east, into central and southern Bolivia and on into north-west Argentina. Now, if the work of creation proceeded from Lake Titicaca to the *north-west*, what were the origins of the peoples of Collasuyu, to the south-east of Lake Titicaca? Were the powerful nations and confederations of nations of Bolivia (the QaraQara and Charka, for example) not created at the same time and in the same manner as those of the other three quarters of Tahuantinsuyu? There is no body of myths that would settle our unease about the Inca disregard of this portion of the empire. One possibility suggested is that the Incas may have taken over and remoulded – that is, retold from the point of view of Cusco – the myths of Collasuyu itself, hoping thereby to incorporate into their own origins the power and legitimacy associated even in those times with the mighty kingdoms and confederations of what is today Bolivia.

One myth that does account for the division of the Inca world into four quarters at the beginning of time is provided by Garcilaso de la Vega in his work, *Commentarios Reales de los Incas*. Garcilaso says that after the waters of the deluge receded, a man (unnamed in this myth) appeared at Tiahuanaco. This man was so powerful that he divided the land into four parts, giving each quarter to one of four kings. Manco Capac received the northern quarter, Colla the southern, Tocay the eastern, and Pinahua the western. This 'creator' of Tiahuanaco commanded each king to enter the quarter assigned to him and to conquer and govern the people who lived there.

We would be well served at this point by summarizing some of the key elements that have appeared in the myths discussed so far. These represent what could be characterized as core, or paradigmatic, ideas, events and relationships that will reappear with striking regularity as we turn to the myths of other places in the empire, especially along the spine of the Andes from Bolivia northward to Ecuador. Because of their widespread distribution in both time and space, they could well represent indigenous – that is, pre-conquest – concepts and thematic principles informing, and giving shape and unity to, mythological traditions throughout the empire.

The first paradigmatic element is the notion that all humanity (within the empire, at least) originated at Lake Titicaca, urged into being there by a supreme creator most commonly identified as Viracocha. Second, one consistently finds that the particular group of people – a 'nation', ayllu or family – occupying a given region will recognize a particular place in the local landscape, such as a spring or cave, as its unique place of origin. Offerings will be made to the place, which will be regarded as a huaca ('sacred place'), for the well-being of the group as a whole. In addition, the mummified ancestors of the group may be stored and worshipped there. The third element is a complementary relationship, which may be either co-operative or more commonly conflictual in nature, between this local autochthonous group of people and a group of outsiders who are believed to have arrived on the scene in the past as conquering invaders. The resulting relationship between locals and foreigners is the defining one for political life within the territory occupied by the two groups. The final paradigmatic element is a principle of ranking, or hierarchy, that suffuses all relationships among peoples, places and histories across the landscape. As we continue, we will see these paradigmatic elements reappear in myths from throughout the empire with notable regularity. For the moment, it is important to examine another theme that underlies the cosmic views of colonial commentators on the Incas.

Pachacuti: cycles of creation and destruction in myths of the ages of the world

A central concept in Inca and later colonial Quechua and Aymara cosmogonic thinking was the notion of regular episodes of the cataclysmic destruction and recreation of the world. This notion is evident in the myths in a general theme of cyclicity that characterizes the succession of events in mythic times.

The cyclical concept is evoked in the Quechua term *pachacuti*, which refers to a 'revolution, or turning over/around' (*cuti*) of 'time and space' (*pacha*). Pachacuti is the term that is often used in chroniclers' accounts of the numerous mythic episodes of the destruction of the inhabitants of the world and their replacement by a new race, as we have seen in some of the origin myths from Lake Titicaca. This theme is well-represented in the corpus of Inca myths collected during the colonial period, one of the best examples being that given by Guaman Poma de Ayala in his *Nueva Corónica y Buen Gobierno*.

Guaman Poma's mid-seventeenth century version of the world depicts a succession of five ages. From comparison with other versions, it appears that the general scheme in the Inca/Andean cosmic vision was of five ages, each referred to as a 'sun' and with each sun/age enduring for a thousand years.

In Guaman Poma's version, the first age began during a time of primordial darkness with a race of humanity called *Wari Wiracocharuna*. The term *wari* refers to a hybrid camellid, a cross-breeding between a llama and an alpaca; *runa* is the Quechua term for 'people'. Guaman Poma glosses this name as the people from the time of Noah's ark who were descended from Spaniards (in addition to its designation of the creator deity, 'Viracocha' was used by Andean natives to refer to the invading Europeans). The people of the first age lived with only rudimentary technology and wore clothing of leaves and other unprocessed vegetal materials. Guaman Poma says that the Wari Wiracocharuna first worshipped God, but they then lost faith and began worshipping Andean creator deities, including two forms of Viracocha – Ticci Viracocha and Caylla Viracocha – and Pachacamac. The first age came to an end in some unspecified manner.

The second race of humanity, called *Wari Runa*, was more advanced than the previous race. The Wari Runa had clothing of animal skins; they practised rudimentary agriculture and lived simply and peacefully, without warfare. They recognized Viracocha as their creator. The second age ended in a deluge.

The third age was that of the *Purun Runa* ('wild men'). Civilization was becoming increasingly complex, as witnessed by the fact that the people of this age made clothing of spun and dyed wool; they practised agriculture, mining and the making of jewellery. The population grew beyond previous levels, with people migrating into the previously uninhabited lowlands. There was a marked increase in conflicts and warfare. Each town had its own king, and the people as a whole worshipped the creator Pachacamac.

The fourth age was that of the 'warlike people', the *Auca Runa*. In certain passages, Guaman Poma suggests that the early part of the Inca empire fell within this age, but elsewhere the Incas are considered to have lived during the fifth age. During the age of the Auca Runa, the world was divided into four parts. Warfare increased, and people lived on mountaintops in stone houses and fortifications, called *pucaras*. Ayllus became common in this age, and decimal administration was instituted. In general, the technological and material conditions of life became far more advanced

The first four ages of the world, according to Guaman Poma de Ayala.

TER3ERAEDADDEIŃS
PVRVNRVNA

ELQVARTOEDADDEIŃS
AVCARVNA

and complex than in the previous age. Guaman Poma does not specify how this age ended.

The fifth age, or 'sun', was that of the Incas. In his chronicle, Guaman Poma gives a description of the major institutions of the empire, including the institution of the kingship, the decimal bureaucracy, the age-grades of the population and the religious organization of the empire. With respect to the latter, the Incas began the worship of what Guaman Poma refers to as the *guaca bilcas*, the supernaturals who were, as he says, 'the demons of Cusco'. The fifth age was brought to an end, of course, by the Spanish conquest.

This brief overview of Guaman Poma's construction of the five ages or 'suns' omits many of the details of what is, in fact, a complex and rather confusing account. Guaman Poma mixes many Christian symbols and sentiments with what appear to be indigenous elements. The latter include references to the creator deities Viracocha and Pachacamac, whom we have encountered before; institutions that are long-attested in the Andes, such as ayllus and decimal organization and an overall structure built around the notion of a succession of pachacutis – creations and destructions of the world. As we will see later, this concept persists in contemporary Andean myths, especially in those concerning the end of the present world and the anticipated reinstatement of the Incas as the rightful rulers of the land.

These comments and the earlier description of the place of the Incas in the five ages of the world prompt us to ask: Who were the Incas? Where did they come from? Answers to these questions were of vital interest not only to the Incas, but also to the Spanish chroniclers, who struggled to make sense of what they perceived to be the bewildering set of events that occurred at the beginning of time as recounted in Andean cosmic origin myths.

Origin myths of the Inca state

E arly in his account of the origin of the Incas, the Jesuit priest Bernabé Cobo alerts us to the fact that, unlike other lineages or ethnic groups in the Andes, the Incas – perhaps because they recognized the political danger involved – were not content with the situation in which every local group had its own place of origin, each one as important as the next. For them, their place of origin was special, and all-inclusive. As Cobo noted, 'The reason why these nations of Peru came to believe so much nonsense about their origin was caused by the ambition of the Incas. They were the first one to worship the cave of Pacaritampu as the beginning of their lineage. They claimed that all people came from there, and that for this reason all people were their vassals and obliged to serve them.' Clearly, the Inca had other ambitions in mind in recounting their myth of origin from the cave of Pacaritambo.

In outline form, the origin myth of the Incas focusing on Pacaritambo is as follows: At a place to the south of Cusco called Pacaritambo, there was a mountain called Tambo T'oco ('window house'), in which there were three windows, or caves. The ancestors of the Incas, who were related as a group of four brothers and four sisters, came out of the central window. The principal figure was Manco Capac, who was destined to become the founder-king of the empire. The Incas set off with people who lived around Tambo T'oco in search of fertile land on which to build their capital. Following a long period of wandering, they finally arrived at a hill overlooking the valley of Cusco. Recognizing by miraculous signs that this was the home they had long sought, the Incas descended from the mountain and took possession of the valley from the local inhabitants.

The principal account that I shall use in elaborating the Inca origin myth is the version given in Sarmiento de Gamboa's *Historia de los Incas*, which was written in 1572. Sarmiento's account is one of the earliest and most detailed versions that we have. As the official historian to Francisco de Toledo, the fourth Viceroy of Peru (1569-81), Sarmiento was charged with compiling a true history of the Inca empire. In undertaking this enterprise, Sarmiento had access to an unusually large number of informants. He tells us, for instance, that he interviewed more than a hundred quipucamayoqs on historical matters, and he provides us with the names of forty-two of these informants. Furthermore, Sarmiento says that upon completing his account, he had his chronicle read in full, in the Quechua language, to these forty-two descendants of the Inca nobility. All of the men, says Sarmiento, agreed that 'the said history was good and true and conformed to what they knew and to what they had heard their parents and ancestors say, which they themselves had heard their own [parents and ancestors] say.' As we will see, much of the 'true history' recorded by Sarmiento falls decidedly under the heading of what we generally classify as mythology.

According to Sarmiento, the origin of the Incas was at a place called Pacaritambo ('the inn, or house, of dawn'; or 'place of origin'), which is located six leagues (c. 33 km) south of Cusco. In primordial times, there was a mountain at Pacaritambo called Tambo Toco ('the house of openings/windows') in which there were three windows, or caves. The central window was called Capac Toco ('rich window'), and the two lateral windows were called Maras Toco and Sutic Toco. Two different nations of Indians who allied themselves with the Incas originated from these side windows. A nation called the Maras emerged from the window of Maras Toco, while the Tambos Indians (whose head lineage seems to have borne the surname Sutic) came out of the window of Sutic Toco. The ancestors of the Incas emerged from the central window, Capac Toco. Sarmiento says that these three groups of people were born from the caves, or windows, of Tambo Toco at the urging of Ticci Viracocha.

From the central window at Tambo Toco there emerged four men and four women who were, according to Sarmiento, brothers and sisters. Betanzos says that the ancestors were paired as spouses. The names of the eight ancestral siblings as given by Sarmiento in the order of their age-grading (with the oldest pair, Ayar Manco and Mama Ocllo, listed first) were:

The Inca king and queen worshipping the cave of Tambo Toco at Pacaritambo.

Brothers/Husbands	Sisters/Wives
Ayar Manco (Capac)	Mama Ocllo
Ayar Auca	Mama Huaco
Ayar Cachi	Mama Ipacura/Cura
Ayar Uchu	Mama Raua

'Ayar' comes from the Quechua word *aya*, 'corpse', thereby establishing a link between the ancestors as mythological characters and the mummified remains of the Inca kings, which were kept and worshipped in a special room in the Temple of the Sun in Cusco. In addition, this same word *ayar* was the name of a wild strain of the *quinua* plant, a high-altitude grain crop of the Andes.

We should note that while all accounts of the Ayars say that the ancestors came from Tambo Toco at Pacaritambo, in the chronicles of Martín de Murúa and Guaman Poma de Ayala we read that the ancestors originally passed underground from Lake Titicaca to the cave of Pacaritambo. In addition, Garcilaso de la Vega included in his chronicle the Inca origin myth that links Manco Capac and Mama Ocllo to the Island of the Sun, in Lake Titicaca.

After the ancestors emerged from Tambo Toco, they allied themselves with the Tambos Indians and prepared to go with them in search of fertile land; upon finding good land, they vowed to conquer the people who lived there. Sarmiento describes this turn of events as follows:

'And agreeing among themselves on this [plan for conquest], the eight [ancestors] began to stir up the people who lived in that part of the mountain, setting as the prize that they [the Inca ancestors] would make the people rich and that they would give them the lands and estates which they conquered and subjugated. From an interest in this [proposition], there were formed ten groups or ayllus, which means, among these barbarians, a lineage or faction.'

The first Inca king, Manco Capac.

The ten ayllus of Tambos Indians founded at Tambo Toco were destined to become the principal groupings of commoners in Inca Cusco. They were complemented in the social organization of the capital by the ten royal ayllus, called *panacas*, which were composed of the descendants of the first ten kings. Shortly after their creation and emergence from Tambo Toco, the eight ancestors set off with their entourage – the ten ayllus of Tambos Indians – walking northward in the direction of the Cusco valley. Along the way, the ancestors tested the earth by plunging a golden bar, which they had brought with them from Tambo Toco, into the soil. They were searching for fertile land that would be suitable to call home.

The ancestors made several stops along their journey to Cusco. During the first of these stops the oldest brother, Ayar Manco (who will later be called Manco Capac), and his sister/wife, Mama Ocllo, conceived a child. At the second stop, Mama Ocllo gave birth to a boy, whom they named Sinchi Roca. This child was destined to succeed his father (Ayar Manco) as second king of Cusco. In Betanzos' version of the Inca origin myth, he says that Sinchi Roca was born in Cusco, after the ancestors had reached and taken possession of the city. From the second stop, in Sarmiento's version, the group then moved on to a place called Palluta, where they remained for a few years. However, becoming dissatisfied with the land there, they decided to move on. The ancestors and their entourage then came to a place called Haysquisrro. It was here that a momentous event occurred that resulted in the separation of one of the ancestors from the group.

According to various versions of the Inca origin myth, Ayar Cachi was known universally as a boisterous, rowdy and cruel character; he was also very handy with a sling. Cieza tells us that Ayar Cachi could launch stones from his sling with such force that he could split hills, the rocks and dust flying up to the clouds. In addition, Ayar Cachi stirred up trouble in all the towns the ancestors passed through, and he disturbed the peace and harmony among the ancestors and their allies. According to Sarmiento, 'the other siblings feared that because of his bad behavior and tricks, Ayar Cachi would disturb and alienate the people who were travelling with them, and that they [the ancestors] would be left alone.'

These concerns led the ancestors, under the direction of Ayar Manco, to concoct a ruse to rid themselves of this troublesome character. Manco told Ayar Cachi that they had left several items in the cave of origin, Tambo Toco. These included a golden cup (*topacusi*), some seeds, as well as an object called a *napa*. The latter had the form of a miniature decorative llama, which, in Sarmiento's words, was an 'insignia of nobility'. (Molina gives numerous examples of ceremonies in Cusco during which the Incas brought out, and worshipped, small images of llamas made of gold and silver.) At first, Ayar Cachi refused to return to the cave. However, Mama Huaco, the most forceful and bellicose of the sisters (and according to Betanzos the wife of Ayar Cachi), jumped to her feet and began berating Ayar Cachi, calling him a lazy coward. Shamed into action by Mama Huaco's words, Ayar Cachi agreed to return to the cave.

On his trip back to Tambo Toco, Ayar Cachi took with him a man from

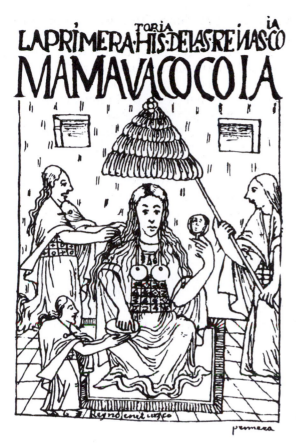

Mama Huaco.

among the Tambos Indians, named Tambochacay ('Tambo entrance-barrer'). Unbeknownst to Ayar Cachi, the other ancestors had persuaded Tambochacay to dispose of the troublesome Ayar Cachi when they reached the cave. Arriving at Tambo Toco, Ayar Cachi went inside to retrieve the articles. Tambochacay immediately closed off the entrance to the cave with a huge boulder, trapping Ayar Cachi inside for all time.

Having rid themselves of Ayar Cachi, the ancestors moved on and arrived next in the immediate environs of the valley of Cusco at a place called Quirirmanta, which is at the foot of a mountain called Huanacauri. Ascending Huanacauri, the ancestors viewed for the first time the valley of Cusco. Heaving the bar of gold with which they had been testing the soil into the valley, they saw the entire shaft sink into the earth. From this indication, as well as by the sign of a rainbow that stretched over the valley, the ancestors recognized that this was their long sought-after home and they prepared to descend.

At this point, the youngest of the ancestor-brothers, Ayar Uchu, was transformed into stone on the mountain Huanacauri. In Betanzos' version of this myth, he tells us that before his transformation into stone, Ayar Uchu stood up on the mountain, spread out a pair of large wings, and flew from the top of the mountain into the heavens. On his return, he said that he had

The view from atop Huanacauri, looking into the Cusco valley.

talked to the sun who told him that Ayar Manco should from that moment on be called Manco Capac ('supreme rich [one]') and that the entourage should proceed to Cusco. There, said Ayar Uchu, the Incas would find good company in the place where Alcaviçça had his settlement. After saying these things, Ayar Uchu was transformed into stone. The Incas later worshipped this stone as one of their principal sacred sites (huacas).

The remaining six ancestors went from Huanacauri to a place called Matao, where Sarmiento says they remained for two years. Betanzos recounts an event that occurred at about this same point in the ancestral journey but at an unnamed place (perhaps Matao?) near Cusco, which was famous for coca and *aji* (chili peppers). Here Mama Huaco, who was herself quite skilful with a sling, struck a man of the town with a stone flung from her sling and killed him. She then split open his chest, took out his lungs and heart, blew into the lungs, making them swell up, and displayed them to the inhabitants of the town. The people fled, and the ancestors proceeded on to Cusco.

Arriving there, they went up to Alcaviçça and told him they had been sent there by their father, the sun, to take possession of the town. Alcaviçça and his followers acceded to this request and made room for the six ancestors. Then Manco Capac took some maize (corn) seeds that he had brought with him from the cave of Tambo Toco, and with the help of Alcaviçça and the other ancestors he planted the first corn field in the valley. Molina gives an interesting account of this final act whereby

Inca vessel composed of replicas of aryballos, ear of corn and digging stick.

the Incas 'domesticated' the valley of Cusco by planting their fields there. He says this field was first planted not by Manco Capac but by Mama Huaco, one of the ancestral sisters. After Mama Huaco died, her body was embalmed and mummified, and the people who were responsible for caring for her mummy made *chicha* (fermented corn beer) from the corn grown every year in this same field; the chicha was given to those who maintained the cult of the mummy of Mama Huaco.

When Manco Capac and his companions finally reached the place that would become the centre of the city of Cusco, the plaza of Huanaypata, Ayar Auca – the only remaining ancestor brother besides Manco Capac – was transformed into a stone pillar. This pillar was worshipped from that time on as a huaca. This left Manco Capac, his four sisters and the boy Sinchi Roca to found and build the city of Cusco.

To recapitulate, in the versions of the Inca origin myth recounted by Sarmiento, Betanzos and other chroniclers, we encounter the various motifs characterized earlier as 'paradigmatic elements' of origin myths in the empire. That is, the ancestors, who initially came underground from Lake Titicaca, had their unique place of origin in the cave of Tambo Toco, in Pacaritambo. This cave, where one of the ancestors, Ayar Cachi, remained entombed, was recognized as an important huaca and pilgrimage site in Inca times. (The ruins of the site are known today as Mauqallaqta, 'ancient town'.) The ancestors went from the cave of origin to the valley of Cusco where, in conquering the local, autochthonous people under the command of Alcavicça, they established the core, hierarchical, political relationship between foreign invaders and local subordinates that came to characterize relations between the Incas in the capital and local peoples throughout the empire from this time forward.

Was the Inca state founded on a ruse?

Before we move on to examine other mythic events that supposedly transpired in Cusco after the conquest of the valley by Manco Capac, we should first examine another tradition of Inca origins from Pacaritambo that projects Inca motives as decidedly more sinister and duplicitous. The basic story-line of this version is that the Ayar siblings decided among themselves

The site of Mauqallaqta, Inca Pacaritambo (left).

to trick the local people of the valley of Cusco into believing that they (the Inca ancestors) were descended from the sun. Manco Capac then fashioned, or had fashioned for him, two plates of gold, one of which he wore on the front of his body, the other on his back. Manco then positioned himself on the hill of Huanacauri overlooking Cusco where, at the moment of sunrise, he appeared as a resplendent, god-like figure. The locals were awed by his appearance, whereupon Manco descended from Huanacauri to Cusco and took command of the valley.

Different versions of this story derive from various sources. Depending on the source, the 'trick' which the ancestors played on the locals can sound exceedingly clever (as it does, for instance, in the version by Martín de Murúa); at its worst, however, the ruse has a sinister undertone, one which implies that the whole rule of the Incas was illegitimate by virtue of this act of trickery played on the people. In this regard, we should specifically note an account of the origin of the Incas contained in testimony given before Vaca de Castro in Cusco, in about 1542, only ten years after the Spanish conquest. This appears in the document called the *Relación de los Quipucamayoqs*, which was drawn up from the testimony provided by four elderly quipucamayoqs, two of whom are said to have been natives of the town of Pacaritambo. The particular version of the origin myth that was apparently told by the two quipucamayoqs from Pacaritambo goes as follows.

Manco Capac was the son of a *curaca* (a local official and head of a high-ranking lineage) of Pacaritambo. Manco's mother had died at the time of his birth, and the boy grew up with his father. When Manco was a boy, his father called him by the nickname 'Son of the Sun'. When Manco reached the age of ten or twelve, his father died. However, since his father had not explained to Manco Capac that the name 'Son of the Sun' was only an innocent nickname, Manco and the 'stupid people' (*gente bruta*) of the town were left with the idea that he was actually the son of the sun. Now, in Manco's household there were two old men, who were the priests of the idols of Manco Capac's father. These men continued to promote the 'hoax' (*patraña*) that Manco was a divine being. Manco Capac came to accept these pretensions, and when he reached the age of eighteen or twenty, he became further convinced by the two priests that he and his descendants were the

Manco Capac standing atop Huanacauri.

natural lords of the earth. Animated by these pretensions, Manco Capac made ready to set off for Cusco, taking with him the other members of his family, the two old priests, as well as his father's principal idol, which was called Huanacauri. This version of the deceitful co-optation of power by the Incas ends like the other version discussed above, with Manco Capac standing on the mountain of Huanacauri dressed in splendid fashion, bedecked with gold, and dazzling the people into accepting him and his family as their rulers.

The chronicler Garcilaso de la Vega added a further twist to the origin myth of the Incas by linking Manco Capac both to Lake Titicaca and to the theme of the first Inca's deceptive identification of himself as child of the sun. Garcilaso says that Manco Capac was aware that the people at Lake Titicaca believed that, following the great deluge, the sun had first shone its light on the Island of the Sun. Knowing this, he made up a fable to the effect that the sun placed his two children, one male and one female, there to teach the 'barbarous' Indians thereabouts how to live in a civilized manner. 'With these and other inventions made for their benefit, the Incas induced the remaining Indians to believe they were the children of the sun and confirmed it by the good they did.'

Stories such as these present the modern reader with the greatest challenges in separating what may have been Inca beliefs and what may have represented events or sentiments imputed to the Incas by their European, and/or Christian commentators. For example, the notion that the fame, prestige and power of Manco Capac, and by extension that of his regal descendants, rested on a ruse, hoax or a trick played on the people looks, on one level, like a politically interested manipulation of the origin myth by those who wanted to call into question the legitimacy of Inca rule. On another level, which may have had some force in the case of Garcilaso de la Vega, those who professed Christianity would have been inclined to see the workings of the devil in native worship of the sun. Thus there would have been in this latter case a profound suspicion of the devil's work in the events that led to the ascendence of the Incas, as 'children of the sun'. Whatever the specific motives and interests of the various chroniclers who recount these myths, there is a sufficient and varied number of sources pointing to solar worship in the Inca empire that we cannot doubt the antiquity and pervasiveness of such beliefs.

A more troublesome and difficult issue concerns the chronological relationship between the worship of Viracocha and the worship of the sun. Some chroniclers suggest that the Inca worship of the sun was a late development, coming only after the expansion of the empire beyond the boundaries of the valley of Cusco and with the maturity of the imperial bureaucratic organization. Others argue that the worship of Viracocha superseded the worship of the sun. Again, the lack of good chronological controls on Inca event chronologies as a whole renders answers to such questions highly speculative.

Myths of Inca state consolidation and expansion

In the mythic history of the Incas outlined thus far, we have followed those accounts that chronicle the events and processes whereby the first Inca, Manco Capac, and his brothers and sisters came to dominate affairs in the valley of Cusco. All subsequent kings of the empire, whether succeeding each other in a single line of succession, as some students of Inca history believe, or whether succession was in dual, co-regal lines, as other students hold, were ultimately descendants of the first king, Manco Capac, and his sister-wife, Mama Ocllo.

We are confronted by a complex set of questions in regard to the succession of the Inca kings following Manco Capac. This includes such issues as, first, the total number of kings that ruled from the accession of Manco Capac until the arrival of the Spaniards in 1532; second, the dates of the reigns of the various kings; and third, whether or not the kings were actual historical persons, or if some (or all?) of them should be relegated to the realm of mythology. We cannot, nor do we need to, enter into all the subtleties and nuances of the various opinions held by scholars on these questions. Rather, as a basis for our discussion of selected mythical events recounted in various of the sources concerning the consolidation of power by the Incas within the valley of Cusco, we can refer to the following list of generally well-attested kings of the empire. Most accounts aver that the last, undisputed Inca to rule before the Spanish conquest was Guayna Capac. At the time of the entry of the Spanish into Peru, succession to the throne was being disputed between two of Guayna Capac's sons (by different women), Huascar and Atahualpa.

The kings of the Inca empire

Manco Capac

Sinchi Roca

Lloque Yupanqui

Mayta Capac

Capac Yupanqui

Inca Roca

Yahuar Huacac

Viracocha Inca

Pachacuti Inca Yupanqui

Tupac Inca Yupanqui

Guayna Capac

Huascar and Atahualpa

The chroniclers give varying amounts and types of information about the different kings and queens of the empire. Some of this information is highly plausible, and the events referred to must have occurred at some time, under one king or another, in the late pre-conquest period. For instance, Manco Capac was said to have divided the population of Cusco into two parts that came to be referred to as 'upper Cusco' (*Hanan Cusco*) and 'lower Cusco' (*Hurin Cusco*), and the populace of the city was indeed divided in this manner at the time of the arrival of the Spanish. Sinchi Roca was said to have commanded people in the valley to cultivate the land for producing potatoes, and the valley has been so cultivated from at least Inca times until the present day. Finally, Mayta Capac was said to have quelled a rebellion by the Alcavicças, who had become restless by the time of his reign. All of these events or actions are plausible historical occurrences, although we cannot say precisely when any one of them may actually have occurred.

On the other hand, such events as those outlined above are jumbled together in the various sources with events that are decidedly more mythical in nature. Here, we should remark in particular two events that I will call 'mythic-historical' (as we cannot be certain of their historical status), for they appear to have been of great importance in Inca informants' accounts of the emergence of the Incas and the consolidation of the empire. The first concerns the war against the Chancas, a powerful nation to the west of Cusco; the second concerns an encounter between a young Inca prince and the creator god, Viracocha.

The attack on Cusco by the Chanca armies and the defence of the city by a young prince was of profound significance in Inca mythic history, for it is said that it was only after this event that the Incas set themselves on the road to building an empire. Some sources say the hero-prince of this myth was Viracocha Inca, the son of Yahuar Huacac, while others credit the event to Viracocha Inca's son, Pachacuti Inca Yupanqui. As the Chanca troops began advancing on the city, most of the residents, including the king, fled. Only the young prince and a few companions remained to defend Cusco. The few defenders were almost defeated in the first two attacks launched by the Chancas; however, in the final attack, with the fate of the Incas in the balance, the young prince received the aid of the rocks and stones in the valley, which were transformed into warriors. The rocks, called *pururaucas*, were worshipped as huacas from that time onward.

The tone and substance of the different versions of this myth in the various chronicles give the modern reader – as they must have given the Inca listener – the sense that the achievement of Inca sovereignty in the valley, a process which set them on the trajectory of empire, received divine sanction when the very stones of the valley rose up to protect the Incas and defend the city. In addition, it is at this point in the mythic-history of Cusco, and particularly in the recounting of the deeds of the various kings, that some scholars argue that our information in the colonial documents makes the transition from primarily mythical to historical. This view credits Pachacuti Inca with the defeat of the Chancas, and it is thought that this event was followed by a significant consolidation and expansion of the city of Cusco and the empire. According to this view, the dates of Pachacuti's reign are given as AD 1438–71. So far, this historicized interpretation of Inca dynastic mythic-histories has not been confirmed by any supporting archaeological data.

Another view of these events, which also regards at least certain elements of the Chanca war as 'real' history, although it does not attempt to attach absolute dates to these elements, suggests that this conflict may actually represent a deep, essentially historical, memory of the Inca rise to power in the Cusco valley. The principal, defining event of this process would have been the Inca defeat of the remnants of Huari control in the Cusco valley. The homeland of the Huari peoples, who were the central Peruvian contemporaries in Middle Horizon times of the Tiahuanaco peoples of Lake Titicaca, was located in the general area where the Chanca peoples were said to have had their seat of power.

To return to the myths of Inca state formation, another signal, mythic event recounted in the chronicles during the same (relative) time period as that subsumed by the Chanca war involved the encounter between the young prince Pachacuti Inca Yupanqui and the creator Viracocha Pachayachachi. This occurred at a spring outside Cusco, called Susurpuquio. As Pachacuti approached the spring on a journey to visit his father, Viracocha Inca, he saw a crystal tablet fall into it. The prince looked into the spring, and he saw on the tablet the image of an Indian wearing a *llauto* (a headdress), earspools and clothing like those worn by the Incas. It had three rays, like those of the sun, emerging from its head and snakes coiled around its shoulders. The figure had the head of a 'lion' (puma) jutting forward between its legs, another lion on its back with its paws around its shoulders and a serpent-like creature that stretched from the top to the bottom of its back.

Pachacuti took the crystal with him when he left the spring, and he used it from that time onward to see into the future. Pachacuti was said later to have come to identify the image on the crystal tablet with the creator, Viracocha Pachayachachi. The prince was so impressed by this vision that he was said to have instituted a religious reform during the time of his reign. In this particular accounting of the hierarchy of deities in the empire (there were other, competing versions), it is said that from the time of the Inca Pachacuti Yupanqui onward, the main temple of ritual and worship in the city of Cusco, the Coricancha, was reorganized to accommodate and display the following hierarchy of gods: Viracocha, the Sun, Moon, Venus, Thunder and the Rainbow. This hierarchy resulted from the replacement of the Sun, which had previously been the supreme deity and image in Coricancha and in the Inca pantheon, by Viracocha, the patron deity of Pachacuti, the new king.

However, another version of the evolution of Inca religion in connection with Pachacuti Yupanqui asserts that this king was responsible for what has been termed the increasing 'solarization' of Inca religion in which the sun replaced Viracocha as the principal deity of the empire. According to this point of view, Pachacuti's rise to power, during which he replaced his father, who bore the name 'Viracocha', was symbolic of this fundamental shift away from the worship of Viracocha to that of the Sun. One topic that is centrally at issue in this controversy is the fact that one of the kings, Viracocha Inca, bore the same name, or title, as the creator. This is account- ed for, in Betanzos' chronicle, for instance, by the fact that Viracocha Inca claimed that the creator appeared before him one night when he, the king, was troubled. The creator calmed him and made him content. The next day, when the king reported this event to his subjects, they stood up and pro- claimed his name to be Viracocha Inca, 'which means king and god'.

Much ink has been spilled over the question of the relationship between Viracocha the creator and Viracocha the king. We cannot resolve the issue here, nor can we easily make the problem go away. This is one area where the mixing, or 'confusion', between myth and history is quite perplexing and, given the nature of our sources (with different chroniclers speaking to different informants at different times and receiving different accounts and explanations), one that may not be resolvable into an absolute separation of these two central characters in Inca mythology.

Questions such as these must have occupied the attention of successive generations of quipucamayoqs and poet-philosophers (the amautas) in Cusco as they recounted, and even on occasion reformulated, myths of the Inca past. What most interested the people outside Cusco, however, although they retained myths concerning some of these imperial preoccupations, were questions regarding their own past. Where did they come from? How were neighbouring groups of people related to each other? And how, and when, did they come to be under the control of the Incas? We turn in the next chapter to some of the few bodies of myths that have been preserved for our appreciation and which address these and other provincial concerns.

Coastal and provincial mythologies

The lords of the north coast and the Incas

The myths of the Ayars and the founding of Cusco and the Inca empire are the principal myths of state origins we have from the Andes, but they are not the only ones. When we turn our attention elsewhere in the empire, particularly to the north coast of Peru, we encounter there tantalizing remnants of state origin myths altogether as complex as those of the Cusco dynasty. Unfortunately, we have only the barest outlines of a few of these myths, including a couple from the Lambayeque valley and one pertaining to the lords of Chimor, in the Moche valley.

Concerning the myths centring on Lambayeque, Cabello Balboa tells us in his chronicle from 1586 of a tradition concerning an invasion of this valley in primordial times by peoples from the sea, to the south, who arrived in a fleet of balsas, or rafts. The leader of what Cabello Balboa calls this 'brave and noble company' of men was a man named Naymlap. Naymlap was accompanied by his wife, Ceterni, a harem, and some forty attendants. The retinue included a trumpeter, a guardian of the royal litter, a man who ground conch shells into powder for ritual purposes, a cook, and many more special functionaries. Naymlap also brought with him a green stone idol, which bore the name Yampallec, a name that is thought to be the origin of the name of the river valley where Naymlap settled, Lambayeque. Cabello Balboa tells us that the idol Yampallec had the figure and stature of Naymlap, thus being the king's double. Naymlap built a palace and a centre of devotion for the green stone idol at a place called Chot. This is almost certainly the site of Huaca Chotuna in the Lambayeque valley.

Naymlap lived a long and peaceful life. When he died, his body was buried in the palace of Chot. However, Naymlap had arranged

Chimu paddle.

Reconstruction of an interior courtyard, Huaca Chotuna, Lambyeque valley.

with his priests that when he died, they should tell his followers that upon his death he took wings and flew away. Naymlap was succeeded by his eldest son, Cium, who married a woman named Zolzoloñi, apparently a local woman (i.e., she is referred to in the document as a *moza*, a common designation in Spanish for a woman from outside a particular, named group – in this case, the group of invaders from the south). Cium and Zolzoloñi had twelve sons, each of whom married, had a large family, and went off on their own to found a different city.

Beginning with Naymlap, there were twelve kings in this dynasty, the last of whom was named Fempellec. Fempellec decided to move the green stone idol, Yampallec, from Chot to a new site, but before he could carry this out, the devil (says Cabello Balboa) appeared to him in the form of a beautiful woman, who seduced him. Following Fempellec's seduction by this sorceress, it began raining – in a part of Peru where it seldom rains – and continued raining for thirty days. After this, a year of drought and hunger set in. At the end of the year, the priests of the green stone idol had had enough. They seized Fempellec, bound him hand and foot and threw him into the ocean – thus ended the dynasty of Naymlap of Lambayeque.

Continuing his recounting of events in the Lambayeque valley, Cabello Balboa then says that 'many days' after the death of Fempellec, Lambayeque was once again invaded by a powerful army from the sea. The leader of this army was a man named Chimo Capac ('lord Chimu'), a name or title which indicates his probable origins in the Moche valley, centre of the kingdom of Chimor. Chimo Capac took control of Lambayeque and installed his curaca (local lord), Pongmassa, in the valley. This man was succeeded by his son, and then by Pongmassa's grandson, during whose period of rule the Incas conquered the area. The valley then continued under Inca control through some five other curacas, who administered the valley on behalf of the Incas. The Inca-Chimu alliance came to an end with the arrival of the Spanish.

We learn elsewhere of another north coastal dynasty, that of Taycanamu, whose home was the Moche valley. Like Naymlap and Chimo Capac, Taycanamu arrived at Moche from the south, on a balsa raft. Several descendants of Taycanamu ruled in succession, each expanding the territory under his control until the sixth or seventh ruler, a man named Minchançaman, was conquered by an Inca lord, Topa Yupanqui. Minchançaman was taken to Cusco, and the Moche valley was effectively brought under Inca control and remained so until the European invasion.

As the Inca empire expanded through the conquests and alliances undertaken by successive kings, the Incas came into contact with rich and vibrant traditions of the origins of noble families and dynasties – as in Lambayeque and Moche – in far flung corners of the empire. The challenge that confronted the Incas in each such instance was not only to incorporate those provincial mythic-histories into imperial traditions but to do so in ways

Moche spouted vessel in the form of a balsa raft with two occupants.

that preserved the sanctity and the centrality of the Inca dynasty. This was the principal task – that is, the continual reworking of local and regional origin myths – that confronted the amautas and quipucamayoqs who were responsible for preserving and reconciling the mythic-histories of Tahuantinsuyu. In the particular case at hand, that of the relationship between the Incas and the lords of Chimor, we have several accounts of how this (or a similar) encounter was considered to have proceeded from the Inca point of view. One such account is in the work of Garcilaso de la Vega, who gives the following account of how the Incas told the story of what happened when the Inca Tupac Yupanqui marched against the once mighty lord Chimu:

'The brave Chimu, his arrogance and pride now tamed, appeared before the prince with as much submission and humility, and grovelled on the ground before him, worshipping him and repeating the same request [for pardon] as he had made through his ambassadors. The prince received him affectionately in order to relieve the grief he was evincing. He bade two of the captains raise him from the ground, and after hearing him, told him that all that was past was forgiven . . . The Inca had not come to deprive him of his estates and authority, but to improve his idolatrous religion, his laws and customs.'

Myths of the Hatunruna (the commoners)

We turn now from the mythologies of peoples of pre-Inca states on the north coast to explore mythic traditions retained by commoner populations in the Inca empire. As was true in the case of the collection and recording of myths in Cusco and on the north coast of Peru, so in the provinces do our sources consist of accounts written down after the Spanish conquest. However, the provincial documentation recounting myths and portraying various aspects of the religious beliefs and practices of people in the countryside tends to be both later and less voluminous than that relating to the same subject matter in Cusco.

Many of the accounts detailing provincial mythologies come to us by way of information collected by local priests during the early seventeenth century who went out into the countryside to root out what the Spaniards referred to as 'idolatries'. This referred to the worship of ancestral mummies, celestial bodies and a vast array of notable features of the landscape, such as mountain peaks, springs and caves. Later, we will examine information from a couple of documents that derives from priests' reports from a few such investigations in the central and northern Peruvian Andes. We will turn first, however, to a remarkable document from the seventeenth century that was drawn up with a similar objective in mind – the discovery of idolatrous beliefs and practices – but which contains one of the most complete and coherent accounts available to us of provincial mythology.

The gods and men of Huarochirí

The document we are concerned with now is commonly referred to as the 'Huarochirí Manuscript'. The province of Huarochirí is located to the east of present-day Lima, in the westernmost chain of mountains in central Peru. The manuscript, written in the Quechua language, dates from around 1608. We do not know who actually wrote the material down (it is likely that it was written by a native), although we do know that its collection and recording were carried out under the direction of a local 'extirpator of idolatries', Francisco de Avila. In order to appreciate the events and actions recorded in this remarkable document, it is helpful to give a general overview of the social and political milieu within which it was produced.

The inhabitants of the region of Huarochirí were predominantly members of ayllus of the Yauyos ethnic and cultural group. The Yauyos ayllus were divided into two parts: *Anan* ('upper') *Yauyos*, and *Lurin* ('lower') *Yauyos*. The information recorded in the manuscript is written from the point of view of a couple of subgroups – the Checa and Concha – of Lower Yauyos. As a general classificatory label of a certain type of people, the 'Yauyos' were considered to be late arrivals to this region, pastoralists who came into the area, perhaps from the south. The invading Yauyos pastoralists established themselves in the Huarochirí area in opposition to the autochthonous population of lowland agriculturalists. In fact, however, it seems likely that the aboriginal farmers of the area were themselves of Yauyos origin. That is, the agriculturalists had moved into this area in remote antiquity, became assimilated, and were then overrun by this later migration of peoples of the same Yauyos ancestry.

Huallallo Carhuincho was the principal deity worshipped by the aboriginal peoples of Yauyos. Huallallo was a fearsome, fire-breathing volcanic deity who was given to the practice of cannibalism. For instance, he commanded that every household in Lower Yauyos should have only two children, and that one of the children was to be given to him to eat. In those primordial times, when Huallallo ruled unchallenged, the climate of the highlands was comparable to the coastal lowlands (the *Yungas*); that is, like the Yungas, the area of Huarochirí in those days was warm, and the land was filled with huge snakes, toucans (a kind of tropical bird), and all kinds of animals associated in later times with the coast. The principal deity of the recent Yauyos invaders was Pariacaca. In the Huarochirí Manuscript, 'Pariacaca', which was the name of a high mountain peak, is portrayed as a huaca (sacred object, or place) who moves about the countryside in the personification of a culture hero, or patron deity.

The mythological accounting of the origins of the world as told in Huarochirí begins after Huallallo Carhuincho had held dominion for some time. The huaca Pariacaca was then born on a mountain top in the form of five eggs that became five falcons that were transformed into five men. These men were believed by the author(s) of the Huarochirí Manuscript to have been the ancestors of the principal families and ritual groups of the recent Yauyos pastoralists who lived thereabouts. The powerful mountain deity, or huaca, Pariacaca challenged Huallallo Carhuincho for supremacy in this area. Pariacaca prophesied that he would fight Huallallo Carhuincho and drive him away. Pariacaca said that he would would fight with water, whereas Huallallo vowed to fight with fire. Their struggle is described in the document as follows:

'Pariacaca, since he was five persons, began to rain down from five directions. That rain was yellow and red rain. Then, flashing as lightning, he blazed out from five directions. From early in the morning to the setting of the sun, Huallallo Carhuincho flamed up in the form of a giant fire reaching almost to the heavens, never letting himself be extinguished. And the waters, the rains of Pariacaca, rushed down toward Ura Cocha, the lower lake. Since it wouldn't have fit in, one of Pariacaca's five selves, the one called Llacsa Churapa, knocked down a mountain and dammed the waters from below. Once he impounded these waters they formed a lake . . . As the waters filled the lake they almost submerged that burning fire. And Pariacaca kept flashing lightning bolts at him, never letting him rest. Finally Huallallo Carhuincho fled toward the low country, the Antis [Antisuyu].'

Pariacaca next fought against a female huaca, a demon named Mana Ñamca, who was an ally of Huallallo Carhuincho. Pariacaca defeated this woman as well, driving her into the ocean, to the west. Pariacaca then set about establishing his own cult. These struggles were the defining set of events in the displacement of the autochthonous agriculturalist population and their deity, Huallallo Carhuincho, by the invading Yauyos pastoralists, the latter of whom were the chief adherents of the cult of Pariacaca.

The Huarochirí Manuscript also attests to the presence of a deity named 'Viracocha', the same name as borne by the creator deity whom we encountered in the origin myth from Lake Titicaca. The compilers of the Huarochirí document claimed not to know whether or not this Viracocha, who was known as Coniraya Viracocha, lived before or after the time of Huallallo Carhuincho. Whenever it was, Coniraya Viracocha was a creator deity. He made the villages in the region, and by his words alone he brought the agricultural fields and terraces into existence. He also created the irrigation canals, an act which he accomplished by tossing down the flower of a type of reed, called *pupuna*, to form the channels.

Coniraya Viracocha went around as a wandering, friendless beggar, dressed in ripped and tattered clothing. People who did not recognize him shouted insults at him. At this time, there was a beautiful female huaca in the area named Cavillaca. She was a virgin, and Coniraya decided that he desperately wanted to sleep with her; however, the beautiful Cavillaca would have nothing to do with him. One day, Cavillaca was weaving beneath a *lúcuma* tree. This is a type of evergreen tree common on the coast, which bears fruit with a yellowish-orange pulp. Coniraya Viracocha transformed himself into a bird and flew into the lúcuma tree. He put his semen into a ripened fruit and dropped it beside Cavillaca. The woman ate the fruit happily, and she became pregnant. Nine months later, Cavillaca gave birth to a boy, still not knowing who had fathered him.

When the boy was one year old, Cavillaca determined to find out who had impregnated her. Thus she called together all the *vilcas* and *huacas* – the powerful male deities, mountains and other sacred places. The vilcas and huacas all came dressed in their finest clothing, each one excitedly saying, 'It's me! It's me she'll love!' Coniraya Viracocha came as well, but he arrived still dressed in tattered clothing. When the vilcas and huacas had all seated themselves, Cavillaca asked which one of them was the father of her child. When no one spoke up, Cavillaca put the boy on the ground, saying that he would crawl to his father. The child crawled along the line of seated vilcas and huacas until he came to Coniraya Viracocha. The boy brightened up and climbed into his father's lap.

Cavillaca became furious at this turn of events; how could she have given birth to the child of such a beggar as this? Enraged, she snatched up the child and headed straight for the ocean. She went out into the sea, near the site of Pachacamac, a great pilgrimage centre and oracle on the central coast (just to the south of present-day Lima). There, Cavillaca and her son were transformed into stone. They can still be seen off the coast today, near the ruins of Pachacamac. Coniraya Viracocha was distressed at this turn of events and determined to go in search of them. He sped off toward the coast, asking all whom he encountered along the way if they had seen Cavillaca pass by.

As it turns out, Coniraya encountered a series of animals and birds on his journey: a condor, skunk, puma, fox, falcon, and parakeets. He asked each one in turn about Cavillaca. Depending on the answer they gave him – that is, whether they gave him good or bad news – he assigned to them good or bad traits and fortune. For instance, when he asked the condor about Cavillaca, the bird said that she was nearby and that Coniraya would surely find her soon. Coniraya told the condor he would live a long life, would always have plenty of food, eating dead animals from the mountain slopes, and that if anyone should kill him (the condor), that person would die as well. However, when Coniraya asked the skunk if he had seen Cavillaca, the skunk said he would never find her, that she had gone far away. Thus Coniraya said to the skunk that he would never go around in the daytime; rather, he would always go out at night, stinking, and people would be disgusted by him. In this way, Coniraya Viracocha performed the creative task of naming the animals and giving them their habits and characteristics just as the myths centring on Lake Titicaca tell us Conticci Viracocha did in his own journey of creation from the mountains to the Ecuadorian coast.

When Coniraya reached the seashore, he went to the site of Pachacamac. There, he came upon the place where Pachacamac's two daughters were guarded by a snake. The girls' mother, Urpay Huachac, was away at the time. Coniraya seduced the elder sister, and then tried to do the same with the younger. Before he could succeed, however, the girl turned into a dove and flew away. Now, at that time there were no fish in the ocean. The only ones that existed were bred by Urpay Huachac, who kept them in a small pond near the site of Pachacamac. In his rage, Coniraya Viracocha scattered the fish in the ocean and since then the sea has been filled with fish.

A pyramid compound at Pachacamac, with Inca temple of the sun in the background.

Coniraya Viracocha never succeeded in finding Cavillaca and her son. Instead, the Huarochirí Manuscript says, he travelled along the coast 'for a long, long time, tricking lots of local huacas and people, too'. It is particularly notable that the exploits of Coniraya Viracocha on the coast are recounted in the Huarochirí Manuscript by people who lived in the high Andes. This mythological link between the two worlds, coast and highlands, prompts us to recognize the intimate relationship between the different but closely related peoples and resources of these two regions. We should explore this relationship more directly.

Viracocha and Pachacamac

Part of the task of mythology in pre-Columbian and continuing into early colonial times was to explore and explain the distinctions and linkages between the two worlds of the coast and the highlands. One of the ways this exploration is reflected in the myths is in terms of the identities of creator deities, such as Viracocha and Pachacamac. These two are seen in the myths in a way like face-to-face revolving mirrors: at one moment they are distinct and separate, while at the next moment they appear to be identical. In fact, the question of the relationship between Viracocha and Pachacamac is further complicated in the Huarochirí Manuscript because the people in this area – midway between the Incas in the south central highlands, on one side, and the Yungas and other peoples of the coast, on the other side – often sub-stituted the highland/coastal opposition between Viracocha and Pachacamac respectively with that between the Sun and Pachacamac. That is, the document cites the Huarochirí view to the effect that: 'In the highlands, they say, the Incas worshipped the sun as the object of their adoration from Titicaca, saying, "It is he who made us Inca!" From the lowlands, they worshipped Pachacamac, saying, "It is he who made us Inca!"'

According to one of the interpreters of the Huarochirí document (Salomon), this manuscript links, at the same time as it juxtaposes, the creator of the highlands (the Sun) with that of the coast (Pachacamac). What is elided in this relationship – although it is evoked in the above reference to 'Titicaca' – is the highland creator deity, Viracocha Pachayachiachic. These seemingly contradictory references to different, yet apparently complementary, creator deities have been the cause of an enormous amount of confusion from the colonial period to the present day. In general, it seems that the creator was identified by different names in various parts of the empire, while retaining a similar, core set of characteristics and performing similar creative works from one place to the next. The latter include dressing as a beggar and punishing those who offend him while he is in this state, naming and assigning typical traits to animals and birds of the realm, and the creation, destruction and recreation of humanity. For the moment, we should turn our attention to Pachacamac, for we have not yet explored the characteristics of this manifestation of the Andean creator deity in any detail.

As mentioned earlier, the name 'Pachacamac' referred among other things to a pilgrimage site on the central coast of Peru, a few kilometres south of Lima. The site was probably recognized as an important oracle as early as the Middle Horizon and was, until the incorporation of the site into the Inca empire, probably known as *Irma*, or *Illma*. When the Incas conquered the central coast, they took possession of the site but retained it as an oracle and a pilgrimage site. In addition, they built a large Temple of the Sun there, installing alongside the ancient oracle a cult with priests dedicated to the Inca (highland) solar deity.

Antonio de la Calancha left us one of the principal myths concerning the deity Pachacamac, a myth in which the Sun and Pachacamac are in intimate association with each other. In fact, Pachacamac is introduced in this myth as the 'son of the Sun', thus placing the coastal deity in a subordinate position vis á vis the highland deity. The myth goes as follows (as summarized in a work by Franklin Pease, see Further Reading).

At the beginning of time, Pachacamac created a human couple, the first man and woman. However, there was no food for them and the man soon died. The woman begged the Sun for help, whereupon he impregnated her with his rays. The woman gave birth to a boy after only four days. Pachacamac was jealous and angry at this turn of events, and he killed the boy and tore him into pieces. Pachacamac then used the dismembered body to provide for the want of food in the land. That is, he sowed the teeth of the corpse, and from them corn sprang up. He planted the ribs and bones, and yucca (manioc) tubers sprouted from them. The flesh was planted and it gave forth vegetables, such as cucumbers, and fruiting trees.

The Sun then took the penis and navel of the corpse and created another son for himself; this child was named *Vichama*, or *Villama*. Like his father, the Sun, Vichama wanted to travel so he set off on a journey. When Vichama departed, Pachacamac killed the woman, the same one whom he had earlier created. This woman was, in fact, Vichama's mother as Vichama was made – by a kind of 'cloning' process – of the penis and navel of the woman's first son. Pachacamac fed the remains of the woman to the vultures and condors.

Pachacamac then created a new human couple, who began to repopulate the land; he also named authorities (curacas) to rule over the people. When Vichama returned from his journey, he reassembled his mother and brought her back to life. Out of fear of reprisal for having killed Vichama's mother, Pachacamac fled to the ocean, sinking into the sea in front of the temple of Vichama/Pachacamac. Vichama turned the people whom Pachacamac had recently created into stone. He later repented of his deed and transformed the stones which had previously been curacas into huacas.

Vichama now asked his father, the Sun, to create a new race of humanity. The sun sent three eggs, of gold, silver and copper. The golden egg was the origin of the curacas and nobles; the silver egg gave rise to women; and from the copper egg came the commoners and their families. Elsewhere along the central and south coast, Calancha reports, it was believed that Pachacamac sent four stars to the earth. Two of the stars were male and two were female. From the first set were generated the kings and nobility, and from the second came the commoners.

The joining of Pachacamac and the Sun in this myth may well represent another example of the process alluded to earlier of the reworking of local myths to reflect a highland, Inca perspective. In this instance, the Sun represented the surrogate for the Incas. What we do not know, of course, is to what degree peoples of the central coast around the powerful oracle of Pachacamac might have actually bought into – that is, retold voluntarily – this imperial reworking of the local origin myth.

As noted earlier, the myth of Pachacamac and the Sun recounted above is recorded by Antonio de la Calancha in a chronicle written in 1638. At about this same time, a momentous process of investigating native idolatries in the highlands to the east of the site of Pachacamac was well under way.

Idolatry and the persistence of pre-Columbian beliefs and practices

The proselytizing of native Andean peoples carried out by various orders of the Catholic clergy began during the earliest days of the conquest, in the 1530s and 1540s, and was both intense and continuous. Nonetheless, by the end of the sixteenth century and into the early seventeenth century, as the clergy moved into remoter regions of the Andes, it became increasingly clear to them that the native peoples in these scattered mountainous settlements were continuing the worship of mountains, 'pagan' creator deities, and ancestral mummies, as well as the sun, moon and stars.

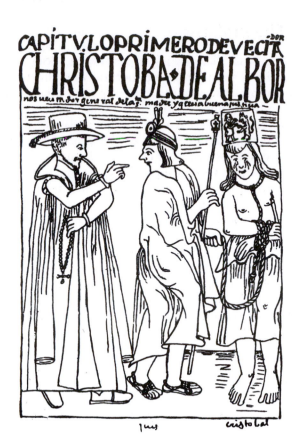

The priest Cristobal de Albornoz (left) directing the capture of an accused idolater.

This discovery greatly concerned the Spanish priests, for it suggested to them that while the armies of Spain had long ago won the battle against the Inca armies, they might be steadily losing the war against the native deities. More drastic and concerted efforts were required in order to root out and exterminate the worship of native idols, 'witches' and spirits. Therefore a number of vigorous campaigns against idolatrous practices were launched between 1610 and 1690, in the course of which the Catholic priests, relying on the support of the local lords (curacas), systematically questioned native peoples about the objects or deities they worshipped, their methods of curing diseases and divining the future, and other 'heretical' beliefs and practices. The records drawn up from these campaigns, only a handful of which have so far been published, are known as *idolatrías*.

The documents produced by the idolatries campaigns represent an unparalleled source of information on many aspects of everyday life, including religious beliefs and practices, in Andean communities at this time. In addition, they provide a background and a foundation for contextualizing and interpreting the great cosmic myths and the myths of the Inca state as the latter were recorded in the earlier 'official' documents and chronicles – based on Spanish inquiries among noble informants – of the Inca past.

The Idolatries

The most illuminating aspect of the idolatry records after almost four centuries is the intimate connection they illustrate between the people living in a community and the host of sacred objects and spiritual entities occupying the landscape around them. One particularly detailed and poignant set of accounts comes from the highlands of central Peru, around the town of Cajatambo. The people in this area, like those in many other parts of the Andes during this period, were divided into numerous ayllus. In Cajatambo, the ayllus were grouped together according to the two different 'types' of people that were considered to inhabit this land: the Guari and the Llacuaz. We will see that the characteristics of, and the relations between, these two types of people were similar to what we saw earlier in the case of the agriculturalists and pastoralists of the region of Huarochirí.

The Guari of Cajatambo were aboriginal lowland or valley-dwelling peoples who had founded the existing towns in the region. The patron deity of the Guaris was a giant god, associated with caves, who is identified in the literature as 'Huari'. These people also worshipped the night-time sun – that is, the sun when it passed through the underworld, moving along its watery passage from sundown to sunrise. It was said that the ancestors of the Guari peoples had come into this area in remote times either from the ocean, to the west, or from Lake Titicaca. The Guaris were primarily corn-cultivators who worshipped sacred amulets, called *canopas*, which were considered to control the fertility of the maize fields.

The other side of the great social divide in the region of Cajatambo was composed of the Llacuaz peoples. These were puna or highland dwelling people whose economy was based on potato cultivation and the herding of llamas and alpacas. The principal deity of the Llacuaz peoples was 'Llibiac', who was primarily a thunder-and-lightning god. The Llacuaz also worshipped the sun of the daytime – the sun as it passed overhead from sunrise to sunset – and the stars. The Llacuaz were considered to be late arrivals to this area, migrants who had come into the territory at some time in the not-too-distant past and had conquered the Guari.

The ritual life in the settlements of Cajatambo commemorated the Llacuaz conquest of the Guari, as well as the subsequent founding of a confederation between the two groups. Each side of this two-part (moiety) confederation adopted certain rituals and ceremonies of the opposing half. That is, rituals were celebrated in a reciprocal fashion: the Guaris celebrated rituals on behalf of the Llacuazs, and vice versa. The two groups also celebrated some rituals and festivals jointly, and they also jointly revered certain sacred objects, as well as numerous places in the landscape that were identified as the burial places of sacrificial victims, the capacochas. These sacrificial victims established links between the local people and the Incas, the latter of whom had been considered by the Guaris and Llacuazs to have been the owners of the entire land.

The various ayllus of Guaris and Llacuazes each had special links to huacas in the surrounding countryside, such as mountain peaks, springs and caves. The huacas were thought to exert influence over the life and destiny of the particular group of people who worshipped them. The most powerful huacas were the high mountains, each of which had its own name, spirit (or spirits), and a particular kinship relationship to other mountains in the region. In addition, any especially large or prominent boulders, called *huancas*, were considered sacred and were believed to represent, or contain the essence of, an ancestor of one or more of the local ayllus.

The mythological traditions of ayllus within the region of Cajatambo were composed largely of stories recounting how the spiritual essences of ayllu ancestors had come to be lodged within the surrounding mountains, rocky outcrops, and other prominent features of the landscape. Stories also told how these sacred places and entities had interacted with each other in the distant past. Another geographical feature that was of great ritual and mythological significance for the peoples of Cajatambo were the many caves, called *machay*, that dotted the mountainsides. As we saw earlier, caves held a place of particular importance in Inca myths about the origin of the first king of the empire. In Cajatambo, caves were the places of origin of the ancestors of the Guari and Llacuaz ayllus, as well as the repositories of the mummies (*malquis*) of deceased ayllu members.

The numbers of ancestral mummies stored in these caves were truly astonishing. For instance, one idolatry account from 1656–8 lists the following numbers of ancestral mummies found in caves, or in abandoned towns around the settlement of San Pedro de Hacas: in Yanaqui, 214 bodies; in Quirca, 471 bodies; in Ayllu Carampa, 738 bodies; and in Ayllu Picoca, 402 bodies! These collections of malquis were worshipped by the living inhabitants of their respective towns. The mummies were dressed in new clothing at certain times of the year, and offerings of food and drink were made to them at planting and harvesting seasons.

The information recorded in the idolatry accounts thus reveals, even a century or two after the Spanish conquest, how people in the Andean countryside viewed the past and the present, the living and the dead, and the land and the people who lived on it as interconnected, continuous and fully complementary. The complementary oppositions between lowlanders and highlanders, autochthonous peoples and migrants, conquerors and conquered, corn (maize) and potato cultivators (and pastoralists), sun and moon and other such divisions that appear in the beliefs of peoples in Cajatambo in the seventeenth century were entirely consistent with similar beliefs described in the earliest chronicles of the Inca empire.

These beliefs, which formed the religious and ideological foundations of myths detailing the nature of relations among ayllus and ethnic groups in the empire, continued to inform the mythological traditions of Andean peoples during much of the colonial era. But beyond a similarity between pre-Hispanic and colonial beliefs and myths, there were also traditions linking the two eras; these were – and still are – recounted in villages throughout the Andes in myths such as those narrating the death, and predicting the rebirth, of the Inca.

The Inca past in the Andean present

Ethnographic studies in Andean communities did not begin in earnest until after the end of World War II. By the end of the 1950s, a number of anthropologists had assembled a corpus of myths and legends from Quechua- and Aymara-speaking communities throughout the Andes. There are two mythic traditions to point to in particular as they will allow us to reflect broadly on the long-term importance of the image and persona of the Inca, as well as the uses to which myths have been put, in the Andean world. One of these traditions concerns a body of myths relating to what we may term the theme of the 'dying and reviving Inca'. Such myths, shared as they are by communities throughout the Andes, represent a source of pan-Andean unity, somewhat in the manner of the cosmic myths with Lake Titicaca as the place of origin that were told in Inca times. The other type of myth that we should look at briefly here concerns the linkage between a local myth of origin and its connection to local and state validation. Interestingly enough, we may again turn in this regard to the uses of myths of origin in the town of Pacaritambo, the origin place of the first Inca, Manco Capac.

The dying and reviving Inca

Many myths about the Incas that are shared broadly throughout the Andes today revolve around the millenarian theme of the return of the Inca. The central character in these myths is *Inkarrí*, a name based on a combination of the terms Inca and the Spanish *rey* ('king').

The myth of Inkarrí is millenarian in the sense that it foretells a time in the future when the Andean world will undergo a cataclysmic transformation involving the destruction of the Spanish-dominated world, which has been in place since the European invasion in the seventeenth century, and the reinstatement of the Inca as supreme ruler. The millenarian overtones here are perfectly in tune with the age-old Andean notion of 'pachacuti', the revolution, or reversal of time and space. A number of versions of the Inkarrí myth were collected in the 1950s by the great Peruvian anthropologist José María Arguedas in the southern Peruvian town of Puquio. One version of this myth goes as follows.

'They say Inkarrí was the son of a woman who was a savage. His father, they say, was Father Sun. That savage woman bore Inkarrí; Father Sun begat Inkarrí.

The Inca king had three women. The work of the Inca is on Ak'nu. On K'ellk'ata Plain the wine, the *chicha* [corn beer] and the *aguar-diente* [cane alchohol] are boiling.

Inkarrí drove the stones with a whip, ordering them about. Afterwards, he founded a city. K'ellk'ata could have been Cusco, so they say.

. . . Inkarrí confined the wind. . . [and] he bound Father Sun, so time would last, so the day would last, so that Inkarrí would be able to do what he had to do.

When he had bound the wind to the mountain [of Osk'onta], he hurled a golden rod from the top of Big Osk'onta, saying, "Will Cusco fit?" It did not fit into K'ellk'ata Plain. He threw the rod far down, saying "It does not fit in." Cusco was moved to where it is. How far off might that be? We of the living generation do not know. The old generation, before Atahualpa, knew that.

The Spanish Inca imprisoned Inkarrí, his equal. Where, we do not know. The head is all that's left of Inkarrí, they say. From the head he's growing inward; toward the feet he's growing, they say.

He will return then, Inkarrí, when his body is whole. He has not returned until now. He is to return to us, if God sees fit. But we do not know, they say, if God is to decide that he should return.'

The decapitation of Atahualpa.

The origins of the myth of Inkarrí as recounted in Puquio and in countless other cities, towns and villages in the Andes seem to go back to events that occurred during the forty years or so immediately following the Spanish conquest. One event was the decapitation of the last Inca ruler, Atahualpa, by Francisco Pizzaro soon after the defeat of the Inca armies in Cajamarca. The other major, traumatic event was another decapitation of a native leader by the Spanish authorities – the victim in this case was Tupac Amaru, who led a revolt against the Spanish in the 1560s and 1570s. Tupac Amaru was beheaded in the plaza of Cusco, by order of Franciso de Toledo, in 1572.

In both these instances of the decapitation of an Inca – or, in the second case, a 'neo-Inca' – the story apparently spread throughout the countryside that the head had been spirited away and buried. In some accounts, the head was taken to Lima; in others, it was taken to Cusco. In either case, once the head was placed in the ground, it is believed to have begun to regrow the body. When the body is complete, the Inca will return, and the world will undergo a pachacuti.

Living at, and using, the Inca place of origin

The town of Pacaritambo, site of the cave of Tambo Toco, traditional birth-place of the Inca Manco Capac and his siblings, lies some 26 km due south of the old Inca capital of Cusco. Having myself lived in this town during more than two years of ethnographic fieldwork in the 1980s, I can attest to the extraordinary interest and pride on the part of local people in the position this village occupies in Peruvian history. People continually point out places in the landscape – a rock outcrop with what appear to be the footprints of a llama impressed in the stone, a depression in a boulder, or a split mountain peak – that are believed to be the visible markings of the passing of the Incas at the beginning of time. A kilometre or so from the town is a small cave, which local residents identify as the site of Tambo Toco. Thus the landscape around the town and cave is a living remnant of the Inca origin myth.

In fact, the status of Pacaritambo as the origin place of the Incas is re-inforced today by the government-issue primary school textbooks, used throughout Peru, which recount a truncated, child's version of the origin myth. This officially sanctioned version of the origin myth is a source of considerable pride for the people of the town, but in addition to the local importance of the continuing identification of Pacaritambo as the origin place of the first Inca, this tradition has on occasion been used by outsiders in some rather novel ways. Perhaps the most striking such instance involved a past president of Peru, Fernando Belaúnde Terry.

Upon first entering office in 1964 Belaúnde Terry visited Pacaritambo in a move that was blatantly intended to incorporate into the foundations of his presidency the legitimacy afforded by contact with the origin place of the first Inca king. The president took a helicopter from Cusco, landing in the plaza in the middle of the town of Pacaritambo. There, he received a tradi-tional wooden staff of office, called a *vara*, shook the hands of local officials,

The cave recognized today as Tambo Toco.

and then helicoptered back to Cusco, whence he returned to the presidential palace in Lima. Today, people who were in the plaza then, and who perhaps shook the president's hand, tell the story of his (literal) whirlwind visit, exaggerating various elements of the story for the benefit of their companions.

Whatever the true character of the Incas in their own day, therefore, and whether or not the head of the last Inca is regrowing its body in the present day, the memory and image of the Incas continue to hold tremendous power and meaning for the people who live in the land that was once Tahuantinsuyu.

Suggestions for further reading

There are a number of recently published books in English that provide good, general overviews of Andean archaeology up to, and including, the Inca empire. These include: Michael E. Moseley, *The Incas and Their Ancestors* (London, 1992); Adriana von Hagen and Craig Morris, *The Cities of the Ancient Andes* (London, 1998); and Jonathan Haas, Sheila Pozorski and Thomas Pozorski (eds), *The Origins and Development of the Andean State* (Cambridge, 1987). Other archaeological studies concerning developments in the Andes leading up to the Incas include: Richard Burger, *Chavín and the Origins of Andean Civilization* (London, 1992); Alan Kolata, *Tiwanaku: Portrait of an Andean Civilization* (Oxford and Cambridge MA, 1993); Katharina J. Schreiber, *Wari Imperialism in Middle Horizon Peru* (Ann Arbor, 1992); and William H. Isbell, *Mummies and Mortuary Monuments* (Austin, 1997).

For archaeological and ethnohistorical studies dealing specifically with the Incas, see Brian S. Bauer, *The Development of the Inca State* (Austin, 1992) and Martti Pärssinen, *Tawantinsuyu: The Inca State and Its Political Organization* (Helsinki, 1992). Still one of the best overviews of Inca culture in late pre-Hispanic times is John H. Rowe, 'Inca culture at the time of the Spanish conquest', in Julian H. Steward (ed.), *Handbook of South American Indians*, Vol. 2, Bulletin #143: 183–330 (Washington, DC, 1946). For a work documenting the relationship between state and ayllu in Andean economic organization, see John V. Murra, *The Economic Organization of the Inca State* (Greenwich CT, 1980). The standard source for studying the social, ritual and political organization of Inca Cusco is R.Tom Zuidema, *The Ceque System of Cuzco: The Social Organization of the Capital of the Inca* (Leiden, 1964).

There have been few good, English-language overviews of the Spanish chroniclers who wrote on Inca myth and history. One of the most authoritative and comprehensive of such works in Spanish is Raúl Porras Barrenechea's *Los cronistas del Perú* (1528–1650) (Lima, 1986). For a set of studies on the native Andean chroniclers, see Rolena Adorno (ed.), *From Oral to Written Expression: Native Andean Chronicles of the Early Colonial Period* (Syracuse, 1982). The reader is also referred to the collection of translated passages from various chroniclers' accounts of Inca myths in Harold Osborne's *South American Mythology* (London, 1968). The best study to date discussing the intellectual and theological backgrounds of many of the chroniclers in relation to their accounts of Inca mythic-histories is Sabine MacCormack's *Religion in the Andes: Vision and Imagination in Early Colonial Peru* (Princeton NJ, 1991).

For works concerning the cosmic myths of origin focusing on Lake Titicaca and Tiahuanaco, see Verónica Salles-Reese, *From Viracocha to the Virgin of Copacabana: Representation of the Sacred at Lake Titicaca* (Austin, 1997); Thérèse Bouysse-Cassagne, *Lluvias y Cenizas: Dos Pachacuti en la Historia* (La Paz, 1988); and Franklin Pease, *El Dios Creador Andino* (Lima, 1973).

For a study specifically dealing with the role of colonial-period residents of the town of Pacaritambo in recounting Inca myths of origin beginning at their home community, see Gary Urton, *The History of a Myth: Pacariqtambo and the Origin of the Inkas* (Austin, 1990). For a general study of the Inca origin myths and their relation to the political organization of the capital city, see R. Tom Zuidema, *Inca Civilization in Cuzco* (Austin, 1990). A good, highly readable account of the Spanish conquest of the Incas that pays special attention to the early colonial history of the Cusco region is John Hemming's *The Conquest of the Incas* (New York and London, 1970).

For an excellent collection of articles dealing with the mythic-histories and archaeological records of the Chimu and other Peruvian north coastal societies, see María Rostworowski de Diez Canseco and Michael E. Moseley (eds), *The Northern Dynasties: Kingship and Statecraft in Chimor* (Washington DC, 1990). On this same topic, see María Rostworowski, *Costa peruana prehispanica* (Lima, 1989). For an excellent overview of the cultural context for reading the Huarochirí Manuscript, as well as a definitive transcription and English translation of the Quechua text itself, see Frank Salomon and George L. Urioste, *The Huarochirí Manuscript* (Austin, 1991). Kenneth Mills' *Idolatry and Its Enemies: Colonial Andean Religion and Extirpation, 1640-1750* (Princeton NJ, 1997) is an excellent study of the idolatrías process and reports. In addition, many of the documents deriving from the idolatry investigations and trials in the region of Cajatambo have been collected in Pierre Duviols' *Cultura Andina y Repression: Procesos y visitas de idolatrías y hechicerías Cajatambo, Siglo XVII* (Cusco, 1986).

Accounts of a few versions of myths of Incarrí are to be found in the short ethnography of Puquio published with José María Arguedas novel, *Yawar Fiesta* (Austin, 1985). For an excellent study of the Incarrí myths, see Mercedes López-Baralt, *El Retorno del Inca Rey: Mito y profecía en el mundo andino* (Fuenlabrada, 1987). On the theme of utopianism and millenarian ideology in contemporary Peru, see Alberto Flores Galindo, *Buscando un Inca: Identidad y Utopia en los Andes* (Havana, 1985).

Picture credits

Glossary

Adad (*Mesopotamian*) Weather god, controller of storms and rain. Son of **Anu**.

Adapa (*Mesopotamian*) Mortal man with divine ancestry, a priest of **Ea**, who loses the chance to gain immortality.

Aeshma (*Persian*) Demon of fury and outrage who assists **Angra Mainyu**.

Afraysiyab (*Persian*) Another name for Franrasyan.

Ahriman (**Evil Spirit**) (*Persian*) Another name for **Angra Mainyu**.

Ahura Mazda (**Wise Lord**) (*Persian*) The ultimate god and creator. Represents goodness, wisdom and knowledge, and opposed to all evil and suffering.

Akvan (*Persian*) A demon, beheaded by **Rustam**.

Alcavicça (*Inca*) A great lord created by **Viracocha**, an original inhabitant of **Cusco**. Helps **Manco Capac** plant the first corn field there.

Alexander the Great (*Persian*) Actual Greek king who conquered many countries, including Persia in 331 BC. Immortalised in Persian literature as an epic hero.

amautas (*Inca*) Official poet-philosophers who recorded genealogies, royal deeds and battles as songs, which they performed before the king and court. *See also* **quipucamayoqs**.

Angra Mainyu (**Evil Spirit**) (*Persian*) Also known as **Ahriman**. Personification of evil, whose aim is to destroy the world of truth and lure all beings into darkness, deceit and lies, assisted by other demons. In constant opposition to **Ahura Mazda**.

Annunaki (**Anukki**) (*Mesopotamian*) Sumerian gods of fertility and judges of the **Underworld**.

Anshar (*Mesopotamian*) A god, father of **Ea**.

Antum (*Mesopotamian*) A goddess, wife of **Anu**.

Anu (*Mesopotamian*) Sky god, sometimes chief god, who appears in many myths. Married to **Antum**, father of **Adad**, **Anzu**, **Ellil** and **Ishtar**.

Anzu (*Mesopotamian*) An evil god, son of **Anu**. Takes the form of a bird. Steals **Tablet of Destinies** and is destroyed by **Ninurta**.

Apaosha (**Drought**) (*Persian*) Shape changing witch, enemy of **Tishtrya**.

Apsu (*Mesopotamian*) (1) Subterranean realm of sweet water, ruled over by **Ea**; (2) in Epic of Creation, primordial god of the waters who mates with **Tiamat**.

Ardvi Sura Anahita (*Persian*) Goddess of all earthly waters. Source of the cosmic ocean and of all life.

Aruru (*Mesopotamian*) Another name for **Nin-hursag**. Mother goddess, creator of **Enkidu**.

Aryans (*Persian*) The peoples of Iran.

asha (*Persian*) Right order.

Astyages (*Persian*) Actual king of the Medes, deposed 550 BC. Maternal grandfather of **Cyrus the Great**, whom he attempts to kill in infancy. Cyrus survives and eventually usurps him.

Atar (**Fire**) (*Persian*) A god, the son of **Ahura Mazda**, closely associated with **Mithra**. Symbol of **Zoroastrianism**. Worshipped in fire temples and at domestic hearths.

Atrahasis (*Mesopotamian*) 'Extra Wise', king of Shuruppak. **Enki** advises him how to survive divine **flood**.

Auca Runa (*Inca*) Warlike race of people created during the fourth of the **five suns**.

Avesta (*Persian*) The holy book of **Zoroastrianism**.

Ayar Auca (*Inca*) One of the eight sibling-ancestors who emerge at **Pacaritampu**. Married to **Mama Huaco**. Transformed into a stone pillar which becomes an important **huaca** in central **Cusco**.

Ayar Cachi (*Inca*) One of the eight sibling-ancestors who emerge at **Pacaritampu**. Married to **Mama Ipacura**. Troublesome personality, so sealed inside **Tambo Toco**.

Ayar Manco (*Inca*) One of the eight sibling-ancestors who emerge at **Pacaritampu**. Married to **Mama Ocllo**. Later called **Manco Capac**. Founds **Cusco** with his four sisters and son, **Sinchi Roca**.

Ayar Uchu (*Inca*) One of the eight sibling-ancestors who emerge at **Pacaritampu**. Married to **Mama Raua**. Flies into sky where meets the **sun**; on return is transformed into stone.

ayllu (*Inca*) A group of people related by kinship, land-holding and ritual ceremonies.

azhi (*Persian*) Demons or fabulous monsters (including **dragons**) which devour people and animals and cause general terror. See **Azhi Dahaka**.

Azhi Dahaka (*Persian*) Monstrous demon, follower of **Angra Mainyu**. Tries to steal the **Divine Glory**, outwitted by **Atar** and **Mithra** and imprisoned by **Thraetona** until the world's end.

Belet-ili (*Mesopotamian*) Goddess of the womb and motherhood. Creates the seven original men and women whose offspring eventually overpopulate the world, and the hero **Ninurta**, her 'supreme beloved'.

Bull of Heaven (*Mesopotamian*) Powerful beast kept by **Anu**. **Ishtar** borrows it to punish **Gilgamesh** when he refuses her advances, but it is killed and disembowelled by the hero.

calendar (*Aztec and Maya*) Intrinsic to cultural life, linked to heavenly bodies, directions, sacred moments and periods: (1) 260-day cycle comprising 21 consecutive day names combined with the numbers 1–13; (2) year of 365 days comprising 18 months of 20 days each, plus final period of 5 days; (1) and (2) ran concurrently to produce a total cycle of 52 years; (3) Long Count (*Maya*) System based on 20, counting continuously from mythical event in 3114 BC.

Can Cong (Silkworm Cluster) (*Chinese*) A god, originally a king in silkworm shape. Teaches humans cultivation of silkworms and silk.

canopas (*Inca*) Sacred amulets of the Guari people, controlling the fertility of maize fields.

capacochas (*Inca*) Sacrificial victims, usually children, from provinces of the Inca empire. Their deaths sealed bonds between central Incas and people of the outlying areas.

Cavillaca (*Inca*) A beautiful female **huaca**, impregnated by **Coniraya Viracocha**, who flees him with her son. They are turned to stone near **Pachacamac**.

Centzon Huitznahua (The Four Hundred Southerners) (*Aztec*) Multitude of brothers of **Coyolxauhqui**, sons of **Coatlicue**.

Chac (*Maya*) God of rain and lightning.

Chalchiuhtlicue (She of the Jade Skirt) (*Aztec*) Goddess of rivers and standing waters, wife of **Tlaloc**.

Chancas (*Inca*) Powerful nation to west of **Cusco**, whose attack on the Incas precipitated the building of their empire.

Chang E (Ever Sublime) (*Chinese*) Moon goddess, linked to **immortality** and rebirth. After stealing **drug of immortality** from her husband **Yi**, she is changed into a toad and transported to the moon.

Chang Xi (Ever Breath) (*Chinese*) A moon goddess.

Chi You (Jest Much) (*Chinese*) God of war and inventor of metal weapons.

Chimo Capac (*Inca*) Leader of army who invaded Lambayeque valley after **Fempellec**.

Cihuacoatl (Woman Serpent) (*Aztec*) Old goddess who grinds the bones of fish-people into flour and mixes it with the gods' blood, thus creating the human race.

Cinteotl (*Aztec*) God of maize.

Cizin (Flatulent One) (*Maya*) God of death, also known as **Yum Cimih**.

Coatlicue (She of the Serpent Skirt) (*Aztec*) Mother of the **Centzon Huitzhahua** and **Coyolxauhqui**; also of **Huitzilopochtli**, whom she conceives after being impregnated by a ball of feathers.

codex (pl. **codices**) (*Aztec* and *Maya*) Book of folded paper or parchment painted with symbolic pictures and hieroglyphic script; an important source of mythology.

Colla (*Inca*) After the **flood**, king of the southern quarter.

Con Ticci Viracocha (*Inca*) Another name for **Viracocha**.

Confucius (Kong Fu-Zi) (*Chinese*) Philosopher who lived 551–479 BC. Taught complex moral code based on *li* (courtesy and reverence) and *shu* (consideration for others). Teachings adopted as 'orthodox way' of China by the 2nd century BC.

Coniraya Viracocha (*Inca*) Creator god of the Yauyos people, a wandering, friendless beggar. Impregnates **Cavillaca** by transforming into a fruit.

Contiti Viracocha Pachayachachic ('God, maker of the world') (*Inca*) Another name for **Viracocha**.

Country of Women (*Chinese*) A mythical, all-female land where virgin women are fertilised by bathing in a miraculous pool.

Coyolxauhqui (Painted with Bells) (*Aztec*) Sister of the **Centzon Huitznahua** and half-sister of **Huitzilopochtli**, who kills her.

Cusco (*Inca*) Capital city and centre of Inca empire, in modern Peru. Founded by **Manco Capac**, his four ancestral sisters and **Sinchi Roca**.

Cyrus the Great (*Persian*) Actual ruler of the Achaemenid empire, 550–530 BC. Survives attempted infanticide by his grandfather **Astyages**, raised by a herdsman and eventually overthrows Astyages, uniting the kingdoms of the Medes and Persians.

Damkina (*Mesopotamian*) Goddess, wife of **Ea**, mother of **Marduk**.

Daoism (*Chinese*) Religion and philosophical system founded in 6th century BC by Lao Zi. Following the natural rhythm and harmony of nature, adherents shun desire, emotion, aggression and interference. *See also* **yin and yang**.

demons (*Persian*) *See* **div**.

Di Ku (Great God Tellswift) (*Chinese*) God associated with bringing music to humans. Marries both **Jian Di** and **Jiang Yuan**.

Dinazad (*Persian*) Younger sister of **Shahrazad**, whom she helps to end **Shahriyar**'s reign of terror.

div (*Persian*) Demons said to live in the northern darkness. Variously identified as (1) evil humans; (2) personifications of **Angra Mainyu**; (3) a group of enemy kings.

Div-e Sepid (white demon) (*Persian*) Arch-demon, killed by **Rustam**.

divination (*Mesopotamian*) Art of foretelling the future by observing animal entrails, the effects of oil on water, the patterns of smoke from incense, the behaviour of birds and animals, the weather or the stars.

Divine Glory (*Persian*) The 'Kingly Fortune', possessed only by legitimate rulers, and lost if they stray from the righteous path.

dragons (1) (*Chinese*) Associated with water and the bringing of rain, immortal and generally benevolent. Dragon-kings rule each of the four seas surrounding the earth, and many lakes and rivers. (2) (*Persian*) *See* **azhi**.

drug of immortality (*Chinese*) Obtained by **Yi** from **Xi Wang Mu**, but stolen by his wife **Chang E** before he can use it.

Dumuzi (*Mesopotamian*) Pastoral god associated with seasonal fertility. A former lover of **Ishtar**, condemned to stay in the **Underworld** but periodically returning to earth. Also known as **Tammuz**.

Duzhyairya (Bad Harvest) (*Persian*) A witch, opponent of **Tishtrya**.

Ea (*Mesopotamian*) Lord of the **Apsu**. Married to **Damkina**, father of **Marduk**. All-knowing instructor of mankind in arts and crafts, and the source of secret magical knowledge. Appears in many myths to offer advice, warnings and suggest solutions to predicaments. Also known as **Enki**.

Ehecatl (*Aztec*) God of wind, an aspect of **Quetzalcoatl**.

eight trigrams (Ba Gua) (*Chinese*) System of divination invented by **Fu Xi**, recorded in a book called Yi Jing ('Classic of Change'), consisting of eight combinations of three broken and unbroken lines (symbolising **yin and yang**), multiplied to make 64 variations of six lines. Each variation has a title and mystical meaning.

Ellil (*Mesopotamian*) Son of **Anu**, replaces him as king of the gods. Keeper of the **Tablet of Destinies**. Instigator of the great **flood** in myth of **Atrahasis** and appears in many other myths.

Enki (*Mesopotamian*) *See* **Ea**.

Enkidu (*Mesopotamian*) A hairy savage man, created by **Aruru**, but civilised after seven nights' lovemaking with **Shamhat** and becomes beloved companion of **Gilgamesh**. His death inspires Gilgamesh to embark on his quest for eternal life.

Ereshkigal (*Mesopotamian*) **Queen of the Underworld**, sister of **Ishtar**. Lover and sometime wife of **Nergal**.

Erra (*Mesopotamian*) God of plague and war, lord of the **Underworld**. *See also* **Nergal**.

Etana (*Mesopotamian*) King of Kish, who lacks a son to succeed him. He rescues an eagle from a pit and is carried on its back to heaven in an attempt to obtain the 'plant of birth'.

Farangis (*Persian*) Wife of **Siyavush**, mother of **Kay Khusrow**.

Fariydun (Thraetaona) (*Persian*) Superhero who destroys **Zahhak** and rules for 500 years of prosperity, harmony and peace.

Fempellec (*Inca*) Last king of **Naymlap**'s dynasty. Tries to move **Yampallec** to a new location, causing environmental disasters, which end when he is hurled into the sea.

filial piety (*Chinese*) In the philosophy of **Confucius** and **Mencius**, the moral duty to honour one's parents and not disgrace them. *See also* **Shun**.

fire (*Persian*) *See* **Atar**.

five suns (*Inca*) Five different ages, each lasting a thousand years and then destroyed. The last 'sun' was the age of the Incas. *See also* **Nahui Ollin**, **pacachuti**.

flood (1) (*Mesopotamian*) Seven-day inundation of the earth sent by the gods to punish mankind, paralleling the biblical story of Noah. Different myths describe how either **Ut-napishtim** or **Atrahasis** receives divine help to survive the flood by building a special boat. (2) (*Inca*) In creation myths of **Viracocha**, a deluge destroys the first race of people; after it subsides the land is repopulated with a new race. *See also* **pachacuti**.

Four Emperors (*Chinese*) Gods of the four cardinal points: Great Whitelight (east), **Yan Di** (south), **Shao Hao** (west) and **Zhuan Xu** (north).

Franrasyan (**Afrasiyab**) (*Persian*) King of Turan and symbol of evil. Continuously tries to overthrow Persian kings to obtain the **Divine Glory**. Murders **Siyavush**, whose son **Kay Khusrow** kills him in revenge.

Fu Xi (**Prostrate Victim**) (*Chinese*) Major god, one-time ruler of the cosmos, who invents writing, the **eight trigrams**, hunting nets and music. Sometimes linked with **Nu Gua** as the first divine married couple.

Garshasp (*Persian*) *See* **Keresaspa**.

Gayomartan (**Mortal Life**) (**Gayomard**, **Kiyumars**) (*Persian*) The first man, created out of earth and bright as the sun. Killed by **Angra Mainyu**, his seed grows into a plant from which spring **Mashya and Mashyanag**.

Gilgamesh (*Mesopotamian*) Semi-divine king of Uruk, who oppresses his subjects until the gods send **Enkidu** to befriend him. Together they embark on heroic deeds, killing the **Bull of Heaven** and **Humbaba**, but the gods make Enkidu die as a punishment. The devastated Gilgamesh embarks on a quest for eternal life. Eventually **Ut-napishtim** directs him under the sea where he finds a **plant of immortality**, but a snake steals it before he can use it.

Gong Gong (**Common Work**) (*Chinese*) Rebellious worker-god who challenges the supremacy of **Zhuan Xu**.

Gu Shan (**Mount Drum**) (*Chinese*) Mythical being with dragon's body and human face, transformed into a bird. An omen of drought.

Gu Sou (**Blind Man**) (*Chinese*) Murderous father of **Shun**, symbol of

moral ignorance.

Gucumatz (*Maya*) Creator god who works with **Hurucan**.

Gun (**Hugefish**) (*Chinese*) Eldest son of supreme god. Steals god's sacred cosmos-repairing soil to save the world from flood, executed as punishment. **Yu** is born from his corpse.

Gushtasp (*Persian*) *See* **Vishtaspa**.

Haoma (*Persian*) (1) God of health and strength, providing rich harvests and sons; (2) medicinal plant with intoxicating powers.

Haoshanha (*Persian*) *See* **Hushang**.

Harpagus (*Persian*) Median nobleman, ordered by **Astyages** to kill the infant **Cyrus the Great**. He is later punished for his disobedience by having his own son killed and cooked.

Hasan of el-Basra (*Persian*) Hero of fairy tale from *1001 Arabian Nights*. Abducted by an alchemist, he is befriended by seven sisters and marries a shape-changing bird-princess.

He (*Chinese*) *See* **Xi He**.

Hou Ji (**Sovereign Millet**) (*Chinese*) God of grain, son of **Jiang Yuan**. Founder of the Zhou dynasty and people, and minister of agriculture in the government of **Shun**.

huaca (*Inca*) Sacred place, often connected with myths of creation and origin.

Huallallo Carhuincho (*Inca*) Principal god of the aboriginal Yauyos people, defeated and driven out by **Pariacaca**.

Huang Di (**Great God Yellow**) (*Chinese*) Supreme god of **Daoism** and ancestral deity of Chinese civilisation.

Huari (*Inca*) Patron god of the Guari people.

Huehueteotl (**Old God**) (*Aztec*) Fire god.

Huitzilopochtli (**Hummingbird on the Left**) (*Aztec*) (1) Fourth son of the creator couple, with creative powers; (2) son of **Coatlicue** and half-brother of **Coyolxauhqui** and the **Centzon Huitznahua**, who try to kill him at birth, but he slays them instead; (3) patron god of the Aztec people and empire.

Humbaba (Huwawa) (*Mesopotamian*) Monstrous giant of the Pine Forest, killed by **Gilgamesh** and **Enkidu**.

Hun Batz and **Hun Chouen** (*Maya*) Twin sons of **Hun Hunahpu**, turned into monkeys by **Xbalanque and Hunahpu**. Patrons of artists, dancers and musicians.

Hun Came and **Vucub Came** (**One Death** and **Seven Death**) (*Maya*) Principal lords of **Xibalba**.

Hun Hunahpu and **Vucub Hunahpu** (**One Hunahpu** and **Seven Hunahpu**) (*Maya*) Twin sons of **Xpiyacoc** and **Xmucane**. **Hun Hunahpu** is the father of **Hun Batz** and **Hun Chouen**.

Hun Nal (*Maya*) A form of the maize god.

Hundun (**Muddle Thick**) (*Chinese*) God of chaos, a pig-like creature with six feet and four wings but no face, whose death results in the creation of the cosmos.

Huracan (**Heart of Heaven**) (*Maya*) Creator god who works with **Gucumatz**.

Hushang (**Haoshanha**) (*Persian*) Mythical king, grandson of **Kiyumars**, who discovers fire, iron, tools, weapons, irrigation, cultivation and the craft of the smith. Father of **Tahmuras**.

Igigi (*Mesopotamian*) Gods of the sky, led by **Ellil**.

Imaymana Viracocha (*Inca*) Eldest son of **Viracocha**, whom he helps with creation; brother of **Tocapo Viracocha**.

Inanna (*Mesopotamian*) Another name for **Ishtar**.

Inkarrí (*Inca*) Modern millenarian myths foretelling cataclysmic destruction of Spanish-dominated culture and the reinstatement of the Inca as supreme ruler.

inti (*Inca*) *See* **sun**.

Isfandiyar (*Persian*) Invincible hero, son of **Vishtaspa**.

Ishtar (*Mesopotamian*) Insatiable goddess of love, sex and war. Daughter of **Anu** or **Sin**, sister of **Ereshkigal**. Also known as **Inanna**.

Ishum (*Mesopotamian*) Vizier of **Erra**.

Island of the Sun (*Inca*) Island shrine on Lake **Titicaca**, focus of annual pilgrimage. Supposedly the place where **Viracocha** created **sun**, **moon** and stars.

Itzamna (*Maya*) Old creator god, married to **Ix Chel**.

Itzlacoliuhqui (*Aztec*) God of stone and darkness, a transformation of **Tlahuizcalpantecuhtli**.

Ix Chel (**Chac Chel**) (*Maya*) Aged goddess of midwifery and healing. Married to **Itzamna**.

Jamshid (*Persian*) Mythical king who rules for 300 years, overseeing inventions. Also known as **Yima**.

Jian Di (**Bamboo Slip Maid**) (*Chinese*) Ancestress of Shang dynasty through her son Xie or Qi, whom she conceives miraculously by swallowing an egg dropped by a black bird.

Jiang Yuan (**Jiang the Originator**) (*Chinese*) Mother of **Hou Ji**, whom she conceives by treading in the toe-print of a god, thus ancestress of the Zhou dynasty and people.

Jing Wei (**Sprite Guard**) (*Chinese*) *See* **Nu Wa**.

Jun (**Foremost**) (*Chinese*) A supreme god of the sky who gives **Yi** his bow and arrows.

Kakka (*Mesopotamian*) Servant of **Anu**.

karshvar (*Persian*) Seven regions of the world, created when the first rain fell on earth. *See* **Khvanirath**.

Kavi (**Kiyanian**) (*Persian*) Mythical dynasty of kings who possess the **Divine Glory** and are constantly opposed by **Franrasyan**.

Kay Kavus (*Persian*) King of kings at the time of **Rustam**. Father of **Siyavush**.

Kay Khusrow (**Kavi Haosravah**) (*Persian*) Son of **Siyavush**, who kills **Afrasiyab** in revenge for his father's murder.

Keresaspa (**Garshasp**) (*Persian*) Hero who fights evil forces and **dragons**.

Khusrow Parviz (*Persian*) Exceptional king who loves **Shirin** and eventually takes her as his third wife.

Khvanirath (**Khvaniras**) (*Persian*) The **karshvar** inhabited by humans. Contains the **Vourukasha Sea** and the **Saena Tree**.

Kinich Ahau (**Sun-Faced Lord**) (*Maya*) Sun god who transforms into a jaguar during nightly journey through the **Underworld**.

Kiyumars (*Persian*) Another form of **Gayomartan**. Perfect ruler of the world who introduces the throne, crown and castle of kingship, also religion.

Kui (**Awestruck**) (*Chinese*) God of thunder in form of a blue, one-legged ox. Director of music in the government of **Shun**.

Kunlun Mountain (**Mt Offspringline**) (*Chinese*) An actual mountain range, supposedly an earthly paradise full of mythical animals and plants, including the **drug of immortality**. **Xi Wang Mu** rules from one of its peaks.

Kurnugi (*Mesopotamian*) The **Underworld**.

Llibiac (*Inca*) God of thunder and lightning, principle deity of the Llacuaz peoples.

Macuilxochitl (**Five Flower**) (*Aztec*) God of games and gambling.

mallquis (*Inca*) Ancestral mummies.

Mama Huaco (*Inca*) One of the eight sibling-ancestors who emerge at **Pacaritampu**. Wife of **Ayar Auca**.

Mama Ipacura (**Mama Cura**) (*Inca*) One of the eight-sibling ancestors who emerge at **Pacaritampu**. Wife of **Ayar Cachi**.

Mama Ocllo (*Inca*) One of the eight sibling-ancestors who emerge at **Pacaritampu**. Wife of **Ayar Manco**, mother of **Sinchi Roca**.

Mama Raua (*Inca*) One of the eight sibling-ancestors who emerge at **Pacaritampu**. Wife of **Ayar Uchu**.

Mammi (*Mesopotamian*) *See* **Nin-Hursag**.

Mana Namca (*Inca*) Female demon and **huaca**, ally of **Huallallo Carhuincho**, defeated by **Pariacaca**.

Manco Capac ('supreme rich one') (*Inca*) (1) Second name of **Ayar Manco**, given him by **Ayar Uchu** on instruction of the **sun**. One of the founders of **Cusco** and first king of the Inca empire; (2) after the **flood**, king of the northern quarter.

Marduk (*Mesopotamian*) Heroic supreme god and creator. Son of **Ea** and **Damkina**, father of **Nabu**. Physically outstanding with four ears, four eyes, lips that blaze fire and weapons including lightning, seven winds, flood and a storm chariot. In the Epic of Creation he creates sky and earth from **Tiamat**'s corpse; and uses the blood of **Qingu** to create mankind.

Mashya and **Mashyanag** (*Persian*) First mortal man and woman, who worship **Angra Mainyu**, thus filling the world with corruption and evil. Their twin children are the ancestors of the human race.

Mayahuel (*Aztec*) Beautiful young goddess of the maguey plant. Seduced by **Quetzalcoatl**, killed by **tzitzimitl** grandmother. The first maguey grows from her bones. *See also* **pulque**.

Mencius (**Meng Zi**) (*Chinese*) Philosopher who further developed the teachings of **Confucius**, emphasising **filial piety**.

Mictlan (*Aztec*) The dark and gloomy **Underworld**.

Mictlancihuatl (*Aztec*) Wife of **Mictlantecuhtli**.

Mictlantecuhtli (*Aztec*) Primary god of death, Lord of **Mictlan**. Depicted as a skeleton, married to **Mictlancihuatl**.

Middle Kingdom (**Zhong Guo**) (*Chinese*) Ancient name for China as the civilised centre of the world, supposedly surrounded by four seas and four outer wildernesses.

Mithra (*Persian*) God who controls cosmic order and protects the **Divine Glory**.

Mixcoatl (**Cloud Serpent**) (*Aztec*) A god of the Milky Way, personifying the souls of warriors which became stars at their deaths.

Monkey King (**Mei Hou Wang**) (*Chinese*) Supernatural trickster hero of China's most famous myth. Attains immortality and tries to seize control of earth and heaven, causing much chaos. Subdued and imprisoned by the Buddha. Subsequently reborn as a god and embarks on eventful pilgrimage to the Western Paradise to bring the Buddhist scriptures to China.

moon (**quilla**) (*Inca*) (1) Divine power behind the queen; (2) the waxing and waning of the moon determined the ritual life of **Cusco**.

Mubad Manikan (*Persian*) King of Merv who covets both **Shahru** and **Vis** and declares war on their kingdom.

Mulliltu (*Mesopotamian*) Goddess, wife of **Ellil**.

mummies (*Inca*) Preserved bodies of past Inca kings, and of ancestors of the **ayllus**. Revering and caring for them

maintained cosmic order and ensured the fertility of crops and animals.

Mylitta (*Mesopotamian*) *See* **Mulliltu**.

Nabu (*Mesopotamian*) God of wisdom, patron of scribes, son of **Marduk**.

Nahui Ollin (**Sun of Motion**) (*Aztec*) The fifth sun, the present world.

Namtar (*Mesopotamian*) Vizier of **Ereshkigal**.

Nanahuatzin (*Aztec*) A diseased, humble god, (1) chosen by the other gods over **Tecuciztectal** to be the fifth **sun**, and transformed into **Tonatiuh**; (2) breaks open Mt **Tonacatepetl**, releasing maize seeds into the world.

Naush (*Persian*) The most evil female demon, often appearing as a mottled fly.

Naymlap (*Inca*) Legendary first king of the dynasty that conquered Lambayeque valley in primordial times. *See also* **Yampallec, Fempellec**.

Nergal (*Mesopotamian*) God of plague and war, lover and sometime husband of **Ereshkigal**. *See also* **Erra**.

Nin-hursag (*Mesopotamian*) The great mother-goddess, sometimes described as wife of **Nergal**. Also known as **Aruru** and **Mammi**.

Ninlil (*Mesopotamian*) *See* **Mulliltu**.

Ninurta (*Mesopotamian*) A war god and patron of the hunt, son of **Belet-ili**, who destroys **Anzu**.

Nissaba (*Mesopotamian*) Goddess of schools and scribes.

Nu Ba (**Woman Droughtghoul**) (*Chinese*) Goddess, bringer of drought. Daughter of **Huang Di**.

Nu Chou (**Woman Deuce**) (*Chinese*) Goddess of corpses, burnt to death by ten suns but reborn, symbolising renewal.

Nu Gua (**Woman Gua**) (*Chinese*) Important creator goddess. Makes cosmos through undergoing 70 transformations. Creates humans from yellow clay and scattered mud. Romantically linked with **Fu Xi**.

Nu Wa (Woman Lovely) (*Chinese*) Goddess, daughter of **Yan Di**. Drowns in the East Sea and is transformed into a bird, renamed Jing Wei.

Ometeotl (God of Duality) (*Aztec*) Creator god possessing both male and female principles. *See also* **Tonacatecuhtli** and **Tonacacihuatl**.

orejones ('big ears') (*Inca*) The nobility, so-called from the golden spools worn in their pierced ears.

Pacaritampu (**Pacaritambo**) ('house of dawn', 'place of origin') (*Inca*) The place where **Ayar Manco** and his seven sibling-ancestors emerge, now a town.

Pachacamac ('maker of earth/time') (*Inca*) (1) Provincial name for **Viracocha**; (2) pilgrimage centre and oracle on coast south of modern Lima; *see also* **Cavillaca**; (3) creator god.

pachacuti ('revolution of time and space') (*Inca*) Regular cycles of time featuring creation, cataclysmic destruction and then re-creation. A feature of origin myths. *See* **five suns, Inkarrí**.

Pachacuti Inca Yupanqui (*Inca*) Ninth Inca king, possibly the prince who defended **Cusco** from attack by the **Chancas**, helped by the **puruaucas**. *See also* **Viracocha Inca**.

pairaka (*Persian*) Witch-like, shape-changing female evil beings, mostly nocturnal.

Pan Gu (Coiled Antiquity) (*Chinese*) A giant, involved in creation. Hatches out of primordial egg when it splits into **yin and yang**. After death his body parts are transformed into wind, clouds, thunder, sun and moon, mountains, rain and rivers, soil, stars, vegetation and minerals. The insects on his body become the first humans.

Pariacaca (*Inca*) Principal god of Yauyos people. Defeats **Huallallo Carhuincho** and **Mama Namco** in battle.

Pinahua (*Inca*) After the **flood**, king of the eastern quarter.

Popol Vu (*Maya*) Major documentary source for mythology. Quiché Maya manuscript written down in 16th century, derived from lost ancient book, augmented by oral tradition. Describes (1) primordial origins of the world; (2) myth of twins, origins of humans and of maize; (3) legendary history of the Quiché.

pulque (*Aztec*) Alcoholic drink made from fermented sap of the succulent maguey plant. Drunk at banquets, festivals and rituals and used as sacrificial offering. *See* **Mayahuel**.

Purun Runa ('wild men') (*Inca*) Race who lived during the third of the **five suns**.

pururaucas (*Inca*) Rocks and stones which temporarily transform into warriors and help the hero-prince (either **Viracocha Inca** or **Pachacuti Inca Yupanqui**) defend **Cusco** when the **Chancas** attack. Afterwards become **huacas**.

Qingu (*Mesopotamian*) In Epic of Creation, monster created by **Tiamat**, who gives him the **Tablet of Destinies**. Killed by **Marduk**, who uses his blood to create mankind.

Queen Mother of the West (*Chinese*) See **Xi Wang Mu**.

Queen of the Underworld (*Mesopotamian*) See **Ereshkigal, Underworld**.

quetzal (*Aztec*) Tropical forest bird with bright green feathers and red underparts.

Quetzalcoatl (Plumed Serpent) (*Aztec*) Major creative god, son of **Ometeotl**, brother (sometimes ally, sometimes opponent) of **Tezcatlipoca**. Sometimes identified as benevolent culture hero who teaches people the arts of civilisation; driven into exile by Tezcatlipoca, with unfulfilled promise to return.

quilla (*Inca*) *See* **moon.**

quipu (*Inca*) Bundles of coloured, knotted strings used to record (1) population and accounting statistics; (2) mythological and historical information.

quipucamayoqs ('knot makers or keepers') (*Inca*) Experts who interpreted historical and mythological information contained in **quipu**s, and narrated them on public ceremonial occasions. *See also* **amautas.**

Rakhsh (*Persian*) Exceptional horse, faithful servant and companion to **Rustam.**

Ramin (*Persian*) Younger brother of **Mubad Manikan**, lover then husband of **Vis**. After Mubad's death, Ramin becomes 'king of kings'.

Rustam (*Persian*) Super-strong hero, son of **Zal**. Together with **Rakhsh** undertakes seven heroic deeds. Defends **Kay Kavus** against **Afrasiyab**, who tricks him into killing his own son, **Sohrab.**

sacrifice (*Aztec*) Tradition established by the gods at the creation, offering their own blood to create the human race and to ensure the sun would move along its path. The sacrifice of human hearts and blood demonstrated mankind's role in maintaining cosmic balance.

Saena (*Persian*) Great falcon which nests in the **Saena Tree**, beating her wings to scatter its seeds. Suckles young ones. Possibly the same as **Simurgh.**

Saena Tree (Tree of all Remedies or Tree of all Seeds) (*Persian*) The 'mother of all trees', source of all plants. Grows in the **Vourukasha Sea.**

Sam (*Persian*) Father of **Zal.**

sapa inca (*Inca*) The ruling Inca king, supposedly a direct descendant of **Manco Capac** and the earthly manifestation of the **sun.**

Scorpion-men (*Mesopotamian*) Terrifying guardians of a mountain gateway through which **Gilgamesh** must pass on his quest.

Sebitti (*Mesopotamian*) Seven warrior gods who march at the side of **Erra.**

Shahrazad (*Persian*) Heroine of the 'frame story' of *1001 Arabian Nights*. Marries **Shahriyar**, but escapes the execution meted out to his previous wives by telling him stories for 1001 nights and bearing him three sons. *See also* **Dinazad.**

Shahriyar (*Persian*) King in the story of **Shahrazad**, who vows to marry and behead a different woman every day.

Shahru (*Persian*) Queen of Mah, mother of **Vis**. Courted by **Mubad Manikan**, who forces her to give him Vis in marriage.

Shamash (*Mesopotamian*) Sun god, judge of heaven and earth. Advises **Etana** in his quest to find the plant of birth.

Shamhat (*Mesopotamian*) Harlot who civilises **Enkidu** through six days and seven nights of lovemaking.

Shao Hao (**Young Brightsky**) (*Chinese*) The white god of light and one of the **Four Emperors.**

Shen Nong (**Farmer God**) (*Chinese*) God who teaches humans about agriculture and medicine.

Shirin (*Persian*) Beautiful daughter of the Queen of Armenia, later queen herself. Beloved of **Khusrow Parviz** and becomes his third wife.

Shun (**Hibiscus**) (*Chinese*) Second ideal ruler and moral hero. His father and half-brother, **Gu Sou** and **Xiang**, try to kill him three times. He survives and refuses to condemn his family's evil intents, responding with exemplary **filial piety.**

Siduri (*Mesopotamian*) Goddess and beer-seller who helps **Gilgamesh** on his way to **Ut-napishtim**.

Simurgh (*Persian*) Legendary guardian bird who raises **Zal**, and gives him a feather to burn whenever he needs her help. Assists **Rustam**, possibly the same as **Saena**.

Sin (*Mesopotamian*) God of the moon, sometimes described as father of **Ishtar**.

Sinchi Roca (*Inca*) Son of **Ayar Manco** and **Mama Ocllo**. One of the founders of **Cusco** and its second king.

Siyavush (*Persian*) Son of **Kay Kavus**, raised by **Rustam**, married to **Farangis**. Murdered by **Afrasiyab**, his death is avenged by his son **Kay Khusrow**.

Sohrab (*Persian*) Son of **Rustam**, whom he has never seen. His father is tricked by **Afrasiyab** into killing him.

sun (**inti**) (*Inca*) (1) The divine power behind the **sapa inca**; (2) a separate deity, father of **Vichama**; (3) a world age. *See also* **five suns**.

suns (*Aztec*) Worlds created and then destroyed by the gods. There were four suns before the present world, each linked to one of the elements (earth, wind, fire, water). *See also* **Nahui Ollin**.

Tablet of Destinies (*Mesopotamian*) Tablets decreeing the fates of men and gods. Their owner has supreme power. Originally belong to **Ellil**, but in Epic of Creation given by **Tiamat** to **Qingu** and then seized by **Marduk**.

Tahmuras (*Persian*) Mythical king, son of **Hushang**. Confronts **divs**, who teach him skills of writing and reading. Also called Takhma Urupi.

Tahuantinsuyu ('The Four United Quarters') (*Inca*) The Inca empire, divided into four regions and embracing many ethnic groups.

Tambo Toco ('house of windows') (*Inca*) A mountain in **Pacaritampu** with three windows. **Ayar Manco** and his seven sibling-ancestors emerge from the central window. The Maras and Tambos Indians emerge from the windows on either side.

Tambochacay (*Inca*) Ancestor of the Tambos Indians who seals **Ayar Cachi** inside **Tambo Toco** on the command of his brothers.

Tammuz (*Mesopotamian*) Another name for **Dumuzi**.

Tamoanchan (*Aztec*) The place where the gods created people.

Tang (**the Conqueror**) (*Chinese*) A king, one of the mythical founders of the Shang dynasty.

Taycanamu (*Inca*) First of legendary dynasty of kings who ruled Moche valley before Inca conquest.

Tecuciztecatl (*Aztec*) Haughty god. Tries to become the fifth **sun**, beaten by **Nanahuatizin** and instead becomes the moon.

Temple of the Sun (*Inca*) The 'golden enclosure' in central **Cusco**, housing the **mummies** of past kings and images of the deities.

Tezcatlipoca (**Smoking Mirror**) (*Aztec*) Powerful, dangerous god, son of **Ometeotl**, brother (sometimes ally, sometimes opponent) of **Quetzalcoatl**. Represents conflict and change.

Thraetaona (*Persian*) *See* **Fariydun**.

Thunupa Viracocha (*Inca*) Another name for **Viracocha**.

Tiamat (*Mesopotamian*) In Epic of Creation, the first goddess, personifying the sea. Mates with **Apsu** to produce four generations of gods. When **Ea** kills Apsu, she calls up a troop of fearsome monsters in revenge but is eventually killed by **Marduk**. He turns half her body into a roof for the sky and the other half into the earth; her spittle becomes the clouds, wind and rain, and her eyes form the rivers Euphrates and Tigris.

Tian Shen (Sky God) (*Chinese*) Ox-like god with eight feet, two heads and a horse's tail. An omen of war.

Tishtrya (*Persian*) Shape-changing god of rains, rising from **Vourukasha Sea**.

Titicaca (*Inca*) Actual lake straddling modern Peru and Bolivia, from which **Viracocha** emerges and begins acts of creation.

Tlaelquani (Eater of Excrement) (*Aztec*) Another name for **Tlazolteotl**.

Tlahuizcalpantecuhtli (Lord of the Dawn) (*Aztec*) Personification of Venus as the morning star. *See* **Itztlacoliuhqui**.

Tlaloc (*Aztec*) God of rain and lightning, married to **Chalchiuhtlicue**; (pl.) four directional gods of rain and lightning, coloured blue, white, yellow and red.

Tlaltecuhtli (Earth Lord) (*Aztec*) Dual-sexed monster, dismembered by **Quetzalcoatl** and **Tezcatlipoca** to make the heavens and earth.

Tlazolteotl (Filth Goddess) (*Aztec*) Goddess of consequences of lust and licentiousness. Also known as Tlaelquani.

Tocapo Viracocha (*Inca*) Younger son of **Viracocha** whom he helps with creation, and brother of **Imaymana Viracocha**.

Tocay (*Inca*) After the **flood**, king of the eastern quarter.

Tonacatecuhtli and **Tonacacihuatl (Lord and Lady of our Sustenance)** (*Aztec*) The male and female principles of **Ometeotl**.

Tonacatepetl (Mountain of Sustenance) (*Aztec*) The source of maize. **Quetzalcoatl** unsuccessfully tries to carry it away. **Nanahuatzin** cracks it open, helped by the four **Tlalocs**, scattering the seeds far and wide.

Tonatiuh (the Sun) (*Aztec*) (1) A sky god, important in the cult of war; (2) the **fifth sun**, transformed from **Nanahuatzin**. Demands the fealty and blood of other gods before it will move.

trigrams (*Chinese*) *See* **eight trigrams**.

twins (*Aztec* and *Maya*) Feared as strange and abnormal. Often appear in myths as monster-slayers and culture heroes. Creators of order, but embody conflict and change. *See also* **Hun Batz** and **Hun Chouen**, **Hun Hunahpu** and **Vucub Hunahpu**, **Xbalanque** and **Hunahpu**.

tzitzimime (sing. **tzitzimitl**) (*Aztec*) Celestial demons of the night, often female, in the form of stars which fight the sun at dawn and dusk, constantly threatening to destroy the world. *See also* **Mayahuel**.

Underworld (*Aztec*) *See* **Mictlan**.

Underworld (*Maya*) *See* **Xibalba**.

Underworld (*Mesopotamian*) Dark, dismal land of the dead, from which none may return. Guarded by seven gates and ruled by **Ereshkigal, Queen of the Underworld**. Also called **Kurnugi**.

Ur-shanabi (*Mesopotamian*) Boatman who guides **Gilgamesh** across the Waters of Death on his way to find **Ut-napishtim**.

Ut-napishtim (*Mesopotamian*) Man who survives the flood by following **Ea's** advice to build a great boat. Afterwards **Ellil** makes him and his wife immortal. Tells **Gilgamesh** where to find the plant of immortality.

Utu (*Mesopotamian*) Another name for **Shamash**.

Vayu (*Persian*) Warrior god of wind.

Verethragna (*Persian*) Shape-changing warrior god who overcomes evil.

Vichama (Villama) (*Inca*) Son of the **sun**. Turns early people to stone, and makes some of them **huacas**.

Viracocha (*Inca*) Great creator who emerges from **Titicaca**. Creates race of giants, then destroys them in **flood** before making humans. In one version, a 'tall white man' who also heals the sick. Also called **Con Ticci Viracocha, Contiti Viracocha Pachayachachic, Pachacamac, Thunupa Viracocha, Viracocha Pachayachachi.**

Viracocha Inca ('god and king') (*Inca*) Eighth Inca king, possibly the prince who defended **Cusco** from attack by the **Chancas**, helped by the **pururaucas**. *See also* **Pacachuti Inca Yupanqui.**

Viracocha Pachayachachi (*Inca*) Another name for **Viracocha.**

Vis (*Persian*) Daughter of **Shahru**, first married to her own brother, then to **Mubad Manikan**, and finally to childhood friend **Ramin.**

Vishtaspa (*Persian*) A king, follower of **Zoroaster.** Father of **Isfandiyar.** Also called **Gushtasp.**

Vourukasha Sea (*Persian*) The source of all waters in **Khvanirath.**

Vucub Caquix (**Seven Macaw**) (*Maya*) Boastful monster-bird who declares himself lord of the universe. Killed by **Xbalanque and Hunahpu.**

Wari Runa (*Inca*) Race who lived during the second of the **five suns**, destroyed by **flood.**

Wari Wiracocharuna (*Inca*) Primitive race who lived during the first of the **five suns.**

Weaver Woman (*Chinese*) *See* **Zhi Nu.**

winds (*Mesopotamian*) Supernatural forces often used by the gods in battles.

world mountain(s) (*Chinese*) (1) Earthly paradise, full of mythical plants and animals; *see* **Kunlun**; (2) in a creation myth, four mountains supporting the domed sky over the flat earth.

world tree (*Chinese*) Grows at the centre of the cosmos, joining earth and sky. Main variants are (1) Jian Mu (Building Tree), brightly coloured trunk and fruit, black blossom, with nine tangles at both crown and roots; (2) Da Tao Mu (Peach Tree) forms ladder to sky, where entry

to paradise is barred by the fierce gods of punishment; (3) Fu Sang (Leaning Mulberry) trunk is 100 miles high with ten suns in its branches.

Xbalanque and **Hunahpu** (*Maya*) Sons of **Xquic** and **Hun Hunahpu.** Great hero **twins** who slay **Vucub Caquix**, defeat death gods and demons of **Xibalba** and then become the sun and moon.

Xi He (**Breath Blend**) (*Chinese*) Sun goddess, mother of ten suns. Later transforms into two separate gods, Xi and He, who officiate over the agricultural calendar in the government of **Shun.**

Xi Wang Mu (**Queen Mother of the West**) (*Chinese*) Major goddess of wild appearance who lives on **Kunlun Mountain** and punishes the world with disease and disaster. Occasionally grants immortality to humans.

Xia Hou Qi (**Open, Lord of the Summer**) (*Chinese*) Son of **Yu** and founder of mythical dynasty of Xia (Summer). Brings humans the gift of heavenly music.

Xiang (**Elephant**) (*Chinese*) Murderous younger half-brother of **Shun.**

Xiang Liu (**Aide Willow**) (*Chinese*) Officer of **Gong Gong**, a monster who spoils crops by polluting soil with his drool. Slain by **Yu.**

Xibalba (*Maya*) The **Underworld**, a fearsome, gloomy place reached by a treacherous path blocked by many obstacles.

Xing Tian (**Heaven Punished**) (*Chinese*) Warrior god who attempts to attain supremacy and is decapitated as a punishment.

Xipe Totec (*Aztec*) God of springtime rejuvenation, and patron god of goldsmiths.

Xiuhtecuhtli (**Turquoise Lord**) (*Aztec*) Fire god concerned with time. Patron god of rulership.

Xochipilli (Flower Prince) (*Aztec*) Patron god of pleasure and arts.

Xochiquetzal (Flower Quetzal) (*Aztec*) Goddess of arts, physical pleasure and love.

Xpiyacoc and **Xmucane** (*Maya*) (1) Old couple, soothsayers, who assist **Gucumatz** and **Hurucan** in the creation; (2) parents of **Hun Hunahpu and Vucub Hunahpu**; (3) Xmucane grinds the maize from which the first men are fashioned.

Xquic (*Maya*) **Underworld** maiden, supernaturally impregnated by **Hun Hunahpu**. Mother of **Xbalanque** and **Hunahpu**.

Yampallec (*Inca*) Green stone idol installed by **Naymlap** when he conquers the Lambayeque valley. *See also* **Fempellec**.

Yan Di (Great God Flame) (*Chinese*) One of the Four Emperors, the scarlet god of fire. Brother of **Huang Di**, father of **Nu Wa**.

Yao (Lofty) (*Chinese*) The first ideal ruler.

yatu (*Persian*) (1) Evil beings; (2) sorcerers and magicians who fight against evil.

Yi (the Archer) (*Chinese*) Hunter god who shoots down nine (or ten) **suns** that threaten to scorch the earth.

Yima (Jamshid) (*Persian*) (1) Mythical king of the whole world, which he enlarges every 300 years; (2) 'King of Paradise', who rules for a thousand years.

yin and yang (*Chinese*) In **Daoism**, two opposing forces. **Yin** is feminine: dark, cold, shaded, heavy and passive, associated with water, the moon and stars. **Yang** is masculine: light, hot, sunny, ethereal and active, associated with fire and sun. Interaction between the two brings harmony.

Ying Long (Responding Dragon) (*Chinese*) Divine avenger and bringer of rain. *See also* **dragons**.

Yu (Reptilian-Pawprint) (*Chinese*) Semi-divine heroic saviour and queller of **floods**. Born miraculously from the corpse of **Gun** in form of a bear; third ideal ruler; father of **Xia Hou Qi**. Inventor of metal and metal working.

Yum Cimih (Lord of Death) (*Maya*) Death god, also known as **Cizin**.

Zahhak (*Persian*) Man who sells his soul to **Ahriman**, murders his father and sprouts two man-eating snakes from his shoulders. Usurps **Jamshid** and reigns in terror for a thousand years; overthrown by **Fariydun**.

Zal (*Persian*) Son of **Sam**, who abandons him in the mountains, where he is found and raised by **Simurgh**. Father of **Rustam**.

Zhi Nu (Weaver Woman) (*Chinese*) Goddess who falls in love with a mortal oxherd. The lovers are separated as punishment, but meet in the sky once a year. Popularised in many folk tales and poems.

Zhu Long (Torch Dragon) and **Zhu Yin (Torch Shade)** (*Chinese*) Gods with snakes' bodies and human heads, who open and shut their eyes to illuminate the north-west region where sunlight cannot reach.

Zhuan Xu (Fond Care) (*Chinese*) Monstrously deformed sky god who orders his grandsons Chong and Li to separate sky and earth for eternity. Attacked by **Gong Gong**.

ziggurat (*Mesopotamian*) Rectangular stepped tower with a temple on top. The ziggurat of Esagila at Babylon was supposedly built by the gods to mark the proclamation of **Marduk** as king.

Zoroaster (Zarathushtra) (*Persian*) Prophet, founder of **Zoroastrianism**.

Zoroastrianism (*Persian*) Monotheistic religion of ancient Persia, founded by **Zoroaster** and teaching of struggle between good and evil. Modern followers in India are known as Parsees.

Index